SEA
CHANGE

FOREWORD BY SIR RANULPH FIENNES

SEA CHANGE

THE TRUE STORY OF WHAT HAPPENED WHEN
THE GREAT-GREAT-GRANDSON OF CHARLES DICKENS
PACKED IN THE RATRACE TO RUN
AWAY TO SEA FOR A YEAR...

IAN DICKENS

JOHN BLAKE

Published by John Blake Publishing Ltd,
3, Bramber Court, 2 Bramber Road,
London W14 9PB, England

First published in hardback in 2003

ISBN 1 904034 78 0

British Library Cataloguing-in-Publication Data:

A catalogue record for this book is available from the British Library.

Design by ENVY

Printed in Great Britain by CPD (Wales)

1 3 5 7 9 10 8 6 4 2

Papers used by John Blake Publishing are natural, recyclable products made from wood grown
in sustainable forests. The manufacturing processes conform to the environmental regulations
of the country of origin.

Every attempt has been made to contact the relevant copyright-holders, but some were
unobtainable. We would be grateful if the appropriate people could contact us.

FOR HOLLY AND MICHAEL

CONTENTS

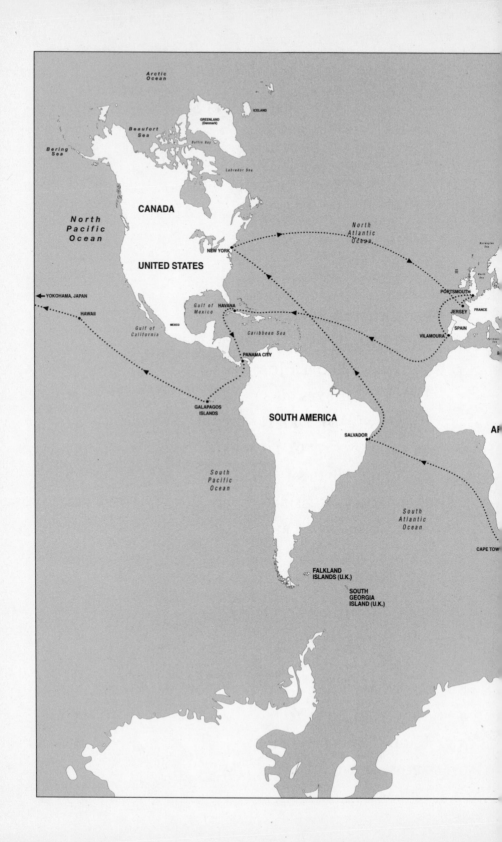

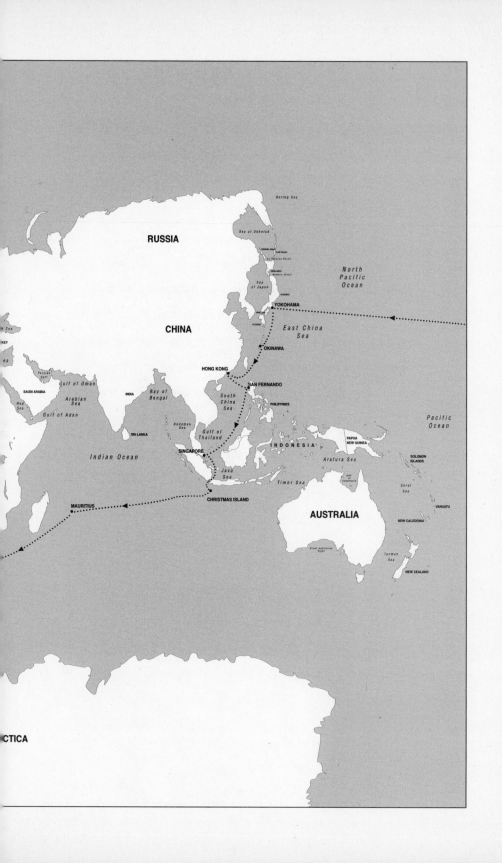

Whatever the miracle is that grants us life, it deserves
to be repaid by exploring, to the very maximum, all that
is on offer in the time span we have been allotted. It is a precious
gift and one that should be honored, not by cowering in a
draught-free basement in case the candle gets snuffed out
prematurely, but by experiencing, to the very highest order,
the very best of every opportunity.

IAN DICKENS

ACKNOWLEDGEMENTS

This is a story of discovery that spans three years. In that time I discovered true friendship from quarters I had not expected, lost 'friendships' from quarters that surprised me, had my eyes opened by the simplest of gestures and experienced kindnesses that took my breath away.

Many of those are described in the following pages.

On the sailing front, I would like to thank the directors and staff at Clipper Ventures, creators of an extraordinary event that changes people's lives: Sir Robin Knox Johnston at the helm, the irrepressible Colin de Mowbray, William Ward, Tim Hedges and Richard Cooper. Also, Liz Green and Nick Crawford, our training skippers, who made learning a joy. Not only did Clipper deliver a great race, they also provided a string of opportunities to keep the wolf from the door when I returned home.

To Stuart Gibson, who ran our race with such elegance. The mixture of competitiveness, focus, dedication, professionalism, humour, humanity, humility and honesty set an astonishing example. You are a unique individual and a privilege to know. To you, Liz, Ben and my godson Oliver, my gratitude is never-ending.

To all of the crew of *London*, who proved to be such inspirational individuals battling against the conditions and, in some cases, their own demons. We have a unique, precious bond and the moments we shared have ensured friendships for life.

To dear Mirella Ricciardi, who urged me to write it all down, and to Brian McLaurin, who responded so warmly when I did. He introduced me to John Blake and turned an idea into a book with disarming ease. Without that introduction this book would not exist. At the publishers, my editors Adam Parfitt and Richard Dawes guided me through the maze with gentle encouragement, reassurance and valued advice, for which I am hugely grateful.

To Barry and Wendy Taylor. Readers will see why you are so loved when they start to turn the pages.

To the numerous family members and friends, who provided such incredible levels of support and encouragement for me, Anne, Holly and Michael. Special thanks go to Marion and Jonathan Lloyd for publishing advice, the loan of their cottage in Norfolk for me to write in and for several days of fearless seafaring skills which demonstrated that only *real* sailors perform off Blakeney Point.

To Mum and Dad, Liz, Nicky and Gerry, whose support through e-mails and letters proved that family bonds are not dulled by miles.

And finally, to Anne, Holly and Michael, whose love, support and selflessness continue to amaze me on a daily basis. I hope you know that it is returned with interest.

Ian Dickens
Elm Farm,
Bedfordshire 2003

FOREWORD

I met Ian fifteen years ago when I was looking for camera kit to document my first polar walk. I had expected to meet a serious and intense businessman intent on grilling me for several hours before agreeing to my requests. Instead, I found an easy-going and enthusiastic supporter who readily warmed to the idea of someone walking through the Antarctic ice with several thousand pounds' worth of kit which might never come back.

But come back it did, and in the expeditions that followed I was able to rely on Ian, as my adventures continued and developed. While I flew off to the most remote parts of the world, he continued to pursue a career in London, but it was clear that a brightly burning flame would eventually ignite in to something more spectacular.

Looking back, I suppose there were a few clues – his desire to hurtle head-first down the Cresta Run seemed to be the height of foolishness to me, but it clearly acted as an antidote to his day-to-day routine behind a desk. I was happy to act as patron for his fund-raising drive to the Arctic Circle and back in the Auto Arctic Challenge Car rally, driving a soft-top MG, which raised over £10,000 for Mencap and Motivation.

Clearly these were mere warm-up acts, and I was not hugely surprised to learn that he was leaving to embark on a round-the-world yacht race. I admit to feeling slightly miffed at losing such a valued supporter – and, by now, good friend – but equally I knew how fulfilling the challenges he would inevitable encounter would be.

Ian's words show an extraordinary and often moving depth of thinking as he observes the valuable lessons his journey presented. It makes this book far deeper than a simple tale of circumnavigating the world under sail, and it is clear that the family genes for communicating have been passed down to him!

It is also clear that he has taken the numerous lessons that all adventurers learn – preparation, team work, mental strength, stamina, an unknown tomorrow, exhaustion, despair and elation and applied them back to the everyday events that 'normality' brings.

He has learned that to go off and test oneself in such a challenging way requires the unstinting support of a loving family. He is blessed with a wife who provides such unswerving support and deserves huge credit for providing the stability for his extraordinary adventure.

This book should inspire a great number of folk who may *think* it's too late for them to leave their desk and follow their wildest dreams into proving themselves wrong.

Ran Fiennes,
Exmoor, 2003.

1

DROWNING

King's Cross railway station is an odd place to start drowning. Especially on a train emerging from a tunnel, on an unremarkable Monday morning in mid-September.

The grime-encrusted brickwork picked up the first glimmers of early-morning light as the slowly turning wheels clanked and ground their way out of the darkness.

A lone green fern grew out of the wall, fed by the meagre rays and the constant subterranean drip-drip from the street above. But the falling droplets would never be enough to deal the fatal blow to my lungs.

Alongside, a diesel-belching 125 crept slowly past, its fly-spattered windscreen heading away from the light, towards a hundred business meetings in Leeds, Bradford, Darlington and Peterborough.

The train stopped with a jolt once more and I watched as the red-underlined, slick first-class carriages of the InterCity paraded their important passengers slowly by. A voyeuristic elongated curtain call from a cast of grey-suited, laptop-tapping, coffee-sipping, *FT*-reading, loudly speaking, telephone-calling management. Their journey had only just started, but even now, at eight in the morning, the jacketless white shirts were already building a heavy sweat of frustration as the telephone signal went down, the secretary was still on voicemail and the e-mail from head office introduced an out-swinger from left of field, creating different ball parks that would need ongoing dialogue before flags could be raised to check for flutterings.

My throat started to tighten a little and I eased my tie open.

In my own carriage, people stirred. Papers were folded, coats collected, briefcases snapped shut and wobbling queues made their swaying way to the door in order to snap up pole position on the race to the tube.

A hiss of air released the eager throng and the seething mass strode off to the exit, carrying me along in a tidal wave of smartly tapping, briskly pacing, eager-to-hit-the-ground-running feet.

Like rivers pouring towards the sea, several further tributaries joined the main current and individuals, with personalities, wives, husbands, children, hobbies, hopes and dreams that existed in mortgaged homes in Huntingdon and Sandy, Biggleswade and Cambridge, Hitchin and Stevenage, became a small amoeba of unimportant matter – a tiny part of a gigantic cancerous cell which carried them in a surge towards a gaping hole in the ground.

They tumbled like a torrent down the steps and swirled headlong around corners, through ticket halls and barriers and on, downwards, into the bowels of the earth.

They filled the underground platforms and packed on to the Circle line train so tightly their breathing had to become unified in order to share the space.

I stood gasping for breath as the current swept me along like a piece of flotsam, bobbing and swirling in the raging confusion of white water that tore a path of its own choosing, taking out anything that dared to stand in its way.

There was no courtesy or queue to get on board the tube train that was now disgorging passengers like projectile vomit. As they poured out of the carriages in a counter-current to the fast-flowing tide, there was the normal jostle, with every man and – more often than not – an even more aggressive woman securing their own place. No 'women and children first' on this Monday morning. People trying to get off were ignored. People with suitcases were glared at. The man who had stopped to help the harassed mother and her pushchair were easy prey to the crowds behind, who swept around the stationary island and looked on smugly through the glass as the train pulled away, leaving him behind on the platform.

But despite my lack of oxygen, I was happy to help a fellow struggler with a lifebelt or two.

We had an entire two minutes to wait, the mum, her baby and I, for the next train – a lifetime in the race to the desk and the podium, with its gold medal, would never countenance such moments of selflessness.

I supposed I should have been bothered by my lack of enthusiasm in not taking the competition seriously enough, but the baby in the pushchair was cute and her mother pathetically grateful that someone had broken the rules.

I made it through the two stops and fought my way back up into the sunlight for the final dash. I was on the surface again now, allowing the current to take me at its own pace as it babbled around the traffic bollards and news stands. Turn right, forty strokes, angle across the road with an inelegant front crawl, along the parade of shops with a nod of a hello to the ironmonger treading water unlocking his security grilles, a nod to the long-serving street sweeper I nodded to every morning, a nod to the *Big Issue* seller, and it was backstroke down the final street before arriving at the steps of my office.

And it was here that the deep-end dangers really began to lurk. Predators with big teeth awaited below the oily calm of the corporate surface that lapped up to the shores of my desk.

It had not always been like that, though.

For twenty very happy years I had done the same journey without too much thought, swimming happily in a unique and privileged environment for an organisation that had the character and personality of a large family firm.

At the head, a jolly, paternal, visionary, larger-than-life character. Shunning further education, he had headed to sea aged sixteen and learnt hard lessons from the deck of a series of rusty freighters that slowly ploughed the waters of the Atlantic, the St Lawrence, the Caribbean and the English Channel. Life was learnt from bar room brawls, from cockroach-infested digs, from over-made-up ladies of the night, from late-night drinking, from smoky cafés in dank and desolate docksides, where grey cranes towered, storage sheds echoed and forklift trucks rolled, on the edges of some of the world's great cities.

That experience left him a unique observer of people, with a wisdom and a wit that made him equally at home with a peer of the realm and a London cabbie.

His name was Barry and I considered it my huge good fortune to join the company he ran, in the most junior of junior positions.

'Sales office order entry clerk, three weeks holiday, starting salary £15,000' was what it said on my contract but despite that lowly start, I was the first person he came to see, and offered a warm welcome to my first Monday morning in July 1979.

For the next two decades his charismatic leadership continued to create an environment that was hard-working, fun, original, creative and, when the work stopped and the partying began, often exhausting.

As the corporate years passed, a mass of opportunities found their way to my door and saw me rise through the ranks to the heady heights of marketing director, representing the interests of the UK company on behalf of the Japanese HQ and its German-based European sidekicks.

I was suddenly important. A bulging deluxe Filofax, the ubiquitous mobile phone, a smart company car, rich holidays and a gently bulging stomach from expense-account lunches in Langans, the Ivy and Harvey Nic's Fifth Floor.

Throughout that time, Barry's attitude remained unchanged and he approached business with the same rare zest allied to an eager desire to squash pomposity. Bullshitters were shat upon and his focus on common sense was liberating to work alongside.

'Why are we doing that?' he would reply to an accountant desperately overeager to complicate proceedings. 'We are doing it because it's fucking obvious, that's why!' No research, no focus groups, no think tanks. Just pure common sense allied to a laterally thinking mind that clearly understood the people he wanted to market to.

But the heady days of the eighties gave way to the hard-nosed nineties, and with the planet closing in on the new millennium, Barry had to endure an ever-increasing number of periods when his head was held under the surface by a new European way of doing things at odds with his own well-proven beliefs.

Forget the success he had managed so well for so many years. In other quarters, a new and 'better' way was being proposed. What had worked well in the UK seemed to be viewed with an ill-concealed envy and, instead of encouraging, nurturing and learning from the example, it was deemed better to wipe the slate clean and introduce a whole series of new approaches led by a European team.

Nothing he saw convinced him that this offered a better future and rather than drown in the cesspit of stagnant waters, he cashed in his quarter of a century of success and struck out for the shore and the freedom of early retirement.

We had forged a special partnership and had created a series of award-winning marketing campaigns that filled the boardroom with an embarrassment of framed riches.

I was devastated to see him go and even more concerned that, with my long-term ally gone, I would probably be next in line for the dunking sessions.

I headed up a project to create a new advertising campaign for all of Europe – a first for our now border-squashing company. After nine trying and rather lonely months, the fruits of the ad team's labour broke in sixteen countries.

A few months later, sales reached new levels of success.

Big mistake.

The success of the work again created a debilitating envy and a nasty campaign of negativity flew towards my desk. I had not followed the European way as I was expected to do, and as Ian-bashing from across the Channel became all the rage, one or two who should have known better in London decided, with a firm eye on their future careers, that it would be useful for them to join in too.

The negativity reached its peak and the marketing campaign that had been so effective was deemed a disastrous waste of time and resource. It was scant consolation when the work was entered into the industry's annual awards a couple of months later and walked off with the top accolades from juries all over the world. By that stage I was well and truly disillusioned with an uncomfortably large number of people who, for twenty years, I thought were on the same side as me.

It was into that bubbling pool that I plunged on that September Monday morning, hoping beyond hope that the weekend had allowed me to put things into perspective. Opening e-mails, listening to voicemails and reading faxes that demanded I report to Germany in the next twenty-four hours to answer yet more charges of nonsense put paid to that. My battles were now almost exclusively against individuals who had the same company name on their business card, and the excessive energy spent fending off the predators seemed such a waste of a beautiful day.

I also had to consider the uncomfortable possibility that the European view was maybe right, even though twenty years of experience shrieked, 'No!' Perhaps the Teutonic vision had a real foundation for a new future and the English oak tree that I was barking up was the wrong one.

Whatever, I did not want to spoil my two decades of valued working pleasure with months of misery that would end up leaving me bitter, twisted and thoroughly fed up.

Clearly, this was a battle I could not win and it would have been easier for my sanity to start looking for another job. But when I shared the concerns with friends, they looked astonished at my angst. So long in one company, led by a visionary leader, had protected me from the ravages of the modern corporation. The scenes I described were deemed completely normal – mild even – compared with some of the shockers that my more battled-scarred mates had experienced on a daily basis.

And if that was sobering, other much more valuable influences came to bear and helped remind me of where my priorities should really lie. A colleague (an unscheming one) was one day perfectly fit and the next doubled up in agony with what appeared to be a back problem.

Tests followed tests and slowly a much more serious picture emerged. It was cancer, an unkind one, and work, home, wife and children all became replaced by courses of chemotherapy, loss of hair, sallow skin and a terrified look in his sunken eyes as the prospect of death before the age of forty loomed large.

Suddenly, being a head of a department or having a smarter car than a colleague or staying in a junior suite rather than a standard room, paled against his desire to simply walk out into the back garden and kick a ball with his young son again.

He battled hard for several months, made it through the longest night, when the family were called to say tear-strewn goodbyes around his beeping, tube-infested hospital bed, and fought his way into the light of a new day and merciful remission.

A farmer from a village near my home, only a few years older than me and a great character, had started to feel unwell.

We went to see him at Addenbrokes Hospital, where he sat, a frightened and suddenly small man, not knowing what had gone wrong. Unbeknown to any of us, a tumour was slowly eating into his brain and six months later this strong, funny, warm-hearted father of a beautiful young child lay ranting in a private mad world at the local hospice.

His funeral was, in the end, a blessing.

A pilot whom I was privileged to meet vanished into the heavens. A brilliant flyer, respected by all who knew him, who flew stunts for Spielberg and charmed all those whose lives he touched, had one slip and his thousands of hours of experience suddenly counted for nothing. His Messerschmitt plunged to the ground and the impact and explosive fire took him away too.

All were people of my sort of age, now being remembered amid the tears, and the fragility of life was brought well and truly home. When one is made aware of such a fragile thread, the rail journey, the tube, the meetings and the unbelievable pettiness of it all are brought into sharp focus.

I was healthy, successful, lucky to have a loving, supportive family and a wonderful home. I had achieved a lot professionally, met enough fascinating and famous people to fill *Hello!*, and through my friendships been privileged to enjoy a number of very special moments.

The back seat of a Hawk jet with the Red Arrows. The Williams pit garage in Japan when a friend became world motor-racing champion. Being at Wembley to see Chelsea lift the FA Cup. Twice. The helicopter trip into the Grand Canyon with a press party. The run up to London in a Royal Navy submarine. The breathtaking descents of the Cresta Run. Learning to fly and gaining my pilot's licence. The many opportunities that had come my way from the people I had met over two decades of corporate life.

My portfolio of achievements was good and I seemed to be respected within the industry for all that I had achieved. Was my existing predicament really so bad that all this was worth giving up, just because a new band of people had new views about how the future should be shaped? And if I did move on professionally, would I simply be exchanging my nine-to-five commuting day for another, perhaps less bright hamster wheel, that even now lurked in the file of an unsuspecting headhunter somewhere in London?

Or perhaps now was the time to have a complete change of direction, sell up, move away, downscale, live simply and opt out of the race that seemed to be more and more dominated by the rats.

The salary, the bonus, the car, the expense account, the opportunities, the travel, the house, the holidays, the large garden, the privileges. Was this really exchangeable, especially when I was not on my own and had the responsibilities of others to consider?

The answer was a mixed-up 'Yes/I don't truly know/probably/I'm not sure/don't be such a bloody fool'. But, with the events at work clashing with the dramas of the cancer ward, the local hospice and a lone Spitfire dipping a saddened wing over a pilot's funeral in tribute, I had at least come to the conclusion that something needed to happen. Something or someone deep in my subconscious was giving me a heavy-handed prod, and chucked a lifebelt on the surface of the swirling water right under my nose.

I grabbed it and started to swim.

2

ADVERTISING WORKS

As an ad man I'd spent much of my time proving to companies that investing money in a fine advertising agency generated an excellent return for them in terms of additional sales.

At the end of the following week, the marketing people at a company called Clipper Ventures could make the same claim to their superiors. They had created a single-page, colour, right-facing ad and booked space in the *Sunday Times* supplement. All they had to do was sit back to wait for a reaction and they didn't have to wait long to get one from me.

A picture of an ocean-going racing yacht storming along under reefed sails on a wave-flecked ocean. A headline beckoning the adventurer. A number to call. The seductive line that offered the bored breakfast-table reader the chance to break away and achieve something truly exceptional. Anyone, the ad said, could earn themselves a place on board and compete in a yacht race that circumnavigated the planet.

It was a potential answer to all my problems – except for one or two minor details. I needed to find £23,000. I would have to take a year off. I needed to persuade my wife that it was a brilliant idea. I would have to tell my children that I would be away in a risky environment for longer than they had ever experienced. My proud parents would have to be told that I would probably have to give up my hard-fought career. The bank would need to know that the mortgage and bills would still be met despite my being (a) out of the country and (b) having no income. I would need to tell work that I wanted out.

Minor problems that were exacerbated by a rather too large overdraft and a less than friendly work environment that would probably not take too warmly to the request of a sabbatical.

But for now all that could wait. All I needed at this stage was a brochure that would tell me more. Once I got that I could start to consider a plan of action that would begin with suggesting to my wife, as subtly as possible, that this was one of my better ideas.

A difficult task to find the right opener and I started to rack my brain for the best way of breaking the news. In Sainsbury's perhaps, as we walked through the produce of the world. 'Look, darling, bananas from the Dominican Republic. Wouldn't it be fascinating to sail there? Oh look, pineapples from Hawaii – did you know that an English-run yacht race calls in at Waikiki? Dolphin-free tuna – so important to protect the ocean, don't you think?'

Maybe not.

Perhaps a wistful look through my father's photo albums, where images of his father and brothers joined Dad on the bridges of a host of great warships. As I looked at their gold-braided sleeves, I could perhaps summon up a misty-eyed detachment that might be translated as a desperate yearning for the sea. A tad too melodramatic perhaps.

Maybe it should be a mid-life crisis style breakdown. Allow it to seep out late one night after several Scotches, with a head-clutching moan of despair and an Oscar-winning delivery: 'I can't go on like this.'

Not unless I wanted to get a firm slap followed by an abrupt demand to pull myself together.

The problem was solved by Holly.

Holly is my daughter – fourteen at the time of this attempted subterfuge and, as is true for any father anywhere in the world, the most beautiful and perfect daughter a father could wish for.

Sparky, fun, honest, stunning, coy and the owner of a long and languid pair of legs that were the first thing I spotted coming down the stairs as I hastily finished dictating my address into the Clipper Ventures mailbox.

'What are you doing?' she asked, wrapping her equally long arms around my waist in a loving hug. Over my shoulder, she studied the hard-working ad, taking in the content with a sweep of the eye.

'Are you thinking of sailing around the world? Cool.'

I had not intended to talk to anyone – even to consider planning anything – until I had seen more details. The race demanded volunteers and there was a selection process to get through. There was no point getting my hopes up, or winding up other people, until I knew exactly what my chances were.

Before I could explain to Holly that she had got the wrong end of the stick, Anne appeared at the front door with a huge clutch of Sainsbury's carrier bags hanging from each arm. One of the bags was ripped badly at the handle and my wife was involved in a frantic battle to deliver it to the floor before gravity took over. It looked like the shopping trip had not been the highlight of her weekend and the tearing plastic was the conclusion of a less than satisfactory hour away from the house. I took in the heavyweight contents of the bag, which appeared to be made up of several large and ripe pieces of fruit from far-flung corners of the world, and wondered if there was a chink of an opening for my carefully rehearsed argument.

The bag finally crashed downwards, spilling melons and mangoes on the floor, and as they rolled away a steady stream of fine Anglo-Saxon, broadcast in a broad Irish accent reserved for such occasions, issued forth amid the exotic trifle that surrounded our feet.

I chickened out, mainly through a sense of self-preservation, but also because my daughter had got there before me.

'Dad's thinking of sailing round the world,' she airily announced to the harassed figure still standing in the door. Holly now also took in that her mum had clearly not entirely enjoyed the aisle tour of the world's food markets and the remark was not timed to be the most helpful. The sound of all the other bags hitting the stone floor in an orchestrated crash made my daughter jump, me tremble and scared the dog, who headed through the polythene jungle out into the sanctuary of the garden.

I had a sudden desire to follow.

There was shock, of course, at the intention of electing to spend a year apart. There was an instant demand to know much more about the year away. What was this event? When did it start? How much did it cost? Did I intend to apply for the whole race or do just one of the legs? How would I raise the money? How did I feel about being apart for the best part of twelve months? What about the job? What about the mortgage? What about the children? What about us?

A whole series of immediately practical questions rather than the much more obvious, 'No bloody way, sunshine.' It was typical of the woman I had been married to for eighteen years, and a complete contrast to the reaction of some of her friends, who over the following months would exclaim, 'But how could you let him?'

Anne viewed their behaviour as downright selfish. 'No, you can't be allowed to experience the thrill of travelling around the planet, because we want you here at home. Get back to work, pay the mortgage, mow the lawn and put up the shelves.' She viewed me as far more than a cash-supplying handyman commodity and was cautiously excited about the magnitude of the trip. And if she was hurt by my decision, then she hid it brilliantly well. Perhaps because she had an ulterior motive.

For the past couple of years, family holidays – paid for by my generous director's bonus – had seen us hoisting sails on board a variety of yachts in the heat of the Mediterranean summer.

Just three weeks before this awkward confrontation, we had nudged gently up to a rough wooden jetty beside a sandy beach in the backwaters of Turkey. Our yacht-handling skills had been viewed with scarcely concealed nervous relief by the owner of a well-used sailing boat with a tatty red ensign flying from the stern. He and his wife, dressed in battered T-shirts and worn shorts, had been busy hanging out a curious assortment of washing as we hove into view.

With a nautical version of 'Janet, donkeys!', they were off the boat and ready to repel anything that looked like it might damage their precious home. The safe arrival of our mooring ropes on the quay had calmed their fears and we had an amiable chat in the warm sunlight.

The couple were two professionals from the UK who had done their fair share in the boardroom and decided to opt out and gently cruise from one hot spot to the next on a boat that contained all they really needed in life. Anne, in particular, had envied that freedom and, long after we had waved goodbye the following morning, we fantasised about one day adopting an equally simple lifestyle.

The days where even a swimsuit would be overdressed. Days free of TV and newspapers, commuting, lawnmowing, council tax, parking fines, speed cameras and party political conferences. Days free of meetings, voicemail, impossible deadlines, the M25, traffic reports, litter-strewn streets, floods, shops that stock Christmas crackers in September, Easter eggs in January and Halloween masks in August. Days free from privatisation, ensuing train crashes, sabre-rattling warmongering and 'Two Jags' Prescott. Days free from an environment where loyalty was no longer valued and blinkered self-interest was deemed so normal that complaining about it was considered to be the start of a nervous breakdown.

The opportunity to do the ultimate journey around the world under the guidance of a professional would be a fantastic learning opportunity and Anne saw the Clipper Ventures idea as a sound investment in her own dream. It was a brilliant argument and one that I wish I'd thought of when faced with that awkward carrier-bag moment of explanation.

There were still inevitable concerns, and over Sunday lunch we began to touch on the issues. How would we pay for the trip? How would the mortgage be met while I was away? What would the separation do to our relationship? How would the children react? What if I fell overboard and didn't come back?

While I had already been rumbled by Holly, twelve-year-old Michael was out doing what twelve-year-olds do. Riding bikes, kicking balls, swinging from trees and dreaming up far-fetched games that were acted out on the village green in front of our home.

He arrived back for lunch, breathless, wreathed in sweat, and headed straight for the sink and a glass of frantically gulped water. Like Holly, he took in the concept with an easy acceptance and, as the debate continued, the materialistic thrills came into view.

As I shared the route, savouring for the first of many times 'Portugal, Cuba, the Galápagos, Hawaii', Holly interrupted me.

'Does this mean we can go to Hawaii?'

'Quite probably, yes,' I guessed, and that was it. As far as my children were concerned, the trip was a definite, and she drifted off into planning bikinis and the bags required to carry them.

Michael held out a little longer and my travel itinerary continued through Japan, China, Hong Kong, the Philippines, Singapore, Mauritius, Cape Town, Salvador, in Brazil, and New York.

One leg away from returning home, he too had found his own Eden, becoming instantly smitten with the idea and wondering whether Nike Town should be the first port of call or perhaps it should be the Empire State. Whatever, it would be vital news to airily lob into the classroom on Monday morning, despite my dire warnings to say nothing at this stage.

I noticed that Anne, trying her best to be hard-nosed about the travel prospects, had visibly wilted when I had mentioned the Galápagos Islands.

But until I had a place on board there was little point in going any further. I had no idea of the criteria the organisers were looking for, and might well find myself on the receiving end of a reject letter saying, 'No mid-life-crisis candidates required. Good luck with the rest of your life up a dead-end street. Kind regards, Sir Robin Knox Johnston.'

Stopping the conversation now would also allow me to open another bottle of red, put the globe on the table for an in-depth study, find where the dog was hiding and tell her it was safe to re-enter the house.

I decided on one thing, though. Should I get a place, I wanted to start and finish the entire race on board the yacht. I had to complete the journey and deal with all the challenges it had to offer. The sensible option (which I had hardly taken in from the ad) of doing a six-week leg, taking the time off as holiday and funding it by cashing in an insurance policy, was far too practical. If you mean to do it, then it should be all or nothing and the difficulties placed in the way would all be part of the challenge.

If we were going to worry the bank and the mortgage company, then let's really give them something to fret about.

I filled up Anne's glass, the children went in search of the atlas and Raggles settled back down in her basket and nodded off to sleep.

3

Easy Goodbyes

Clipper Ventures, true to their promise, sent through a pack of information and an application form a couple of days later. Meanwhile I had been to the website and was already hooked by the adventure. I really did hope that Sir Robin, the man at their helm, had a soft spot for middle-aged businessmen trying to find more from life, because I now wanted this very much indeed.

Anne and I filled out the forms, thinking long and hard about the testing questions that asked for a very honest, warts 'n' all opinion about myself. These were clearly the ones that would give an insight into my personality and provide clues as to whether I was made of the right stuff.

We agreed that a cheeky response was the best approach, and that summed me up anyway. If they were looking for a bunch of military-style squaddies, with fun and banter banned, then perhaps the event was not for me.

I stuck it all in an envelope with a good-luck pat and Michael hurtled across the green on his bike to the postbox, demonstrating a fearful disrespect for the laws of gravity and tyre adhesion.

When the post arrived a couple of days later, among the envelopes was one with a Clipper Ventures postmark. Not an A4 folder full of information this time, just a simple regulation envelope with what felt like a single-page letter inside.

Suddenly I was sixteen again, looking at the faces of my parents, knowing that the O Level results would either thrill or disappoint. The affected lack of interest, the studied indifference from around the breakfast table, belied the nervous anticipation in the room. As in the days of exams, I wanted to run and hide under the bed or lock myself in the loo before reading if Sir Robin had made the grave error of deciding I was not even worthy of an interview.

First I opened the bank statement and the long line of numbers adding up to one big OD suggested that knuckling down to earning more cash was the sensible option for the next few months. Or decades.

Reader's Digest offered an escape route in the next envelope, advising me that I had been selected to win at least a million. There was some tedious small print regarding the purchase of a book that detailed fascinating facts about 'healing plants of the world'. So confident were *Reader's Digest* that the money was virtually mine, I wondered if Lloyds might take the 'YES' sticker as down payment against the overdraft, and was tempted to stick it to the bank statement before posting the whole lot off again.

The third envelope could wait no longer, so I opened the life-changing communiqué and read its content. Never has anyone been happier to receive an invitation to the small market town of Olney and have the potential of adding £23,000 to their bank-account burden. While Anne, Holly and Michael whooped their enthusiasm, I too had to admit to feeling just a trifle happy. After all, with *Healing Plants of the World* in my bookcase, my financial problems might be well and truly solved for ever.

On the train to King's Cross I dreamt of what might be. The problems at work that had been getting me down so much were suddenly hugely diminished and I realised how badly I wanted this new chance. The fields of Bedfordshire gave way to the suburbs of north London and, as row after row of terraced houses crept by, I was off in a frenzy of escape, in the midst of a sun-kissed distant ocean with dolphins splashing all around. The whole idea was wonderfully romantic.

The romance continued when I offered to kiss Clipper's marketing manager.

We met a week later in a small industrial estate on the outskirts of Olney, in an office about as far from the sea as it was possible to get. Sitting nervously in the company's reception area, eyeing a couple of other candidates suspiciously, I wondered how to approach the impending grilling. Here was yet another new experience for a man who thought, rather too arrogantly, that he had experienced most of what life had to offer. My interview technique had become decidedly rusty and I had no idea of where the probing questioning might go.

In the end it turned into a really good chat, which I enjoyed hugely. After an hour in which my technique had included a mild dose of pleading, the interrogator looked at his watch, snapped his pen shut and uttered the immortal line, 'Thank you, we'll let you know.'

I was completely in the hands of someone else and it left me feeling distinctly uncomfortable.

A couple of days later another letter arrived from Clipper. It contained three paragraphs, the most important of which started with the word 'Congratulations'.

If I was ecstatic, so too was Anne, even though she was entering the foothills of a deep journey of discovery. Ever practical, she was acutely aware of the potential pitfalls that lay on the paths ahead. This was not just an idea any more, a fantasy played out over a bottle of wine. This was real, a black-and-white absolute fact that could be life-changing in ways that might unearth our deepest fears. But she remained totally and utterly positive, despite that troubling prospect.

Touchingly, Michael and Holly were also nothing other than completely thrilled and their excitement matched my own. While Anne, as an adult, could think things through with a practical logic, the children were surely allowed to have selfish moments of feeling sorry for themselves at the year-long loss of Dad. Their reaction was such a spontaneous act of support that tears pricked my eyes as they smiled smiles of real happiness for my adventure. I was going to be away from home for the best part of a year to follow a personal dream, but not an ounce of selfishness entered their thoughts.

When I spoke to my new best friend at Clipper to thank him for his brilliance in character judgement, the offer of the kiss was laughingly dismissed and replaced with a couple of much more practical issues.

Paying the money and booking up for training.

I had yet to resolve how we might pay for it all, but still Anne remained completely positive. She was adamant that, having come this far, I would be mad to turn the opportunity down, no matter what problems work might put in my way to quash the dream.

'You'll kick yourself for ever if you don't do it,' she admonished, fully aware of the responsibilities I had towards her, the children, our home, Lloyds Bank and, if they were lucky, *Reader's Digest*. For several weeks there was a small niggle that refused to go away, especially late at night as I tried to get back to sleep. It whispered words like 'irresponsible', 'fool' and 'idiot' as an incessant nag. But Anne had quietly spotted the signs and was already heading them off at the pass.

I e-mailed Barry in his retirement idyll of Miami and he concurred with Anne's view. We had kept in regular contact and he knew that work was becoming an increasingly challenging experience for me. He also knew that the longer I stayed a part of it, the unhappier I would become. But he urged me to do the race for far bigger reasons. He and Wendy, his spiritual and visionary wife, knew that the journey would offer a set of experiences of such clarity that my eyes would be opened in a way they had never been opened before. Whatever the future held, no one could take away the experiences that sailing around the world would provide.

My parents were also completely on side. Dad loved the idea of another family member going to sea. He loved the idea of the seamanship involved and the scale of the journey. More importantly, both my mother and father thrilled to the boldness of my decision, recognising that I felt able to turn my back on convention and dare to dream a completely impractical dream.

They had watched with growing dismay, they now confided, the pressures a modern directorship puts one under. They could not understand the amount of travel, the meetings, the punishing schedules that were asked of me and, like any parent, they worried at the toll it might be exacting on their son. There he was, perfect material for being struck down by one of the dangers that come stalking people in their mid-forties. A narrowed artery struggling to deal with high blood pressure, perhaps, or a sudden tumour (as my poor workmate had demonstrated). Or maybe an exhaustion-driven nodding off at the wheel, ending in a somersaulting, horn-blaring wipe-out on the A1 in the middle of the night.

They saw my decision as nothing other than a truly positive step and realised how difficult the debate must have been to arrive at that point. Any doubts were hidden well and a letter from Dad was hugely supportive and full of unconditional parental love. Already my adventure was unleashing emotions that would have probably otherwise remained unsaid and the honesty that resulted from it was hugely moving and very precious.

The difficult bit was sharing my plans at work. The easy answer was to simply leave and the past few months had made that a temptation, but life is rarely so simple. I had a mortgage and bills to pay, and a family to keep fed, warm and healthy during my year away.

I decided to go for the sabbatical option, even though it would mean that I would have to return to an environment that was rather less than enjoyable. But who knew how I might feel after a year away – perhaps the break and a new perspective might be beneficial all round and I could approach another decade with renewed energy and a grander global vision. That ought to appeal to the Germans, surely?

In the business press I noticed several articles where visionary companies spoke about the benefit of holding on to valued individuals and paid them while they went off to recharge. I carefully cut them out and added them to the early-morning rehearsal of words in front of the mirror before the now tedious dash to the train.

I sought out my new boss in his newly decorated MD's office and put the idea to him across his grey wooden desk. I tried not to hide anything and attempted to enthuse on the energies that the trip would bring. The pieces about sabbaticals that had handily appeared in the press to help my cause delivered a faint glimmer of hope, despite the heavy sighs that dominated the meeting rather too much.

At this early stage in his appointment, it was clear that anything that rocked the boat would be frowned upon from above. The easy option for him was to stay safe and follow the path of least resistance. But, having worked alongside me for several years, he heard a nagging whisper urging him to do better than just dismiss my request out of hand. At the end of the consultation he agreed to think about it for a while, and a couple of days later I was called back for the decision.

Unfortunately, it was the two-letter version.

No.

No, a sabbatical would be unacceptable. The achievements and the market successes, the loyalty and the passion, the desire to come back and continue were all acknowledged, but the answer was 'No'.

If I wanted to go, then it would set a precedent and everyone on the board would want to be off. While none of my fellow directors had ever previously hinted at the desire to spread their wings and set about discovering new vistas, I had to accept that perhaps they might be tempted.

I felt there was an element of brinkmanship being played. Told no, I might simply dismiss the idea as a dreamy aberration, forget about the magnitude of sailing around the world and knuckle down to drowning every time I pulled into King's Cross.

If that was the case, it was a complete misreading of my character and the burning desire that was becoming an all-consuming inferno. My mind was made up and, with Clipper assuring me of my place, I was going to be on the deck of that yacht when the start gun fired, no matter what it took. The flickering of the flames could clearly be seen from the other side of the grey desk and the awkwardness that it generated suggested that my single-mindedness was hardly helping make for a perfect corporate day.

'Nothing changes,' I told him, hoping beyond hope that Anne agreed. I would resign if I had to, but still hoped that we could work some sort of deal. With my head light from the euphoria of the moment, I walked back to my office and wondered how on earth I might find the money – not just to fund my place, but also to keep the family surrounded by bricks and mortar, heat and fish fingers, petrol and tins of Winalot while I was away.

At least the unhappy meeting had closed with the agreement to give it even more thought, and the man in charge was at pains to point out that he wanted to reach a fair conclusion if he possibly could. But until that could be resolved, he asked me to keep the plans to myself. He did not want the other directors to know and he certainly did not want a boat-rocking session with his superiors from across the water.

That was fine, except when it came to my most immediate colleagues. Not only did I owe it to them to be honest, but the person who would take on most of my responsibilities in my absence was the person I had employed and nurtured for the past five years. She had become a loyal and trusted friend and, quite apart from wanting to ensure that she was happy to enter the lion's den, I wanted to be completely straight with her as I planned my own future.

I organised lunch and nervously told her that the world's oceans awaited me. She had seen me struggle in recent months and had been supportive in the increasingly lonely battles, so was well placed to appreciate why I wanted this dramatic change. And while I gabbled on about what a great opportunity it was for her career, she stopped me short, held up a hand to attract a passing waiter's eye and ordered two glasses of champagne.

While the company decided how it was going to see me on my way, I took out an additional loan on the house in order to pay my £23,000 crew member's bill, hoping beyond hope that the future would deliver a solution to fund it all.

After several more months we finally agreed on a package that would allow me to leave but generously acknowledged my length of service and contribution to the company. My position would be made redundant and the resulting deal would provide enough funds (with careful housekeeping) to keep Anne and the children housed, fed and warm for my year away. The dog might have to get used to the cheaper offering of Sainsbury's own brand of diced rabbit in gravy, though. And despite the supposed secrecy, by the time the announcement was made, the entire company knew all about my plans.

By then I was sporting the giveaway skin colour of a man who had spent several weeks at sea with other like-minded volunteers likewise completing their training. More telling than the healthy skin tone was the healthy persona that went with it.

The dark-rimmed, sunken eyes. The close-to-the-surface anger sparked by political games. The bubbling frustration caused by a surfeit of meetings in too many different locations with not enough time between them. The daily backlog of a hundred e-mails and mailbox messages. The ever-ringing mobile and the stream of urgent faxes that drove the breakneck pace of an average day. All of that had blissfully disappeared for a few precious days as I faced my new future and loved what I saw.

The issues that seemed so important had folded themselves up and found a tiny recess in my mind where they remained wonderfully undisturbed. With them went the nine-to-five routine of commuting, the familiar London streets that marked the route between station and office, the sandwich bar with its unchanged lunchtime menus and the ongoing tedious exchanges between one department and another.

All of this had been replaced by the growing camaraderie of a bunch of strangers who arrived, from a broad mixed bag of backgrounds, at the quayside, intent on giving nothing less than their all.

Every applicant for the race underwent an identical training programme and no matter if it was a crew member's first, tenth or one-hundredth time on a boat, we were all starting as equal. I was amazed at the numbers who had no sailing experience at all yet threw themselves at the course with real gusto.

The training was designed to be as tough as possible, but the harder the instructors made things, the more inspirational the performance from this unique group of people. No matter whether it was three in the morning or three in the afternoon. No matter whether we were soaking wet, tired or confused. No matter whether someone was making a lunge to the rail to be gloriously sick in front of the rest of the crew or making a fool of themselves by cocking up a manoeuvre. The only thing that existed on board was a committed level of support and a desire to help each other through whatever surprise came next.

A larger-than-life gynaecologist, used to the high proportion of teenage mothers Newcastle produces, would break off her conversation, lean over the side, throw up, make a typical nurse-like comment about lunch being just as good on the second tasting, laugh enthusiastically and then look for the next job to do. Down below, three university students sat in a line, looking for all the world like the three wise monkeys. With impeccable manners, they politely asked if perhaps the bucket might possibly be passed down to them, before burying their head and adding to the content. The retching sound from one would set off his neighbour, while the third, rather than simply letting supper go on to the deck, would make a polite request for the bucket to be passed on in readiness.

Through sail change after sail change, working twenty-four hours a day with just a few hours of snatched sleep, we pounded through the waters of the Atlantic until we were exhausted. Exhausted from the physical exercise, exhausted from the vomiting, exhausted from the amount of information we were being bombarded with and exhausted from the lack of a full night in a stable bed.

Yet, exhilarated and completely alive too, alert and more awake than I had been in years, I was inspired by the supporting, laughing, encouraging help that lifted moods and got us working together as one. Strangers became brothers and by the time we set foot back on dry land, the group had become a really unified team.

Social barriers vanished and I was deeply, deeply inspired by the generosity of the personalities I shared my training with. After just one week, I knew without a shadow of a doubt that I had made the right choice and, with life looking far less jaded, I returned to the office with a definite spring in my step.

I was humbled once more, but this time in the corporate world, as my day of leaving drew closer. After so long with one company I wondered if I might suddenly crumble in an emotional heap when the moment came to say goodbye. Setting that process in motion, I had written to all the contacts that filled the bulging pages of my Filofax, from Ackerley via Lichfield to Young. I had been amazed at their responses, which ranged from the 'I always knew you were barking (Ackerley, A.) to 'Wow, what an adventure – you'll be following in the steps of my great-great-great-grandfather (Lichfield,

P.) to 'What a sad day for the company and what a great moment for you' (Young, R.). I was applauded for my decision to think big and brave, rather than make the more predictable step of safely sidling from one desk to another, and congratulated for taking a dive into the unknown.

Much of this sentiment came from individuals for whom I had a huge respect, having followed their own adventures with ill-concealed envy via e-mails, postcards and letters dispatched from an exotic collection of foreign fields over the years. Chris Bonington and Ran Fiennes urged me onwards and upwards. Mirella Ricciardi, the artist behind the seminal photographic book *Vanishing Africa*, grasped my decision with a passion that was frightening. Judy Leden, the women's world hang-gliding champion, wrote a dedication in her book encouraging me to 'go on taking risks' and giggled down the phone when I told her I was. Adrian Thurley – another pilot, ex-Red Arrows – was equally thrilled at the prospect, as was the company president, who wrote a personal letter of warm support from his eyrie high up in a glass tower in the Shinjuku district of Tokyo.

If these responses were humbling, the icing on the cake came in August 2000 – a couple of months before the start of the race, when I was asked out to dinner by my advertising agency. We met at Kettners restaurant in Soho and it was clear that something was up. Jeremy Bowles, our account director, was full of over-the-top innocence and bonhomie. Sarah Gold, our account handler, could barely conceal her excitement and my work colleague Sara, who was set to inherit my day-to-day problems, puffed nervously on more cigarettes than usual.

These people had kept me sane for the past year as we fought our advertising battles and they were all trusted friends. Despite my agency's reputation as one of the most creative in Europe, the most imaginative nicknames they had managed to create for each other were 'Bowlsie' and 'Goldie'.

Bowlsie and I had worked together for twelve years and had been thick as thieves through all of them. Not only had we worked hard to create a whole series of award-winning campaigns, we had played hard too. Watch Damon and Georgie Hill giving Murray Walker the first opportunity to talk to the new world champion at Suzuka and behind them you will find Bowlsie and I making complete idiots of ourselves for the benefit of our friends viewing back home. Look at a time sheet for the Cresta Run and you will find the names Bowles and Dickens on it somewhere. Look through a hotel register in Arles, Las Vegas, San

Francisco, New York or Burgh Island in Devon and you will find our presence immortalised. Scan the East stand at Chelsea or high up at the Nu Camp or at the away end of the San Siro or somewhere in Wembley and you'll spot us. A bar stool just about anywhere in London will have a tale to tell, and if I had been through some tough times recently, the compensation was a valued friendship.

Given such a close bond, I guessed that Kettners was not going to be a quiet drink and an early night, but was still unsure what their nervousness was hiding. After a studied yawn from Sara and yet another whispered conversation on her mobile, it was suggested that perhaps we might move on to Groucho's for another drink.

Rumbled.

I knew that none of them was a member and the club has a distinctly superior attitude to visiting guests. I knew this because Bowlsie and I had been kicked out a couple of years previously for daring to use a mobile phone from the club's dining room. It was apparently strictly against the rules.

Once in the club, my posse of friends urged me up some back stairs and then, rather curiously, shoved open the door of the Gents and pushed me in. The curious part was that they followed – girls as well as boy – and then started to undress me.

I had a panic-laden vision of being pushed naked on to a stage where a series of strippers would set about humiliating me as my mates cheered. It was not something I really wanted to endure and a good scuffle in the confines of a pair of urinals ensued. In between breathless lunges, they promised that nothing untoward was about to happen. They just wanted me to wear something a little different for whatever awaited me in the club.

Out from a suit bag came the outfit of a Royal Navy ordinary seaman, circa 1942, and as my suit, shirt, trousers and tie were stuffed away, I was transformed into a jolly Jack Tar with huge bell bottoms and jaunty cap.

Dressed as a sailor out for an evening in deepest, gayest Soho. Ha, bloody ha!

I was led to a door and, amid a lot of stage coughing and banging, it swung open and I was pushed through, to be greeted by a great cheer.

I stood, mouth agape, taking in the scene in front of me. I had anticipated that there would be a bit of a work send-off and had expected to see familiar faces from my office, the agency and one or two other companies I worked closely with. What I hadn't expected was the breadth of the turn-out and the generosity that such a commitment involved.

As I scanned the room, I could see photographers David Bailey and Bob Carlos Clarke. Alongside them were Richard and Susan Young, Jane Bown and Barry Lategan, chatting amiably with Carol White, head of the Elite Premier model agency. Judy Leden (who hates coming to London from her Derbyshire home) was there, as was Charlie Shea Simmonds, leader of the Diamond Nine Tiger Moth display team. There were Damon and Georgie Hill, giggling at my outfit, mingling with Ron Smith, who had come up from the Isle of Wight especially for the night. By the time he got home it would be way past midnight. Mountaineer Paul Deegan was there; so was TV presenter Chris Packham. Everywhere I looked, I saw the faces of people I had worked alongside over the years, and they all had happy, smiling, laughing faces, genuinely pleased to be able to share the moment.

There were speeches, of course, and as I stood on a chair I spotted more and more precious people who had made time in important schedules or travelled long distances to say goodbye. I was truly humbled by what I saw and taken aback by such simple and genuine signs of friendship. It meant a huge amount to me and I was moved to tears by such kindness.

The party flowed and everyone seemed to have a great time as I went from hug to kiss, handshake to embrace, toast to banter and back to hug again. One hard-boiled ad man said goodbye with tear-filled eyes, clearly expecting me to be washed overboard somewhere far away, and saw this as the last opportunity to say a proper farewell.

It was a fantastic night – especially as Anne had been smuggled into the club (thank heavens the stripper fear had been unfounded) and she was as touched as I was to witness the generous outpouring of support that filled the room.

Perhaps I had become too close to the job and, as it became an all-enveloping task, I had been unable to stop and appreciate the numerous good qualities of the people around me. That extended to my family as well, and the exhausted and drained father who sat silent in front of a large glass of red wine at the supper table every evening, too tired to speak or truly listen to the playground news that was being shared with him, had clearly missed so much.

Bugger. Maybe I was wrong to leave after all.

Too late. The deal was done, the letters written, the lawyers happy, the Germans ecstatic, the President sad and I guessed that my still-warm seat had designs already on it.

If the sole result of my decision was to witness such honest declarations of support, then that alone was already enough, even if the race itself were to turn into some sort of ghastly nightmare. The leaving party had been a bit like attending my own funeral, where I could look down and witness the people I care about, saying all the nice things that the pressure of everyday life normally holds back.

4

GETTING A PROPER JOB

I had a couple more days of work in London before I was formally
due to leave, but I took advantage of the last holiday allowance and
headed off for a final break with the family. We rented a simple little
cottage beside the sea in Norfolk. The four of us pottered over picnics
on Holkham beach, strolled through the narrow streets of Holt, sat on
a steam train to Sheringham and had long barbecues on the pebbles at
Salthouse. Some gentle sailing through the muddy creeks out into
Blakeney Pit was a fun prelude to the challenges ahead and as we
headed out into the North Sea chop off Blakeney Point, I was urged to
pay attention to the skills of the skipper at the helm.

There was a lot of ribald banter from my cousin and her husband
as I trimmed the small tan sails of their tiny open boat, and they were
laughingly adamant that the shingle spit just off the starboard beam
was a test equal to that of the Cape of Good Hope. Marion and
Jonathan may well have been right, although I imagined that off the
African coast there would probably be fewer boats crammed with
day-tripping, ice-cream-licking seal-spotters watching us slip
purposefully by.

Behind the happy-family-on-holiday image lay a growing
momentum of departure. We all knew that the moment was fast
approaching where serious goodbyes would have to be said and no
one wanted to face up to the prospect. We pretended it would never
come and put on brave faces, laughed overeager laughs, and the
hands that gripped mine on either side held on with extra strength

as Holly and Michael refused to let go. The goodnight hugs were extra firm as the days were counting down but, while they struggled, my focus remained firmly on the adventure ahead.

We were able to test the emotions again in a trial separation, when I went off to complete the last part of my training, competing in four races around the British Isles. The entire fleet came together for the first time and we headed for the start line of the first twenty-four-hour event.

The eight entries in the Clipper Ventures race – each a sixty-foot, cutter-rigged ocean-going yacht – looked the part, badged up with sponsors' names, along with the colours of the eight UK cities who were supporting the boats. On board *London Clipper*, with our blue and red stripes, the crew who would share so much together over the next year set sail as a team for the first time.

Unfortunately, our skipper was not with us. Stuart Gibson was the name the website listed as the man in charge and the fact that he was currently paddling a sea kayak around the frozen wastes of Alaska suggested he was not shy for a bit of adventure.

As it turned out, circumstances worked in our favour. A missing leader forced us to work harder to forge a team and a really strong spirit of togetherness began to take hold on board. The drafted-in training skippers commented on it as we bashed around the English Channel, rounded Land's End and fought our way up the Bristol Channel, before returning to Southampton via Plymouth. By the time we returned from the final race to Jersey with Stuart now with us, we were well on the way to establishing a solid bedrock of stability among the eight individuals signed up to go the whole way around the planet.

Just like the earlier training, I was amazed and moved at the sacrifices people had made in order to get on board. We were a real mixed bag of individuals from a broad range of backgrounds, jobs and disciplines, with ages spanning forty years.

There was Ellie Matthewman, an A&E nurse turned marketing consultant who had sold her flat to raise the funds. With a buyer found in July, she had to move out and now listed her UK address simply as 'London Clipper, Shamrock Quay, Southampton'. All her possessions were in her mum's attic, the boot of her car or on board the boat. Already this was her home.

There was Jane Gibson, a young PA who wanted to get away from a desk in London, see more of the planet and hone her small-boat racing skills. She too would sell her flat to pay for it all and, while the vital buyer was sought, her parents agreed to underwrite the participation fee.

There was Alistair Baxter, already known to one and all as Ali Baba. A larger-than-life, shaven-headed, fanatical Arsenal supporter, he was the sort of chap you would cross the road to avoid if you saw him heading out of the tube station on his way to his beloved team's Highbury ground. But crossing the road would have led you to miss out on meeting the most gentle, perceptive, deep-thinking, funny, caring, gregarious and huge-hearted football supporter in London. Flogging advertising space for a series of struggling medical journals, wall calendars and the occasional tray of dodgy perfume had earned him enough commission to find a place on board.

Fast becoming his chief partner in crime was Andy Howe, fresh out of Westminster School and university. Backed by his parents, Andy energised the boat with the enthusiasm of an on-heat spaniel and his flashing smile and ready friendship proved deeply infectious. His parents were no doubt expecting that the trip would enrich his education, but they had not bargained for the fact that Mr Baba would be sharing the bunk opposite their son for eleven months. A tragedy, especially when one considers the cost of a private education.

Anna Kellagher kept the girl-power momentum rolling and, like Andy, she seemed to enjoy a ceaseless supply of energy and enthusiasm for any and every task, no matter what time of day or night. A research scientist, she brought a constantly analytical mind to every problem on board and was quick to offer a solution to any problem that presented itself. The job could go on hold for a year and she was happy to rent out her London flat while she was away. As a result, she was homeless too. All across the fleet of clippers, parents who had long celebrated the day when their house was their own again, suddenly found that the kids were back in town.

The Fire Service had said goodbye to Alan Wells with the usual gold watch affair. But after years with his beloved brigade, Alan was adamant that an immediate departure to the bowls club was not for him. So while the other early retirees went for their flannel fittings, Alan was at the chandler's getting kitted out for a final adventure way more alarming than those found on Blue Watch.

I added my cashed-in career to the single-minded list of personal sacrifices on board and was joined by the final member of the team.

Watching this curious collection of individuals with an incredulous eye was Akira Sato, a talented sailor from Yokohama in Japan. Aki had read about the race in a Japanese yachting magazine, applied for a place and flown to the UK for an interview. His sailing credentials were impeccable, his agility on a boat second to none, his fitness and age perfect, but his English was, unfortunately, dreadful.

This was a race crewed primarily by English speakers and clear communication was of obvious importance. In a crisis it was essential and lives might even depend on it when the shit found the fan – an inevitability at some point over the next eleven months.

Sadly, Aki was turned away, and as he left the Buckinghamshire office, eight thousand miles away from home, he tried to recall how to arrange a taxi and a train ticket back to the airport. But, like everyone else on board, Aki had the same determination and was not going to be beaten. He managed to order a taxi and negotiate the rail system back to Heathrow.

But, instead of returning crestfallen to continue his white-coated role researching cosmetics in Japan's industrial heartland, he took a flight to Canada, begged a bed from some friends, resigned from the job that had made his parents so proud and set about learning the language.

Two months later he was back in England and in front of the MD of Clipper Ventures once more. 'Now will you take me?' he asked in impeccable English, and was warmly welcomed on board. And now that Aki was with us, Ali Baba set about quickly expanding his vocabulary by teaching a medley of songs dear to the Arsenal faithful.

We had yet to sail an ocean in serious anger, but already here were a bunch of people who inspired intense levels of respect in each other, and wherever you looked there was a bigger sacrifice and a larger effort from someone else.

As you would expect from a skipper in such a race, Stuart Gibson's sailing credentials were impeccable. Not only was he a sound sailor, he was also a good teacher and a well-balanced manager. This last quality was essential when the team needing management was the mixed bag of strong-willed personalities already described. For each of us, the environments where we were the experts, the people in control, the people making decisions, had been replaced by a totally new way of living and working.

Ellie had been the boss when an ambulance, its blue light flashing, arrived at her A&E department, and she had taken control of injured patients and weeping nervous relatives. Anna had run her team of scientists with a rod of iron as they peered into microscopes and deepened their understanding. Alan had been at his happiest when the alarm sounded and the Blue Watch team swung into action down the pole, each knowing the job he would have to do when his much-missed appliance arrived at the shout. Ali was the one who made the decision about how much he would charge for a page of advertising and who he would target next.

None of us knew anything about living together, crammed within the confines of a sixty-foot length of fibreglass. Our lives had never centred around the narrow bunks, with no separate cabins or snore-proof doors, that were now the core of our home. And as the boat went to sea on practice sails to try to turn a group of individuals into one cohesive, finely tuned team of round-the-world sailors, we all struggled to acknowledge each other's skills and new-found abilities. We were all experts, we all had an opinion, and, as we watched someone else attempting to complete a task, we all had better ways of doing it. As a result, a steady stream of helpful advice was offered on anything and everything taking place on board.

The furling of a sail, the process of putting a reef in the mainsail, the packing of a spinnaker, the coiling of a rope, even how much water to put in the kettle when it came to a tea break, were all tasks enthusiastically debated. And while we were all quick to offer lots and lots of advice on everything, we were distinctly uncomfortable about receiving it. Tell a strong-willed person that there is a better way of achieving a goal and more often than not their views will become more firmly entrenched and more and more obtuse.

I saw a whole series of glorious parallels with the boardroom I had left behind, as our early behaviour mirrored the attitudes that exist in work places the length and breadth of the country.

Stuart was the man who faced the daunting task of managing this powder keg of personality, and in addition to ensuring that his charges made it around the world faster than anyone else, uninjured and still speaking, he had other highly charged emotions that dominated his every waking moment.

Clipper had approached him with the offer of skipper, but the chance to complete the trip that all sailors dream of was at odds with a rather more pressing responsibility. Back home in north Wales, in a small stone cottage overlooking the sea from a gentle hillside, lay a tiny bundle of kicking, gurgling blue-eyed baby who had been born into the world at the same time as I had been celebrating my departure from work. Overseeing baby Ben Gibson's every move was his proud and practical mother, and as she watched her first-born suckle contentedly at the breast, her mind was filled with the thought of losing her husband for the best part of a year – the first and most important year of their fine young son.

Stuart's decision had been a desperately hard one to make. Liz Gibson came out of the same mould as Anne and was adamant that if the opportunity was presenting itself, then he should grab it with both hands. Liz is a local GP and an immensely practical and honest thinker. Baby Ben would not be aware that his father was not around and as long as he was fed, warm and dry, then the child would be blissfully unaware and blissfully happy. And while Stuart could accept that fact, he still desperately wanted to be a part of that first year. To see his son grow, smile his first smile, utter his first 'Da-Da' and take his first step. And while Ben did not have a clue of his dad's impending departure, Stuart most certainly did. Like any first-time father, he was racked with guilt and, despite Liz's eager support, still had his doubts.

We secretly wondered if he might even pull out before the start and did as much as we could to persuade him to stay. We showered gifts on him for the impending christening; we worked harder than any other boat to prove our eagerness; we offered him breakfasts and dinners, drinks in the bar after training and an ever-present eagerness at the sights, sounds and experiences that he would lead us through as we discovered the planet. In the end it was probably a close-run thing, but Stuart stayed, and in between the pangs of guilt he began to demonstrate the skills and qualities that would inspire such devotion and loyalty.

I returned to work to fulfil my last two days behind a desk in London, and felt comfortable as the office floor gently rolled from long days at sea. After I had completed the King's Cross route for the last time and sunk slowly into my huge leather executive chair, a steady queue of people came to my door for an audience.

They issued long diatribes about individuals who had created political mayhem over the past couple of weeks and complained and whined and demanded that action be taken. It was true that certain people seemed to be behaving in a less than helpful manner, but even as the earnest beseeching went on across the desk, I had an urgent desire to giggle uncontrollably. This was all suddenly very silly and spectacularly unimportant.

I still had to make one last visit to the ad agency over in Knightsbridge and, with a couple of hours to spare before the warm white wine moment of departing speeches in a boardroom packed with awkwardly shuffling staff, I strolled away from the slowly crawling traffic and meandered through Hyde Park. Drawn towards the placid peace of the Serpentine, I sat on a park bench at the water's edge and reflected on the year that had just past.

It was a year ago that I had decided on a major change and now the moment had come when the salary stopped, the Club Class travel and grand hotels were over, the company car was no more and the expense account a thing of the past. I had no more need of a suit, a briefcase, a diary or a secretary to manage it. I had no politics to fight, no battles to win, no meetings to attend, no e-mails to collect or mailbox messages to respond to.

As twenty-one years of sitting in an office came to an end, I sat in the warm September sunlight and felt more content than I had felt in years. For an hour I sat there, oblivious to everything else in the world as the traffic hissed through the trees, the inbound jets to Heathrow lowered themselves out of the sky and a group of young children from a playgroup excitedly fed bread to the ducks. Serious workers were at work, leaving the park for American tourists, pensioners leaning on their sticks, lovers walking hand in hand, a well-heeled rider and her horse cantering through the sand and the odd rower out on the lake showing off to an adoring partner. We were each content in our own world and happy to be able to have the time to simply watch the afternoon unfold.

That was it. Being a 'grown-up' was finally over. Now I could seriously go to work and start playing.

The task of preparing the boat began in earnest and more crew came to join Ellie as *London* became our new home. I lived on the boat during the week, going home at weekends to be with my family. On board we lived like gypsies, grabbing whatever bunk might be available and falling asleep to the gentle slap of the passing tide in the River Itchen. Shamrock Quay, at the back end of Southampton, is not a glamorous marina and, nestling under the building work of the city's new football stadium, we went about our daily tasks, fitting in with the other jobbing workers who made their living from boats at this functional, practical yard.

The daylight brought with it a heavy damp dew, which made a perfect alarm call. By 06.30 most of the crew had stumbled over the rough yard in a half-dressed, half-awake, yawning stumble and queued to get the hot water. Lines of steaming naked bodies emerged unselfconsciously from the cubicles and, as we towelled ourselves dry, the tasks for the day were discussed.

While one person was planning to go deep into the bilge, another would be hoisted high up the mast. Another would be off on a sail-repairing course while another couple, in a different classroom, would consider the complex issue of global routing.

Spanners and pliers were not the work tools for most of us and we set about learning the workings of our boat with a splendid cack-handedness. Fingers were sliced open, hammers dropped from the top of the mast, vital bolts plopped into the oil-laden foul bilge water and the bravest soul took a first nervous screwdriver to the flushing mechanism of the two heads, or on-board lavatories.

In between bouts of manual labour I went off to meetings that discussed provisions and drew up a shopping list for fourteen people's breakfast, lunch and dinner over seventy days, with no fridges to store it all in. I learnt how to service and repair the on-board diesel generator and main engine after a day of lectures in a lathe-turning, oil-smelling fabrication shed, and returned to the boat clutching a certificate of competence that meant as much to me as any advertising award.

More lessons on fixing followed at a two-day first-aid course. I could hardly believe that it was me snapping the stethoscope shut and deflating the blood-pressure collar, injecting apples with a series of practice syringes and learning how to stitch a wound using sutures on a mortally wounded ripe pear. In between the laughter prompted by a series of dreadful bodge jobs, the Army medic giving the lectures offered some sobering advice.

'If anyone receives a serious blow on the head and damages their skull,' he said, aware that the class had pencils poised and were ready to frantically scribble down the solution 'you might as well not bother.'

The nervous new sailors looked at each other and the colour drained from the upturned faces as he continued. 'Unless a helicopter is within thirty minutes' flying time and the patient can be stabilised, then basically they are dead meat. That's it, lecture on head injuries over.'

And just to make sure we were completely up to speed, he reminded us that for about ninety per cent of our journey a helicopter would be way out of range. Suddenly I wanted my crew mates to take the greatest possible care. On the training races we had already seen two crew airlifted from the deck of *Liverpool* and flown off to hospital in a coastguard Sikorsky. One of our own crew had got her fingers caught in a shackle when a line released suddenly and her screams could be heard on boats a quarter of a mile away.

A fully powered-up sixty-foot sailing yacht carries awesome loads, and I shared the dangers with the rest of the crew as we ate supper that night. Anne had already asked the crucial question and, in seeking the answer, I had established that there were two body bags on board. But out in the tropics, where the heat is intense, burial at sea for the soul that got it wrong was the probable answer.

Thank heavens Ellie was on board with her A&E nursing skills and I hoped and prayed that she remained undamaged throughout. If she got hurt, my two days of learning would be brought to bear and, quite frankly, the idea terrified me. I vowed to keep a special eye on her and pad her bunk with cotton wool if necessary.

5

HARD GOODBYES

My last weekend at home was supposed to provide plenty of quiet time for just each other, but it never really materialised. We had a mound of paperwork that needed sorting – this was the last chance for eight thousand miles and at the bottom of the large pile was a final draft from the solicitor. No matter how practical it all was, seeing the title 'Last will and testament' still brought me up short. There, in black and white, were all the details that would ensure a trouble-free handover of everything that related to me, should the unthinkable happen and the Army lecturer's prophecy came true.

We changed the subject quickly and moved to the huge world map taking pride of place in the mission control centre of the kitchen. Holly and Michael joined in, their fingers pointing at the stopovers where they would be on the quayside and we would be reunited as a family. The Galápagos stop was already booked and the long journey via Amsterdam, Curaçao, Guayaquil and Quito, with an arrival time of 23 December, already promised a Christmas like no other.

From there, Mike's finger trailed left, across huge areas of blue, traversing the Pacific to the edge of the map, before picking up from the opposite side and continuing left again, past the Far East, over the Indian Ocean, to finally pause on the small island of Mauritius. The idea of his spring half-term holiday seemed too far off to be real and the May arrival time was worryingly distant for all of us. The journey continued again, heading up to the more familiar seaboard of North America and ending with an excited jab at the black dot marking New York. If Mauritius was a distant thought, then the next summer holidays were a lifetime away.

Through the kitchen window I could see my turbo-powered, metallic paint-clad, alloy-wheeled, air-conditioned director-style car with its leather seats and CD changer. But not for much longer. I had no need for it and it represented a massive bucket of travel vouchers that would get the family to the three locations already booked. Anne's first task after I had gone, was to go and sample the delights of negotiating a fair price for it. She had already put one over-cocky salesman in his place and, with the help of a friend in the trade, I knew that she would get a decent amount of cash.

We worked through all the practical details that needed sorting and, as we did, I continued to be fuelled by a surging energy that willed the adventure to start. I knew that the emotions of departure were bubbling beneath the surface, especially for Anne, but selfishly I shooed them away. Partly out of excitement and partly out of fear over what would be unleashed if I truly addressed them.

If I had been more in tune with the rest of the family's emotions, we would have spent the evening at home in front of the fire. Instead we were at the local pub, where another jolly farewell party was in full swing. The bar was full of Tiger Moth pilots from Charlie's Diamond Nine display team, who were due to perform their last-ever public display the following day. They had also generously agreed to overfly the start as a special farewell for me and my boat the following weekend.

And while I enjoyed the ribald toasts, the warm wishes of good luck, the backslapping and the offer of another pint of Greene King, Anne was really struggling.

She was being asked the same questions by well-meaning friends and as she tried to cope with yet another explanation as to how she would cope on her own, the armour was finally pierced. This tough, brave, sassy woman, who had offered nothing other than unconditional support and love over the last twelve months, had to flee the bar. Eventually she emerged from the Ladies, eyes red raw, attempting to play it all down with a watery grin and a heavily chewed lip. It was clearly a real struggle to be there and watch another round of goodbyes. In such a fragile state, each farewell was like a nail through her heart and, true to form, I was horribly oblivious of how difficult it all was for her to endure.

So focused was I on what lay ahead for me, I had been blindly ignorant and unthinking about what it might be like for other members of the family. I just wanted to get on with it, put the waiting and the training behind me and put into practice all that I had learnt. Surely everyone must be thinking the same way?

It was a child's simple observation that finally opened my eyes and brought me back to earth with a bump. I was sitting on the floor at home, half watching crappy TV, enjoying a glass of red and a slice of pizza cooked by Mike, in the way that our regular Sunday-evening routine dictated, when he turned to me and said, 'Dad, do you realise this is the last Sunday night we will spend together for almost a year?'

In typical twelve-year-old-boy fashion, he'd made a simple observation, not one designed to open a wound or to crave attention – just an honest and practical passing comment.

Now, just when I needed to be in reassuring hero-father mode, I almost let it all go and was perilously close to sobbing like a baby in front of them all.

I headed back to the boat on Monday morning and used the time on the train to draft letters to Anne and the children, which I would leave as a surprise on their pillows. Once again the jangled and exposed nerve of emotion kicked in. Writing letters, particularly to your son and daughter, as you go away for nearly a year, placing yourself at the mercy of the oceans and trying to reassure and not patronise, proved unexpectedly hard. It was supposed to be a positive missive reassuring them of the adventure to come, but as the words came out, the sheer breadth of separation really took hold and as I bashed at the keys during the familiar journey down to the capital, tears streamed down my cheeks. At least it gave the commuters something to think about, especially as the regulatory uniform of suit, tie and briefcase had been replaced by a bright-yellow foul-weather jacket, T-shirt and kitbag.

I clearly no longer conformed and was delighted that the seat next to me was carefully ignored for several stops, before someone was brave enough to take it. Stepping out of myself and seeing the picture of my usual day as if for the first time highlighted what the year ahead was all about. Some things would be truly easier to miss than others and I thrilled once more at my decision.

The scene that greeted me when I stepped back into the marina car park looked like a Tesco truck had exploded. Everywhere there were great piles of cans, pack after pack of tea bags, vast catering drums of coffee, stacks of loo rolls, jars of Marmite, tubes of tomato puree, bag after bag of pasta in every conceivable shape, plastic packages of rice, box after box of Weetabix, Corn Flakes and Frosties, and a great pile of cartons of the long-life milk that would wash the cereal down over the next three months.

This was the result of my shopping list, and now supplies to keep fourteen people fed and watered for three meals a day for seventy days had to be squeezed on board. Everything in cardboard had to be de-packed and repacked. Every label on every tin had to be removed and the contents marked with an indelible pen. With no fridge or freezer on board, the location of milk, butter and cheese had to be selected carefully and the whereabouts of every single piece of food had to be logged so that we knew in which corner of the boat it could be found.

The entire crew formed a long chain and over the course of a day the piles of stores slowly dwindled. By eight in the evening we were done, by which time not an ounce of extra space could be found under the floorboards, under bunks, in lockers and in the galley itself. The newly painted last coat of anti-fouling had now vanished under the waterline and *London* sat lower in the water than we had ever seen.

We had wanted to spend at least a day back out at sea, working up the first-leg crew so that we were truly prepared for the start. But with the daily work list showing no sign of diminishing, time was running out. There were numerous small tasks of boat maintenance still to be done, route planning for the first seven-day leg down to Portugal still to be prepared and all the spare parts that had been ordered had still to be delivered and stowed.

The sea would have to wait. Stuart was less than happy and, with a full complement of crew on board for the first time, we were all equally anxious to work ourselves up into a well-oiled racing machine. Thirty thousand spectators were expected at the start and, on top of that, our every move would be watched by the all-seeing TV and still cameras of the assembled press. We were all eager to do it right.

Danny Farmer had already hung up the ignition keys to his London taxi and joined Gary Bower on board. They would both leave the boat in Hong Kong, having taken her halfway around the world. James Landale would be with us through to Hawaii, before a General Election would force him back to his role as political correspondent for *The Times*. Patrick Seagar had left his florist business for the seven weeks that it would take to get to Cuba and photographer Roy Riley would be leaving us in Portugal, having used his Nikon to capture the drama of the first leg for the news pages.

The last week flew by and while the rest of the crew took *London* round to the start base at Port Solent, I jumped on a train and headed for home for the very last time.

Everything I needed to pack was already on the boat and my locker was stuffed full of the tiny wardrobe of clothes that would see me through the year. I had nothing left to take, other than my toothbrush and the family, who would travel back with me in readiness for the race start. It was a Thursday evening and we lit some candles and had supper as a family, the dog sitting close to Michael, waiting for the inevitable spillage from his plate. We talked as we normally did, joked as we normally did, ate and drank as we normally did and went to our beds as we normally did. It was a Thursday, just like any other. Everything was normal, routine, unexceptional, except that it would be my last night in the house for eleven long months.

In the morning I had my usual cup of tea, shared a biscuit with the dog, took a shower and listened to 5 Live on the radio. As they went through the regular time checks, I knew that the same commuting faces would be lining up along the platform waiting for my old train. I knew that in London the office shutters would be rolling up about now, the mainframe was being switched on for the day, and I knew that the traffic on the M25 was building up badly around junction 19.

I ate the breakfast I normally ate and waited for the children to appear from their bed, as was the norm for a weekday morning. A watery sun shone, picking up the glossy sheen of freshly ploughed brown soil in the fields beyond the garden. The season was turning and for the first time in my life it would all happen without me. The morning continued just like any other. Holly arrived pyjama-clad, bleary-eyed and hair in spikes, closely followed by Mike. I got an absent-minded kiss on the cheek and a vague hug before they settled down to eat and the radio continued to offer its time checks and M25 traffic updates.

It was all perfectly normal and just a little unreal, until the dog was driven off to stay with friends for the weekend and we were reminded that this was my last few minutes with all that was familiar.

A clock had started ticking and the excitement of the previous months were replaced with a nerve that grew more raw as the second hand rotated. When the taxi arrived, Anne, Holly and Michael piled in, while I went to each bedroom in turn and left my notes on the pillow. Just doing that had my eyes stinging furiously, and as I took one last, long look inside before closing the door on my home, something became firmly lodged in my eye. Well, that's what I told the taxi driver.

He left us at the station and a few late commuters eyed us suspiciously. 'Children out of school, man dressed like something off a tin of John West salmon, strong-willed woman who refuses to let go of his hand. Very odd. Very odd indeed.' But it did ensure that we got most of the carriage to ourselves. After heading into London and then out the other side, the train made its slow and steady progress towards Portsmouth. A ticket inspector stamped the four tickets, only three of which were returns, but if he thought it odd he kept it to himself.

We had agreed that on such an emotional weekend the idea of Anne carrying my precious family around the busy motorway network as she headed for home was an extra we could all do without – hence the train. And even though it made sense, I looked at them lost in their own thoughts and tried to stave off a whole horror list of train crashes, taxi smashes and house fires that chose that moment to come and test my resolve.

Down at the marina there was the usual buzz of activity and I got stuck into it all, happy to have something to occupy my mind. The family went off to explore, and when we met in the evening at the hotel we were back on to an even keel, still steadfastly ignoring the dreaded moment that would take place just twenty-four hours later. While the kids abused room service, Anne and I went to a pre-race party attended by all the crew.

Try as we might, the party mood failed to truly kick in and no matter what we had to drink, both of us were unable to enjoy the moment. We snuck off into the night and had a last look around *London*, sitting proudly at her moorings. A full moon shone across the water and the sounds of the party drifted towards us as we looked at what would be my home for the next year. We stared intently at her suddenly small and vulnerable confines, willing them to yield at least a flavour of the adventures that we would share together, but she was asleep for the night and refused to indulge our whims.

We were back the next day, Holly and Michael spending time around my bunk before we stepped ashore. The next time they would be on board would be in the Pacific, and as we walked slowly away I turned to catch Anne placing a kiss on her hand and then transferring it to the hull at the approximate position of my bunk. The red eyes had returned and I looked quickly away, pretending not to notice such a small yet intimate act of love. The kiss was not just for me, it was also for the boat, and already Anne was demonstrating the deep-seated respect and bond that a sailor develops for his craft. I was hugely touched, and once again the tears pricked heavily in my eyes.

Back at the hotel we were almost at zero hour. We had agreed that goodbyes were going to be said on the eve of the race and that, having said them, I would go and join my crew mates on board. It would allow race day to dawn as the first day of our adventure and, while I could focus on what lay ahead, my family could tick the first day off the diary, which would mean the year until my homecoming was already a day shorter. The last thing any of us wanted was a protracted departure at the pontoon, where the time would linger and the act of letting go mooring lines, making the gap between quay and hull slowly widen, would be too cruel to endure. We would be surrounded by curious onlookers and embarrassed crew and it was far too public a place to conduct such an intense parting. The privacy of a hotel room would be so much better.

The hotel was one in a series of identical faceless buildings that dot the outskirts of most major towns in the UK. Dreadful muzak played through the luridly carpeted reception and floated around the green-waistcoated and name-badged staff. Debbie controlled reception, her sing-song voice greeting the weary traveller. Darren stood by with his luggage trolley, and in the bar Kevin and the rather racy Chantelle poured pints and dispensed packs of peanuts.

It was horribly impersonal for such a personal moment and our final supper took place in an overlit carvery, where a line of red lights squeezed the final juices out of the tired and overcooked meat. Mandy struggled with the corkscrew and poured the wine to taste with a shaking hand. Bread rolls were dispensed with an equally nervous double-spoon manoeuvre by John and, while I wanted the meal to last for ever, there was an equal desire to rush away from this dreadful attempt at being 'posh' as quickly as possible.

Then suddenly the plates had gone, the bill had been signed and we were back up in the overheated bedroom, with its trouser press and kettle. The dreaded moment could wait no longer.

Hugging Anne was fine. She was being strong and uttered nothing but positives. Michael was fine too, holding on to his emotions with a firm grip, as he became my man of the house for the year. His hug and kiss were hugely open, warm, loving and giving. And then the father had to say goodbye to the daughter. She rushed into the tightest embrace and as her head pushed hard against mine, sobs racked every part of her body.

And at that point I was undone. All the bravado and the excitement and the single-minded focus simply evaporated away. As she sobbed I attempted to control my own sobs and not let out howls of anguished pain. She shook and I shook back and our tears mingled into a soggy mass on the swirly-patterned carpet.

Eventually we had to break apart and with my family framed in the doorway I walked away down the long corridor, a steady stream of salty droplets pouring down my cheeks. I was oblivious to the guests who emerged from their rooms and oblivious to the people in the lift.

Across reception, Debbie and Darren smirked at each other and just as I headed out through the revolving doors into the welcoming darkness of the night, Anne's family appeared, ready to join in the start-line celebrations. I could only offer the crassest of welcomes and they clearly understood the private turmoil I was going through. I stumbled into the back of a taxi, consoled that family would soon be enveloping family, under the watchful gaze of Kevin and Chantelle.

Back at the boat my crew mates were returning in similar states of raw emotion, and as I stepped on board Ellie took one look and enfolded me in a huge hug. I headed for my bunk and discovered that the emotion was not yet done. Balloons were festooned from my tiny locker and three cards sat on my sleeping bag. Anne had written words of unconditional love and support. Michael had added a joke and a crude drawing of the boat – a token of his method of dealing with the situation. Once again Holly knew exactly how to hit the spot, and as I opened the card a pack of tiny gold metallic stars fell out.

She asked me to sprinkle a few of them on to the ocean every time we arrived in a port. Furthermore, I was asked to look deep into the vivid skies every night and say goodnight to the heavens, as she would be doing from her bedroom, snuggled high up under the thatch, back in Bedfordshire.

The emotion continued. I defy anyone not to lose it completely when they read a note that starts, 'To my dearest Daddy' and goes on to say, 'This is one of the hardest things to do ever! Saying goodbye to a Daddy like you.'

For the second time in half an hour I lost it totally and wept unashamedly. Others on the boat must have heard but, in the most caring show of respect, they left me alone and ensured that new arrivals were aware, via a series of gently whispered words of warning. I spent a long time at my bunk, unable to talk to anyone, opting instead to sort and re-sort kit that had already been sorted.

With red-rimmed eyes I eventually went up on deck just as Patrick appeared on the pontoon, and in the darkness I watched as his wife and daughters went through a ritual identical to my own. Eventually the girls in his life headed off into the night, like a group of mourners stumbling away from a fresh grave, and Patrick stepped blindly through the crew in the same emotion-laden state as myself and headed for the sanctuary of his bunk.

All of us had been on the same roller coaster and, despite an attempt to have an alcohol-free night, we ended up opening a bottle of wine and helped each returnee with gentle and very touching waves of support.

Goodbyes against the backdrop of such an immense passage of time and potential danger were new to all of us. The morning goodbye on the way to the train, or the casual farewell before a day in a boardroom somewhere in Europe, had always been conducted with a vague thoughtlessness. A quick peck on a cheek, an absent-minded hug, an all-too-easy 'Love you' and I was off, hitting the ground running with a briefcase and a loaded appointment book. More often than not, some of the family would not even be awake for such partings and it bothered no one. I would be back later and because the journey had been so matter of fact, so routine, the welcome home would be equally lacking in intensity.

'Darling. My God, how brilliant. You've returned. Fantastic. Wonderful. Look, children, this is your daddy. Do you remember him from this morning? God, it's amazing. You got the 17.55 from King's Cross? How was it? Come in, come in. Sit down, relax, have a drink.'

Hardly surprising that this never happened. But its absence only emphasised a brand-new and intense experience that had ambushed us all. It also revealed another new facet, where work mates – ones who were still comparative strangers – went out of their way to ensure that their colleagues were cared for and treated with the greatest sensitivity. Everywhere we turned, it seemed, important lessons were being learnt about a life that had been conducted in a climate of growing cynicism and tarnished values but was now being viewed as something virginally new.

All these lessons and we had yet to set sail.

6

READY, STEADY, DRIFT!
PORTSMOUTH TO PORTUGAL
15.10.00–22.10.00

A thin sun bathed the Port Solent Marina with a rich autumnal glow, making start day perfect for the visiting spectators. For the sailors, though, the only thing we were interested in was wind. And at that hour not a breath of it stirred the glassy surface that led down to the Solent and the start line.

But it was only six o'clock and there was plenty of time for a breeze to arrive before the midday gun signalled the first thousand-mile race down to Portugal. Even at this early hour the shower block was packed and filled with good-natured banter between all the crews, who had endured a restless night. Steaming, towel-clad forms shook hands with others with shaving-foam-covered faces. 'Have a good one!' were the repeated parting words, and out of sight of the spectators and the families a true spirit of togetherness existed among these amateur gladiators.

As the sun rose and breakfasts were cleared away, the fleet began to prepare for the momentous departure. Families who had opted for the quayside farewell lined the pontoon, and as I watched the grasping hugs I was glad that we had said our painful goodbyes in private. And while the last-minute leavers concentrated on trying to be brave in such a raw environment, the rest of us untied our lines and allowed the broad white hull to slip slowly away. In the intensity of the moment, no one had really taken in that the act was severing our final connection with the UK for the best part of a year.

In the marina's lock we offered ourselves up as a perfect goldfish bowl to the crowding TV cameras, brave-faced parents, press photographers and eager voyeurs. Poor Stuart had to endure this moment to finally hand over his two-month-old son, who was oblivious to the attention being focused on him. The tiny sleeping form had stayed on board for as long as possible, but now he was handed over to Liz.

As they embraced yet again, a final warm, proud and gentle kiss was placed by the father on his baby's forehead. The press, spotting the value of the picture, moved in for the kill. A hundred shutters rattled to the motordrive's command and captured the moment for the benefit of the world. Stuart looked like he was ready to hit someone, as the things most precious to him were transformed into a commodity that would flog a few more papers the following day.

The lock gates opened and we motored out of the marina with 'Jerusalem' playing loud from *London*'s speakers. We had wanted to give our boat a proud signature tune, and as the choirs built and the brass section bellowed, we felt we could not have picked a more rousing and emotional choice. *Glasgow* had gone one better, though, and stole the show completely. On her foredeck stood a lone kilted piper and as the green and yellow hull slipped through the water, the swirl of the pipes sent the familiar refrain of 'Speed Bonny Boat' back across to the waving families. The melancholy lament sent the hairs on the back of my neck alive and the ever-present emotion bubbled to the surface once more.

We came down the river to Portsmouth surrounded by a mass of spectator boats and formed up on the towering grey hull of HMS *Glasgow*, who had slipped her mooring to become our guardian stake boat. In a giant armada, the Royal Navy led us out of her most famous harbour and we must have made an impressive sight as the Round Tower slipped by, crammed full of frantically waving spectators.

My grandfather had witnessed this scene so many times in his naval career and then watched with pride as his sons had grown into the role, commanding their own ships. Now it was my turn to make such an exit and I was sure that the ghost of my grandmother joined her husband to witness it all once again. Waving a hanky and wishing God speed to her grandson would have been a routine that was comfortably familiar.

They would have been doubly thrilled, as another grandson, my cousin Mark, stood on the flight deck of the destroyer waving enthusiastically down at the race fleet. Unlike me, he had joined the family 'firm' and, ignoring the decorum that was supposed to go with his commander's uniform, he marshalled Anne, Holly and Michael into view at the guard rail, where they waved and hollered with unbridled enthusiasm. His help in getting them on board such a privileged vantage point had been the perfect foil for the emotions of the day. If I was having an adventure, so too were they, and while the sights and sounds on board the warship would no doubt appeal to Michael, the attentive care from the uniformed crew would prove equally popular with the women in my life.

Waving is an odd thing.

A wave is only complete if acknowledged by a wave in return, so that communication is established. Having made the connection, all you can then do is wave some more, so that is exactly what we did. I waved at Anne and Holly and Mike and they waved back. I waved at Mark and I waved at his wife, Debbie. I waved at Aunts Audrey and Mary, whose naval-officer husbands would have loved the moment. They all waved back. I waved again and they waved too. They waved at me and I waved back once more. I gave a ten-second burst of waves and they responded with a slow, fifteen-second salvo, as if they were at a Pink Floyd concert, so I responded once again with a double-handed rejoinder.

Then a spectator boat passed by with a full commentary spouting from the tannoy about the crew of *London*, and sisters and nieces and nephews and in-laws and outlaws all waved enthusiastically, so the trade-offs started all over again.

It is a mute and pagan form of connecting and after a bit you wonder what else you can do. Perhaps a back-handed wave, or a windscreen-wiper flip or a through-the-legs Ministry of Silly Waves version, to keep the communication fresh and interesting.

And then Charlie and the team centred their Tiger Moth display right overhead and gave a beautiful send-off with the tightest and sharpest formation, waving from their cockpits on the downwind flyby (I employed a simple, strong, forearm sweep for this moment in order to return the greeting) and Charlie very sweetly ensured that the formation took in the Royal Navy on his circuit as well, so that Anne, Holly and Michael could be acknowledged too.

On either side, the other seven sixty-foot racing yachts surged through the water, with sponsors' flags flying proud alongside the individual colours of *Glasgow*, *Liverpool*, *Bristol*, *Plymouth*, *Jersey*, *Portsmouth* and *Leeds*. Behind us sailed Clipper Ventures' corporate fleet of ten 38-foot racers and around them all buzzed a grand-prix grid of wave-bouncing ribs. Ahead lay a further massive fleet of around two hundred yachts, motor boats, dinghies and gin palaces that had secured a waterborne vantage point to watch the start. With the Tiger Moths departing, helicopters took over the skies and the beach around Southsea Castle was awash with spectators.

It all blurred into an amalgam of sights and sounds, with only a vague awareness of the number of spectator boats all around us, the twenty thousand people watching from the shore and the downward-pointing TV cameras from overhead, and thumping helicopter blades and radio calls and clock watching, as I gave the countdown to the crew. And then, in the midst of all the confusion, an echoing 'BANG'.

Off went the start cannon in a great blast of blue-black smoke, up went a huge cheer and suddenly all that had gone on before – not just the previous few hours, or the previous day, or the farewell party, the engine-servicing and first-aid courses, the maintenance period of the last month, the training races of the month before, but also the previous September, when I replied to Clipper's ad and explained to the family why I thought it a good idea, and before that all the self-important politics from the work place – all of my past fell by the wayside and we were a racing yacht, off around the world, with every crew member playing his or her part to make it happen to the best of our abilities.

No one heard the buzzing helicopters. No one waved, oblivious now to spectators. No one took in the armada around us and everything came to a culmination of expectation, focus and concentration that, gratifyingly, saw us cross the start line in first place.

Except the whole thing was a bit of an anticlimax as there was still not a breath of wind and the pent-up energy and potential of our ocean-racing yacht remained, well, firmly pent up. All that training and preparation and readiness to show off our brave, heeled-over, ploughing-through-the-water-at-a-ridiculous-angle skills would have to wait for the secret, over-the-horizon land and in the meantime we could hear, uncomfortably, the peals of laughter coming from the shore as the spectators took in the ridiculousness of the moment.

We lolloped over the line in first place, drifted a bit, created some apparent wind from the movement and managed to turn around the first mark. The tide stream heading out of the Solent gave us some more apparent breeze and we made it past HMS *Glasgow* at

Top: The first night of the race and *London* has to suffer the indignity of anchoring off Cowes when the wind dies clean away. In the background, three further racers attempt to claw their way back against the tide in order to pass the correct side of a race mark.

Bottom: *London Clipper* beating against a Force Seven in the Bay of Biscay.

Top: Up the mast to fix a broken spinnaker halyard, as *London* continues to race south towards Portugal.

Bottom: Dawn in the middle of the Atlantic, *en route* from Portugal to Cuba.

Top: Dawn in the Atlantic, and the previous night's errant flying fish are cleared from the deck.

Bottom left: Turning 45 in the middle of the north Atlantic – as good a place as any for a party.

Bottom right: The eleventh of the eleventh, and at eleven o'clock local time the crew observes two minutes' silence, complete with home-made poppies, mid-Atlantic. (*Back row, left to right*) Aki Sato, Jane Gibson, Andy 'Radar' Wilkinson, Anna 'Nick Nack' Kellagher, Patrick 'Pancake Pat' Seagar, Ali 'The Baba' Baxter, Andy 'Chairman' Howe, Alan 'Gringo' Wells. (*Front row, left to right*) James Landale, Elaine 'Miss Ellie' Matthewman, skipper Stuart 'Stug' Gibson, Gary Bower, Danny Farmer (aka 'Fanny Darmer') and 'Daddy Dickens'.

Top left: No matter if it is 2.00 pm or 2.00 am, *London* continues to race. A full moon watches our progress as we speed towards Cuba.

Top right: The logistics of buying provisions for the next leg: this shop was in Colon.

Bottom: Filthy conditions at the start of race three to Panama. So much for the sparkling image of the Caribbean!

Top: An illustration of the type of drama we dipped in to when ashore.

Bottom: The giant gates of the Gatun locks look like something from a James Bond film set, and herald the start of the Panama canal.

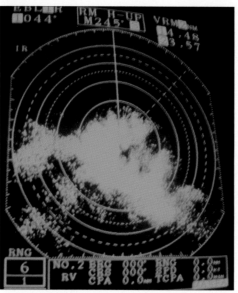

Top: The Pacific Ocean, and with the spinnaker harnessing good winds, coupled with good swell and good waves, it means excellent surfing. These are the greatest sailing conditions in the world, and Danny Farmer and I are clearly enjoying them.

Bottom left: A night-time squall, six miles across and directly overhead, fills *London*'s radar screen.

Bottom right: Thanks to the generosity of Barry and Wendy Taylor, I get to swap my bunk for some five-star luxury in Honolulu.

Top: A Booby does an exploratory fly-by in the Pacific to check if *London* is a good place for a kip.

Bottom: The ocean's loss is the crew's gain as we get our first fresh meal after three weeks of living on tinned food. Pacific Ocean, 300 miles south-east of Japan.

Top: Bayside Marina, Yokohama.

Bottom: A spectacular sunset in the South China Sea, *en route* to Hong Kong as I sail waters patrolled by my grandfather and uncles some 70 years before.

Inset: Sarah Beaugeard from *Jersey Clipper*, Akira Sato, Alan Wells and Gary Bower help me investigate an appropriate bar in Hong Kong. It turned out to have no link to Dickens whatsoever and instead of book-lined walls, numerous TV screens pumped out global sport to a mass audience of pint-clutching ex-pats.

Gilkicker Point at a snail-like pace and then attempted to head over to Cowes for the next mark.

It was here that the wind gave out completely and we watched, helpless, as the tide pushed us past the wrong side of a vital buoy which, if missed, would mean disqualification. We tried to combat the problem but the tide was stronger than our headway. In the end we were forced to throw out an anchor to stop drifting even further away and then wait an agonising five hours for the tide to turn, in order to drift back towards the start. And still not a breath of wind blew, so it was anchor time again in order to wait the outgoing tide once more, before we could slip past the correct side of the buoy.

What a ridiculous moment. Here we were, at the beginning of a thirty-six-thousand-mile odyssey, anchored two hundred yards off the shore of Cowes, enduring snide comments from passing weekend sailors. 'You haven't got very far, have you?' or 'You're going the wrong way – Portugal's over there' issued forth from a steady stream of smirking homeward-bound locals. How funny these jibes were, especially when we heard them for the twentieth time, and our sides almost split with mirth. Our patience, just three hours into the race, was being sorely tested. The dictionary suggests that 'frustrating' should be the word to use, but it was not nearly expressive enough to describe the moment.

But even though we were at anchor, there were still problems to resolve. The generator decided to choose that moment to pack up and Stuart and I spent three fume-filled hours down in the darkness of the aft watertight compartment, attempting to coax it into life. All our efforts failed and, as it powered up the water maker, the boat went on to immediate water rations while we were still within a few hundred yards of a land-based tap.

With the cynical yachtsmen firmly tucked up for the night and lost in a land of dreams that took them out to where the albatross flies, the merest hint of a breeze finally whispered its way around the sleeping houses of Cowes and crept out across the water to us. In the small hours of Monday morning we eventually got going, unseen by anyone and in the darkness of the night, we sniffed the first real breeze off the English Channel. A few hours later and the lights of England slipped lazily over the horizon as we entered an alternative world where time takes on an entirely new dimension.

In a normal week the seven days have a structure and a personality. Monday is dreaded, Wednesday marks the halfway point, Friday means a big night out and the weekend is for football scores, dinner parties, lawnmowing and lie-ins. Ashore, radio alarm clocks were introducing Monday morning to the groaning masses, while out at sea, on board the racing fleet, the week took on a completely new structure, with its own unique agenda, rules and foibles that were not structured by diaries or timetables. Mondays, Wednesdays and Fridays still existed, but they did so in a parallel universe where time stood still.

And if time had stood still, the front-runners had certainly not. Two boats had just managed to slip around the windless mark before marooning the rest of the fleet and because of the lack of wind and a heavy dose of bad luck, we were now fourteen hours behind the lead boat. And in our diary-free, timeless home, other problems started to test us as we tried to play catch-up.

Over the next few days we sat in the confined space of the generator room, trying again to fix the duff engine, bleeding diesel, stripping electrics and bypassing solenoids, but all to no avail. Showers were definitely off, but at least we would all grow smelly together.

We smelt a faulty propeller-shaft brake burning out its disc pads in choking plumes of blue smoke and had to revert to a much more seaman-like solution of strong rope and secure knots to solve the problem.

We saw the bilge fill with sea water, pouring in somewhere around the engine exhaust system, that required constant bailing.

The spinnaker halyard snapped with a loud bang, dumping the sail into the water and just as we finished that 'all hands on deck' drama, the team on watch played midnight fishing with a boathook to recapture the topping lift after a shackle sheared at the end of the boom.

We watched as Stuart pummelled the computer screen when it failed to give him weather updates and we tried to restore the wind-reading instruments that suddenly decided to uncalibrate themselves on the cockpit display. Gary reached for the rewiring kit when the compass lights gave out for no apparent reason and Ali cursed the skipper of a large French trawler fleet who decided to motor across our bow at two in the morning, oblivious to our presence somewhere off Ushant Point.

Ex-nurse Ellie marvelled at Anna's swollen, bruised forehead and two black eyes, gained from being pitched into head-butting a forestay in the middle of the night, and we watched alarmed as Aki, Danny and then Andy were sent, cannon-fodder style, up the seventy-foot mast to fix the broken spinnaker halyard.

Aki went first and at the top of the pendulum-swinging mast he was tossed around like a rag doll as he tried to sort out the lines. The impact of his body hitting the mast was so great, his sailing boots were shaken from his feet and plunged into the sea with a loud splash. Danny volunteered to replace him and was gingerly raised aloft. The poor chap also lost his grip and he too was swung out over the ocean, before returning, legs either side of the mast, in a bollock-smashing moment of agony.

Then up went Andy, our testosterone kid, who loved the added thrill of danger. He too slipped, coming back down with blood pouring from a wound caused by impact with the upper mast spreaders that required a couple of stitches to staunch the flow. I watched and took notes, while Ellie conducted the operation. It looked a lot trickier than repairing ripe pears – especially as fruit tends not to howl out in agony when pierced with a sharp suture needle. Stuart joined in as another trainee doctor and administered a tetanus jab to Andy's mooning backside. As the patient lay face down on the engine cover awaiting the shot, the rest of the crew clustered around and helped Stuart's aim with a series of helpful observations. And at no point did anyone think it was anything other than completely normal.

We decided that enough damage had been done for one night and agreed that the problem could wait until the hopefully calmer morning. The selection process for such perilous trips was based on crew members' weight, since they needed to be winched aloft, and, realising I might be the next 'volunteer', I set on a crash course of heavy eating at breakfast. It didn't work, though, so up I went, hanging on for my life, threading new halyards at the top of the mast and then going up again half an hour later to check if they were free-running. And although I am not a great fan of heights, the view from such a lofty vantage point was breathtaking.

It seemed that bad luck was in the ascendant as we battled to overcome all the difficulties that came our way. But battle we did, with a never-say-never Blitz spirit, and as each day brought a new problem we dealt with it, dispatched it and challenged the gods to try us some more.

London beat through Force Eight storms that sent several of the crew to their bunks with debilitating seasickness. The foredeck crew struggled up at the bow to change sails. Stuart took flyers on the weather and bucked the fleet trend by pushing out to meet the weather fronts in the Atlantic, in order to get a broader reach across the Bay of Biscay, and we had a collective teeth gnash when those fronts failed to materialise and wind shifts took us in the wrong direction.

The two watches alternated through nights of rain, spray and prolonged tiredness as we raced for longer than we had ever endured in our training. But, through all the problems, there remained an incredible focus, spirit, commitment and desire that saw us make up all the lost miles, and more, as we came back through the fleet.

It provided a huge test, which we passed with flying colours.

And, by electing to live life at such extremes, we enjoyed rewards that were correspondingly inspirational. We were the only people in the entire world to sail under a harvest moon in a heaven alive with pinpricks of starlight and criss-crossed with shooting stars reflecting on a phosphorescence-creaming sea, and hear a gentle 'plop' in the water just a couple of arm lengths away from where we sat. There, in the moonlight, swam a lone dolphin, keeping us company in the long night. We sat awestruck by sunsets and sunrises that no one would ever see from land. We saw schools of whales alongside the boat and marvelled at the breadth of the vast grey-black backs that lolloped out of the water right alongside us.

We watched, fascinated, as the torpedo-like wake of a large male whale headed straight for us, a rippling, oily, eight-foot-across shimmer of water betraying the beast's presence as it nosed forward, diving at the last minute and giving our keel the gentlest of nudges as it passed by below. We ran for the birdwatcher's guide to identify two large brown boobies, flapping their huge and heavy wings, far out to sea. Anna fed an exhausted sparrow that came out of nowhere, in the middle of nowhere, and settled in the cockpit, hopping from crew member to crew member and sharing the Alpen and Weetabix breakfasts we were eating. We baked fresh bread, we made pancakes and challenged each other to produce the best supper on board. And no matter which team was on watch, the crew drove the boat with more stamina and willpower than we thought possible.

As the Bay of Biscay gave way to the coast of Portugal, the bows of *London* headed back in from the Atlantic and for forty-eight hours Stuart, Gary, Ali and I battled with the elements at the wheel. One hour on, one hour off, in two different watches, we ran, under spinnaker, in a Force Eight blow with a huge following sea. The knife-edged course needed was marginal, and could easily have resulted in an on-the-side broach, with the boat blown over nearly horizontal, or in a mass of sail cloth tangled around the forestay. It required a massive amount of strength and commitment.

With my hour on the wheel done, I headed for my bunk but struggled to find a position comfortable enough to let sleep come. Muscles that had never been tested over such lengthy periods by such powerful forces shrieked in agony, no matter how I lay in my narrow 'coffin'. And just when the burning ache subsided a little, it was my turn back at the wheel, for another sixty-minute workout. But everyone, as they had from the start, delivered and did so big time. So much so, that *London* set a Clipper Ventures speed record for the leg of 17.4 knots – amazing when one considered the thirty tons of hull, fourteen crew and several hundred tins of baked beans that we carried.

Whether it was 14.00 or 02.00, the boat was being driven with the same dedication and focus, which was why, twenty miles from the finish, we rounded Cap St Vincent, Europe's most westerly point, and found ourselves reeling the competition in at a rare rate of knots.

The towering cliffs, with their dramatic lighthouse, were a spectacular landfall, and as we rounded them close in to shore and headed east down the Algarve coast, the Mediterranean came to greet us. The last remnants of the onset of a British winter fled and a warm sun baked down on to a glistening azure-blue sea that revealed two of our competitors just a few miles ahead. We knuckled down for one final push as the sun dipped into the ocean behind us and the race carried on into the night. In light and fickle winds, *London* slowly narrowed the gap and then overtook first *Jersey* and then *Portsmouth*. From being more than a hundred miles behind in last place, we had worked our way up to third.

At the end of our first race we had beaten *Liverpool*, *Glasgow*, *Leeds* and *Jersey* and just missed grabbing *Portsmouth*'s scalp by a mere twenty seconds after a thousand miles of racing, thanks to a wind shift in their favour just a mile from the finish. Fourth, after all our difficulties and problems, was a result we were mighty proud of, and with 'Jerusalem' pouring out of the speakers we motored in, breaking the silence of a sleeping Vilamoura. Back on dry land, we wanted a beer, we wanted to party, we wanted to celebrate our safe arrival, but the bar owners and restaurateurs had other ideas. In the hotels and timeshare apartments clustered around the harbour, clocks, watches and radio alarms were showing 02.00, and for the landlocked the rules said 'sleep'.

When the sun rose we were truly back amid normality, where people and shops and supermarkets and traffic reports and lawnmowers and newspapers from home and all-day fried breakfasts existed, and the secret world beyond the horizon faded to a distant blur once more. Already, after just a few days, we were questioning whether true normality really existed ashore. By comparison, the simple reality of living where the planet was at its most raw was startlingly attractive and honest.

I got to a telephone in a huge hotel that towered over the marina, amused at the memories that it brought back. A year ago I had been there, suited and booted, for the annual winter sales conference. Reps with their golf bags, PowerPoint presentations that looked at profit margins and retailer incentives, earnest messages from the sales director at black-tie banquets, all echoed like ghosts around the foyer. Now the staff looked down their noses at the boat bum in shorts and T-shirt who had dared to enter their marbled halls in search of a phone.

The mere seven days that had passed since the emotional departure felt like seven weeks, so varied and intense had been our experiences. I connected up my laptop, sent off e-mails to announce my safe arrival and attempted to try to convey at least a little of the drama and intensity of what we had been through.

I spoke to home and learnt that our journey had been dutifully watched on the web and, with twelve-hourly updates provided by Clipper, they had been able to share every high and low. My father, who for years had dismissed computers and e-mails as the devil incarnate, was especially fascinated by the level of information on offer and had spent the week standing at my brother's shoulder, poring over the facts on his screen. Like an anxious admiral back in Whitehall, he became immersed in the race, zipping from the official Clipper site to weather sites, to satellite pictures and back to the race site again. At seventy-four he decided that a laptop was now a must and, much to the amazement of the family, went off to PC World, bought the kit, signed up for an e-mail account and logged on. The town of Crowborough is a fair distance from the sea, but, from that point on, all the maritime sites in the world came flooding into East Sussex and on to the bridge, from where he directed operations.

The weekly shop, the allotment, the *Telegraph* crossword, all the day-to-day routines that fill the life of a retired couple, were replaced with real adventure. Mum stepped on to the bridge too and they settled down to run the race with as much involvement as if they had been on board alongside me. From home, similar stories were relayed and the official website was getting an amazing number of hits, as friends logged on to chart our progress. The on-board diaries that I was writing for *The Times* On-Line seemed to be hitting the mark and, with James Landale filing regular pieces for his paper, our every move and emerging emotion was shared by an enthusiastic audience.

After a week at sea living in such an intense and public environment, the crew headed for the sanctuary of hotels, as hot water, a steady bed and personal space were suddenly hugely sought-after commodities. Despite having enjoyed the luxury of the five-star gaudy conference hotel the year before, I prided myself on readjusting to life after expense accounts and negotiated a room for £30 a night including breakfast, in a slightly less impressive building in a backstreet. No minibar, no welcome bowl of fruit, no luxury bath stuff and no global TV, but it was fine. In fact, after my bunk, it was luxurious.

But years of living at someone else's expense is a hard habit to break and I used the room phone without a second thought, checking for e-mails every hour out of force of habit. I wanted to share my digital pictures and fired them off down the wire, thinking nothing when the large files took an age to send. While my laptop clicked and buzzed, I took a bath and fell asleep in the warm water. My pictures were still making the journey forty minutes later.

When I checked out of the hotel after three days and returned to my bunk, the bill for the room came to a very respectable £95. However, I feared that Anne might be less impressed when the credit-card statement came through, demanding a further £350 for the communication charges. Breaking the corporate habit would clearly be harder than I thought.

We had a five-day stopover to recharge our batteries, but Portugal was hardly a holiday. With so many parts of the boat failing on the run down, we had our work cut out to complete the long list of fixes before the race start.

Day after day, every boat in the race fleet was a hive of activity as the late sun-holiday chasers watched us at work. Lots of Brits were in town taking advantage of the half-term holidays and a regular stream of questions were directed at anyone in Clipper team kit.

I hired a bike and zipped through the crowds along the bar-lined waterfront where the red-skinned package-tour crowds sat and ate plates of baked beans and read their *Sun* and *Daily Mirror*. I became a familiar face at the two local chandlers as we sought all the vital bits we needed and tried to contain my frustration at the repeated shrugs of the bored girl behind the counter.

'Do you have one of these?'

Shrug.

'Where can I get one?'

Shrug.

'Is there another town nearby that might have one?'

Nod.

'How far away is it?'

Shrug.

'Do you have a telephone number for the other shop?'

Shrug.

Very frustrating days, made all the more frustrating by trying to complete jobs with a lack of knowledge and an even greater lack of the right tools.

Our spinnaker pole had been bent and needed repairing. Clipper were adamant that we had to do it ourselves and I spent two absolutely bloody days with a recalcitrant hand drill, salt-encrusted pop rivets and a useless pop-rivet gun, trying to effect a half-decent repair.

In the end Alan and I took it to a local sail loft, where a helpful Canadian surf dude allowed us to use his workshop. His world was one of calm tranquillity, and surrounded by whitewashed walls with white ceilings and white floors, we finished the repair, to the buzzing accompaniment of sewing machines stitching together yards and yards of crisp white sail cloth. The radio played gentle music and the dude's female colleagues looked shyly over their hard-working machines, casting coy and blushing smiles in my direction.

At the very end of the stopover I got just four hours to myself and after the hard work of the previous few days, plus the rigours of several weeks at sea ahead, I was determined to maximise it.

For £10 I rented myself a Lambretta and with sunglasses clamped firmly to my face I zipped away from Vilamoura to find a bit of peace and quiet. I took the coast road and screamed along at full throttle, revelling in the freedom of speed, escape and solitude. After about fifteen miles the concrete eyesores started to dwindle and the coast turned rocky and dramatic. Following my nose took me to a small deserted beach in a sandy bay and I found a sheltered rocky cove bathed in the warm October sunshine. Perfect.

I stripped off and immersed myself in the cool of the sea, luxuriating in the freedom of the moment and then lay in the sun, reading, sleeping and daydreaming for a couple of hours of blissful relaxing solitude.

On the way back I followed my nose again and when the tarred road ran out and became a dusty track, I continued to follow it, winding my way through vineyards of rusty-leafed vines and deep-green orange groves, where the fruit hung heavy and lush on the branches. Wizened old olive trees filled fields lined by crumbling stone walls and the occasional dog was startled by my buzzing scooter as I zipped through rundown farmyards.

As I rounded one corner it was my turn to be startled. Peering over the hedge at the curious noise were four outstretched necks attached to the biggest ostriches I had ever seen. It was the last thing I had expected and my journey home nearly ended in the ditch.

The break from the race was minuscule, but even so, getting away from the boat and having time for myself was an essential thing to have done. I felt much better for it as we reconvened for a crew dinner to say goodbye to the ever-smiling Roy Riley. He had been allocated to *London* by *The Times* to cover the race start and, as well as sending back daily images for his employers, he had become an indispensable and popular member of our team. Despite our best efforts, 'The Thunderer' was adamant that Roy was needed back in the capital and as he headed gloomily for the airport, a cab heading in the opposite direction carried a slightly more excited fare. Andy Wilkinson joined us from the UK and *London* was ready to go back to sea.

7

In The Wake of Columbus
PORTSMOUTH TO CUBA
28.10.00–22.11.00

We motored out the following morning to enthusiastic waves from the holidaying Brits and headed towards another start line with no wind. In the short time before the off, we still had to test the generator and ensure that we had a functioning water maker. With fingers firmly crossed, everything seemed to work and we hoped that it was a good omen for a more reliable crossing.

Up to thirty spectator boats, including the impressive racing catamaran *Club Med*, milled around us as we sailed in the lightest of breezes to jockey for the best starting position and a shy wave from a nearby yacht was delivered by my bashful friend from the sail loft as she steered close by our stern quarter to give an unexpected farewell.

A TV helicopter careered desperately low over the water filming the action as its blades beat up a mini-whirlwind on the surface. As with the Portsmouth start, the gun went off in almost zero breeze. And again like Portsmouth, we were first across the line and set off at an agonisingly slow pace, leading the fleet westwards towards Cap St Vincent.

Several inshore race markers had to be cleared before we could set a course south towards the trade winds. The final buoy, just off the Portuguese coast at Lagos, was timed to perfection, our course hard on a now brisk breeze taking us just the right side of it. We tacked through the wind, bore away and launched the spinnaker in one swift piece of crew action. To the watching spectator boats, it looked very sharp, very satisfying and very professional.

As the long trawl south began, a school of dolphins came leaping across the waves to bid us farewell. The late-afternoon sun glistened on the shards of water dripping from their backs and bathed them in a surreal halo of golden mist. They swam with us for several minutes before turning north again and we watched them head effortlessly away back towards Europe. Their fins, lit by the setting sun in the west, burst in and out of the water until all that could be seen were numerous fizzing balls of fine spray betraying their presence.

Stuart produced a bottle of rum to toast our impending adventure. The first tot went straight over the side as a peace offering to Neptune and we toasted his and each other's health for the days and weeks ahead. The bottle passed from Jane to Ellie, Andy and Ali as it worked its way around the boat. Each gulp was preceded by an individual message of respect to the ruler of the seas, delivered through a series of impassioned oratories to the undulating surface. Aki joined in, despite being fiercely allergic to alcohol, and we hoped that Neptune did not catch the screwed-up face of total disgust as he did his bit for tradition. The laws of the sea were now being observed and the creeping warmth from the spirit energised the boat – even though it would be the last alcohol we would touch until we stepped ashore again in Cuba.

The tactic for crossing the Atlantic is to head south for the trade winds. The November routing chart for the ocean showed that the winds and currents down towards the Cape Verde Islands were more useful for our journey and all the manuals on board confirmed the view. One even commented that Christopher Columbus's route is a hard one to improve upon. Out on the ocean, despite all the aids from radar, GPS and Met reports, the basic environment clearly remained untouched by man's inventive progress. The sea will always be the sea and would behave in exactly the same way this century as it did for adventuring seafarers five hundred years ago and will go on doing so five centuries hence.

We truly were travelling in Columbus's wake and it put things firmly into perspective early on.

So south we went. The days turned to night and night turned back to day again as the first week crept by and we remained firmly on the eastern side of the ocean, tracking in horribly light breezes down towards latitude 25, longitude 25.

Madeira came (and went) painfully slowly in the night, with the shore lights twinkling away in the distance on one side of the boat while *Portsmouth*, half a mile away on the other side, sailed along far quicker in a selective patch of breeze.

I tried my mobile telephone to see if I could get a signal from the shore and was overly cross to find it not working. Like a junkie trying to kick a habit, weaning oneself off the all too readily available communication bandwagon was proving exceptionally hard.

I tried the radio instead. Lying in my darkened bunk, I slowly rotated the dial of my small Sony receiver, tuning into a mixed bag of German, French, Spanish, Portuguese and African stations. They delivered a familiar mush of chat, Europop, classics and, in the case of the African stations, religious wailings and chants.

Out on the ocean, some two hundred miles off the Saharan coast, radio waves that had started out from a transmitter on the roof of some dismal downtown station, where a lone presenter worked through his tedious play list, hurtled through the night sky. They sped unseen over the low rooftops, skidded past mighty sand dunes, skimmed invisibly over the canvas shelters of sleeping Bedouins, where the dying embers of campfires swirled up into the cold, inky blackness and camels strained uneasily against their tethers. As strong as ever, the signal continued onwards, projectile-like, towards the pounding surf at the shore before heading out across the waves like a skimming Exocet, until it finally homed in on the vague shape of our small and insignificant hull. Spotting the weak red lights shining from the portholes out across the cold, still ocean, the sound swirled past James on the helm, tumbled down the companionway steps beside Stuart, hard at work on tactics, and crept into the sleeping quarters before finally settling at the aerial in my narrow bed.

The signal brought with it a contradictory feeling of warm comfort and complete loneliness. For the first time, I really felt homesick and very far away. It was essential that such negative moments should be banished without delay, so I have to thank the 'dove from above' who arrived on board later in the night and literally knocked some sense into me.

I was on the helm at 03.00, feeling a little sleepy, a little groggy and a little out of focus, when 'WHAM' was followed by 'FUCK' and then 'THUMP'. Out of the jet-black darkness in the middle of nowhere, my temple was struck a firm yet fluffy blow as something white and soft careered past my saucer-wide eyes.

It scared me witless and my shaking hands fumbled for a torch. There in the yellow beam sat a stunned and very confused baby dove, complete with comic-book stars swirling around his head. He sat where he fell, eyes half shut, feathers puffed up, and for several hours each helm change was conducted with Tom and Jerry-style tiptoe movements, so as to avoid treading on him.

The next morning he was still with us and ready to partake of breakfast. Weetabix went down well as he hopped from Ellie to Patrick, happy to be stroked. He steered well clear of me, though, casting an evil eye in my direction, believing that it was my sleepy-eyed helming that had steered me into his perfectly innocent trajectory.

As the sun set on the following evening, he took off and completed a couple of circuits of the boat. Although his final approach and touchdowns still looked a little shaky, he made it intact back to the deck. After a final pre-flight ruffle and with a departing crap, the bird flew off into the night. We wished him a safe journey and hoped that his night vision had improved enough to prevent him headbutting the less forgiving side of a passing supertanker.

After a week at sea the race fleet started to split up, with *Portsmouth* deciding to head west first. As each day passed, more and more of the fleet peeled off, until just *London* and *Glasgow* remained heading south. It meant that we gave up our lead position, but the stronger trade winds would allow us to quickly catch up again.

The weather faxes we tuned into every day from stations in Boston, New Orleans and Germany showed a confused picture. A late-season hurricane had crossed the Atlantic ahead of us and was tracking north, splitting up the usually regular trade winds. Everything pointed at its continued track northwards, which would ensure that the more reliable winds would re-form behind it. Bizarrely and breaking all weather patterns, the huge low then decided to track south again. The net result was that the power source we expected refused to blow while further north the isobars at the edge of the storm provided excellent drive into the sails of our competitors.

The result quickly dropped *London* to the rear of the fleet and as each day's radio schedule came in, we plotted our rivals' progress with a growing despondency. Down where Columbus had found the best winds, we sat in a frustrating and debilitating slop as the gap between us and the leader steadily increased. But it was all right for Columbus – he wasn't racing.

At the helm, I became absorbed with the challenge of such light weather conditions. With one's face up to sense and feel any wind, the merest puff on the cheek indicated something to be seized upon. Gentle turns on the wheel allowed the puff into the sail and all eyes looked at the speed instruments to see what it delivered. Every tenth of a knot was viewed as a major achievement and as the thirty tons of boat started to move, the forward motion created additional breeze. That, too, helped fill the sails and the wake started to bubble a murmur of approval as the hull crept slowly through the water.

And then, just when we thought we were on our way, the gust died, the boat rolled upright like a beached whale and the sails flapped their taunting tattoo once more. The noise of slapping cloth for hour after hour is the strongest form of torture and the entire boat grew irritable and frustrated from the repeated reminders of slow progress echoing through the hull.

Eventually we too turned west, but on half the breeze expected. Our faithful spinnaker, up since Portugal, kicked us along at just seven or eight knots, giving daily runs of around 170 miles. It was the best we could manage, but if the conditions continued we looked likely to arrive several days late in Cuba, still some three thousand miles away.

Down in the tropics, the boat settled into a simple routine. Shorts and T-shirts replaced the foul-weather gear and day after day the sun sparkled on a benign ocean. Images of grey, windswept Atlantic seas were dispelled as we rolled along on a surface that the weekend sailors on the Solent would be happy to play on. The only difference was downwards, where beneath our fragile hull lay nineteen thousand feet of sea water.

The nights brought blessed relief from the beating sun and were introduced by the warm-up act of spectacular sunsets.

Evening after evening we gazed on golden clouds with shafts of rich light striking the sea and setting it on fire. We looked in awe at the beauty of our surroundings and a click of a camera shutter would capture a perfect scene for an Evangelical poster displayed in the window of a religious curios shop somewhere in the American Bible Belt. The glorious shafts of light descending from the heavens would be reproduced on fine art paper and accompanied by an earnest headline proclaiming, 'The magnificence of God's Creation is with us always' – at $5 a go. Praise the Lord and amen to all that.

And then after the religious moment, our day gave way to the night. Before the moon rose to spoil the party, the stars came out to play with the most amazing intensity. The starlight was so bright it illuminated the distant horizon in the dimmest of glows and we gazed upwards in awe at Cassiopeia, the mother of the heavens. From that start position,

Stuart established Taurus and Gemini, Perseus and Andromeda for us. At Anna's insistence and with the help of a Dorling Kindersley pocket guide for the amateur astronomer, she told the tales of Lyra, Hercules, Cygnus and Pegasus, adding them to the more familiar Milky Way and Orion's Belt, complete with its red and dying sun.

The sky went on for ever and the night watch sat, necks straining, in complete reverence at the display. Mirroring it, the sea was determined not to be outdone and the phosphorescence churned up by our passing cracked and exploded beneath the frothing wake. Looking down in the inky-black water was like observing a thunderstorm from above the clouds and when the froth of the wake subsided for a moment, the sea surface, just a couple of feet away, looked like the lights of a giant city viewed from a thousand feet up.

Phosphorescence is microscopic dots of tiny life and, like the stars, these are minute pinpricks in a giant firmament that has never-ending grades of scale. These are fractals, where small becomes big and scales of size transpose. Each luminous burst in our wake was tiny and insignificant when compared with the might of the ocean. The ocean itself became tiny compared with the might of the solar system playing on for ever above our heads. It followed then that the heavens were perhaps an equally small speck in some way vaster plan beyond comprehension. Perhaps all of that, all that we survey, all that we are – from prehistory to cavemen, the Bronze Age, the Tudors and the Stuarts, the industrial revolution, to the brave new information age – was like one small bursting piece of phosphorescence that had flashed and burned and then discarded in our wake.

And then it is another new day. The vaguest of vague suggestions of a small glimmer of a slightly less dark night was hinted at from the east, now astern of the boat as we bobbed along in the mid-Atlantic. The glimmer gained in confidence and provided just enough light to reveal the dark and ominous shapes of clouds. A little more time and the sky itself shifted gently from black to the deepest of velvet blues, which in turn became royal and then powder blue, with a splash of ochre for good measure, as the first vestiges of sun appeared. The clouds went from sinister black to warm and welcoming orange-peel glows before complementing the blueness of the sky with the pastel yellow of a stone farmhouse in Provence. And as the sun finally climbed up over the horizon and the first fingers of warmth tickled the sunburn on the back of my neck, the clouds turned whiter than white and proclaimed that the day could now commence.

Although it was impossible not to be amazed by the vastness of the planet going about its business, no host of angels came trumpeting hallelujahs out of the clouds at me. There was no doubt that what we were witnessing – the creation and its constantly evolving beauty – provoked deep-seated emotions and soul-searching thoughts. It was far bigger, though, and far greater and far more limitless than the conveniently packaged, neatly presented parcels offered by the religious conventions I had grown up with. Yes, I was moved and inspired and humbled beyond belief, but with a magnitude that was impossible to contain in one thought or dedicate to a single being. Kneeling at a dusty pew to recognise this magnitude seemed too shallow an offering to acknowledge what surrounded us. So I looked and thought and looked some more and had no answers, other than to view it all with an intense humility.

It may not have been a religious moment, but it was a deeply spiritual one.

Down below in the galley, the crew members on mother watch started their daily chores, providing breakfast, baking bread and cleaning the boat. After two weeks at sea, most of the fresh food had gone and what remained had healthy levels of mould. The carrots were black and slimy but an energetic scrape of the first three or four layers revealed a perfectly edible vegetable. Ditto the onions and potatoes. Mould was scraped off the butter that was still solid, although in the heat, most of the tubs had turned to a liquid and greasy ghee.

Increased inventiveness was applied to the tins of stewing steak, minced beef, Spam and greasy corned beef. Forget the niceties of sell-by dates, pre-washed veg or refrigerated food. Blind eyes were turned time and time again, meals were wolfed down from the practical plastic dog bowls and, with second helpings popular, no one seemed to be coming to too much harm.

Everyone took turns at mother watch and it provided some delightful pairings. Our on-board political correspondent from *The Times* and the Cockney Cabbie were destined to spend the watch together, conjuring up the day's culinary delights for the hard-working crew. Back in reality, Danny and James would probably never mix. One would hail a cab and say, in his best Old Etonian, 'The House of Commons', before settling back to look at his notes and consider what questions he might put to Tony or Gordon. Up front, the cabbie would eye up his fare in the rear-view mirror and possibly mutter, 'Tosser!' under his breath.

On a boat far out at sea and away from the self-important life onshore, the office junior had become as valuable as the office senior. The forklift-truck driver equal to the royal chauffeur. The pauper as valid as the prince and the director as humble as the down and out.

And, to prove the point, down in the galley James and Danny were getting on famously. Danny had never been to the ballet but was eager to go, so James made immediate plans to organise tickets and form a party of two when the race was done. The public school boy, mirrored by the East Ender, sharing thoughts and views, jousting wit against wit, listening and learning as they juggled with the toast, powdered egg and industrial-size jars of Marmite. To the crew munching their breakfast, the easy relationship was no surprise, but the outside observer's eyes would have been opened, with important lessons learnt and the essential quality of humility clearly demonstrated. It provided a firm reminder of the qualities that existed all around us and I wanted to capture the moment for when we splashed back down into the real world again.

What a difference a year had made. Twelve months before, almost to the day, I had undertaken a week of true corporate stress. Instead of having Sunday lunch with the family, I was at Heathrow, clambering on board a Tokyo-bound 747, which took twelve long hours to arrive at Narita Airport. Because of the time change, it was Monday when I arrived. I checked into my hotel, enjoyed a business dinner with my Japanese colleagues, had an all-day meeting on Tuesday and headed back to Narita early on Wednesday morning. Gaining time coming west, I was back at Heathrow on Wednesday afternoon and after a two-hour wait was on a flight to Portugal. In Lisbon for eight that evening after a slight delay, I sprinted to another desk and just made the connection to Faro, arriving at the sales conference hotel at midnight. Before I could relax, we went straight into a rehearsal for the following day's presentation, before flying home on Friday, my week complete.

And now I sat, bereft of suit, tie, briefcase, company credit card, car and expense account on our slow-moving racing yacht in the middle of the Atlantic.

Occasionally I spotted a vapour trail steaming through the stratosphere overhead as a jumbo at thirty-five thousand feet cranked along at around five hundred knots per hour. In the time it took one of the passengers to turn away from the window, remove their headphones and consider whether to have the Chablis or perhaps go straight to the red, they would have travelled the same distance that was taking us an hour of blood, sweat and tears to achieve.

To sail the Atlantic is to work every single tiny inch of it. Every foot, yard, furlong and mile had been worked for and each passing wave was a mini-achievement as we trimmed and helmed with the utmost care, in an effort to make *London* go faster.

A thousand miles from anywhere, petrels skimmed the waves, flying with inch-perfect precision above the slight swell. Shoals of flying fish broke the surface in a great shimmer of silver and a few days earlier a large whale had squeezed past in the opposite direction just a few yards from our hull. It was like passing a juggernaut in a tiny country lane, and the whale showed as much interest in us as any bored long-distance trucker might.

To begin with, the slow pace proved uncomfortably frustrating to a mind conditioned to getting somewhere in the quickest possible time in order to meet hectic schedules. Of course, *London* was still chasing speed and our focus remained sharp. We had just learnt that you only need to worry about the here and now.

Look after the seconds and the minutes will come to you. Look after the minutes and the hours will tick by. Look after the hours and a day will pass. Eventually, at some point in the distant future (that we had long since stopped worrying about), the days will have turned to weeks and a distant smudge of coastline will appear.

As the passing jumbo receded, the vapour trail crumbled to nothing and the bored passenger returned to staring out of the window at the mass of ocean beneath his wings, I realised what a privilege it was to travel this way. The journey truly was our adventure, rather than what awaited at the destination.

Still we headed west, chasing the departed jet and still we languished in seventh place, one ahead of *Glasgow*, as the trades continued to refuse to kick in. Cuba seemed no closer but time stood still. One day it was Saturday and in the blink of an eye it was Saturday again.

We marked key anniversaries, subconsciously trying to give the timelessness a structure. On 31 October, and due on watch, Andy, Gary, Danny and I gathered like naughty schoolboys at the forward hatch. It was pitch-black outside and we crept unseen up on to the deck. Shrouded in white sheets, we stood ready and, at a whispered 'Now', the light of a torch was played upwards as we giggled our way through a series of ghostly wailings. Ali and his cockpit crew were completely unprepared and assured us that it was a truly scary Halloween moment.

My birthday came and went and balloons and cards appeared, along with a cake, complete with candles, baked by Ellie, which we consumed at an impromptu cockpit tea party. With such vast quantities of time and space, uninterrupted by ringing phones, bursting Filofaxes or a document-strewn in-tray, my mind went back to childhood birthdays and images long forgotten came flooding back with a very real clarity. Because we now had the luxury of great swathes of freedom where the day-to-day clutter had been removed, I was having recollections of the most amazing detail. Wrapped up in the rat race and in ourselves, I began to appreciate how little time we have to take stock, look and enjoy where we have come from and enjoy what we have achieved.

Weekends and holidays, because they are so precious, take on an intensity all of their own, so that even when we are relaxing there is a pressure and urgency in doing so. There was a dawning realisation that it had been years, decades actually, since I last really, *really* had the time and the uncomplicated freedom to open up my mind.

And over that time so much had slipped by. Busy being a corporate success, I had become blinkered – most crucially as my children grew and developed. What had already gone was gone, but I decided, mid-Atlantic, to set myself some new priorities as a dad for when I came home. I couldn't backtrack in order to read the bedtime stories I was too tired to read before, but giving time and attention to my family, and really appreciating their precious qualities, lay ahead as exciting discoveries.

The eleventh of November came around and I was determined we should mark Armistice Day by observing a two-minute silence. With the aid of a red felt-tip pen, I created a set of reasonably accurate paper poppies for everyone to wear and as the GPS clock ticked down to 11.00 local time, a short blast on the yacht's foghorn marked the act of remembrance.

Everyone stood stock-still, caps removed, and the only sound to be heard was the hissing of the wake, the creaking of rigging and the gentle hush of the wind in the sails. At 11.02 the foghorn went off again and a CD selected by James brought the sounds of 'I Vow to Thee, My Country' into the cockpit. The words – and the recording – were stunningly beautiful, and when it was all done there was discreet wiping of eyes. It had been a moving moment and later we all agreed it was a good thing to have done.

As the mid-Atlantic came and went and the Caribbean islands started to get encouragingly closer, we began our race up through the fleet. The weather fax showed that the unsettling low had finally cleared off to the north and the trades were re-establishing themselves. After weeks of seven or eight knots of boat speed, we were back up to twelves and fourteens as the wind grew to a steady twenty-one knots. At last the spinnaker was properly filled, and as the sea zipped by rather than languidly crawling, it felt like we were escaping. The long-awaited winds had come in the night and, as Stuart looked in on our 02.00–05.00 watch, a full moon crept up over the horizon ahead and lit a large flare path of light, down which we careered gratefully.

The northerly boats, who for so long had held the advantage despite ignoring all the advice given by the routing books, were now stuck in a large hole with not a breath of wind as the high settled over them and were frantically trying to get south. As each twelve-hour radio check came in, we ticked off another scalp, until only *Plymouth* and *Portsmouth* lay ahead and it was clear that we were catching them as well.

Squalls were now the name of the game and during the night a watch member regularly checked the radar, where the active clouds appeared as a vivid and fast-tracking green blob. During the day we could see the active cumulus building and frothing upwards, soaring into the blue sky at an alarming rate. Underneath, a heavy grey smudge indicated torrential rain and, more worryingly, winds that would be gusting at thirty-five to forty knots. We practised squall drills, where everyone would go to an appointed position in order to alter course, run before the wind and if necessary drop the spinnaker before the incoming maelstrom could shred it.

Stuart advised us that if we got caught it would be a noisy, confused ride, with very little time to think. He took me to one side and began to discuss man-overboard drills, just in case he was the one swept into the ocean. I was both flattered and worried when he asked me to take charge of the boat should such a disaster happen. He wanted to be certain that someone could deal with the situation and co-ordinate the crew's efforts in order to get the yacht quickly back to him. He assumed that my flying skills had developed a heightened level of coolness for such high-pressure situations. Clearly he had never seen me land Charlie's Tiger Moth.

I played out the situation many times in my head, getting the lookouts in place, the dan buoy out, the GPS man-overboard fix set, the engine started, the spinnaker dropped, retrieval systems ready and a reciprocal course steered against a wristwatch, in order to bring us back to his point of departure. As with my first-aid training, I really hoped I would never have to use it for real.

So the only clouds on our horizon were the clouds on our horizon. The Inland Revenue, council tax, parking tickets, speed cameras, double yellow lines, on-the-spot fines, 'don't walk on the grass' notices and nanny-state EU regulations – none of those nonsenses existed here. All that mattered was the squall cloud up ahead that was developing upwards and starting to tower over us. It was only a cloud, a mixture of rising warm air reaching its dew point and forming into vapour. An entirely natural and pure phenomenon that might be benign or might be vicious. A phenomenon that could shred our sails, broach the boat, send people into the sea and create a mini-disaster area. Or it would just provide some welcome relief from the sun.

And when all was done, it would fizzle away and be eaten up by the heat of the day.

What a moment of pure relief to realise that such occurrences were all we had to worry about and what a contrast to the day-to-day concerns that existed on dry land. E-mails into the boat brought news from home that emphasised the purity surrounding our floating home. It had not stopped raining since we left England, the south was badly flooded, petrol delivery strikes were still disrupting lives, a train had crashed at Hatfield and foot and mouth was starting to close down the countryside. I had commuted through Hatfield every day of my working life and when I learnt that it was a 125 express that had gone off the rails, images of carriages with their important red markings, full of urgently communicating businessmen, came flooding back.

Drowning at King's Cross, I had stared in through their slowly passing first-class windows wondering if life could be offering more, and now here I was, free and content, out on the ocean. And as we were blown gently along, the ground-up pulp of twisted seats and bogey wheels lay strewn across the rain-sodden sleepers back in Hertfordshire. Amid the wreckage, inside a blood-stained, fashion-labelled suit jacket, a mobile phone urgently rang, trying to rouse the lifeless soul who had been simply trying to earn himself a living.

Apart from a couple of torrential soakings from monsoon downpours, our simple life continued. The good winds carried on blowing until we made landfall at Hispaniola, with the high mountains of the Dominican Republic revealing themselves as a dark blue smudge on the horizon off to port.

We had seen little wildlife for several weeks, but now the sea was suddenly full of jumping, leaping excited dolphins. A couple came and rode the bow wave – large Atlantic spotted ones – who quickly put out the word. In minutes we were surrounded by an exuberant display of unbridled joy as twenty-five or thirty of these stunning creatures showed off all around the boat.

Up in the air, the ever-present wave-skimming petrels and shear-waters were joined by an exotic-looking tropicbird. Pure white, with a rich-red beak and a long streaming wisp of a tail, it circuited the boat, looking down with curious interest, before flapping lazily away. Even butterflies joined in the fly-by, blown in on the warm breezes from the shore thirty miles away.

The charge through the fleet was still on. Race leader *Plymouth* was only fifty miles ahead, and somewhere over the starboard horizon lay the Portsmouth-sponsored yacht. With the Atlantic basically crossed, our route started to track north-west towards the Old Bahaman Channel and the chart showed that the exotic pleasures of Nevis, St Kitts and the British Virgin Islands were just a half-day's sail away. As if to prove their presence, a lone coconut bobbed past in the afternoon swell.

Spinnaker gybing was the tactic now and it was good to have some action return to the boat – we had been sailing in a straight line for some eighteen days. As the channel started, the fleet was funnelled into a narrow band of water and one morning as the sun rose, there, about three miles behind us, lay *Portsmouth*. We had clawed our way up to second place and were still closing in on the lead boat.

The next five days had us locked in bloody combat with the crew of *Portsmouth*. We would gybe one way, they another. For twelve hours we would hold the advantage and for the next twelve it went in their favour. Under the cover of darkness in a pitch-black night, we crept up once more and as they came abeam around half a mile away, Andy and Stuart got out the Aldis lamp and flashed in Morse code across the water, 'BOO.'

There was a small pause as they translated our signal, before a two-letter response – 'F' followed by 'O' came flashing back.

The gloves came off.

As the two boats closed on each other we could see that

Portsmouth's spinnaker was shredded, with the top third streaming out free from the masthead. She had pushed too hard in the conditions and paid the price with a top-to-bottom rip down the sail. Desperate not to lose their advantage, they hoisted a jib and took to a luffing match, forcing us to sail higher and higher towards the edge of the channel, where the shallows start and the razor-sharp coral lies only a couple of feet beneath the surface. With four hundred miles still to go, it was a legitimate but slightly desperate move to make and showed that, despite the long weeks at sea, they had lost none of their competitive spirit.

We went back into our 'strongest helm' strategy, which had worked on the way down to Portugal and really aided our progress. Now it was Stuart, Andy Wilkinson (now universally known as 'Radar' following his prolonged periods staring at the screen), James and I who took the wheel for an hour each on a rotating cycle through the days and nights. The decision rankled a little with a couple of the crew – with everyone paying a considerable sum to be on board, they not unreasonably expected an equal share in the running of the boat. But all of us were in a race, all of us wanted to win and all of us had agreed that Stuart should run the boat to reflect that desire.

Having anticipated such a problem back in Southampton, I had proposed a mantra (no more mission statements now) that would help to keep us all thinking in the right way. Stuart had readily agreed to it and, around the boat, laminated A4 posters asked the simple question, 'Does it make the boat go faster?' If the answer was 'yes', then none of us could take issue with a decision. The same applied if the answer was 'no'. If one person on the helm could shift the boat through the water quicker than a colleague, then the answer was clear to see. However, it would take a big dose of humility and some serious soul-searching for the unlucky individual missing out on their time at the wheel – no one could be expected to be truly happy when a particular skill got the thumbs down.

But despite the inevitable grumbles, we fought on as a crew, following another boat mantra shared by Sir Robin on the eve of the race start. 'If you follow this simple rule,' he had explained, 'you will get around the world intact and still be talking to your colleagues at the end.' His pearl of wisdom was: 'The boat should come first, your crew members come second and you should come last.' We had printed that up as a poster as well and I could only wonder how such a belief would be received back in the corporate world. 'Your company comes first, other departments come second and you come last' would have people choking on their espressos all over London.

And while those far-away machiavellian boardroom manoeuvrings continued, our own battle raged as the wind started to shift. Neptune was sending out a timely reminder of what the seas could do and within a couple of hours we had downed the spinnaker, made a foresail change and put in first one, then two reefs to the mainsail. The boat heeled hard over, huge waves pummelled into the cockpit, foul-weather gear dripped wet and the bow crashed into the huge waves that were being whipped up by a strong northerly. After weeks in the tropics it came as an uncomfortable shock.

In the middle of all this mayhem the hatch flew open and there was Danny on mother watch. Alan and he had gone into battle with a rolling galley and despite the spin-dryer effect down below, here they were offering us tea and freshly baked scones, still warm and dripping with butter and jam. Such thoughtfulness really lifted the spirit and illustrated that no matter what position you happened to be fulfilling on board, you truly could help make the boat go faster. And Danny had done all of this despite being terribly seasick in his whirling, oven-hot environment. It was an inspirational example, where he had put his own discomfort last and illustrated exactly what Sir Robin had been getting at. And Danny being Danny, he waved away the enthusiastic thanks from the soaked crew with a blushing humility, threw up once more and then stumbled back below to help Alan with the washing-up.

The battle with *Portsmouth* continued, although in truth we were more focused on the conditions rather than each other. We both took another five miles out of *Plymouth* and, as dawn came up on our last day at sea, *London* remained firmly in touch with second place.

In a last attempt to seize the advantage, we raised the heavyweight spinnaker, which proved to be a real handful in the huge seas. Two helms had to wrestle with the wheel in order to keep a straight line and surf down the steep faces of the waves. Any normal sailor would be taking down sails and altering course for a more comfortable ride in such conditions, but we were now racers, putting our foot down hard on the accelerator and coping with whatever the conditions might throw at us.

Portsmouth took a direct route up the coast, while we headed out to sea a little in order to give us a faster angle of sail towards the finish. Now it was a drag-race dash to the line and up ahead we could see her sails getting ever nearer as we closed in. The first tower blocks of

Havana appeared on the horizon and as the shore grew closer we could see lines of palm trees being pounded by a huge surf that was smashing into the shore. We got a radio message from Clipper Control advising that the finish line had been moved because of dangerous conditions at the marina entrance and as a result seven miles were lopped off the course. Suddenly we were running out of time.

In the end *Portsmouth* pipped us again by a mere fifteen minutes. An amazing end to 4,700 miles of racing and third place on the podium was a result that left us feeling pretty happy. With Patrick at the helm, we downed sails and rode in on alarming breakers towards the land, the depth gauge showing zero as we surfed down a narrow channel and into the calm waters of the Hemingway Marina. The crews of *Portsmouth* and *Plymouth* gave us a long and protracted round of applause as ice-cold beers were thrown on board by a smiling Sir Robin and our feet finally touched dry land after twenty-six days at sea.

Castro's khaki-clad conscripts went through their immigration paperwork as hugs and kisses went round the boat. Ellie hugged Jane, who kissed Patrick, who embraced the Baba, who kissed Alan, who hugged Danny, who embraced Gary, who kissed Anna, who hugged James, who kissed Andy, who embraced Stuart, who kissed Radar, who embraced Aki, who hugged me. And then we repeated it all until every permutation had been exhausted. Stuart had the added reward of being able to step ashore into the arms of his wife and have the triple whammy of a hug, kiss and embrace. Ben, now three months old, was also there to welcome his dad, although our skipper's joy turned to dismay when the child burst into floods of tears at the strange and bearded apparition who was showering him with kisses.

Liz Gibson had brought out mail and I settled down in the cockpit, oblivious suddenly to all that surrounded me, as I immersed myself in letters from home. A long missive from Anne, photographs and long chatty exercise-book pages from the children had my total attention. There was nothing new or particularly exciting to share but the contact and the sheer normality of the news had me reading and rereading the precious pages. I had not expected to shed a tear over stories about the school bus, a football match, rehearsals for the end-of-term play or the state of the garden, but I did. The time and energy spent in writing the letters was in direct proportion to the pleasure that they gave, and with my mind uncluttered by the day-to-day tedium that clouds one's vision, the news that they shared meant everything.

Living a normal routine back home would have meant that such moments would have remained unmentioned. And if they had been, probably the best I would have managed at the end of another tough day at the office would have been a grunt of vague acknowledgement from behind a large glass of red. The gap between us may have been several thousand miles, but we were communicating better than we had ever done in our entire lives.

I put the family's letters back into the precious envelope which carried the touch of their hands and returned to the party that was developing around me. We sat in the warm sunshine, laughing, elated, hugging and getting very quickly and very happily drunk, as the crew reflected on twenty-six days shared together, crammed into a sixty-foot sliver of a lozenge surrounded by three thousand miles of purity.

We had sailed the Atlantic Ocean.

Four thousand seven hundred miles of open water.

A great wilderness that plunges nineteen thousand feet to the seabed.

A yawning chasm that divides two giant continents.

A divide that splits cultures.

A sea that has remained unchanged – completely unchanged – since the first brave sailors decided to try to conquer it.

A wilderness that for days on end showed no sign of life.

A wilderness that was in a constant state of flux as the gods randomly chose how it would behave on a particular day.

And we had just sailed across it.

God, that sounded sexy. We had to say it again, accompanied by great cheers.

We had just sailed across the Atlantic.

I knew every single inch of it as we had clawed and battled our way, oh so slowly, across its mighty back. And to have studied every inch of it was to know it in the most intimate fashion.

Gone were the great broad brushstrokes that modern travel brings, where you can cross such a divide in just a few hours, with only enough time for some lunch, a movie and a bit of a kip.

Out there in a small boat, we knew – really knew – and lived each second, each minute, each hour, each day and each night, for week after week. And at that pace one had the luxurious benefit of swathes of time without distraction, to consider and appreciate and be awestruck by the magnitude of the journey.

We motored away from the immigration pontoon and tied up beside a lush green lawn, where a ramshackle band played us ashore, smiling locals carried trays awash with rum punch and Cuba welcomed us in the only way it knows how.

We moored within sight of the Caribbean and beaches lined with coconut-festooned palms, their huge fronds swaying in the breeze. With the salsa band playing and the rum working its magic, it all seemed an age away from the start in Portugal. And that made it a lifetime away from those dark, wet November evenings back in London as shoppers began the annual scrum of planning for Christmas and the tube was dank, bad-tempered and cold.

I checked into one of the marina hotels and was frustrated to discover that the telephone refused to work. Down in reception the story was the same, and while it would mean that my communication budget would be safe after the Portugal scare, I was desperate to make calls and announce my arrival.

In the end we were all forced to use the satellite phone from the boat, unavoidably hearing each other's personal and emotional reunion conversations. The satellite meant a lengthy delay as voices travelled deep into space and, when I finally got through, our words tripped over each other somewhere high above the coast of Long Island. We tried to get the hang of this new and slow way of talking but it was all deeply frustrating and I realised that my love affair with modern communications showed no sign of cooling.

The navigation station on board became the boat's public call box and it was from there that I filed my weekly dispatch for *The Times* website, sharing those frustrations with the outside world.

London Diary, Tuesday, 28 November 2001

> *Hello, my name is Ian and I am a communications junky.*
>
> *I'll say it again as Nursey at the therapy centre assures me it will help.*
>
> *Hello, my name is Ian and I have become so used to a mobile phone, an internet access line, an international switchboard, a phone in my hotel room, the ability to pick up a handset and dial numbers anywhere in the world and talk to the people that I love, when it is removed from me, I go cold turkey.*
>
> *When one completes a transatlantic crossing, there are a million and one thoughts, observations, feelings and emotions that you are so eager to share. Try doing so*

from Cuba and those emotions remain firmly with you.

Mobiles do not work, hotels charge $6 a minute (and that is only when you are lucky enough to get a line). The reception staff look on in uncomprehending pity when you react to the news that you can't make a call until the morning – or if the line is still U/S, maybe the day after.

And then, on the lucky moment that you get through and a ringing tone begins, you hear the heart-sinking click of an answerphone that tells you that the number you are trying to call 'is not in right now, so please leave a message'.

Quite apart from wanting to tell people about the trip and let them know that they are missed and loved, I want to share the magnificent, exciting, thrilling, vibrant and oh so alive island that is Cuba.

Despite its dodgy telegraph poles.

The entire fleet has fallen for Havana. Its crumbling grand architecture, its falling-down backstreets, its Brave New World pre-fab high-rises, its F. Scott Fitzgerald grand hotels and the bars frequented by Hemingway, have all sown an active seed.

The people are warm, the salsa that blares from every radio, street café and bar is oh so addictive and the 1950s Buicks, Chevys, Cadillacs and Pontiacs that somehow continue to rumble through the streets add a bizarre time warp to the proceedings.

The Cubra Libres, the Mojitas, the Daiquiris and the Pina Coladas have all played havoc with brains weaned off alcohol for three long weeks, but what the heck – we've sailed the Atlantic, so we've earned it.

Today, I rented a car and headed for the country. We passed by lush sugar-cane plantations, hilltops thick with palm trees and small villages. We eventually arrived in a hustling main street of a small town, just as school finished, and walked down the rough main street that looked straight out of a Wild West film set. We were truly the strangers in town, but a local hotel provided an excellent supper which the profusion of flies seemed to enjoy as much as us.

On the way back, in the dark, communication

frustrations came to the fore again. There were no road markings, no signposts and no street lights as we tried to retrace our fifty-mile journey. To help matters, cyclists (and there are hundreds of them) don't bother with lights. As we progressed, it appeared that several cars and trucks had also decided that rear-facing illumination was a bore, causing sudden swerves of avoidance. Doing so brought us, on several occasions, into the path of a truck devoid of headlights. I suppose it was lucky that the two cars we passed on a dual carriageway had their lights on, as, without signs or markings, we were unaware that we were heading east down the west-side carriageway.

And once that little problem had been resolved (with the help of the local finger-wagging police), we only had to skid to a stop one more time in order to navigate round a field of Friesian cows that had decided that the main arterial road into Havana was a good place for a kip.

Some parts of Cuba communicate better than others, though. Yesterday, there was a mass rally peopled by adoring and dutiful school children, massed ranks of soldiers in fatigues and the great and good of Havana, who had gathered in their hundreds of thousands to hear Castro speak. We could make out the word 'Americano' being offered in the heated diatribe and knew that his views were being heard, as the political rally stadium has been deliberately built right underneath the glass edifice that is the American Embassy.

It would appear that on some occasions you don't need mobiles, satellites, international exchanges or e-mails in order to get your message across.

The ride into town from the Hemingway Marina was twenty minutes on a race track, bouncing along the potholed roads in an ancient Buick held together by pop rivets and welds. The road passed stilted river shacks looking for all the world like something from the Mekong Delta. It went down wide avenues lined with embassies where stunning-looking hookers touted for business at every set of traffic lights. It ran along the coast, where the Caribbean pounded the breakwater, sending great spumes of water crashing across the road. Miami lay just ninety miles to the north and, despite the treacherous line of water, the lure of the promised land still attracts a small fleet of homemade rafts.

The Lido Hotel, a cheap offering from the *Lonely Planet* guide, became my latest bunk substitute. At $20 a night the room looked out on to a brick wall a couple of inches away. The dimly lit corridors were painted a drab green and images of Alcatraz with an echoing cry of 'Dead man walking' followed me as I locked myself in each night. And still there was no phone. Outside, the fantastic architecture of once-grand buildings lined the main streets as ancient American cars honked their way past fleets of pushbikes and vast humpbacked 'camel' buses stuffed full of locals.

The Hotel Nacional offered the F. Scott Fitzgerald timewarp experience. Beyond the vaulted marble-cool hall, a twilight breeze rustled through the palm gardens, bringing the gentle sound of a group of local strolling musicians. A sugar-cane press beside the outdoor bar cranked into action, pouring freshly squeezed treacly juice into a glass. It was followed by fresh lemon juice and a profusion of mint leaves, which were energetically crushed with a wooden pestle before ice, sparkling mineral water and a huge slug of white rum were added and stirred. This is a Mojita, and Ellie and I sampled several of them as the moon rose over the now languid sea.

At every street corner, opportunistic workers from the cigar factory tried to sell their stolen contraband. Romeo y Julietas complete in huge aluminium tubes magically appeared and a brisk exchange took place. I don't smoke, but the temptation of the preparation, the ritual, the thick smell and the glowing embers was too much. I sat, in a gentle stupor, puffing away and sipping my cocktail, immersed in the moment as we waited for supper. The table filled as the rest of the crew joined us from a varied selection of Havana's budget lodgings, and we began the sad task of saying goodbye to the crew who had completed the first leg.

Earlier I had headed off to meet the two new members of the team, eager to ensure that they felt loved and part of the boat from the moment they stepped off the British Airways jet. It was odd being in an airport, where global destinations echoed from the tannoy system. It had taken us three weeks to arrive from Europe, but as I looked at the constantly clattering departure board a whole raft of suddenly exotic cities lay just a few hours' flying time away. I felt a million miles from all that had been familiar for so long, but there was the British Airways flight turned round and pointing back at London, just twelve hours away. Twelve hours on board the yacht would cover an on watch, a sleep period, a couple of meals and another on watch. If the winds were good, we might crack a hundred miles. For the same donation of time, I could find myself on the Piccadilly Line, clattering through Acton Town away from Heathrow and reading the latest forthright views from Linda Lee Potter in the first edition of the *Daily Mail*.

I decided, on balance, to stay where I was and led the jetlagged forms of Keith Shakespeare and Neil Tweedly out to the cab rank and on through the sultry Caribbean night to our riotous party. It was hard to say goodbye to Patrick and Andy, both of whom had been in at the start of our dramatic learning curve. They had contributed hugely to the success of the boat and Patrick's determination to cook pancakes, complete with flamboyant tossing action whatever the weather, had endeared him hugely to the crew. He was going back to his wife and daughters and for a moment I was deeply envious.

Radar's wife had come out to Cuba to meet him, and despite putting sailing at the very bottom of her list of enjoyable pastimes, she was already deeply engrossed in his plans to sell their house, buy a yacht and sail off with their young family for a year. She could clearly see how the three weeks on board had changed her husband and was drawn in by the energy and enthusiasm from the *London* crew. Their life-changing discussions continued as we swam lazy circles in the marina pool, oblivious to the fact that it was three in the morning and the rest of the world was asleep. If three weeks caused such a transformation, what on earth might eleven months do for my own plans?

Life ashore was wonderfully comfortable, but as if sensing our rather too easy return to civilisation, the weather took a turn for the worse. The wind got up, the clouds blocked the sun, rain started to fall and the palm fronds blew out horizontally in the misty air. Back at the marina, the fleet was a hive of activity as we prepared to go to sea again.

The melancholy weather set the mood for more goodbyes. Stuart had to endure the repeated agony of saying goodbye to Liz and Ben once more. Ali waved a tearful farewell to his girlfriend, Anna waved a tearful parting to her aunt and we all waved a tearful goodbye to our departing crew. Patrick and Andy were melancholy too, and the thought of watching 'their' boat set sail without them on board reminded me why I had signed up to complete the entire circumnavigation.

The weather worsened and there was some doubt about our even getting out of the marina as the wind whipped up an energetic swell. The next leg of our journey had been dismissed by the armchair pundits as 'an easy cruise through the Caribbean' but the sea state and darkening sky suggested otherwise. We rolled out into spectacular breaking waves, but despite the lumpy ocean, the mood on board remained despondently flat.

8

CARIBBEAN BLUES
CUBA TO PANAMA
01.12.00–08.12.00

A gentle blue-sea cruise was probably exactly what was needed to remind us what the ocean could offer. It would provide the perfect pick-me-up for homesick, lovesick or seasick souls. But the sea has a perverse sense of humour, seeking out any chinks in the armour at exactly the time you least need it.

Forget the idea of the thousand-mile race to the Panama isthmus being a high-season, steel-band-swaying, melodic cruise south in balmy conditions. Neptune puffed up a brisk blow at the start and then waited for night to fall before playing his trump card. We crossed the line in last place and the site of the fleet up ahead finally galvanised the boat into action. Putting personal emotions aside for a while, we worked the helm hard and trimmed the spinnaker well in a large following sea, working our way up to third place. Neptune was watching, though, and despite a liberal pouring of Havana Club over the side to appease him for this leg of the journey, he snuffed out the sun and brought on the darkness with a sly grin and a wicked chuckle.

The night did not so much fall as come crashing down in a hurtling, confused, windswept maelstrom of a storm. Thick clouds meant that we were careering along in absolute blackness, trying to keep the spinnaker safe in the screaming, rolling, invisible sea. Vast joules of light caused temporary blindness as lightning cavorted all around us and the scream of the wind in the rigging was temporarily outdone by ear-splitting cracks of thunder mingling with the hammering of torrential rain on the coach-house roof.

A line connecting the spinnaker pole to the boat snapped and had to be replaced in the wild ride. In the middle of the night Aki crawled gingerly out along it until he was sat astride the end of the pole, which pitched and rolled alarmingly over the boiling black ocean. He did so with a complete trust in his colleagues, and back in the cockpit every one of us fulfilled our roles to ensure the job was completed quickly and without harm to him. A man overboard on such a night would mean almost certain death, as there was virtually no likelihood of locating him in the heaving swell.

The huge squalls that were causing such challenges brought hour after hour of Hollywood-style rain. From somewhere just out of camera shot, a series of hoses sprayed in our faces and the downpours were so intense that the mast top disappeared from view. To make matters more uncomfortable, our foul-weather gear gave up the unequal struggle, letting water seep into T-shirts and shorts. Below deck, the moist, humid air quickly developed into a healthy mould as fourteen irritable crew members tried to climb into their heeling, bouncing, damp bunks in a futile attempt at sleep.

For Keith and Neil it was a baptism of fire. As their bodies desperately tried to adjust, a green pallor quickly became evident on their faces and they declined to partake of the sweet-smelling curry on offer from the rolling galley.

In the thick, tar-black night we continued to crash along blindly at twelve knots, hanging on to the wheel and trying not to wrap the spinnaker. The ever-present lightning continued to momentarily illuminate a wildly tossing sea as the thunder crashed through the clouds, and just to make life completely bloody, the soaking red ensign flying from the stern took to delivering stinging slaps across the face of the helm. I would not have minded so much, except that I was on the wheel at the time. And as if to remind me that such thoughts were not following Sir Robin's valued mantra of putting my own discomforts last, an incoming flying fish leapt out of the night and dealt me a smack on the side of the head. Not only was it a lot harder than the earlier incoming Atlantic Ocean dove, it was a great deal smellier too.

Despite our best helming efforts, Stuart was the first to wrap the spinnaker in the confused winds and the remainder of our first long and very trying night at sea was spent unravelling three similar gigantic knots, made up from seventy feet of bulbous and soaking-wet sail cloth.

If the mood had been flat at the point of departure, it was totally horizontal now that the race was under way. Having gone back into the promised land of baths and cooked breakfasts and televisions and bars and phones – even though they rarely worked – and communicated with loved ones once more, the pain of leaving had been intense.

Stuart and I had a long heart-to-heart at the nav station sometime after 03.00 and although we both knew the positive answers to our negative emotions, it was none the less a difficult period of gloomy doubt. Our race start had been poor and the first fifteen hours had been less than enjoyable. We were convinced that our cock-ups had put us to the back of the fleet again, although the mood lifted a little when the morning radio schedules revealed that the other boats had experienced an equally bad night. All around us, kit had broken, sails had been rent in two and much more serious wounds were being licked.

But, despite that, things remained depressed – especially when our communication kit packed up and the chance to talk to home via e-mail was denied. The rain refused to let up and as we headed southeast towards Grand Cayman in third place, the thought of racing in such trying conditions excited no one.

Curiously, the sight of the island as it passed by the port beam two days later brought a calming influence to our troubled thoughts. We had yet to shed the comfort blanket of civilised life, and having endured a series of intense hardships, we were helped by it to appreciate what we previously viewed as mundane. The simple sight of a tree-lined shore, of cars travelling along the coastal roads, of high-rise and low-rise buildings, of neon lights and landing aircraft reminded us that the connections to home were never that far away. We lined the rail and took turns peering through binoculars, sniffing the air and allowing our thoughts to travel across the three miles of water, taking us into an environment that was more comfortable and familiar.

With that much-needed tonic spreading through the crew, we got our act together and the boat slowly settled back into the familiar routine we could follow and rely on. In addition, we also had something to truly focus our thoughts. Our nemesis, in the shape of *Portsmouth*, once again appeared over the horizon, readying themselves for another titanic battle in an effort to inherit the last podium place from *London*.

For three days we stayed locked in combat. On some occasions they would draw level and on others we would struggle to build a quarter-mile advantage. Every step up to the helm brought huge responsibilities and the focus and concentration needed to build on the work of the previous driver were immense. Stuart selected his choice helms again and four of us drove the boat as fast as we could, through the long, damp days and nights. Our rivals gave us no respite and the whole boat ran on the competitive edge hour after hour, day after day and night after night. There was no let-up, and having concentrated like grand-prix drivers for four hours, the outgoing watch would collapse into their bunk and sleep like the dead, before coming back on deck to do it all again a few hours later.

We were determined to break their resolve and on our sixth day at sea we finally built up a three-mile cushion. It proved to be just enough. All that work and effort had put us on the front side of a huge wind hole and as we sailed away on a gentle breeze, *Portsmouth*, still clearly visible, ground to a miserable halt. Twelve hours later our advantage had shot up to ninety-five miles, and what was more, we found ourselves leading the race. Away to the west, *Liverpool* and *Bristol* languished in a similar wind hole and with Panama one day away, our prospects looked suddenly very healthy.

The soggy clothes that festooned the bunks below decks, the damp sleeping bags and mould-encrusted pillows, the lack of showers and the walls dripping with condensation didn't bother anyone now. A good position in the twelve-hourly radio updates provided a better tonic than any illegal narcotic and being in the lead meant *London* was on a real high.

These progress reports provided an all-or-nothing experience for the crew. Positive news and the delight was greater than winning the lottery. But a loss of miles against the fleet made us feel as if a favourite dog had just died, so glum was the mood. Such highs and lows were mentally exhausting to a crew with a single-minded aim to their every input. We wanted to win but knew just how fickle the ocean could be. With that in mind and trying to temper our enthusiasm, we looked at the positions of our nearest rivals and agreed that the only way they could beat us was if the wind turned and came from the west.

Keeping a firm check on any desire for early celebrations, we consulted the routing charts and the pilot books to understand the chances of this happening and were encouraged to see that at this time of year there was a one per cent possibility. The weather forecast predicted south-easterlies, which seemed to confirm that view. Surely we were home and nearly dry and the fabled yellow winner's pennant, along with eight valuable championship points, would be ours.

Two hours later the wind turned and came in from the west. Neptune, it seemed, might be getting more regular offerings of rum from our rivals.

In our own bit of sea, we lurched from thirty-five-knot squalls to vast wind holes where we sat and slopped and tried to eke out some form of forward motion, desperate not to wallow and allow the remaining fleet to catch up. *Bristol* and *Liverpool* had crept ahead again, blown towards the finish line by a fluky turn of the breeze.

And while we battled with these frustrations, I was lost in a daydream of thoughts. My mind was back in London, knowing that Dad and Uncle Cedric and cousins Henry, Mark and John, along with a whole host of Dickens descendants, were making their way through a narrow passageway in the heart of the City, off Cornhill. They were heading towards the old city chop house where the male members of the family hold their annual lunch. This regular pilgrimage to the George and Vulture, immortalised in *The Pickwick Papers*, is a highlight of my Christmas and the warmth of family togetherness, fuelled by large quantities of port, makes it a lunch not to miss.

To mark the moment, I appeared for the watch beginning at midday dressed in jacket and tie. Bearing a crest depicting a vulture and a bone to represent poor George, the tie was the same as worn that day by all present at the gathering in London. I had brought a bottle of port for the occasion and in the middle of the ocean, we drank a heartfelt toast to 'families'. Just to be on the safe side, Neptune had the first tot and this provided a bizarre yet comforting moment during which the expanse of miles between my family and myself briefly disappeared.

And a day later, after the most amazingly intense sunset, where the sky was filled with reds and blues, purples and surreal greens, the call of 'Land ahoy' went up as the dark shape of a Colombian mountain appeared off the port bow. A few hours after that we slipped by the fairway buoy under the darkness of night and drove through the huge concrete breakwater that marks the entrance to the amazing Panama Canal. The harbour, several miles across, was full of ships. Every shape and size of freighter rode at anchor, their huge rusting hulls dwarfing the two clippers who had beaten us to the finish line.

We had another third place and another podium position for a crew who had rediscovered the ocean and the raw honesty that racing over it provided. And with no family coming out to this stopover, there could be no melancholic departures hovering over us as we looked forward to relaxing ashore once more.

As we sat at anchor out in the bay the following morning, a huge squall was building. The familiar towering black clouds swept in and we were quickly engulfed in yet another freshwater deluge. With no showers for a week and conditions down below becoming riper by the moment, the whole crew took advantage of it. As the rain swept down, the crew emerged in swimming kit and frantically soaped away before the squall dried up. All around me, hair was awash with suds and a motley collection of beakers, bowls, hands and buckets captured the water running out of the scuppers, in order to rinse it all away. In the warm air, it provided a fantastically invigorating wake-up call, and with the quantity of water running off the boom filling a large bucket in seconds, we gave ourselves repeated dousings.

Aware that from the next boat a camera was being trained in our direction, Stuart and I each filled up a bucket, pulled out the waistband of our trunks and sent several gallons downwards. The camera clicked, the crew laughed and we headed for towels to dry off. With the boat secure and me washed and dried, I made a quick call on the sat phone to tell home we had safely arrived.

It was Saturday morning in the UK and the family would probably be in the kitchen pouring cereal into bowls, putting bread in the toaster and feeding the dog surreptitious titbits under the table. A couple of rings and Holly's voice came echoing across the world to our curious location.

'I've just seen a picture of you taking a shower,' she said.

'Really?' I replied, wondering what she could be talking about – not thinking for a second that it was from the moment on deck a few minutes before.

'Yup,' she said. 'You and Stuart pouring water down your trunks – we've just seen it on the website.'

In the time that it had taken me to finish my bath and dry off, the next-door boat had downloaded the digital picture on to their computer, dialled up the satellite, sent it on its way to race HQ back in Southampton, where the duty officer opened it, chuckled and decided it was one for the website. A click on the forward button sent it to the website technos, who downloaded, dragged and clicked and put the site back to live. A nanosecond later a sleepy daughter in Bedfordshire woke up, wondered where her dad was, logged on and joined in the fun on deck, a mere ten minutes after the camera had snapped.

The world had suddenly become a wonderfully small and intimate place.

Despite dire warnings from Clipper HQ about the evils that lay ashore, we decided that fresh supplies would make life a little more comfortable on board while we waited for clearance to transit the Panama Canal. Colón offered the shops, but muggings, shootings, rapes and murder supposedly lay in wait the moment we stepped on to dry land. The town, according to those in the know, was supposed to live up to its rather inelegant name and even without the risk of murder, I imagined that the twinning committee in the local council struggled somewhat. I made a mental note to suggest that the charming Kentish hamlet of Pratts Bottom might be a good place for them to start.

A few brave souls in the fleet moved away from the sanctuary of our boats, wondering if the natives would be friendly and secretly thrilled at the opportunity of another new experience diametrically opposite to all that was familiar. Armed with a harmless collection of string shopping bags, James and I pushed up to a drunken-looking jetty and gingerly stepped ashore, looking nervously for the hidden sniper. No salvo of gunfire jabbered in our direction and no roughly jabbed knife pierced our corporate Clipper clothing. So far, so good.

And with no Vietnam-style, AK47-toting welcome committee, we were able to look around us and take in the planet that our very own lunar module had settled. Beam me down, Scottie – I want to explore Colón.

Everywhere I looked in what seemed to be a fetid backwater of a marina, there were rotting hulks of yachts. Beautifully carved wooden prows and once erect masts now lay peeling and snapped. The *African Queen* must surely be hanging off one of the rough and twisted wooden pontoons, held afloat only by the green and rotting mooring lines that ran down into the infected water.

There was a corrugated-roofed shack, colonial style, that housed a surprisingly smart air-conditioned bar. Like the water, its patrons were flotsam and jetsam. Shaggy-haired men and kaftan-wearing, over made-up women lined the bar, drinking local beer at $3 a pitcher. It looked like they were as much a part of the place as the light fittings and faded black-and-white photographs. They were friendly, though, and no one confronted us with a snarling demand for our wallets. Bulging bellies and florid complexions were beacon giveaways that their ocean-gypsy dreams had stopped there, content to fester and die. 'Maybe next year' seemed to be the mantra, as their boats lay half prepared and incomplete.

Beyond a barbed-wire compound, railway lines and a giant container yard lay the town. A town that exists from the proceeds of traffic going through the nearby canal yet, despite the influx of American dollars, life clearly remained pretty poor and basic. Each supermarket, housed in the crumbling remains of old cinemas with fading 1930s-style frontages, seemed to boast an armed guard at the door and the sight of the guns was a sharp reminder of Clipper's warning.

In the streets, kids played, kicking a ball that scattered the small army of feral cats busy scavenging through the slum dwellings. Air horns from fleets of buses mingled with tapping diesels as ancient American high school transport, now brightly painted and luridly adorned with favoured girls' names, came rattling into the bus station.

It was Mother's Day, and despite the basic living conditions, the town was out to party in its finest clothes. A brass band rocked its way down the main street, followed by young girls in white holy communion frocks. This is a deeply Catholic country and the driver who collected me from the grandly named Panama Yacht Club crossed himself every time he passed a church.

His taxi was perfectly adequate, apart from being a pick-up, where his passengers sat in the open flatbed behind the cab. A humid, sticky wind blew through my sweat-sodden T-shirt and, as we sped through the ramshackle town towards the biggest supermarket, I wondered if the large chrome rear bumper held on with bailing twine would complete the journey before it fell off.

We were 1,225 miles from Havana, the gap between home had widened even further and again the journey was delivering experiences way beyond my expectations as we dipped in and out of a series of extraordinary diverse cultures and lifestyles.

Even supermarket shopping delivers revelations when it is done on the wrong side of Panama and from it I developed a great new marketing ploy, which I am now happy to share with Mr Tesco, Mr Sainsbury or Mr Waitrose.

This subtle retail idea, picked up from the Rey chain of food emporiums that service the people of Colón, will guarantee a massive increase in sales, if the UK bosses are wise enough to use it.

Like many shops in the town, the Panamanian chain had stationed an armed guard at the door. Not a regular security guy with just a radio, a uniform and a readiness to lend a helping hand at the checkout when an additional packer is needed. Here the food chain insist on a blue serge-wearing, heavily sweating, mean-faced maverick, armed with a huge – really huge – sub-machine gun.

If the recruitment policy has worked, they will have picked a slightly suspect character with a hint of an unbalanced background and a nasty twitch to his finger as he strokes the trigger just a little too energetically. He is the sort of person who can never be fired because there is no telling the consequences – should the bosses be foolish enough to upset his fragile nature.

He is not to be messed with and this is where the tactical marketing ploy comes into play. He stands by the checkouts scanning the trolleys coming through and shifts the steel weapon from huge hip to huge hip, just to make sure the shoppers can see it.

If the trolley content is poor or the value is too low, then his eyes narrow, the beads of sweat drip faster and the first round in the chamber starts to brace itself for the firing pin. Sensitive shoppers in Panama spot the signs and, knowing how to make the guard's day, they scurry back to add more, much more, to their trolley before venturing back to the frontline of the checkout.

All across the Home Counties, nervous shoppers would have to double up on cream fondants, fill another bag of kiwi fruit or go for something really obscure like double water chestnuts in brine, in order to get out of the door unscathed. It could earn millions of extra revenue and, as a marketing man, I share the concept for what it is worth.

We clearly pleased the guard as our bulging trolley was pushed back to the cab. In addition to the fresh meat, fresh vegetables and exotic fruits, James and I had spotted the bargain of the week and brought several bottles of it to please our fellow crew. Champion Gin, with its yellow label depicting a boxer delivering a knockout punch, has yet to make it into Harrods food hall, but at 95p a litre, we felt it had to be sampled. Five hours later, as the moon rose over the murky green waters of the bay, it delivered its KO to Ali Baxter, who had manfully attempted to work his way through the second bottle, long after everyone else had been beaten into submission.

Nursing large hangovers, we went ashore for breakfast, which was taken on the veranda of the club, as yet another monsoon downpour hammered on the corrugated-tin roof. We were due to leave the berth to ride at anchor, and then later the nose of *London* would slip into the first lock of the canal and make her way towards the Pacific.

Christmas was just fifteen days away and I waited with eager anticipation to see Anne, Holly and Mike on the quayside in the

Galápagos. James had rung home from the air-conditioned yacht-club bar and spoken to his parents. They had just returned from a performance of Handel's *Messiah* at Worcester Cathedral and good strong images of a traditional English Christmas flooded towards the equator. We could imagine the cold, damp air, the thick overcoats, the glistening stonework, the soaring sounds playing out through giant windows on to streets alive with Christmas lights reflecting over dark, wet pavements. The congregation would be buzzing with the growing anticipation of the coming holiday and the supper, stiff drink and log fire that awaited their return.

Two months of racing had already elapsed, with six thousand five hundred of the thirty-five thousand miles completed. Each stop had brought a series of memorable events that were so far removed from all that was familiar, and every day brought an insignificant, but none the less poignant, adventure to my door.

There had been the warm, warm welcome given to us by the Hemingway Marina yacht club, at the race prize-giving back in Cuba. The splendidly large and profusely sweating 'El Comodoro' gave an impassioned speech, which sounded like we were being asked to rise up and join the revolution. When the nervous translator shared his words in English, the pulpit-thumping, hand-waving oration turned out to be a much less impressive message that merely said, 'On behalf of the people of Cuba, welcome to our country.'

There was the moment of drama just after our hungover Panama breakfast, when a powerboat in the marina caught fire. As the blaze quickly took hold, a chap came hurtling down the pontoon, dived on board and a few seconds later emerged through the smoking front hatch with a sleepy young girl in his arms. Father and child stood at the bow, refusing to jump – either because they could not swim or because the waters were so deeply unpleasant. We had been warned not to even think about taking a swim, as a miniature worm, capable of crawling into any choice of body orifice, lurked beneath the surface. Once it was content in its new home, tiny spiked barbs ensured that it was there to stay and a surgeon's knife was the only way to remove it.

In the end the heat from the flames forced the man and child to jump, and to add to the drama, a crew member from one of the clippers decided to effect a dramatic rescue. He dived into the water and helped drag the man and his frightened daughter the few yards to the shore.

Alan Wells, our ex-firefighter, was delighted. The local brigade arrived and he looked on with a critical eye as the 'watch' reacted to the 'shout'. The local boys did their stuff under his excited scrutiny, leaving behind a melted and distorted black hull which sat, sadly steaming, in the water. Anti-worm tablets were dispensed to the victims, and Alan talked us through the observed procedures, leaning nonchalantly against the Panamanian 'appliance' before the fire crew returned to their station – each trying to work out what the critical English yachtsman had been trying to convey to them.

There was another curious moment that I stumbled into, back at the marina in Cuba. Tied to one of the quays was my dream boat. Wooden-built, with lots of polished brass and old-fashioned portholes, and gleaming from lavish amounts of attention, this elegant old cruiser looked like a romantic way of tripping gently around the world. An American flag hung from its stern and I was eager to get on board and have a look below. A pair of children's shoes showed that she was lived in, but whenever I passed by, looking for a hopeful invitation, there was no sign of anyone on board.

Walking back to *London* late one evening, I was once again taking in its graceful lines, when a hatch was suddenly thrown open, spilling yellow cabin light out into the darkness. A figure flew up the companionway in a rabid rage, turning back to the light and shouted back down, 'Fuck you ... No, fuck you ... No, listen, lady, FUCK YOU!' before slamming the hatch shut and extinguishing the warm glow.

The American owner saw me standing there and in a slurred voice, clearly the worse for a few drinks, decided to download his problems, revealing a plot of epic-movie proportions.

He had sailed to Cuba a few years earlier, had met a girl and fallen in love. He returned regularly and she became pregnant, giving birth to a son. I had seen them by the pool, she a stunningly beautiful woman with jet-black long hair and flashing, vibrant eyes. The child was a cute, tanned three-year-old who doted on his mother with the same uncomplicated love that she gave him.

The couple had agreed that the only place for a future was in America and each time the beautiful boat sailed back into Cuba to continue the love affair, its owner gently probed to discover whose palms needed to be greased to keep people quiet about the illegal escape.

He told me that he had parted with several thousand US dollars to marina officials, who make it their business to know what is going on all around the boatyard. He had built a false wall to create a padded secret compartment at the back of the boat for his lover and child to hide in should they be accosted by Cuban or American patrol ships as they made their illegal dash.

Except that the stunning woman now had cold feet. She could not bear the risk to her son and had decided that it should all end and they should remain, unhappy, in Cuba. It was in response to that decision that he had flipped and involved me in his mini-soap opera.

I saw him the next morning preparing to sail and asked if his cargo was complete. He looked a little taken aback, forgetting for a moment that he had shared this deep, deep secret. Yes, they were on board, and half an hour later my dream boat dipped through the surf at the marina entrance and pointed up towards the American coast.

Their story stuck with me and as it replayed amid the worn-out boats in Panama, I rather hoped that Julia Roberts might take the lead when someone buys my screenplay. With such intense fantasies and Oscar-winning dreams whirling in my head, it was probably time to leave.

We slipped from the ramshackle quay mid-afternoon and rode at anchor to await our pilot for the transit through the Panama Canal. Despite the seediness of Colón, there was a raw and unpretentious honesty about the place and I had enjoyed dipping into the backwaters of lost dreams and rotting hopes. What's more, I had not been shot and the only thing that had mugged me was a glass too many of Champion Gin.

The pilot arrived and asked us to head off towards the line of neon lights that crawled up the hillside ahead. We motored through rich, lush rainforest lining both banks of the narrowing channel, as a full moon rose behind the sharp, pointy fronds of silhouetted palm trees. Behind us, a giant banana boat, all white and yellow logoed, towered over the entire scene as we edged slowly towards the Gatun locks and the canal's entrance.

Take a banana out of your fruit bowl and have a look at it for a moment. Seriously, do it, because its arrival in your hand marks the end of an extraordinary journey.

The vast ship behind us had taken many months to build at an arc-welding, steel-banging boatyard somewhere industrial. Its huge tanks were brimming with fuel for the backwards and forward slog across giant oceans. The captain had in his safe the wage bills for the crew on board. Somewhere in the ship's wake there was a small army of dockside workers and crane drivers whose job was to load the cargo and, far ahead, a similar, rather better-paid army awaited the vessel's arrival. On waterside industrial estates, cavernous cold-storage depots manned by forklift-truck-driving dispatchers awaited. In turn, they would load up fleets of diesel-eating juggernauts ready to head for the M3, M4, A14 and M25. And ready to greet them, another small army – this time of retailers, with stores to fill, staff to pay and overheads to beat. The Panama Canal speeds up the process of delivering bananas, even though the transit of that vessel alone would add another $50,000 to the shipping costs.

All that effort. All that manpower. All that cost. All that burnt energy. Just so we are able to peel a banana in the UK and add it to our cereal. Or throw it away because it has become a little too black.

And the yellow fruit that hopefully you are now gazing at with renewed awe and respect will have cost the princely sum of just a few pence. The giant white ship behind us stood as a towering monument to consumerism, but for such an unimportant sliver of fruit the whole process seemed suddenly hugely absurd. And while there will be defenders of the tiny islands where bananas keep the economy going, I still can't quite work out why a banana sells for just a few pence, when by rights it should cost several pounds. It would appear that someone in the chain is getting a raw deal.

The canal is an extraordinary feat of engineering. Running up the gentle hillside ahead of us were three enormous locks on a scale way bigger than anything I had envisaged. Forget what you might have experienced on a narrow-boat holiday on the Grand Union or even the Manchester Ship Canal. These locks were like something out of a James Bond film set, capable of swallowing giant supertankers whole and still leaving room for more. Vast gates, towering walls, giant arc lights and an extraordinary railway system that shunted up and down on either side of the flights greeted us. The high-powered little trains spewed out coils of thick steel hawsers that pulled the bow of the ship into the lock, while a sister engine tugged backwards on a similar hawser, braking hard on the stern. By this method the towering holds of bananas were gently eased upwards away from the Atlantic.

Far above us, workers in hard helmets and life jackets peered over the edge of the towering concrete walls and threw down heaving lines with pin-sharp accuracy. Our mooring lines snaked back up towards them and we were as secure as we could be. Seven hundred and fifty tons of lock gates swung effortlessly shut behind us and everyone prepared to defend *London* from the unyielding walls, as twenty-six million gallons of water flooded into the chamber in just ten minutes.

To a twenty-five-thousand-ton merchant ship held tight by the dockside railway system, the massive influx of water was a minor irritant. For a suddenly very small and vulnerable racing yacht, the incoming rush caused massive eddies and swirling currents that sent the hull rolling and spinning upwards. We lined the wall, pushing off with all the strength we could muster, using boathooks, paddles, spinnaker poles and bare hands to stop the upper part of the mast hitting the unforgiving sides.

Ten minutes later the front door of the first lock eased open, the funicular railway whistled its signal backwards and forwards and the giant ship in front of us was gently tugged into position on the second tier. Alongside us in a parallel lock, the banana ship rose in unison and behind us on the lower flight another huge merchant vessel was lining up to join the queue. A hundred thousand dollars earned in just a few minutes.

As the third lock gates swung open we motored away from the arc lights and the radio signals and the Spanish shouts and the tooting engines, now busily shunting back down the hill to collect another ship and entered the calm oasis of Gatun Lake. This vast, man-made affair provides the water for the locks and is fuelled by the regular heavy downpours that the nearby dense and constantly breathing forest helps to create. With a huge full moon illuminating the surface with a steel-blue glow, we followed the roadway of red and green flashing lights that marked the channel, and crossed the placid surface.

Away in the distance, above the banks of rainforest, distant mountains sat in silhouette against the rich velvet blackness of the star-filled sky. Over the regular beat of the engine and the gentle splash of freshwater on the hull, the sounds of the jungle came to us across the lake. We all spoke in hushed tones, like tourists in a cathedral, and were lost in the sheer tranquillity of the moment. OK, so the race route avoided Cape Horn, but this was still a rich, precious and, because it was night time, intensely private and intimate moment of travel.

The path through the lake twisted and turned before entering a narrow cut through a steep-sided gorge. On several occasions we were forced to squeeze close into the dark and mysterious shoreline, as a towering steel hull sluiced by at great speed, heading towards the opposite ocean. In the distance a bloom of light pollution indicated the next set of locks that dropped back downhill towards the Pacific, and the twelve-mile trip across the isthmus was almost over.

Our pilot had been monosyllabic throughout the transit, miserable that his relative newness to the job only allowed him to control the passage of small boats. He looked up with ill-concealed envy and resentment at his more senior colleagues as they controlled proceedings from the wings of the lofty bridge on the merchant ship behind us.

With the descent complete, a strong current took us downriver and the first hint of a swell from the Pacific nudged *London*'s bow in greeting. In the darkness, we swept under the huge steel span of the Bridge of the Americas – the only thing that connects the two vast continents – and found a mooring buoy off the Balboa Yacht Club.

The morning sun revealed pelicans languidly flapping through the early light and large manta rays broke the surface inches from where we ate breakfast. Away in the distance, a vast Panamanian flag hung from a huge pole on a conical hillside and the first commuter traffic of the day headed for the nearby airport.

Behind a line of palm trees, the tips of Dallas-like skyscrapers marked the brave new world of Panama City, now free but still very much influenced by the Americans' recent presence. The Caesar Park hotel, with its mini-Vegas-style casino, obligatory slot machines in the foyer and 'have a nice day' attitude, was happy to take my credit card, and a couple of days of five-star luxury, complete with instant communications to home, recharged my jaded batteries. A nearby Chinese laundry took care of my festering clothes and mouldy bedding. A backstreet watch shop fitted a new battery to my blind wristwatch and an optician had a valiant go at fixing my broken sunglasses.

A taxi ride around town cost $1 and the teeming streets seemed happy, safe and full of hope and energy as they aped the familiar brands of the first world. Several giant McDonald's outlets indicated how much 'progress' had been made and the economy was clearly working, because the supermarkets stocked bananas.

We revictualled the boat at a well-stocked, gun-free Costco, filling seven huge shopping trolleys. Fourteen thousand dollars ensured that all the boats had enough creature comforts to take us on to Honolulu at the end of January. Ali, Aki, Keith and I missed out on the frivolity of the prize-giving party, complete with dancers in national dress and a rather fey British Ambassador, as we endeavoured to stow all the food before the sun could get at it. And while Ali searched through the boxes of incoming stores for more bottles of Champion, the rest of us took a look at the supplies that had been with us from the start.

The products purchased from Bookers Cash and Carry in Southampton were still going strong. Between us we spent a joyful couple of hours cleaning up tubs of butter and long-life milk that had travelled the oceans on bilge-class tickets.

At first sight the mould-encrusted and soggy packaging seemed to have 'bin' written all over it, but a bit of a wipe and a nervous sniff under the lid suggested that there was still potential and the butter, which had melted, set and melted again, stayed with us. So did the slightly green milk cartons, which continued to provide a liquid that its bovine donor might just still be able to identify.

All those niceties, like sell-by dates, were ignored and even the most appalling student would probably turn his nose up at the state of some of what lay on board. But on it went, as we prepared for the next leg out into the Pacific towards the Galápagos Islands.

In my hotel room, high up on the fourteenth floor, old habits died hard. The ridiculously overpriced minibar should really be avoided, but I plundered the contents anyway, enjoying the curious combination of a gin and tonic with a Toblerone chaser. The telephone was a fully functioning, totally reliable little number, a by-product of America's recent occupation that allowed me to plug in my laptop and pick up e-mails that had been waiting since I left Portugal six weeks before. In the office world, leaving an e-mail unread for more than an hour was a mortal sin. And as I knew the in box would only contain words from people I liked and who liked me, I dialled up expectantly with all the excitement of a small boy on Christmas morning.

A list of bold-type headings formed on the screen and I eagerly checked to see who the messages were from. Some of the names I had expected to see failed to materialise, but were adequately replaced by ones that were warm surprises.

There were numerous messages of support and, within them, deep-seated emotions, shared with unselfconscious honesty. I was touched by the depth of feeling that these people gave me and it was clear that they were sharing, experiencing and understanding much of what I was going through. In every case the words came from sensitive souls with creative minds supported by spiritual beliefs and as they shared my journey, so I too had my mind opened by theirs.

Peter and Mary Le Coyte, Pam Roberts, Barry and Wendy Taylor, Anna Tully, Mark Cranmer, Bowlsie and Goldie, Chris Bonington, Judy Leden, Michael Hoppen, Zelda Cheatle, Cathy Davies, Nikki Gordon, Ali Sanders, Kathryn Fowler and Christine Horowitz all flowed into my hotel room and their encouragement meant a huge amount. Their contact and support remained consistent throughout the year and revealed a depth of friendship that I had failed to appreciate in the mad schedules of the average day.

The same applied to my family, for equally special were the messages of uncomplicated love from brother, sisters and parents that chased me around the world. Had I been at home continuing a more mundane routine from nine to five and easily available at the touch of a few buttons, the honest and open exchanges would probably not have been even considered, let alone shared. It was a sound reminder that no matter how busy our individual lives become, it is a special thing to tell a sibling they are loved and, in turn, provide an opportunity to respond with an equal amount of love.

There were plans for a big night out in Panama City and the hotel bar filled with a variety of clipper crew members. Despite our being fierce competitors, the spirit of togetherness was great and the fleet ashore was one huge and very happy family. Relationships were starting to flourish in several quarters, and in people who had battled with the world at its wildest, the desire to continue the adrenalin high buzzed with a fierce intensity.

A laughing, noisy, enthusiastic mass whirled their way out into the night and, in a sudden attack of sensibleness, a few of us decided to opt out. Gary, Neil and I were all in the same hotel and instead of copious beers and a greasy late-night burger in a series of smoky bars, we chose to take the hotel elevator up to the top floor.

Gentle music tinkled through the cut-glass crystal and carefully laid-out silver as we entered the lofty dining room overlooking the darkened ocean. Several whispering, hand-holding couples looked up vaguely in our direction while white-coated waiters attentively refilled half-empty wine glasses.

The atmosphere wrapped us in its warm, secure blanket and we settled down for our first really civilised meal since leaving the UK. After such a long gap, the food offered an intensity and variety of flavours previously missed in the world of business lunches, where eating in fine restaurants had become commonplace. The staff were gently caring and looked after our dining requirements with a professional and discreet eye.

We hardly spoke as the crisp, sharp crunch of a chilled, water-dripping iceberg lettuce mingled with the strong tangs from a gently drizzled thick dressing, which even now was being soaked up by a sprinkling of firm brown croutons that sat collectively on expectant china plates placed on three immaculate linen table mats. A dusting of black peppercorns ground into heavy specks, a sliver of anchovy with its salt-laden ocean flavours, and a sharply chilled white wine to clean away one taste and replace it with an explosion of further delights, completed the ensemble and left us in a state of heady and silent rapture.

The main course replaced the starter and every raised fork brought another combination of mouth-watering tastes. A more complex red filled in the gaps and added to the enthusiastic messages going from taste bud to brain. When the last of the crimson sauce had been mopped up by light and sweet-smelling newly baked rolls, making our plates look sparklingly clean, fresh, strong coffee and a warm, pungent fume-rich brandy rounded off a precious and memorable time at the table. The weeks of brown stuff from a tin, served up in a plastic dog bowl, receded to a far-away place and we sat grinning stupidly at each other in a cigar-smoke haze of complete and utter contentment.

And, after this perfect dinner, three delighted customers took the lift down a couple of floors, turned the key in the lock, slipped between cool cotton sheets and fell into the deepest of sleeps, uninterrupted by watches, alarm clocks or urgent calls of 'All hands on deck.'

9

DOLDRUMS DECEMBER
PANAMA TO THE GALÁPAGOS ISLANDS
15.12.00–21.12.00

Race day was hot, with an already strong sun burning into skin we thought had become acclimatised. There was nothing to fend off the heat, and because it was time for a race start, sod's law dictated that any chance of a breeze looked non-existent.

With mainsails lazily flapping, the fleet headed west under motor and watched the natural harbour full of merchant ships waiting on the Pacific side of the canal slip slowly behind. One Panamanian rust bucket sent us on our way with a football-terrace series of blasts on its horn and the *capitán* emerged to gave us an enthusiastic wave of farewell as if he were standing on the terrace at Stamford Bridge.

The placid surface was occasionally broken by small patches of bubbling, frothing disturbed wavelets, which were quickly pounced upon by the ever-cruising pelicans.

Something huge and hungry was patrolling the depths, forcing the smaller fish right up to the surface. The boiling sea was a shoal of fish literally running out of space and in their efforts to avoid being eaten by the foe from below, they got snapped up by the pelican from above.

We motored onwards, rather than start the race in the windless calm that could possibly delay our arrival in the Galápagos until after Christmas. The unforgiving sun gave way to a still, warm night and around 23.00 the instruments indicated the first whiff of a breeze. All eight boats prepared for a Le Mans-style start, where the fleet would motor slowly along in a line-abreast formation.

When everyone was happy that no advantage was being taken down the line, engines were cut, the mainsail provided the drive and, after a countdown on the radio, the fleet readied itself to race. As the designated minute clicked up on the GPS, a radio call confirmed the start and on eight sets of bows the crews guided their jibs up the stay. At the mast, eight sets of muscles hauled on the halyard for all they were worth and eight sets of cockpit crew loaded up winches and brought in the sheets until the power of the wind began to drive the yachts forward.

On board *London*, Andy and Aki worked the bow together as a fast-moving foredeck team. Anna and Ali heaved at the halyards with all their might, sweating the sail up the mast. Back in the cockpit, Ellie and Jane quickly had the lines attached to a winch and tensioned to a level that was shouted back down from the foredeck team.

With the sails up, James and Danny stood at one winch, Gary and Alan at another, hauling in the sheets and whipping the thick lines around the drum for grinding in. They watched the raised and circling hands of Aki and Andy calling for a tighter trim in each sail and whirled the winch handles at breakneck speed until a clenched fist from the bow indicated it was enough. Behind them Keith and Neil loaded up the running backstay on yet another winch, while sandwiched in the middle, eyes aloft checking its shape, I eased and hauled on the mainsail, making constant adjustments to the wind. And, behind us all, Stuart surveyed the scene from the wheel as he guided the rapidly accelerating hull through the water.

Every member of the team was on deck with a task to fulfil and they all did a stunning job. Across the fleet, no one had set sails quicker or more efficiently and *London* led the pack on into the darkness. The routing for this short leg of a mere eight hundred miles was still of vital importance and the path we chose over the next twenty-four hours critical. Around the equator, what little wind there is moves directly upwards – which was of no use to our sailing boat trying desperately to get blown across the ocean.

We were approaching the infamous Doldrums or, to give it its grown-up title, the Intertropical Convergence Zone. This is a constantly shifting area of nothingness, where boats reliant on wind will sit and slop for days on end, causing great frustration to a racing crew who thrive on progress. If wind does kick in and the ITCZ has shifted to a different part of the ocean, the tactic is to grab hold of it and head straight for the Galápagos. If the nothingness of the

Doldrums is upon you, the best bet is to crawl south and pick up the more reliable trade winds blowing in from Ecuador.

In the night, we watched *Liverpool* and *Glasgow* opt for the direct route, while the rest of the fleet, led by *London*, spun their wheels over to port and headed south towards the equator, where we hoped for a more consistent breeze.

For two days the wind further north kept up a consistent blow and both *Liverpool* and *Glasgow* quickly built up a sixty-mile lead. Meanwhile we slapped and slopped in the most frustrating of light airs, helming by the wind indicator at the top of the mast, turning the wheel to follow the ever-changing directions as the wind backed, headed and did everything possible to hamper our progress.

To make matters worse, the nights brought vast squalls that filled our radar screens with a massive green blob of electronic reflection and settled firmly overhead for hours at a time. The foul-weather kit, which had now grown a coat of black mould, provided scant protection from the onslaught, and we sat in a sodden and sullen silence struggling to go anywhere.

Despite the close proximity to the equator, cold-water currents chilled the night air, and thermal gear, packed before leaving the UK in the autumn, was given a surprise wake-up call. As watch leader, I tried my best to keep attention focused in order to get whatever boat speed we could muster from the trying conditions, but when one achieves an hourly distance of just a tenth of a mile, it becomes very hard to keep motivated.

In such frustrating conditions, patience starts to wear thin and when tiredness is added to the cocktail, thin lines grow taut and eventually snap. And to prove the point, I was on the receiving end of an unexpected and uncharacteristic outburst from Stuart.

A squall had looked like it might rush in and blow away our spinnaker. Stu was up on deck watching proceedings nervously and shouting back orders to ensure the sail was preserved. If we could keep it up, then we would maximise boat speed, but if the squall caught us out, the sail would explode from the sudden onslaught. Up at the mast, he peered through the night-time rain, watching the surface of the ocean for telltale signs of an incoming blow. As he watched, shouting course instructions back to the cockpit, we all followed his lead to the letter.

Normally, the helm looks aloft at the wind indicator at the top of the mast, but so intent was I on obeying the shouted word, I failed to do so. As a result, the wind was placed on the wrong side of the boat and any racing efficiency vanished in our slowly moving wake. To make things worse, the lights of another clipper slipped effortlessly by half a mile away on a completely different breeze and our winning position vanished.

Stuart's dummy was firmly spat out in an intense moment of late-night bollocking. He ranted at our inept attempts to sail the boat halfway efficiently and, quite rightly, the focus of his diatribe was me. It was my watch, I was supposed to be in charge, so I had to take the rap.

I was cross with myself for not having the confidence to see the situation develop. I was cross that, as a result, I had lost a position, and I was cross that my crew mates had to endure criticism, when all they had done was to follow Stuart's instructions. We all festered in the wet, cold, flapping darkness and stewed in our own individual moments of sulkiness as the minutes ticked by to the watch end. Three hours later, at 02.00, we were back at it, but Stuart's mood had not improved, the conditions continued to tease and taunt some more and, to cap it all, a sore throat, headache and wheezy cough told me I had the start of a cold. It truly was a bloody, miserable moment.

Away in the distance and free from the localised squalls, two more of the fleet slipped by and there were renewed knots of tension as the conditions probed and piled pressure on us all.

It was no one's fault that we were moving along so slowly and badly against the rest of the fleet. This mocking weather had delivered itself to our door and all we could do was deal with it as best we could.

I was secretly delighted that the rota for mother watch showed I was on duty the following day. Someone else could stand in the firing line and, for the first time in the race, I had no desire to go on deck.

After three hours of particularly poor sleep, I got up early to start preparing the crew's breakfast. Stuart was already at the stove frying eggs and offering to take my place for the morning's duties. With the eggs spluttering nicely, he rummaged under his bunk, found the rum and decided that a morning toast to Neptune was needed. The large tot poured into my coffee mug was a clear peace offering and we exchanged a rough bear hug of embarrassed reconciliation before taking several further large gulps of the very smooth and warming Havana Club.

The toasts to Neptune went around the boat several times and the gloomy mood was lifted. The King of the Sea seemed to respond to the offering, because over the next twelve hours the barometer fell as a gentle breeze turned into a brisk blow.

In the trying conditions of light and variable winds, we had gone through a huge wardrobe of sails, trying to match the canvas to the wind angle and strength. And with the winds constantly shifting, sail changes were happening every ten to fifteen minutes. Not only was this trying for the on-watch crew, it was also difficult for the people trying to catch some sleep below. Decks banged, winches ground, running feet pounded and echoed through the boat and sail bags crashed through the open hatch, falling on to sleeping forms.

But, with stronger winds, the game of running down through the sail wardrobe, from the No. 1 foresail and staysail, to the Genoa, to the wind seeker, looked like it was over for a while. To make the foredeck more cluttered, the wind had sometimes shifted to the beam, so the spinnakers had also been pressed into action – sometimes the lightweight sail, sometimes the heavier All Purpose. The net result left the deck cluttered with a huge choice of sail bags.

Now back under 'white sails', trimmed in tight on a close-hauled beat, we even had to put a reef in the main as the wind grew and the hull positively sang at the freedom of escape from the angst-filled area of the ITCZ. Our progress was at last good and the latest radio schedule showed that we were in third place, behind *Jersey* and *Bristol*.

Liverpool and *Glasgow*, who had gambled on going direct towards the Galápagos, now found themselves firmly stuck as the Doldrums shifted, and were already fifty miles behind us.

The gap to the leaders was small and we knew from bitter experience what a wind hole in the night or a bad squall could do. Perhaps the next time, though, it would work in our favour, so we kept pushing just in case the opportunity came. As well as keeping a sharp eye on the weather, there was also a need to spot fishing lines, having chanced upon an unmarked set miles from anywhere, acting like a barrier on our chosen path. The locals didn't appear to bother with anything helpful like a marker buoy and the twig-like sticks attached to the hazard were almost impossible to see, even in broad daylight.

Glasgow, *Portsmouth* and *Liverpool* all managed to get ensnared on similar nets and the skippers of all three boats had to don mask and snorkel and go over the side to cut themselves clear. Martin Clough, *Portsmouth*'s skipper, had just clambered back on board when a large shark came to see what all the commotion was about. Martin is a no-nonsense Yorkshireman who had proved a particularly tenacious competitor and we mused on who would have found the encounter more scary. We rather felt that it would have been the shark that turned pale.

The islands on our chart now started to draw closer at a much healthier rate and we plotted the close fight between *Jersey* and *Bristol* going on ten miles ahead of us. It was clear that they were sacrificing direction in the interest of speed and their heading was taking them well north of the rhumb line to our destination.

As a result of this tactic, it looked like they would be forced to tack, allowing us a clear opportunity to close the gap. For two days the good wind stayed with us and we knuckled down for some focused sailing.

The nights continued to bring magical pleasures. As we drove onwards into the blackness, the moon was hidden behind thick clouds and the only illumination in the ocean was a huge green burning wake of churned phosphorescence trailing from our stern. Speeding towards us was more broken flashing plankton, disturbed by the underwater rush of several fast-moving dolphins. They stayed under the surface and as they sped effortlessly towards the boat, great tubes of green marked their trace, looking like torpedo trails, as they twisted and turned around us. Away in the distance, a much bigger blur of green lumbered along at the same speed as our yacht and gave away the presence of a massive whale, who decided to swim with us for a while.

With ninety miles to go, just after the sun had come up, there in the distance, off our starboard bow, was another clipper. The fleet were all racing to a designated point in the chart, right on the equator, that would serve as a finish line should the Doldrums cut back in and cause the fleet to still be floundering at sea when Christmas Day arrived.

It looked like there would be no danger of that, as the good wind still blew, and we dipped into the investment of sailing hard on the wind over the previous days. Thanks to that effort, we could now bear away to the designated mark, put the wind on the beam, hoist the spinnaker and really play catch-up. The team made giant inroads and as we closed in on the yacht and the waypoint, the binoculars revealed the red and grey stripes of *Bristol*. The gap was down to just a mile and the race to the finish was on.

A giant turtle that was swimming near us seemed oblivious to all that, though, as our racing yacht bore down on him at nine knots. His glistening shell gently bobbed in the swell and two huge flippers languidly paddled away, trailing a large tangle of seaweed as he showed us the way towards Christmas ashore.

In the skies above him, frigate birds, tropicbirds and giant brown boobies criss-crossed the sky and, away in the distance, sudden huge splashes broke the surface, revealing the giant and glistening triangular forms of twisting, spinning manta rays.

A sudden explosion of sights and sounds mingled with the excitement of another grandstand finish and the sight of watching the GPS count down to 000° 00.000′ before replacing north with south was hardly taken in.

Traditionally, crossing the equator demands giving full respect to Neptune and a court should be convened to introduce new subjects to the laws of his domain. The crew had already showed him the deepest respect and the earnest sentiments and promises that accompanied each offering of rum demonstrated that he was held in awe. Wigs and costumes and pans full of evil-looking porridge-based sludge had been prepared for the messy moment and just when we were ready to show him our full appreciation, we had a real race on our hands.

Hoping Neptune would understand and continue to give us the winds we had hoped for just another day, we postponed the celebrations. Stuart, ever suspicious, even had a loud chat with him, explaining our predicament over the rail like an orator at Hyde Park Corner, flinging his arms theatrically in order to emphasise a particular point. Huge promises were pledged in order to show our respect, but, true to form, Neptune took the wind away.

Reefs were shaken out, the sail wardrobe – now all on deck again – was fully employed, and the lightweight wind seeker was once again searching for puffs on a listless sea. Our momentum and the apparent wind that came with it took us along at around three knots and delivered the best sight of the day. Up ahead, also with no breeze, lay the lead boat, *Jersey*. At least the ocean ruler was playing fair and we wondered if *London* was going to repeat our last-minute dash to the line in Portugal.

On that occasion it was *Jersey* who were pipped by us and their mood on board had plummeted. They had been in the lead on the race to the Galápagos for the last three days and, with the finish so close, must have started to believe that the win belonged to them.

The three crews did all they could to eke out whatever speed possible and the gaps stabilised to a mile and half a mile. We decided to think bold and take a different course to the yachts ahead. Following would simply provide the same conditions and, with boats so equal, it was unlikely that the gap could be closed any more. A look at the chart indicated that a strong current in the south would help our cause, so we turned away and headed off on a route of our own. We watched to see if they would match us, but they stayed firmly locked in battle with each other and pretty quickly disappeared over the horizon.

Neptune liked this fighting spirit and decided to give us back the wind again. With the current doing its bit, we were right on track for the finish line and knew that the two yachts now well to the north of us would be forced to tack. Suddenly it really looked like we were in with a chance of winning.

The finish lay ten miles ahead and as the Galápagos archipelago started to reveal itself through the haze, the sails of *Jersey* and *Bristol* finally reappeared to the north.

As we all converged yet again, *Jersey* were sailing tight inshore and, try as we might, the gap remained just under one mile. For the last few hours the winds returned to their whispering mode and an intense sun beat down on a calm and sparkling sea. Behind *Jersey*, things were a lot closer. We were now just a length behind *Bristol* and our two boats tacked back and forth across the same path. On some occasions the tacks brought us so close we missed a collision by just a couple of feet.

Yet, despite the close proximity after a week at sea, the two crews failed to acknowledge each other, each one concentrating intently on getting the maximum out of their boat. What little breeze there was came on the nose and we close-hauled our way towards the finish. It put the bulk of responsibility on the helm to keep as close to the wind as possible, without pinching and losing speed. I had the dubious privilege of carrying the can and stared intently at the wind indicator and the sail shape, to ensure we were getting the best from the conditions.

All of *London*'s crew lined the rail in order to keep the hull performing at its optimum and occasional calls of support for my efforts came back to the cockpit.

'Nice driving, Ian,' shouted Ali.

'Go on, my son,' added Danny.

'Doing well,' said Neil.

Beside me stood Stuart, both our heads craning upwards, constantly monitoring every tiny wisp of wind. After the first hour I could feel the unrelenting sun starting to eat into my skin. By the end of the second hour I knew that I should be plastering protective lotion all over it and when the third ticked by I was red raw from overexposure. But none of it mattered while we concentrated hard on the single most important thing on our planet – to gain second place. Stu offered quiet guidance and encouragement, monitoring the instruments and our speed, suggesting small adjustments and whispering his tactics.

Slowly, oh so slowly, we moved up on to *Bristol*'s stern quarter and then mast and then bow. Now we could steal her wind and suddenly we were in the driving seat, covering their every move as the finish line drew closer. To the delight of the crew, we moved ahead until clear water sat between us, and when *Bristol* tacked in an attempt to get us to cover the move, Stu held firm and we drove on to the line.

It had been an incredibly intense period at the wheel and when we finally crossed, the feeling of relief and elation at coming second was immense.

We all danced jigs and hugged and cheered before motoring over to a delighted *Jersey* and giving them three well-deserved cheers. *Bristol* eventually crossed the line a couple of minutes behind us and when they motored up to acknowledge our success, I could see the helm I had done battle with slumped in the cockpit, being consoled by his team mates. When we got ashore I made sure that he would be the first person I would buy a beer for.

And with the excitement over we could stop focusing on the race and take in our surroundings for the first time. Here we were, at an island that was the closest I have ever been to paradise. Pelicans plunged into a turquoise sea and sea lions swam cheekily around the boat, their huge eyes looking up at us looking down.

With *London* riding at anchor in Academy Bay off the island of Santa Cruz, we dived off the stern and cooled in the waters of the Pacific. The buzz from another good result was an intoxicating drug and the brotherhood and camaraderie that we all felt for each other burned intensely.

And for me, the excitement was fuelled by the fact that we had arrived two days ahead of schedule. It meant that I could make the journey to the small airport and witness the Tame Airways jet, inbound from Quito, swoop down from a clear blue sky and make a perfect touchdown, complete with a precious cargo.

It was bringing my family to me for Christmas.

Which was just what I always wanted.

10

SANTA ON SANTA CRUZ
THE GALÁPAGOS ISLANDS TO OAHU
15.12.00–21.12.00

No sooner had we dropped anchor than a small fleet of boats came out to visit us. On the first came the magnificent George, the smoothest operator in town. Standing at the bow of his water taxi and waving his Panama hat graciously in the air, he welcomed us to his home.

'Hi, my name is George. Anything you want, you come to me, I organise.'

Someone mentioned beer and he was on the case. Ice, too, was sorted, as were numerous hotels, scuba dives, trips to the highlands and trips to see giant tortoises.

I needed to get to the airport and before I knew it there was a bus ticket on its way. All before we had even set foot on dry land.

Getting ashore involved either some frantic waving or a blast or two from the foghorn. Eventually a lazy wave of an arm from a small open motor boat at the quay indicated that the taxi was on its way. A fleet of tyre-clad craft offered the service for a few of America's prized cents and wound their way between the visiting yachts, local fishing vessels and deluxe cruise ships that introduced the Galápagos archipelago to the tourists of the world.

The following morning I took one of the taxis to the shore, strolled under the trees, rich in exotic blossom, that lined the edge of Academy Bay and climbed on board a rickety and overloaded bus for the airport.

A mixture of travellers and locals chatted amiably as we swayed out of town and headed up into the highlands. Occasionally a white pick-up – the standard transport on the island – roared past with a friendly wave and a hoot to our driver. On the other side of the island a small ferry transported us across a narrow channel and another bus finally stopped at the corrugated-metal building that served as the main terminal.

A trail of black jet exhaust and the twinkling of a distant landing light heralded the arrival of the jet from Quito and I hoped beyond hope that the complicated journey from Bedfordshire to here had gone without a hitch. I paced to and fro as the pilot took an age to taxi to a stop and I watched as the first passengers walked out into the sun. My eyes darted from the front steps to the rear, frantically searching for the three figures whose embrace I so desperately wanted.

Whenever we fly as a family we avoid the ridiculous scramble that always kicks off the moment the seat-belt sign goes out. But on this occasion I wished that Anne had muscled people out of the way to be the first in the queue. As it was, they were the last off and my heart skipped a beat as the familiar figures picked their way down the steps and on to the tarmac.

When they left Heathrow for Amsterdam and the KLM flight to Ecuador, we had been slopping along in the Doldrums down in fifth place. They would have no idea that we had arrived, so my presence at the airport would be a complete surprise.

Last out of the aircraft meant that they were last through immigration and last in the baggage hall. The half-hour wait was desperately painful, and as people hugged and greeted each other around me, I looked on enviously at their sharing of emotion.

Finally my family made it through and as they walked towards the exit of the terminal, I slotted in behind them, observing my children and bursting with joy at being together again. I was spotted by Michael, who let out a strangled cry and buried himself in my arms. Holly tumbled in as well and the tears that I had last seen at that oh so painful goodbye in Portsmouth sprang forth again in a show of unbridled happiness. Anne completed the huge group hug and the driver who had come to meet them beamed at the sight of such an emotional reunion.

The trip back into town was an explosion of news and I could not let go of the three sets of hands that held on tight and confirmed that we were truly together once more. They were captivated by the scenery that flew by and entranced by the first glimpse of Academy Bay, where the much-prayed-for vision of *London* rode at anchor.

The basic but adequate Sol y Mar hotel welcomed us with great warmth and as Holly and Michael settled into their room on the other side of the road, Anne and I said hello properly for the first time.

Out beyond the gently blowing muslin curtains at our balcony, the sounds of the sea whispered into the room. It may have been December, but a warm sun caressed the stone floor and we kissed properly for the first time since my departure from home. I had waited an age for this moment and Anne responded with an equal urgency.

The kisses became more intense and as the waves lapped against the rocks outside, a stream of discarded clothes lay strewn in a line towards the bed. Despite the months apart, we prolonged the moment, exploring and rediscovering each other with a deep-seated desire. Three months of fresh air, exercise and physical challenges had honed my muscles, so I was in better shape than I had ever been. Anne explored, commented, explored some more, and laughter mingled with the intensity of the moment.

This was a reunion to dream of and we were both lost in the glorious pleasure that our touches were giving. As we rediscovered each other, our bodies were shamelessly exposed to the afternoon light that streamed in through the windows overlooking the ocean.

Unfortunately, it illuminated – rather too blatantly – a tableau that Michael walked in on.

I assumed that Anne had locked the door and she assumed that I had. So eager had I been to emulate the desire so popular among sailors, I had not even considered that we might be disturbed and had stripped off without a second thought. The sound of the door opening gave us a nanosecond's head start over Michael and the scream of 'GET OUT' that echoed around the hotel and out across the town scared him rigid.

The shout was followed by a desperate lunge and the poor, shocked boy was propelled back outside with his eyes still out on stalks. Anne was horrified and burst into tears. Michael stood on the steps at the end of his ten-thousand-mile journey confused and bemused and, to make matters worse, I found it very funny and wanted to laugh. The sensuous nudity of a moment before suddenly seemed cold and embarrassing and I awkwardly got back into my shorts and T-shirt as the tears continued to roll down Anne's face.

Despite my best attempts, she remained inconsolable and as well as trying to calm her I was also acutely aware that Mike would be in need of reassurance. For any twelve-year-old, the idea that your parents

actually still have sex is a difficult enough concept, but catching them
at it was not something he really needed to see. He is a sensitive chap
and I knew he would be horrified that the interruption could tarnish a
holiday that he knew carried such deep expectations.

Leaving Anne still desperately upset, I went to find him. He was
scared that I was going to be furious and was clearly relieved when I
told him not to worry. We talked and agreed about the courtesy of
knocking on doors before barging in and left it at that. I really felt for
him, though. Here he was, in deepest Ecuador, miles from the
familiarity of home, surrounded by curious wildlife and desperate to
share the excitement of it all with us. He was totally blameless and I
gave him a massive hug of reassurance.

An early supper seemed a good idea to try to move things on. We
all ambled down the road to an open-air restaurant, where pizza and
a bottle of red were ordered. Anne still dabbed a soggy tissue when she
thought no one was looking and Mike and I kept catching each other's
eye, trying not to giggle. Life was far too short to let the moment get
to us, especially as we only had a few days together. I thought that the
fact we had been caught was more funny than sad and the only way
forward was to laugh.

By morning Anne had agreed, particularly after we finished what
we started, but this time behind a fully bolted and barricaded door
with a handy chair wedged under the handle as an extra precaution.

We woke up to Christmas Eve and the curious sensation of spending
it on a pure white beach that stretched for ever, under a sun that beat
with equatorial intensity. No logs to split, no fires to light, no turkey
to prepare and no carols from King's College on the radio. As our lazy
day gave way to night, we returned to the hotel, collected a series of
packages and took a water taxi to join the rest of the crew. It was the
first time the family had been on the boat since Portsmouth and here
she was, still safe and sound, many miles away from home.

There were a lot of emotional people on board *London* as our party
increased in volume and Christmas Eve gave way to the first minutes
of Christmas Day.

I was emotional because we were reunited and continued to give
each other huge, warm, limpet-like bear hugs. My fellow crew
members were emotional because in my family's zealously guarded
baggage were surprise packages from home. Suddenly loved ones far
away were brought very sharply into focus and the poignant
envelopes and gift-wrapped offerings that came out of a huge red

Santa stocking were received with a masochistic eagerness. There was a definite double edge here: everyone was thrilled to have fresh contact with home, but as each package revealed itself, the grateful recipient had his or her heartstrings very firmly tugged.

If you think that brave round-the-world yachtsmen don't cry, think again. Our skipper's young son had communicated with his dad via a poignant tiny blue handprint on a Christmas card. Neil's slightly older boys had each picked a St Christopher and worn them for several days close to their young hearts before adding the gift wrap, as a token to keep their absent father safe.

Andy looked at a card, realised that his niece could write her own name for the first time and shared the news with Ellie, who was deeply engrossed in a letter from her mum. It was enough to send the emotional jangle over the edge, and all around the boat the tears freely fell.

People were overwhelmed by the emotion-laden words in numerous letters of love from home, and all the guilt of taking part in a round-the-world race came roaring to the surface once more.

Never mind that the equatorial sun bathed the days in a warm glow. Never mind the passing pelicans, sea lions, manta rays and gently swimming turtles. Never mind the warm welcome ashore. All of that would have been happily exchanged for a 'beam me up, Scottie' moment with the Queen's Speech, a mince pie or two and, most importantly, the company of those we love.

The families who sent such packages might have felt guilty at the tears they caused, but there was no need. The presents were perfect and hit the emotional spot that the recipients wanted hit, with all the accuracy of an Exocet. When the party ended, a slow-moving water taxi picked its way through the sleeping boats and delivered an unusually quiet crew, lost in thought, back to their hotels, B&Bs and lodgings on dry land.

By the morning, the usual buzzing mood had been restored. The entire fleet assembled in town and headed off in a fleet of pick-ups to a hacienda high in the mountains. Mike thought it great to sit in the flatbed and roar along the straight and empty roads, shouting, 'Feliz Navidad!' to the villages we passed through. A giant barbecue with tables full of fiercely celebrating crew from all eight boats created a party to remember, and when the prize-giving came, Anne was asked to present the second-place red pennant to Stuart and the crew.

The afternoon wore on and the swimming pool was soon full of fully clothed individuals. Despite protesting that I was with my family and therefore out of bounds, the Baba and Danny, Gary and James, Anna and Aki picked me up effortlessly and lobbed my kicking form into the air. I landed with a loud splash and surfaced just in time to see Mike follow my trajectory. My son was considered part of the crew and as a result my mates reckoned he should receive identical treatment. They thought the same should apply to Holly and Anne too, but hadn't bargained for their sudden turn of speed across the hacienda lawns. Mike loved being included in my new family, and in the heat his soaking clothes were quickly dry. This was a truly alternative Christmas where adults behaved like kids and no one got a ticking off for being overexcited.

Boxing Day will live with us all for ever. Wearing flippers to propel us along, we slipped off the side of a glass-bottomed boat into the Pacific – Michael on one side of me and Holly on the other – and snorkelled our way towards the shore. Out of the deep blue shot a huge grey shape, which stopped just short of our masks, its huge eyes as wide as saucers, its whiskers pushed back by the waves. It was a young sea lion, eager to inspect our gently paddling forms. Satisfied that we were an attentive audience, it came back with a few mates and they looped and twisted and splashed and turned, before coming back to check us out again. Staring back were three pairs of wide eyes crinkled into smiles of real pleasure at this impromptu showing-off.

Beneath them swam a lazy turtle and a manta ray suddenly lifted itself from the seabed, shook off its sand camouflage and flapped away to a hidden rocky shelf. Even sharks – small tintorellas with white tips on their fins – did their methodical, efficient, sleek body twist as they curved and circled a few yards beneath our feet.

Attractive though mince pies are and much as I love a spot of Stilton and port with repeated showings of *The Great Escape*, days could not get much more perfect than this.

Our short, precious holiday continued. One day we were on a fleet of ancient mountain bikes, riding through a cactus forest to the breathtaking Tortuga Bay. Another day and it was on horseback to see giant tortoises in the wild.

A great blur of desolate beaches lined with sunbathing seals, huge iguanas and blue boobies, who watched with minor interest as we stepped among them. Memories of tiny hermit crabs, who would lift up their minuscule homes and scuttle across one's hand when a gentle warm breath was blown upon them. Picnics that were joined by tiny birds, happy to hop across us to collect a few crumbs. Loud splashes as pairs of pelicans peeled away into a dive and smashed into the water again and again for their lunch. Extraordinary moments of simple but very real pleasure.

It had to end, of course, and the ticking clock hung like an executioner's axe above my head, counting down to when we would say goodbye again. When the moment came it was every bit as hard as in Portsmouth and my daughter's vice-like grip and trembling, shaking body were enough to leave me a red-eyed wreck once more. Anne walked down to the quay with me and as the water taxi motored away I waved until I could see her no more.

But two hours later I was back again. Rumours were rife of a serious problem between the skipper and crew on *Liverpool*, which the other skippers were frantically trying to resolve. As a result, our start time had been put back by three hours and with this sudden reprieve I could come ashore again. Saying goodbye was a lot easier second time round.

After intense negotiation worthy of the United Nations from Stuart and his fellow skipper Paul De La Haye, it transpired that the only solution would be to fly a new skipper out from the UK. And as Clipper wanted the fleet to stick together we found ourselves on the Galápagos for another three days.

It meant that we could have one more precious night together with the chair wedged under the door handle, before the return journey back to the airport for a happy and dry-eyed (well, nearly dry-eyed) farewell. I stayed to watch the entire departure, seeing the family climb the steps of the aircraft, spotting the window where a frantically waved orange fleece made a last connection and then willed the Linea Aerea del Ecuador 727 into the air and watched it set course for the mainland, a thousand miles away. I would not see them again for five long months and felt very alone on the bus journey back into the town of Puerto Ayora.

We drove past too many places too alive with happy memories that were still too fresh. The echoing sound of Anne, Holly and Michael came as distant laughter, pouring out from the cafés and ice-cream shops, T-shirt stalls and bars that we had frequented, as their spirits lingered on the island. It was all too painful, so I went back to the boat and concentrated on getting ready for sea.

A small freighter, spendidly rusty, had dropped anchor in the bay. Her waterline was low and every available space had been taken up with supplies for the island. The ship came in from the mainland once a month and a fleet of DIY wooden barges bobbed on the water as the dubious-looking derricks lowered down an odd collection of island needs. A wooden bed frame preceded a brand-new Japanese pick-up. Hanks of bananas, a pushchair, TV sets and disposable nappies followed. Car tyres, engine spares, diesel fuel and oil. Straw hats, shoes, peanuts and cans of Coke. All were lowered and then rushed ashore, where ancient trucks waited to take the precious goods to a series of storage depots, manned by leathery-skinned, broken-toothed locals.

Back on *Liverpool*, the mutineers sat around in awkward groups. Some, it seemed, had not engaged brain before opening mouth and had forcefully voiced dissatisfaction about how their boat was being handled. The way they led the complaint clearly compromised the skipper's integrity and he was left uncertain on whether he could rely on his team in moments of crisis.

It gave us the opportunity to review our own boat and we were very satisfied with what we saw. We had a group of people acutely aware of the pressures that the race brought and who sorted out potential problems with maturity and thought. We had a skipper who was fair, professional and firm when needed and very entertaining when the moment was right. It made us even more determined to nurture what we had and build upon it.

With *Liverpool*'s departing skipper making a quiet exit to the airport and his replacement still jetlagged, we slipped away from our moorings on New Year's Eve as the town prepared for the night's celebrations. On doorsteps and in backyards the finishing touches were being added to the life-size effigies that are stuffed full of fireworks and then set alight as the clock ticks down to a traditional Ecuadorian midnight celebration. These often depict politicians and burning them symbolises the removal of all that was bad in the outgoing year.

Because of our delayed departure, it was agreed that the fleet should motor for the first twenty-four hours to catch up on our schedule. So while we covered the first few of the four thousand-plus miles to Honolulu, it gave us the opportunity to cruise gently along the coastline of Santa Cruz and then on to Isla Isobel as the sun set and appreciate the extraordinary archipelago in all its glory.

A turtle bobbed past on its back, two crusty-scaled flippers flapping a waved goodbye as we passed. Blue-finned tuna leapt out of the water in semicircular arcs, like a spinning disc at an old-fashioned fairground rifle stall. Boobies and frigate birds swooped overhead and the sun slowly set, bathing the islands in a rich pink light, so that the extinct volcanos looked for all the world like they had had new life breathed into them.

Someone realised that it was nearly midnight at home, so we set off on a frantic and (for the first time in years) sober rendition of 'Auld Lang Syne'. *Leeds* was nearby and we shouted greetings across the still, calm water as the sun was finally snuffed out by the night.

At midnight local time, beneath stars shining with an incredible intensity, we slipped into the new millennium proper as 2000 became 2001. For the heavens, it was a minor moment in the history of time. For the crews, it was another special, private, privileged moment as we silently swigged from a shared bottle of champagne and reflected on our unique and remote location for such a moment.

A year before I had been crammed with the family in a crush of a million people on London's Embankment to watch the fireworks, as the world celebrated around us. Now, on the other side of the planet with just a handful of its inhabitants as witnesses, fireworks appeared again. Away in the distance, a Galápagos cruise ship acknowledged the hour and red flare after red flare arced lazily up into the ink-black sky. At least we hoped they were celebrating and not relying on our passing as the only hope of rescue from a sinking calamity.

New Year's Eve parties can be so depressing sometimes.

So many hopes and dreams exist in those frantic moments of celebration and I wanted to connect and be a part of what was happening at home. I tried to call Bowlsie but I got an answerphone. I tried my best friend Jem, who we had joined in London the previous year, but his machine was on as well. In a flash of inspiration, I remembered that I had a note of Anne's hotel in Quito and tried that.

This time success, even though I was surprised that she was on the line a nanosecond after talking to the operator. The reason became clear because she was talking from reception, surrounded by police and hotel security, as a waiter was handcuffed and led away.

The family bedroom had been robbed of all their cash

The waiter, realising that Anne, Holly and Mike were all in the dining room, slipped out for a pass key and then helped himself. As the firecrackers went off in the streets outside, Anne spotted the loss and, unabashed at the potential pitfalls of involving the local police, demanded that they investigate the theft.

It takes balls to brazen it out when people all around are jabbering in a foreign tongue, but she held firm. The local Poirot established the culprit and he was led away spouting insults at the 'Inglés' family clustered together around reception. And all this from a woman who used to get concerned at driving the twenty miles from home to Milton Keynes.

The money had been recovered, so we were still able to wish each other a happy new year across the echoing satellite connection. Afterwards Anne shepherded our precious babies back to a double-locked and security-chained room and I clambered over heaps of sails to my bunk.

At 08.00 on 1 January 2001 the fleet readied themselves into a line-abreast formation for another Le Mans start, and as the klaxon sounded, the crews set to, raising and trimming the sails in an effort to pick up an early advantage.

London's team proved their worth again, inheriting an early lead that we were to maintain and build over the next two weeks. The wind was light, though, and our speed was only looking respectable thanks to a conveyer belt of a current that carried us swiftly to the west.

A distinct pattern had started to emerge on the first few days at sea. Once again the boat slipped into a mood of melancholy as shore comforts were missed and family pined for. I was laid low by flu and slept for fourteen sweat-filled hours as the fever burned its way out of me, before passing the bug on to James and then Ellie. We had to relearn how to live together and provide the necessary space below decks, working hard on biting tongues when faced with each other's foibles.

Our old nemesis *Portsmouth* was still in touch with our lead, which had quickly grown thanks to the still, strong currents. Missing out on the travelator of fast-flowing water, *Leeds* had been left behind down in last place and we built a ninety-mile advantage in just a couple of days.

I was eager to keep the watches really sharp and focused on sail trimming in order to break the back of *Portsmouth*'s resolve early in the race. It was frustrating to have that desire and then watch a trimmer staring vacantly out to sea lost in thought rather than concentrating on the wind in his sails. As valuable seconds were lost, the management skills learnt from twenty years in the corporate world were bought into play again, in an effort to maintain the best possible speed.

During our fourth night at sea another lapse of attention allowed our rival to close the gap to just a couple of miles. This time it was my fellow watch leader James who took the brunt of Stuart's annoyance and was on the receiving end of a pretty frank bollocking. Being a thoroughly good chap, he took it all on the chin and immediately immersed himself in our available options.

While *Portsmouth* had been creeping up on us, the wind had imperceptibly shifted. James had spotted it and a speedy debate ensued. We could either match *Portsmouth*'s course or, under cover of darkness, change our sail plan, use the wind shift and continue to drive due west with the wind on the bow.

With the yachts being identical, every little advantage made a difference, and eager not to broadcast our intention, we made the sail change with no deck lights or torches. The SAS would have been proud of our subterfuge and we watched pleased as *Portsmouth* slipped away to the north, having missed our move. No doubt their watch leaders would be on the receiving end of a similar bollocking the next time their skipper came on deck, only to find we had slipped away in the night.

Our plan was to stay heading west in the strong currents all the way to longitude 130W. Heading north from there would allow us to re-cross the dreaded Doldrums at its narrowest and provide a better wind angle to beam reach the thousand miles north to the Hawaiian islands.

The plan seemed to pay off, as each day's radio sched revealed an increased lead. We were a comfortable two hundred miles ahead of our main rivals, *Plymouth* and *Bristol*, and all was looking fair. The others had not discovered our conveyor-belt current and one by one gave up the chase and headed north towards the Doldrums.

We watched and waited for their progress to be stunted by the dreaded no-wind zone of the ITCZ and were amazed to see their journey continued completely unhindered. First *Plymouth*, then *Bristol*, *Jersey* and *Liverpool*, crossed it without even a hiccup and when they set course for Hawaii we knew they were all in with a shout for the race win.

Portsmouth and *Glasgow* were not so lucky and for three days they sat and slopped, making pitiful progress as we continued to head west. The trade winds needed to blow at their best and for three days they did exactly that, giving us a record twenty-four-hour distance covered of 270 miles. And then, just when we needed the blow most, it stopped and died.

It stopped and died despite the forecast saying it should be blowing. It stopped and died despite the January wind chart showing consistent strong winds from the south-east. It stopped and died and allowed the northern fleet to romp ahead and eat into our precious lead. And we had still to transit the Doldrums.

In between the days and nights of pushing hard, the sights and sounds of the ocean continued to visit us, although we were much more blasé about the shoals of flying fish – now about as interesting as a flock of sparrows or the ever-present, wave-skimming boobies.

One thing the crew never tired of was dolphins. They always seemed to appear when I was on the helm, denying me the chance to grab a camera to try to capture their exuberant, sleek beauty. One day, a week out of the Galápagos, the sea boiled as maybe seventy or eighty dolphins criss-crossed around the boat, leaping, splashing and, in the case of one young inexperienced performer, belly-flopping in and out of the ocean. They stayed with us for twenty minutes and, as usual, spirits soared and moods were lightened by their presence.

Carried away with the need to impress, a large red-footed booby made several attempts to come in and land for the night but rather foolishly chose the masthead as his touchdown spot. Repeated approaches, with lots of flapping, took place before he settled very awkwardly on to our wind indicator arrow.

The booby's flight manual did not brief for such landing grounds and he was forced to cling on for grim death as the arrow spun round and round under his weight. Trying to look really nonchalant as the red and green nav lights at the top of the mast lit his swirling journey, the determined bird refused to let go, despite the head-spinning unexpected ride.

From below, the revolutions looked like a wild disco strut as the shaking feathered form was lit red, then green, then red again as he spun ever faster. We cheered loudly when the Travolta of the Pacific finally gave up the ghost and was flung off into the darkness of the night.

We continued to push west as hard as we dared and had the spinnaker right at the edge of its loadings. A weak helm meant that the sail and its support pole were given increasingly stern tests of endurance as it cracked and popped as a result of heavy-handed steering. Stuart winced every time it happened and in the end I had to talk to my watch and gently suggest that some people were not up to the testing challenge the winds were presenting.

I was delighted when the argument I offered was understood and the watch went into a self-policing role, taking themselves off the helm when they were unhappy with the accuracy of their performance. It made life harder for those of us left, as we had to double our time at the wheel, but if it meant that the boat went faster, then everyone was happy.

We still led the race by some sixty miles but the northern fleet were slowly making ground as they headed straight for the finish line, with every one of their miles logged as distance made good.

Our game plan was religiously followed, though, and eventually we got to our planned point of 130 degrees west before turning north towards the dreaded ITCZ. Stuart, remembering his angst on the way to the Galápagos, went around the boat shaking everyone by the hand and apologising in advance for the foul temper he knew was coming.

We fully expected a transit of at least a couple of days and all the data told us that the zone was still about a hundred miles to the north. Two miles later and we were in it, cursing the supposed up-to-the-minute computer technology that had given us duff gen.

And the surprise of going into it was just as surprising as popping out the other side a mere eight hours later. We had kept moving throughout and when the grey clag above our heads disappeared and the stars shone over a trade-wind sky, we dared to believe that our lead could be held to the finish.

It was 14 January – Michael's birthday – and when I spoke to him on the £3-a-minute sat phone from the nav station, the crew sang a noisy 'Happy Birthday' down the wires. From the middle of the Pacific, the message of love hurtled effortlessly back to our bedroom at home, already strewn with the discarded remnants of gift-wrapped presents. Presents that I had not had a hand in choosing or buying, yet the heartfelt thanks he offered left me humbled at the generosity of my now teenage son. He knew all about our dive to the north from the website and had already added it to the growing trail crawling across the huge map on the kitchen wall.

Our lead was down to just ten miles, but if the wind favoured *London* we would be better placed for the long drag to Oahu and the finish line at Diamond Head.

We should have learnt by now that such optimism is fatal. The wind immediately shifted and for day after day we ran through a horrendous patch of deeply unhelpful weather.

Large wind holes sat overhead and in the end our lead vanished to first *Plymouth*, then *Bristol*, *Liverpool* and *Jersey*. And when the wind holes decided they were bored with the game, it was a vicious squall that took their place. As the wind increased, it was all hands on deck to tear down the spinnaker and hoist the safer set of white sails. But such tactics don't win races, so we took risks and flew spinnakers in winds that were far too strong.

It put a huge amount of pressure on the helms and my hands were very quickly bleeding from a whole host of blisters rubbed raw by the constant work at the wheel. Poor James took my place at the helm and failed to spot a squall creeping up from astern. It hit with tremendous force in a blaze of forty-knot winds and torrential rain that reduced the visibility to just a few yards.

The wind powered up the sails and pushed the boat around to windward with all the ease of a giant flicking a feather. It was impossible for James to control *London* and as the bow came closer to the wind, so it loaded up the sails even more, until the boat could not withstand the pressure.

Down below, we lay in our bunks and felt the boat heel further and further over, looking at each other over the bunk lee cloths with wide-eyed amazement. The vinyl side walls are tied in place once you have clambered into bed and are designed to stop the occupant rolling out. As the heel continued, they were fully tested and when we looked out of the downwind porthole all that could be seen was a murky-green sea pressing hard against the glass as it tried to invade.

The only way to spill the wind was for the hull to be laid flat in the water and, sure enough, the heavy bulk of our yacht was pushed further and further down until water was creaming down the deck, fully submersing the downwind side of the hull. Great crashes came from the galley as knives, tins, pots and kettles launched themselves into a now vertical drop across the cabin.

With the wind spilt from the sails, *London* attempted to get up again, like a wounded gazelle trying to escape the jaws of a savaging lion. For a moment it was completely silent.

Then up she came, great sprays of water draining off the mast spreaders in an attempt to settle on the water and shake herself clear. The spinnaker, which had been free of wind, was suddenly presenting itself again and the tempest burst back into the still sheeted sail with the wail of a banshee. In a great bang of atomising sail cloth, the spinnaker gave up the ghost in the face of such a massive punch and our power source lay in tatters all over the foredeck.

The shout went out for all hands on deck and we toppled over the lee cloths and dashed to the cockpit wearing whatever we had been resting in. It was pouring torrential amounts of rain and my deck attire of boxer shorts and T-shirt (plus life jacket) was not an ideal choice. Everyone set to and the damaged sail was quickly gathered and replaced by the heavyweight spinnaker. Aki was sent up the mast to gather the top of the damaged sail, now flying untethered like a giant kite. It was no mean feat in the swirling maelstrom and the quick response to the disaster was down to exceptional crew work. Everyone had slotted straight into a vacant position, seeing what was needed and building an instant line of communication with the crew at the mast, on the foredeck, handling sails below or, in Aki's case, swaying around precariously seventy feet above our heads.

Stuart had taken over the helm as we all performed, and with *London* back under way again, he insisted that James get back behind the wheel. Like falling from a wayward horse, the best way to rebuild confidence is to get straight back on, and while he guided us out of the maelstrom, the sail-repair team set to work.

There is little enough space below decks anyway, but when seventy foot of wet sail is spread out, the challenges really start. The sail had ripped down both edges, as well as tearing clean across the top. To make matters worse, the sewing machine decided to pack up, so the whole repair would have to be done by hand, a needle and palm the only helpful accessory to complete 160 feet of precise stitching.

The repair team of Jane, Ellie, Anna and Aki put themselves into watches and for the next forty-eight hours they worked in shifts, slowly piecing it all back together again without a break. It meant that the team sailing the boat was reduced, but everyone pulled their weight and no one complained at the extra hardships we were put under.

Such moments were truly inspirational and I looked at my colleagues with unabashed warmth and respect.

While the stitching continued, so too did the squalls and a day later we were caught out again. In a sudden gust, the helm was beaten and down we went again, the repair team rolling out of their seats. This time we knew what to do and as well as hanging on from a cockpit on its side, we released the spinnaker sheet so that when the wind tried to fill the sail again all it got was a lot of flapping. But it had been a close-run thing and the fixers nearly had a second sail waiting for them, just as they came close to completing the first.

One particularly stubborn squall decided it would be amusing to hold us in a stranglehold grip. For five hours no wind came and it rained harder and harder as the cloud sat vice-like above us. To begin with, the rain resembled a monsoon in its intensity. As time passed it became heavier and heavier until a seemingly solid sheet of water was pouring from the sky. And it stayed pouring for hour after hour. With all the work going on below, heavy condensation quickly built up and bedding turned into a permanent state of advanced wetness, making any form of rest deeply uncomfortable.

Stuart had sat with the other watch throughout the deluge and when supper time came they all trooped below, soaked to the core and very unimpressed with what Neptune had delivered. Stu's parting shot as he headed for his bunk was, 'You decide on the sails.' Normally he had overseen the selection and it was clear that the unrelenting downpour had tested his patience to the full. I was eager to go for the gossamer-light wind seeker in order to harness what little breeze there was – at least if we could get moving we might start to drive ourselves out from under the huge cloud. Such a choice posed a risk in case the wind suddenly kicked in again, but I reckoned we had little to lose.

Oddly, some of my watch seemed to resent someone other than the skipper taking a decision and their efforts to change the sails to my choice were less than enthusiastic. We got the boat on the move again, though, and zero knots developed into a healthy seven. The wind was starting to kick in again, so it meant a sudden and difficult drop of the fragile sail and an equally hard launch of the spinnaker. My tactics to achieve it were less than textbook, but with a lot of swearing and more choice opinion, we got the job done and drove out of the squall, on into a star-filled night.

Such progress did not seem to impress and one or two of the more negative thinkers could not wait to share a whole host of criticisms, which were aimed in my direction. And when Stu was supportive of my decisions, it seemed to annoy the doubters even more. Having seen the crew perform so selflessly when the boat had broached, I was less than impressed by such negativity and it was hard not to share my sense of frustration.

The honeymoon period of respect between us all, so strong since the start in Portsmouth, appeared to be on the wane and we would have to be careful not to lose the strong camaraderie that had stood us in such good stead until now. The negativity took me back to the trials and tribulations of office life and I wondered briefly if my new environment was turning out to be exactly the same as the old. But a review of all we had achieved so far clearly indicated this was not really true and tiredness was the real problem. The ever-present need to push to a hundred per cent without even a second's let-up was starting to take its toll.

With a damaged sail and all the squalls, we had quickly slipped down to fifth place, some 130 miles behind the lead boat. The outlook for the remainder of the race looked bleak and a tired and increasingly bad-tempered crew hardly helped.

To make matters worse, we lost our communication system. Mother watch had been struggling in the stifling sweatshop conditions at the cooker and had opened an upwind porthole for a few minutes to deliver a much-needed breeze. A sudden roll and a breaking wave chose that moment to slam into us and several gallons poured in through the window, straight into the back of the computer. Out in a trice went the telephone, wind information, tracking system and e-mails from home. And everyone's mood was dragged down a little more.

So *London* did what *London* did best. We took a deep breath, picked ourselves up, dusted ourselves down and started all over again.

Day after day and night after night, we pushed like we had never pushed before. Equipment was pushed to breaking point time and time again as the entire team worked with deep intensity as the stern-quarter waves did their best to throw us off course. This was surfing country and with the stronger helms only doing the driving, we were picking up wave crest after wave crest and surfing down the fronts like a roller coaster cresting the top of the rise and hurtling downhill.

Our hourly distances started to increase and the gap to the lead boats started to reduce. For several days and nights we worked without let-up, until the third- and fourth-placed yachts, *Jersey* and *Liverpool*, were just five miles ahead.

The nights were particularly challenging, as the helming was done by feel alone. With no moon, the pitch-black sky offered no clues about incoming waves and we had no idea of what might be lying in our path. It was like steering a sports car down a country lane with no headlights, driving as fast as the accelerator will allow and reacting in an instant in order to negotiate an unseen bend or a hidden humpback bridge.

And watching it all, unimpressed, were a million pinpricks of far-travelled light.

Here we were, two thousand miles due south of Los Angeles. Above us, scudding dark cumulus clouds in different layers gave a 3D perspective to the heavens and added to the grandeur of the scale. Dappled low-level fluffs, mid-layers of stratus, high wisps – they all criss-crossed in the eerie light, with a large swell reflecting weak beams as the stronger planets shone out across the ocean.

The clouds began to part from the highest point directly above us, revealing more and more pinpricks of light until the sky was bare and shining at its most brazen. To the north, the Plough traced the shape of an upside-down saucepan, clear as a simple illustration in a child's astronomy book.

At 03.00, as the globe gently spun, the fabled Southern Cross made its first appearance low in the horizon to the south and created an astral picture unique in the world. Yet another new sight, a new experience, a new emotion on witnessing the trademark signature of both hemispheres, was revealed to a mind that thought it had little more to see.

The Southern Cross is beautiful. As all designers know, simplicity of form is all and elegance comes through understatement and minimalism. The constellation was not a big, gaudy number that tracked across a huge sky. It did not have colour or rings or comet trails. It was just a simple cross, standing upright against the darkness of the southern hemisphere of our planet and no matter whether you follow a religion or are fiercely atheistic, you could not fail to be moved by such a simple, elegant and understated shape as it signals out across the water towards you.

Big, confused seas with a large underlying swell and creaming breakers hitting us beam on continued to make steering a challenge. But once you start to understand the rhythm and appreciate the patterns, you begin to anticipate what will come next.

On one day I helmed for three hours without a break as Stuart was busy and Ali was on mother watch. After half an hour I felt completely tuned in and the remaining two and a half hours were spent in a near trance as my inputs merged with the waves and I talked the language of the ocean. Such moments were deeply uplifting and despite the heavy seas, I felt it was possible go on for ever. I did another three hours in the afternoon and by the end of the day my muscles and fingers were stiff from the strain. It had been a good, satisfying day, though, and at the next radio sched we found that *Jersey* and *Liverpool* had dropped behind us again and *London* was back in third place.

Up ahead, a towering blue-grey shape loomed high above the large banks of cumulus and it took us a little while to establish the perspective of what we were looking at. It was the massive mountain on Maui and the sight of land spurred us on in the still-pounding seas.

Maybe the realisation that the race would soon be over made us lose focus just a little. Whatever the cause, a spinnaker halyard was suddenly released off its winch as several tons of load blew the sail away under the front of the boat. Ellie had the line and, without thinking, tried to grab it to stop the fall. The power of the sail dismissed her futile effort with a shrug, dislocating her thumb in the process. Despite the intense pain, she had the presence of mind to slam on the rope jammer and the spinnaker was stopped just short of going under the hull.

That problem was fixed and then a guy rope snapped. That too was solved and then the up haul gave way. The loads we were putting the boat under were intense and the kit on board was starting to give up the ghost. A dislocated thumb was a mighty lucky minor injury when the consequences could have been so much worse. Lines under such pressure can whip out like a blade and sever a limb in the blink of an eye.

Ellie's medical training came into play again. She was exceptionally cool, explaining to Stuart how to put the right-angled digit back into place. They looked at each other, watering eye to watering eye, and 'CLICK', back it went.

We were less than twenty-four hours from the finish and *Jersey* and *Liverpool* were just six miles behind. The wind shifted again, which favoured their angle of attack against ours, and suddenly the chase was on again.

Stuart ignored the watch system and instead picked the strongest individuals to perform where they performed best as we ran through an intense final night at sea. We gybed up towards Molokai and around the northern tip of the island he took us on a win-or-bust course over a large patch of shallows where a strong tide was running against a big wind. I had my hands full at the wheel, trying to keep things pointing in a straight line as the foredeck and cockpit crew co-ordinated the tricky transfer of spinnaker from the starboard to port tack. We pulled it off in conditions described by Stuart as 'at best marginal' and placed ourselves firmly between our pursuers and the finish line, now a mere fifteen miles away.

But still the challenges were not over. The wind then decided to die again. It died clean away and we sat on a rolling sea, watching in frustration as the masthead lights of *Jersey* and then *Liverpool* closed on us. *Liverpool* came abeam and it looked like our hard work to get on the podium would be for nothing.

But then a mere hint of a breeze was pounced on and we worked our sails hard to ensure every ounce, every tenth of a knot was chased, in order to regain the advantage.

With three miles left to run and with the sun rising behind us, we looked to be in control again. All that was needed was one more spinnaker gybe and the manoeuvre was started for the final time. After such an intense three weeks at sea and holding on to such a fragile advantage, Stuart implored us to do it with real care. No sooner had the words left his lips than one of the huge aluminum poles under the control of an overeager crew was brought forward too soon and it pressed hard against the spinnaker.

Everything went into slow motion and an appalled crew watched the spar push harder into the sail cloth up at the bow. Way before we could rectify the mistake, our giant all-purpose spinnaker exploded into long shards of ripped and shredded material, which rippled back down on to the deck in a mass of pieces.

Stu was incandescent with rage. He rampaged up and down the foredeck yelling every swear word he could think of, cursing and foaming at the elementary mistake. We were equally appalled, but there was still time to salvage things. The shreds of cloth were quickly gathered, the lightweight spinnaker was sent up from below and launched quickly in place, on the new tack. The choice was completely wrong for the brisk breeze and it strained at the tethers, looking very likely that it, too, was ready for an early burial.

Our cock-up had allowed the other yachts back into the race and the three boats embarked on a direct drag race to the line. As Diamond Head and the tower blocks of Honolulu came closer, we failed to see any of it. The mood was horribly flat and the foredeck team leader was in tears at the mistake, convinced that it was his fault. Behind us, *Liverpool* sat menacingly off our stern, while *Jersey* opted for an inshore route in an effort to capture a different patch of better breeze. In the end we held on by just a couple of hundred yards and added another third place and six points to our championship tally.

But there was no cheering, no hugging, no elation at the end of our three-week, four-thousand-six-hundred-mile voyage. We were flat, despondent and angry for letting down our boat. There were a few half-hearted handshakes and we continued to try to console the inconsolable.

The loss of the sail was the fault of no individual. Whatever happened on board was a shared responsibility and if we aimed to win together, then we also had to be able to lose together. There was nothing other than complete support within the team, no matter what disaster had taken place, and no accusing fingers were pointed at guilty parties.

Mooring lines and fenders were prepared in silence and the sails were dropped and stowed with no one issuing instructions or providing the ribald banter that normally flew around the deck.

'Jerusalem' played as it usually did, but the assembled voices soaring from the CD were left to sing on their own this time around. As we stepped ashore on a Sunday morning, fresh flower leis were placed around our necks and large Mai Tai cocktails were pressed into weary hands by a smiling reception committee. But no one was really in the mood to party and as the cameras flashed and the applause rang out from the assembled spectators, we could still not really appreciate our good, solid third place.

I stood on the pontoon completely spent, having had no sleep during the night and was only vaguely aware of a couple who were heading through the throng towards me. Clearly, my shattered body was imagining things as the grinning pair looked exactly like the smiling form of my old boss Barry and his wife Wendy.

When a large arm went around my shoulder and I was hugged in a huge, bear-like embrace, the jaded mood was replaced by one of genuine delight. They had booked a holiday on the island specifically to coincide with my arrival and when the hugs and laughter eventually stopped, they stepped back and took a long look at me.

I felt exhausted – both physically and mentally – after the challenges of the last three weeks. But they took in the faded clothes, the friendship bracelets, the shark's-tooth necklace, the bleached hair, the tan and pronounced that I 'looked fantastic – younger and fitter and more complete' than I had ever looked in the office. And with such compliments ringing in my ears, the tiredness fell clean away.

Barry being an ex-merchant seaman, I thought he might want to see my boat, so I gave him a helping hand on to the deck and led him below down the companionway steps. He took in the tiny galley strewn with the previous night's half-finished mugs of coffee and hot chocolate. He took in the pile of sails stretched out across the floor, dripping wet from the Pacific's onslaught. He took in the damp sleeping bags, the mould-encrusted pillows, the three-week-old socks pegged up under the rotting vegetable nets and the damp and curling photographs taped to the walls of my bunk.

He took it all in with a long, slow gaze, before turning back towards me.

'Dickens,' he said, 'you're fucking mad.'

As a greeting, it was not set to go down as a classic, worthy of repeat within the august walls of the Royal Geographical Society, but it meant a lot just the same.

Back in the sun, and taking large gulps of fresh Hawaiian air, Barry left me to it, promising to return in a few days' time, when we would have lunch or perhaps dinner, somewhere along the Waikiki strip.

If I had a warm welcome ashore, so too did Stuart, who stepped into Liz and Ben's arms. Ali's parents were there too, as was Neil's wife and much-missed young sons. All around me, hugs of tearful reunion were taking place and with feelings running so high on board, the tears fell particularly easily. And although we decamped as a crew for an all-American breakfast complete with large Bloody Marys and tried to capture a sense of achievement, the mood remained tense.

It was clear that extended R&R was required to rebuild our shattered bodies, which had been taken to the limits physically and emotionally over the toughest leg of the race so far.

A few of us found a reasonably priced hotel, discovered that a Starbucks and a McDonald's sat halfway between our bed and the boat and settled back down to the delights of life on land. Three days of intense boat maintenance were needed before we could go off and holiday and the crew returned the following morning, refreshed from a full night's sleep and long hot showers, clutching brimming grande lattes and yolk-oozing Egg McMuffins.

The kit on board *London* had been pushed hard and everything was stripped down, checked, repaired, greased, cleaned and inspected. Our two shattered sails were removed to a nearby sail loft, along with the shredded remains from several other boats, and across the fleet the crews worked methodically away, under the warm Hawaiian sunshine.

Stuart was still unhappy and called a crew meeting for a frank and honest debrief. His main concern was a lack of awareness of the huge forces working on the boat. For day after day the fully loaded kit had been stretched to breaking point and he, more than anyone, knew the consequences should something eventually give. With lines under a massive load, one break could cause a catastrophic accident and terminally wipe out one of his charges.

As amateur crew from the 'ignorance is bliss' school of sailing, we had demonstrated a scant disregard for such dangers and the pressures on Stuart, as the man responsible for our well-being, were starting to tell. It was clear that Liz had experienced a difficult night as he shared the angst with her, and the sight of his growing son brought all the insecurities and guilt bubbling to the surface once more.

Loved ones, like Liz, could have taken the easy option and asked us to return home at the first sight of a chink of doubt. Instead they continued to offer nothing other than the most selfless support. Partners reminded us of the bigger picture, far removed from the intense day-to-day experiences of our last days at sea, and could view the adventure with objectivity. We had finished in third place, we were up to third place in the championship, we had already sailed safely over ten thousand miles and as a crew we were loyal, supportive and eager. A skipper could surely not ask for more.

Stuart was still smarting, though, and it was clear that the ten days ashore, with sleep and family, sunshine, good food and days far away from the boat, were an essential requirement for all of us.

A few days later I was up to my arms in bilge water and grease when Danny called down to let me know that someone was on the quayside to see me. The bilge pump would have to wait and I blinked out of the darkness into the sun, wiping the muck absent-mindedly on to a T-shirt. There stood Barry and Wendy again, grinning like Cheshire cats and eager to share some news.

'I won't keep you,' Barry said. 'But Wendy and I have been thinking. I have decided to become "Le Patron" to your efforts and can't bear the thought of you living in such cramped conditions while we are here.'

Barry had signed my expenses for years and had seen a steady stream of receipts from grand hotels, smart restaurants and exclusive clubs pass over his desk, yet here I was, living like a bum.

'We've decided to put you up in our hotel for a weekend of gentle rebuilding,' he told me. 'We want you to be our guest, so a room is booked and we'll come and collect you on Friday.'

My protests – admittedly quite feeble – were waved away with a dismissive hand and we agreed a meeting time that would ensure I was in the hotel for an excellent lunch. And with that, my grinning sponsors were off with a cheery wave, leaving me clutching a brochure detailing my new weekend home.

Down below, I relayed the news to my crew mates and when

James saw the leaflet he reckoned that the Mandarin Hotel was, without doubt, the best on the island. What else should I have expected from Barry?

In between the fixing I shot off into town to the familiar stores of Gap, Vans and Banana Republic to replace my fading seafaring clothes with a few things slightly more respectable for the five-star surroundings. Trousers of my usual waist size slipped down around my ankles in the changing room and it was a good feeling to slip on a size that had last fitted some ten years before.

My new outfit caused a fair amount of comment in the fleet. Having lived as one big family for four months, we all knew each other's wardrobe intimately and any new item of clothing, a new pair of shoes, a haircut, even painted nails, were spotted, admired and shared with shipmates when they met in the bar at the end of the day.

I waited for Barry's car, bags packed, in sweet-smelling pressed clothes like an anxious school boy at the front door of his prep school, waiting for the Rolls-Royce of a favourite uncle to sweep up the gravel drive and whisk him away for a weekend of ice-cream-laden treats.

We travelled along the coast road, climbing up the edge of Diamond Head, where I could see the ocean stretching away to the distant horizon. This was my home and as long as I could see it, I felt comfortable and at ease. From a distance, the placid blue surface stretching away towards a towering cloud horizon looked gentle and inviting and its magnetic pull had clearly worked its way into my soul.

And then a palm-lined drive, a uniformed concierge, an air-conditioned marble hall and the smiling greeting of a name-badged Mandarin reception operative welcomed me to the hotel. Barry carried my bags, purely so he could see my face when we walked into my room. And he got what he wanted.

A huge four-poster, big enough to fit half the crew, sat far away across the thickly carpeted space. Armchairs, tables, TV and radio, telephone and trouser press, bathrobes and wardrobes lined the walls. The marble-clad bathroom, with not one but two huge tubs and a thick plate-glass and chrome-clad shower, was big enough for a gentle stroll. Piles of thick, white, fluffy towels were stacked on chrome racks and beside the sink were bottle after bottle of lotions and shampoo, along with grooming items, a shoe-cleaning set and a sewing kit.

Back in the main room, a large fridge was stocked with beer, wine, champagne and brandies, and above it, a phone connected direct to room service. With my eyes still out on stalks, Barry made a quiet and secretly delighted exit and I flew through the air, landing on the soft and welcoming cushion of the giant mattress.

Despite having taken such rooms for granted over so many years of corporate life, I viewed it all as if for the first time and appreciated – really appreciated – all the attention to small details that had previously been dismissed as the norm.

We had lunch, strolled along the stunning beach, watched the tame dolphins in the vast hotel pool take squealing kids for rides and went back to the room to prepare for dinner. I called room service and introduced myself with an order for tea. After supper I introduced myself again and ordered a half bottle of wine. By lunchtime next day we were on first-name terms and still the novelty of wading through a luxurious menu refused to wear off.

Barry knew the island well and we set off in the car to see the sites. The north shore beckoned and we drove up to join the dudes hard at play amid the pounding surf. The waves were roaring in after an unrestricted build, developed over several thousand miles of ocean, and as they hit the shallows they curled into massive breakers.

Great pipelines of sea came rolling over, the wind picking up the crests and sending them fizzing away in a cloud of steam-like spray. A small army of surfers waited in the swell, half a mile offshore, for the perfect wave and when it was ready they were off, up and away.

Their grace was balletic as they raced down the huge rollers, disappearing into a weirpool of foam and then bursting back out and up the wave face again. There were no posers here. The sun-bleached hair, the grunge dress, the boards carried on beaten-up bikes, the back-to-front caps, the perfect girl on the arm, were not worn in a mere attempt to aspire to a lifestyle. These people *were* the lifestyle that the disaffected youths of New York and Santa Monica and Miami and Newquay and even Milton Keynes aped with such varying degrees of success. There were no fakes, as only the genuine were capable of taking to the sea and walking back home again to tell the tale.

Getting to the north shore had taken us through a vast central plain of rich red soil, where acre after acre of fields offered up pineapples to the sun. For some reason I had always imagined the rich sweet fruit hung from the boughs of mighty palms and was embarrassed to discover that they sit on top of compact little plants, just a couple of inches off the fertile soil.

The fields were owned by the Del Monte corporation and a faceless brand advertised by a man in a white suit suddenly became a real place of farm workers, planting and picking to a tractor-ploughing deadline.

After the pineapples came coffee plantations. Protected by tall conifers from the strong trade winds, they looked like the apple orchards of Kent. Through the gaps in the screen, we could see the rich red cherry-like buds that protect the bean inside, the plants ripe for picking in the eighty-degree sunshine. On the sheltered slopes of neighbouring Hawaii, the Kona district boasted field after field of similar plantations and yet another brand name came alive.

Next to the coffee plantations came fields of tall sugar cane, swaying under pressure from the warm winds, and I took it all in like a small boy on his first trip to the country. What was mundane to the locals became a thrill of discovery to an impressionable forty-five-year-old, whose nose was pressed firmly to the glass of our speeding car.

Honolulu is also Pearl Harbor and the exotic-sounding Pearl City. Such wonderful names are now for ever tarnished, with the image of a harbour full of pearls destroyed by the ferocious Japanese surprise attack of 1941. Like Dunblaine or Lockerbie or Hungerford, the innocence and anonymity of this jewel-like place was for ever shattered and its name is now only ever recalled in hushed tones of reverent respect.

On the seabed lay the US battleship *Arizona*, which blew up and sunk in just nine minutes at the height of the battle. The navy run a free tour to the memorial straddling the rusting hulk, which is the grave to some twelve hundred sailors. Oil still weeps from the entombed engines and the visiting sightseers who surrounded us pondered awkwardly over whether to take pictures or not. The Japanese visitors in our tour group at the memorial (and there were many because this is an easy holiday destination from the Far East) took it all in and wondered what was being said by the florid, middle-aged Americans from Wisconsin and Milwaukee who hid their faces behind constantly blinking camcorders.

A memorial lists all those killed in the explosion and several sets of surnames showed brothers who died in arms. The Free family lost both a father and son, and their bodies lie together for ever in the waters of the natural harbour. On a separate memorial stone were the names of crew members who survived the attack and have lived with an irrational guilt at being blessed with a normal lifespan. As natural causes have crept up and taken them, their ashes have been returned to the shipmates who have been in their thoughts for every day of the past sixty years.

Barry's tour continued, always with the sea somewhere in sight, and concluded at a Buddhist shrine, where a large bell in the garden tolled out across a placid lake and echoed through a small wood complete with babbling stream. Trees and well-kept green lawns, alive with flowers, brought forgotten smells to life and they were inhaled with a new intensity of fresh discovery.

My weekend of luxury was almost over and despite Barry's protests I insisted on paying for my extensive indulgence in respect of the fridge, the telephone and my mates in room service over three wonderful days.

I took one last shower and stood under the powerful jets, letting the pleasure of hot water cascade over me for a final, luxurious time. I had one last skim through the huge choice of TV channels and wavered at the fridge door, debating whether to give it a last clearance before heading downstairs to the waiting car.

I was delivered back to the boat like a sulking small boy and as we stood on the quayside I wondered about trying to persuade Barry and Wendy to plan a trip to Japan, so we could do it all again. Their generosity and care had been unbelievably thoughtful and they had given it all with an uncomplicated love. No wonder I was loyal to the man for two decades of professional life.

The boat, when I stepped back on board, was empty, which helped the mood, and I settled back to pumping sea water on to my toothbrush, eating stale cereal out of a dog bowl and drying myself with a damp and mouldy towel after a cold flannel wash from a bucket in the galley.

With more days of complete freedom ahead, I hired a mountain bike and zipped around the island, working my unfit legs hard on the climb up to Diamond Head, and looked down past the lighthouse to where the finish line had been. The sea had become my home, my office, my sleeping companion, my ally, my foe and, like the islanders, I was drawn to it, reminded of it and inspired by it, from all points on the island.

Since before the start I had vaguely wondered about some lasting memento that would be a permanent reminder of my year away. Much to Holly's amusement, I had thought about a pierced ear – especially when I learnt that sailors added the rings whenever they went round one of the infamous capes. A ring in the left ear indicated a west-to-east passage, while a ring in the right lobe meant that you had gone round the Cape against the prevailing winds. My daughter helpfully pointed out that such tradition was a thing of the past and rings in ears could now be interpreted as coded messages of one's sexuality.

Amazed that she knew such things, I let my mind wander instead towards the idea of a tattoo. And now there in front of me, as I sat on my bike in the Hawaiian sun, was a Waikiki tattoo parlour, open for business.

I walked in on impulse, and when the assistant said that there was no need to book, I threw caution to the wind, selected a scorpion design to match my star sign and decided on a suitable part of skin for the curling insect to inhabit.

I wanted it to be discreet rather than ape the Jolly Jack Tar hairy-arm approach, where deep-blue snakes for ever crawled towards elbows and girls called Erica remained adored on a broken and blood-dripping heart. We agreed that the top of my leg was a suitably hidden place and the work began of tracing the design on to my skin and then embellishing it with a variety of blue and white inks.

The artist worked quickly and creatively as my skin was pricked a million times with the buzzing needle and the swirling scorpion slowly took shape. As he worked, I told him about the yacht race and he repeatedly paused to let out a low whistle or exclaim, in a long American drawl, 'Man, that's crazy.' He proved to be an excellent audience and allowed me to download the intensity experienced over the last few months.

Back at the yacht club, our boat was looking a real mess and a pony-tailed Vietnam vet with the most spectacular case of builder's bum was struggling to get the electrics to work in the way they should. And while he ferreted around under the floorboards, the soaked communication equipment had been replaced at the nav station. But, despite the hard work, it all still refused to perform and the instruments that gave wind readings and wind angles continued to offer nothing other than blank screens.

With rolls of wire and toolboxes hastily stowed, we went out for a training sail to get us and Phil Varney, our sole new joiner, up to speed. As we approached Diamond Head, the sea picked up, the wind rose and we struggled to put in a reef and control the wild bucking of the boat. Not only had the long lay-off dulled our sailing slickness, the increased awareness of the dangers of our environment following Stuart's lecture had us approaching our tasks with renewed respect.

As we motored back in, Ellie sat on her own, clutching the hand that was injured on our approach to the island and talked quietly to

Stuart. The workout had been painful and the nurse in her knew that something was wrong. We stopped at the fuel jetty to fill the tanks and Ellie left the boat straight for the local hospital.

So not only was the boat in poor shape, the crew appeared to be falling apart as well.

The race started the following morning off the crowded beach of Waikiki after a great send-off from the Honolulu Yacht Club. A PA system had been set up and as we motored out, each crew member was announced to the watching crowds. The American at the mike milked his part to the full with a fanfare introduction.

'*London Clipper*, Alooooooooohaaaaaaaaaa.'

His English pronunciation was wonderfully left-field. As the yachts slipped by his position, Martin Clough, the skipper of *Portsmouth*, became 'Martin Clo'. Paul De La Haye from *Jersey*, was rechristened Paul D. Lehaya and I became Ian Diekins.

We motored out with a reduced crew, some of whom were walking wounded, on a boat that was still not one hundred per cent. We did so with Andy at the top of the mast, fixing a replacement pair of spinnaker U-bolts that had only recently arrived. We did so with no instruments. We did so with a spinnaker repair that the sail loft were unhappy to guarantee. We did so without a working salvage pump and we did so without a functioning e-mail system.

James, Keith and Neil had headed for home and with only Phil arriving, we were down to eleven. Eleven became ten after the hospital told Ellie her wrist had a hairline fracture. She was adamant that she would ignore the medical advice and set sail, and she did, but steering, trimming and winching were ruled out for her. Ten then became nine and a half when Danny succumbed to a bad back, putting on a very brave face as he dealt with what was obviously a considerable amount of pain.

All in all, it was not the ideal way to go to sea with four thousand miles ahead and winter typhoons brewing off the Japanese coast.

Once again, saying goodbye to crew members was hard – particularly to James Landale, who had sailed with us from London. We had worked together as watch leaders from Panama and I had really warmed to his company. Between us we could quote long passages from classic *Monty Python* sketches and shared a similar sense of humour, poking fun at the pompous and finding laughter in just about any situation. His attitude as a fully paid-up and committed member of the crew had won friends throughout the boat and his return to cover the upcoming general election for *The Times* was clearly not filling him with enthusiasm.

Not only were we losing a good man, his columns detailing life on board would cease and, worst of all, his wife, sailing on *Jersey*, would continue in the race until Hong Kong. All in all, the thought of a flight back to London did not make him the happiest man in the yacht club as we said our goodbyes.

11

ALOHA GOODBYA
OAHU TO YOKOHAMA
04.02.01–27.02.01

The start was a lively one, with a brisk wind sending us upwind towards the beach, screaming for right of way over the port-tacking *Portsmouth* and *Leeds*. We also missed a large whale whose tail broke the surface just a few hundred yards behind the surfers riding in towards the pink classic façade of the Royal Hawaiian Hotel.

The fleet were really on it and rode down to the mark in close company before bearing away and setting spinnakers. We gave one final wave to the spectator boats, which were getting a serious rolling on the huge swells, and we were free to set our course for Japan. The seas were big and *London* was quickly back into surfing down their faces as the island of Oahu slipped back down into the sea. Its mountains were bathed in a wondrous afternoon light and, with the skyscrapers hidden from view, we could have been off the coast of the Scottish Highlands.

Back where we belonged, the yacht positively sang again. In harbour, especially when in bits, boats lose their soul and we were all caught up in the intoxication of a great sail. It seemed like the shore had never been visited and the routine that had developed over five months at sea continued uninterrupted.

We headed south towards the trade winds and watched with confidence as the rest of the fleet stayed north. Not only would the warm weather caress us for longer, but we planned to watch with a smug pleasure as our rivals sailed into a series of forecast wind holes and stopped dead in their tracks.

Heading south took us through a band of squalls and in the light of a brightly burning full moon we watched the ghostly apparition of a lunar rainbow forming in front of the dark clouds ahead. It was a perfect arc, milky white and translucent, with just a hint of a coloured band at one edge as the night-time rain combined with the moon to reveal a phenomenon none of us had seen before.

Up ahead, off the port bow, lay the beautiful Southern Cross while astern, off the starboard quarter lay the Plough, with its arm pointing at the North Star. The sea whispered and fizzed past the hull, and the rigging creaked easily in the swell, but the watches struggled as tiredness took its toll. As usual, it took a few days to get back into the routine and the long first night was a real challenge as we tried to concentrate and not nod off at the helm.

Help was at hand from a regular shattering of the peace by the starting of the generator, which now needed to be fired up at least six times a day. The electrician at the yacht club in Honolulu had failed to find the cause of a persistent power drain and the problem had come to sea with us.

The generator, located underneath the cockpit, had a steady, low-revving beat. It sounded like one of those two-carriage local trains that sit smoking on a side platform in Leeds or Manchester, ready to take damp commuters to their terraced homes in obscure suburbs. Sitting wrapped up in foul-weather gear, hood up and collar fastened as the rain beat a steady and amplified tattoo on my ears, it was easy to wander away to the bleak platform at Bradford interchange and picture the desolate late-night scene. A whole head full of memories from numerous meetings up north as I waited for the express home were now triggered by the simplest of sounds.

Heading west in the rather lacklustre trade winds, we watched the weather faxes come in and waited with a quiet confidence for the northern fleet to grind to a halt. The expected large wind holes were clearly developing and at each twelve-hour radio schedule, we were surprised to see the progress still being made. Surely, it was only a matter of time.

Day after day the steady journey of *Portsmouth*, *Jersey* and *Bristol* was monitored and we silently endured the snide comments that came across the crackling SSB (single side band) radio as the other boats questioned our tactics in heading south. We sat where the wind was supposed to be blowing but didn't, while two hundred miles away the fleet roared along at two hundred miles a day where the forecast showed an isobar-free zone of stillness.

For several days the tortuous sound of the mainsail flapping one way and then the other as the fluky breeze gusted, died and gusted again, delivered its familiar tease. The flap shook the boom, and the shock was transferred to the mast and from there to the stays and halyards. The whole boat banged and shook, getting to even the calmest of souls.

The music playing out from the boat's speakers stopped soothing and began to irritate. To calm the fevered brow, the ideal solution would be to take a walk, but with only sixty feet of deck and a watch to run, such escape was impossible. There was no running away, no glass of wine to hide behind, no bracing stride through the countryside or a locked bathroom door with an overflowing tub of warm water. The only way to deal with the situation was to face it squarely and accept our lot. As the moon came up, Ali sat on the foredeck quietly playing his mouth organ, and the melancholy sound fitted the mood perfectly.

For a while the idea of cruising rather than racing looked attractive. The pressure of a race result would be removed, we could motor through these periods of calm and arrive to a deadline decided purely by our whim. Shall we divert to Easter Island? Oh, all right. What about staying here for a week longer than originally planned? Why not. Shall we go to Japan or China or Indonesia next? Whatever.

One day, in my own boat, I shall follow that thought process and luxuriate in the memory of those pressured moments where every second had a vital significance to the outcome of the race.

Another fifteen degrees west went by and we were at the international dateline. Sunday, only a couple of hours old, vanished into the ether and became Monday. Twelve hours behind the UK became twelve hours ahead, and our bow started pointing towards home rather than travelling away. Loved ones now could look down at their feet, bore an imaginary hole through the earth's core and there we were, 180 degrees around from the Greenwich Meridian, truly on the other side of the world.

Valentine's Day arrived and in a haze of Barbara Cartland pink we sent messages of love to two suddenly very popular crew members. Andy Howe had settled into the nav station and refused to budge until he got the telephone and e-mail system working again. After two days of frustration he found the problem, sorted it, and we got our first influx of messages from home. It happened just in time for the crew to send a flurry of love messages, flower orders and whispered 'bunnykins' conversations to wives, girlfriends, boyfriends and lovers.

The other popular crew member was Gary. A meticulous workman, he set to with a methodical approach to try to solve our instrument problem. He and Stuart traced wires under floorboards, through cupboards, around bunks and into a variety of worn and damp junction boxes. They found five separate points where the wiring had chafed badly, all missed by the electrician in Hawaii, so they set about rewiring the entire boat.

Racing over long ocean passages with kit under immense load was a sure-fire guarantee that breakages would happen. Part of the attraction of the event was thinking creatively, finding an often lateral solution to make do and mend. However, as each day went by and something else broke, there was a growing sense of frustration. What really rankled was that after two weeks on Oahu, we went back to sea on a boat unequal to the competition. With the fleet so evenly matched, having fully functioning instruments gave an immediate advantage to our rivals, and that, for a boat desperate to do well, left us unhappy and downbeat.

After two days with wire and pliers, Gary hit the button and on came at least some of the systems. He had done a fantastic job and deserved the warm praise he received from all the crew.

The wind-speed indicator told us that a gentle twelve knots of breeze was blowing – ideal conditions for our repaired medium-weight spinnaker. We gingerly hoisted it and watched as our speed through the water rose to a rather languid seven knots. A squall loomed up on the radar and we sat in a steady drizzle, bracing ourselves for the large gusts we knew would eventually come. Long before any rise in wind speed, the sail decided that enough was enough, and with a lazy, farting sound it ripped from top to bottom.

In the cockpit, nobody moved. Mouths hung agape as we struggled to take in what had just happened and eyes darted between each other and the flapping cloth at the bow, not believing that the sail could have gone. Someone eventually broke the silence with a feeble cry of 'All hands on deck' and together we brought down the tatters in a mist of unreality.

The sail cloth was like tissue paper and a gently prodded finger went through the material like a hot knife through butter. It had given up an unequal struggle with the tropical sun and after six hundred hours of flying under an unrelenting sky, the weakened material could take no more. There was no point in even trying to make a repair and the loss of such an essential power source was added to the growing list of problems winging their way daily back to race HQ by e-mail.

As we progressed west, the northerly boats were still leading the way and we watched anxiously for signs of them turning north towards Japan. The moment that happened, we would be well and truly out of the reckoning, sitting at the back of a long queue of eight yachts.

And while we watched the fleet carefully, we also continued to monitor the weather faxes. When a large low developed off the Chinese coast, a sudden direct path from our southerly position towards Tokyo was clear to see along a broad band of isobars. But if we had spotted it, so, surely, had the other boats, and we debated long and hard as to how long the low would last and how reliable the weather information was. Having come south to supposedly benefit from the trades, would we be wise to leave them and then lose a potential advantage later on in the race?

As one of the watch leaders, I found it good to be a sounding board for Stuart's thoughts and we debated the pros and cons of making the sudden dive towards the cold weather. In the end we agreed that it made sense, turned the boat northwards, retrimmed the sails and crossed our fingers.

At the next radio schedule we were relieved to see that no one else had made the move and our progress through the fleet was sudden and dramatic. *London* crossed the paths taken by the leaders, now off to the west and a thousand miles from anywhere, we passed the bow of *Leeds* by just a couple of hundred yards. Our two boats, following two separate strategies from two different directions, occupied the same small patch of ocean for a few minutes and, in the middle of nowhere, the two crews lined the rail to watch and wave at the chance passing. Five minutes later *Leeds* was a distant speck on the horizon and the next time we looked she had disappeared and the ocean was just ours once again.

We were convinced that our course was the better one and with the crew on a high, *London*'s familiar drive up through the fleet could commence.

One evening, as the wind grew in strength and the sea started to build, the emergency alarm went off on the Galaxy Satcom C set. All the boats were linked automatically to a satellite and storm warnings services, information to mariners and simple messages from race HQ came into the yachts via this system. Maydays were also reported and such emergencies triggered the frantically bleeping alarm.

I sat at the nav desk looking at the computer screen and learnt that a thousand miles away to the north an unknown vessel had collided with a

Vietnamese fishing trawler. The message reported that eight of the trawler's crew had been recovered alive but three others were still missing. A search was being instigated and all local shipping was asked to assist.

Too far away to offer any help, we none the less felt keenly for the safety of our fellow mariners. We were all of one community now, as the bonds of the sea stripped away borders and prejudices. Every vessel in the Pacific that had received the message hoped, with a real fervour, that the search would be successful, but outside, as the wind increased and the large swell began to rise, the chances on such a black, moonless night would be very slim.

Twelve hours later the Satcom C bleeped again. The search was being downscaled, but none of the three had been found.

I looked up at the star-filled night sky and knew that the planets surveyed the scene with an emotion-free detachment. The heavens had witnessed it all before and nothing could surprise, shock or move them.

The sea is the same. Its behaviour directly relates to the weather, which can bring either sparkling and gentle or wild and confused waters. It has no emotion, though, and sailors understand that. It is what it is, will behave however it wishes and if it is too much for the craft you happen to be in, then bad luck.

The sea takes without malice – if you choose to ride on its back, then you need to understand its simple rules.

I had no doubt that the poor three souls from the fishing boat accepted all that sailors believe and understand. Even so, my heart bled for them as they floated in the cold winter waters, feeling their strength ebb away as life, hard struggled for, started to dwindle and dim.

Alone on a vast ocean, they would have looked up to the heavens for help. Maybe way above them, through the surf's spray, they saw the lights of a passing jet, its passengers engrossed in a movie or taking another glass of wine, oblivious to the drama thirty thousand feet beneath their wings.

Maybe they saw the lights from vessels searching for them and, despite knowing that their cries were being whipped away by the wind, cried out anyway, in one last desperate burst of energy for help, while knowing deep down that the battle was almost over.

Their frightened eyes would have searched the heavens for one last time and locked on to the ever-present simple shape of the Southern Cross. How apt that this elegant sign should shine out a distant and last blessing as the waves finally closed over the white, upturned faces, mouths formed in a silent final gasp as the sea invaded them.

Through the watery layers, the cross would still have been visible, swimming in a misty blur of varying clarity, before a last trail of bubbles exhaled from the nose, sending a little stream of phosphorescence swirling upwards.

Those bubbles still contained the final trace of life, and as they reached the surface, the slick, black, stalking sea released the last breath they contained. That small pocket of air, with its smell familiar to a wife, a child, a mother (each still blissfully unaware onshore), that exhaust of a life, was finally free to rise towards the heavens.

I thought of all those business lunches taking place in London's smart restaurants, where the 'think healthy' main course of fish would be consumed without a second thought. The earnest talk about profit and loss, the power games, sales forecasts and new product innovations. The irritated wave at the waiter for interrupting at the wrong moment and the extravagant air scribble on an imaginary pad to summon the bill. All this while the provider of their food sank lower through the layers of water and finally settled on the seabed.

I made a promise to myself that when I got back to that world, I would always pause before I ate, to appreciate the three lost fishermen whose lives, as I looked on, ended on an unremarkable night somewhere insignificant in the middle of nowhere.

Our progress north continued well and we moved up from last place to a more challenging fifth. As the wind increased, a large Pacific swell developed and we began beating to windward in conditions that became more challenging by the hour. But we were only fifty miles behind the leader and quietly confident that *London* was well placed.

And just as we dreamed for another drive through the fleet, the steering collapsed. It did so with a loud crack as the four high-tensile bolts that clamped the steering quadrant to the rudder post simply snapped in two.

The helm could do nothing as the bows pushed up into wind and settled into a hove-to position. We were perfectly safe, because there was nothing to hit for several thousand miles, and as *London* wallowed in the swell, Stuart and Gary disappeared below to check out the problem.

Had it happened while we were surfing waves under spinnaker, the story would have been very different. The boat would have been broached, laid flat on her side, and with no opportunity to correct the course, controlling lines could have broken and people easily been hurt.

The emergency tiller was slotted into place and the helms kept us into wind while the repair work started. We could have started sailing again straight away, using a system of lines and winches to control the impossibly heavy tiller in the trying conditions, but the boat needed to be kept flat for the work going on beneath our feet.

Eventually, in the dark and rolling low compartment, Gary and Stu managed to remove the steering quadrant, stripping away the steel control wires, pulleys and joints and bringing it all out into the main cabin. Two of the bolts had sheered flush with their mounts and because there was nothing to get a purchase on, were firmly jammed. After using every tool in the box and every piece of lateral thinking going, the only option was to drill them out.

We had a battery-driven drill on board but it took three time-consuming sets of recharging and five blunted drill bits before the broken stubs finally gave up the fight. And, with the bolts drilled out, the holes then had to be re-tapped. By the time all that was done we had been drifting for twelve hours and our fifty-mile disadvantage had suddenly become one hundred and fifty. There were some kind messages of support from our fellow competitors as they raced away, but this was our problem and in the middle of the ocean no one else was going to sort it out.

The drift had taken us away from Japan and back out into the wilds of the Pacific. The winds continued to increase and several sail changes were needed to de-power the boat as we limped along under the emergency steering. Trying to control a heavy yacht, still moving at racing speeds, with the temporary tiller took three people and a lot of co-ordination. Because of the intense weight on the rudder, two lines went from the tiller to both port and starboard winches. Two crew either eased or tightened their line at the winch to alter course and did so under the instruction of a third watch member, who checked the compass and sailed to the wind angles.

And while they were busy concentrating in the cockpit, more crew were up on the foredeck, where ice-cold water crashed over the bow, filling sea boots, invading collars, sleeves and salopettes. But the wind strength demanded that sail changes had to be done, so, with boots squelching with icy water, we wrestled with the frantically flapping sails, struggling to flake them directly into the sail bag as they came down. Arcs of spray whistled over our bent backs as we toiled over the wet cloth, resembling wind tunnel models as the spray shaped itself to our contours before blowing off into the night.

The fleet was now heading well into a northern-hemisphere winter and bodies long acclimatised to the tropics were in for a rude shock. All the time we had sat in the trades, the sun shone and T-shirts and shorts were the norm. Since our lunge north, more and more layers had been added and we sat wet and cold, as the wind chill set in.

To make matters worse, the winds refused to be anywhere other than on the bow. With the steering repaired and regularly checked, we were forced to beat for day after day while the heavy weather stuck doggedly with us. The swell and waves combined to make a sea some thirty to forty feet high and our bow launched itself off the wave tops before going into a freefall drop and crashing back down again with an almighty thud.

The repairs to the steering could not stand such an assault and after a couple of days of abuse, the quadrant once again shouted it had had enough. We had to hove to once more while the initial work took place, and then went back to the familiar underpowered crawl forward as three crew worked the emergency tiller for the second time.

We were down in sixth position but still looked in good shape as both *Leeds* and *Plymouth* continued their search for the trades in the warmer airs of the south. *Plymouth* lay one point ahead of us in the overall standings, so by maintaining the status quo we could still move up to second place.

Each day we looked at the chart and estimated that the finish was around three days away and each day something happened to dampen our optimism. If it wasn't the steering, then it was the wind coming from exactly the wrong direction. After having too much wind, we had too little and our daily distance started to dwindle alarmingly.

On one day we were completely becalmed. The sea was glass smooth, whereas twenty-four hours earlier it had been a maelstrom. The sails flopped languidly in the stillness and both watches tried everything possible to harness something – anything – from the ocean. There was nothing to be had, as not a breath of wind blew, and so we took to our bunks to catch up on sleep as Stuart and Phil kept watch together on the tranquil sea.

As the hours crept by, we stewed and fretted over losing even a consolation sixth place. Still without a glimmer of a breeze, we sat and stared into the deep, deep water (the Mariana Trench, a few hundred miles away, is the deepest water in the world), watching a family of yellow-finned tuna swimming around the boat. There were five in total, stunningly beautiful. A line went out in an attempt to produce something fresh for supper and I was delighted that our fishing skills were not up to bringing one of them on board.

A pair of albatross had been tracking us for several days and they continued to glide effortlessly around the boat. In the rough weather they had looked like fast jets flying through the glens of Scotland. Skimming the surface of the tall seas with millimetres to spare, soaring up the wave faces and then plunging down behind them, the majestic birds weaved a path through the constantly changing waters. Their vast wings never flapped once and the beady eye that took us in as they did yet another run right alongside us belonged to a king of the air.

Every day brought a breathtaking flying display and I thought of poor Mark, whose brilliant flying skills had been beaten when his Messerschmitt had got away from him. His death had been one of the shocks that had forced me to look out from beyond the safety of my desk and, as I watched the albatross perform, they reminded me of him. Here was the kind of aerial display that left one speechless, aware of witnessing something extraordinarily special.

It was impossible not to follow every soaring dive and turn, and the memory of the young pretender from the Hanna family was brought very much alive. Brought alive by such a glorious bird flying so stunningly well and free in such a beautiful and unique environment far away from the trials and tribulations of everyday life.

If a soul lives on and comes back as another being, then for a skilled pilot the albatross is the ultimate way of returning. The freedom and beauty of the moment was the best tribute I could think of and it left me uplifted as I remembered a fine flyer and a good man.

The reflective mood lasted as long as the calm, and the next day we were back into storm sails and gusts of forty-six knots across the deck, battling with a turmoiled sea once more. Down in the living area a large pool of water had suddenly appeared, and raising the floorboards revealed why. Our bilge was full to overflowing and the boards were now lifting from the pressure underneath. We clearly had a major leak, but before we could deal with that, we had to pump out the boat.

Normally one would simply turn on the salvage pump to rapidly expel the water. Our only problem was the pump had been disconnected because of yet another fault. It was another glitch we had identified since leaving Portugal and were still waiting for an expert to fix it.

The flooded bilge had risen to a level where it invaded the storage area containing all the medical supplies and associated equipment. All were now unusable owing to water damage and if anyone had an accident there was not a lot we could do to help.

Catastrophes often come about through a build-up of smaller, individual problems, rather than one cataclysmic happening. We were racing, and without any instruments it would be easy to push the boat too hard in too much wind. With the boat fully powered up, the steering could give way, the boat broach, lines snap and people caught in the whipping backlash become seriously hurt. The medical kit was now out of use because we didn't have a functioning salvage pump for the bilge and our telephone, to contact the outside world and summon assistance, did not work. All of a sudden, a chain of events could put a life at risk.

We began to communicate daily with the Clipper office and, without getting hysterical, made it clear that we expected action on arrival. The responses were positive and we waited, rather hopefully, for a toolbox-toting reception committee to meet us on the quayside in Yokohama.

Although I wanted nothing more than to romp up the Solent again at the end of our amazing journey, I decided I would have no hesitation in walking away when we arrived in Japan if I still felt unhappy about the state of our boat. I owed Anne, Holly and Michael that, at the very least.

With Japan only fifty miles away, we hit another huge wind hole and watched with dismay as *Plymouth* took a hundred miles off us in just twelve hours. To lose another place so close to the finish, after all that we had endured, would have been too cruel. Stuart and I looked at each other with growing concern as the hours ticked by. He could see that I was almost beside myself with the frustration of it all, and laughed out loud in sympathy. Two hours later it was my turn to do the same, when his patience also cracked.

Finally, a breeze kicked back in and we were on our way. But salt was still to be rubbed into raw wounds and the blow went around on to the nose again. It played into *Plymouth*'s hands as they came up from the south, but it forced us into a series of tacks that suddenly doubled the time until our expected arrival. This was becoming too painful for words and with another day at sea suddenly thrust on us, Stuart retired to his bunk threatening to resign or end it all, a steady stream of swearing coming up the companionway steps from his cubby hole of a cabin.

But just as we thought all was lost, I found that I could steer five degrees higher, then another five, then another ten, as the wind shifted, and finally we were back on course, romping home over the final twenty miles and crossing the finish line just before the sun rose over the mountains of Japan.

The rising sun delivered a peerless winter morning, with Mount Fuji snow-capped and proudly dominating the crisp and cold vista. The scene was straight out of a traditional pastel-coloured Japanese woodcut, and as we dropped sails and motored down Tokyo Bay, the end of a tremendous adventure came to a close. We had completed the Pacific Ocean and another vast slice of the planet could be ticked in the 'done that' box.

We had covered some nine thousand miles since slipping under the Bridge of the Americas in Panama the previous December and had sweated through every single mile of it. If we were proud of crossing the Atlantic, the sense of achievement in dealing with the feisty Pacific and arriving in the Far East brought a much deeper sense of satisfaction and pride.

The yachts already in gave a rousing welcome for our sixth place and 'Jerusalem' blasted out across the industrial landscape as we came alongside to an early-morning can of Asahi Super Dry beer. There, wrapped up warm on the quayside amid the clapping crews from five of the clippers, were Liz and Ben, and we knew straight away that Stuart would have a happy stopover. The sight of a team of immaculately dressed Japanese engineers waiting smartly beside our berth almost resulted in an equally big kiss of welcome from the crew.

They swarmed on board as soon as the lines were attached and started to attack our long list of reported problems. *London* was getting the attention she deserved, and for all of us that was the best possible ending.

12

TURNING JAPANESE
YOKOHAMA TO HONG KONG
VIA OKINAWA
10.03.01–27.03.01

After so many stopovers bathed by warm tropical sun, Japan provided a slap-in-the-face reminder of an English winter. February in the Far East offered the unwelcome UK combination of grey, cold and wet. When the skies weren't sending down rain they opted for sleet or snow instead.

As we worked on getting *London* shipshape again, crews hurried back and forth between the warmth of the Clipper offices and the chilled yachts, wrapped up in layers of thermal clothing.

A cosy shower block proved a popular if unconventional resting place, with some of the crew electing to sleep on the hard slatted benches under bright lights rather than in the cold dampness of their boat. A door led to a series of hi-tech loos with heated seats, and throughout the stopover each one would be locked as the occupant sat and enjoyed the glowing sensation.

I had been to Japan on business several times, but now it was a good feeling to have arrived by sea rather than on the grim twelve-hour flight to Narita, normally followed by a long train journey into the madness of the city. I knew my way around and led a party of crew mates into town, where Ellie guessed at a suitable restaurant, Anna picked a supper from a hard-to-understand menu and later Danny and Phil sang their hearts out as we applauded their vocal skills over several Asahi Super Dry beers in a Shinjuku karaoke centre.

Clipper had set up a reception at the very British British Embassy – an explosion of Laura Ashley in the Orient, where tourist delegations from *London*, *Liverpool* and *Glasgow* did their bit for the local travel journalists. The selected crew were supposed to mingle and tell tales of the ocean, but, with elegant canapés and free drink on offer, the cluster of men around the bar in ill-fitting and wrinkled blazers was entirely predictable.

Yokohama was Aki's home town and he headed for the comforts offered by his family, happy to be able, for the first time in five months, to converse in his mother tongue. But while he felt at home, the rest of the fleet were certainly not. Simple tasks like working a cash machine (assuming you had managed to locate one), making calls from a public phone box or knowing what the stacks of tins at the supermarket contained all needed explanation. Aki's holiday was spent in a whirl of translations at the hospital, post offices, banks and supermarkets as a hundred and twenty people sought advice. His long-awaited break became a stressed-out day and night of questions and the demands being made of him were a little unfair.

The one place his services were not required was in the coffee shop at the Bayside Marina complex. Delight at finding a Starbucks, identical in every way to the one in Honolulu, provided the pathetic reassurance of a familiar comfort blanket. The grande latte that steamed and frothed in the cup was identical to those being consumed on the King's Road in London, on Broadway in New York or on Sunset Strip in Los Angeles.

The local yachtsmen gave us a party to remember, with members of the Bayside Marina Yacht Club bringing food and drink from their homes to help celebrate. Everyone had to do a karaoke party piece and our hastily rehearsed traditional Japanese miners' song, taught by Aki on watch changeovers during the previous few weeks, went down a storm. The partying continued on board an Oyster 55 and I fell in love with the idea of cruising again.

Unlike our stripped-out and basic clippers, the Oyster was crammed full of luxuries. It had a huge aft cabin with a sumptuous double bed. It had headroom and heaters and air-con and fridges and bow thrusters and electric winches and self-furling sails. A crew of two could manage to sail one and the boat was so spacious it offered all the delights of a well-designed apartment. This example was a long way from the yard in Ipswich where the luxury yachts are built and the only thing preventing me from popping in and writing a cheque was the trifling matter of around £600,000.

I left the party when Danny started to teach our hosts an English song. The sound of 'Two Rittle Boys' came floating through the chill night air as he led yet another laughter-filled chorus. The next morning the yacht club's secretary hummed away under his breath and mouthed the words, determined to remember the Rolf Harris classic for ever.

Outside, it was a bright but bitterly cold winter day as the fleet readied themselves for sea. As a sharp wind tossed the waters of Tokyo Bay into a harsh chop, it was clear that the race start would be testing on both crew and kit. Aki's parents were there to say goodbye and as he headed away from home they watched and waved, their emotions hidden behind a mask of inscrutability.

'Jerusalem' rallied the boat to action as we motored back up the bay, behind which Mount Fuji rose up through the yellow pollution haze coming off the city. The wind was freshening all the time and even in the bay, we were down to three reefs in the main and a No. 3 jib as the hard-heeling yachts tacked around each other at the start line.

In a crammed bit of water intersected by pilot launches, tugs, ferries, coasters and fishing boats, our fleet roared across the line for the week-long race to China and Shanghai. We watched each other at fantastic angles of heel as the downwind portholes disappeared beneath the incoming sea and the helms struggled to control the fully powered-up hulls.

I was at the wheel for the start and found that my right wrist was beginning to buckle under the pressure. It felt like I had taken a hefty blow from something and a large lump was starting to take shape. For the moment, though, such discomforts had to be put to one side as we beat out into an ever-increasing wind in a sea that was steadily building in size.

The area was frantically busy with shipping, so *London* was forced to tack out of the way on numerous occasions as large vessels showed scant regard for the rules of right of way. Huge bow waves crashed over their decks and when the resultant spray cleared the sixty-foot-high sides of a supertanker hull it was clear that we were in for a tough ride.

Darkness fell, leaving a dramatic silhouette of Mount Fuji against a threatening sky, and we plunged headlong into the wildest night of our journey so far. Our instruments, now working again, had shown winds of thirty-five knots at the start. The numbers had steadily climbed to first forty, then fifty and finally up into the sixties as we battled through the night.

The wind shrieked, howled and wailed across the decks, battering into us. *London* launched herself off the top of huge waves, going into vertical freefall before crashing with a body-jarring smash down into the troughs. At the bottom of the dive, our fragile home stopped dead in its tracks and the force of the smack felt like the fibreglass moulded hull was ready to split in two. As I lay in my bunk with the crashing, smashing, rushing weirpool of water just a few inches away from my ear, sleep was impossible.

Getting up to go on watch meant putting on salopettes, a life jacket, life harnesses and gloves, which in turn meant that, for a few seconds, it was impossible to hold on. On one occasion I was propelled across the galley with all the force of a car crash and smashed into a metal bar, which left me winded and doubled up in pain. There was no time to complain, though, so with bruised ribs I clambered up the companionway steps and out into the wildness of the night.

The other watch had sat cold and miserable in the foul conditions and they trooped below looking thoroughly fed up. Not only were the conditions tough, the amount of shipping had given them several close calls. At one point Andy had called out nine contacts picked up on the radar and Ali and Stuart were forced to tack to avoid one, to almost immediately gybe to avoid another and then to heave to so as to avoid a third. On numerous occasions freighters had passed within a couple of hundred yards and a stream of curses were hurled towards their darkened bridges as we lost time to the race leaders.

It seemed daft for an entire watch to suffer in the extreme conditions, so I worked a rotation with one crew member on the helm, two keeping lookout from the relative protection of the companionway spray hood, another at the nav desk watching for radar contacts and the last person keeping dry and warm and grabbing a little sleep. Every half-hour we would rotate, with the chilled helm going below to thaw out.

Clambering out to take over the wheel, the helm stood vulnerable to the onslaught of the storm. Getting there required a tightrope-balancing act where, for a few nervous seconds, the safety harness was clipped, unclipped and then clipped again on the cautious journey down the rolling cockpit. A brief handover with shouted advice about the compass course from Ali and there I was, alone at the stern of the boat, at the mercy of the whims of the ocean.

At the wheel, with hood pulled down and collar pulled up, Ellie, Gary and I stood face to face with the night, staring into the darkness.

The three of us were treated to regular showers of icy spray, which hit us with all the force of hurled gravel. Sometimes, as the others ducked beneath the shower hood, the droplets hurtled over them and hit my face like darts.

Once or twice a minute a much bigger influx invaded the cockpit, but with salt water stinging my battered eyes it was impossible to spot. Suddenly I was completely immersed by a solid wall of water and everything became soaked through. Sailing gloves designed to withstand moisture rolled over and surrendered. Boots filled up, foul-weather gear became as effective as a sieve and in the bitter wind chill I was soon fighting for warmth.

The waves were lit by a steely-blue moon and mixed together in a confusion of white horses, white streaks, spumes of spray, towering peaks and deep, dark valleys.

Hit head on, the hull launched itself into a suicide leap. Hit beam on, the boat rolled so far that the stanchion tops of the guard rail vanished in a swirling, frothing, fizzing mass of hungry water.

Down below, anything less than perfectly watertight gave up the battle and beds, books, food cupboards and clothes were all leaked upon by a sea trying its hardest to invade. There was little point in getting undressed for the off watch, so bunks were full of oilskinned, life-jacket-wearing, dripping-wet, exhausted bodies. Several people had their head in a bucket as a violent seasickness took hold, and the mere thought of food made them retch.

Good old Danny was on mother watch (his turn always seemed to coincide with the toughest conditions) and despite the bucking-bronco galley, he produced beans on toast, mugs of tea and heavy doses of his infectious East End humour as the helms came down below, dripping, shivering and with eyes stinging, physically shattered from their efforts.

For the helm, nothing could be heard above the noise of the wind and I concentrated hard to keep the boat moving, to keep the seas on the bow and to keep racing. We still needed to race as hard as ever for position, irrespective of the wind, and on top of that the radar showed the constant presence of shipping to be avoided.

The wind continued unabated throughout the night, tearing into the spray hood and ripping it clean off its mounts. The crashing and leaping, jarring and rolling continued as we battled our way through the low pressure, the weather fax looking like someone had left a giant thumb print on the chart, so close were the isobars.

Sitting at the nav desk, water streaming from my face, with soggy gloves prised off frozen fingers after another half-hour spell at the wheel, I heard a radio call go out from *Jersey*. In the wild sixty-five-knot winds, *Leeds* had been forced to turn back with her mainsail blown out. *Liverpool* had the same problem and her crew were in the process of replacing it with the bright-orange storm tri-sail – not an easy task in the atrocious conditions. She was also heading for Yokohama, along with *Plymouth*, who was limping back towards the coast under the same sail plan.

On board *Glasgow*, things were a lot more serious. As the storm developed, their helm reported a curious motion to the clipper. Skipper Ed Green came on deck to check it out and was alarmed to find a sloppy wallow to the steering action. The large generator room beneath the cockpit, where the steering gear is housed, was found to be already half full of water, contained by one of the watertight doors.

At that point they were hit beam on by a huge wave and the ingressed water was thrown to one side. The weight shift pushed on the hull's downwind wall and for a dreadful moment it seemed that the yacht was about to turn turtle. And then to make matters worse, the mainsail snapped in two, sending lines on a lethal thrash around the cockpit. But still the wind was not done and to make the crew's night completely miserable, the wheel, whose control mechanisms were now fully submersed in the flooded compartment below, gave up the ghost and simply came off in Ed's hands. Within just a few seconds, a cataclysmic chain of events had put the lives of the whole crew under very real threat.

With *Glasgow*'s generator flooded, the batteries could not be charged and, one by one, instruments and then the radio started to fail. A frantic telephone call from *Jersey* to Sir Robin's hotel bedroom took place and after a sleep-interrupting, blurry-eyed assessment, the decision was taken to abandon the race and recall the fleet.

Dawn came up on the wild sea, where the winds still gusted at over sixty knots, and now for the first time we could really appreciate the size of the waves. They were the real danger, as a breaking crest coming into the cockpit arrives with several tons of damaging clout. A cubic metre of water weighs one ton and on several occasions much more than a cubic metre crashed into us, filling the cockpit. At those moments all you could do was brace hard, shut eyes, hang on and pray. When eyes were opened again, you hoped beyond hope that all the other bodies were still with you, hanging on for dear life. Such was the power of the waves, you could never be sure.

Although the race was over, we still had to deal with the seas and picked our moment to spin the hull around on a wave top and point back towards Japan. We did so with a deep respect for our boat and with a new-found confidence in her ability to ride the savage ocean.

With the wind now behind us, the deafening shrieks reduced to a more gentle whistle, and as the sun brought warmth we could take stock of how we had fared. *London* had been in third place, which was good. Much more important at that moment was how we, as a group of individuals, had performed in conditions that are officially categorised as 'survival'. Stuart was full of praise and we were quietly proud of our efforts during a storm that had brought new experiences not just to the amateur volunteers but also to several of the skippers in the fleet.

Glasgow limped for home with *Jersey* shadowing her every move, while a coastguard helicopter came and went, making periodic checks. The fleet gathered on the pontoon to greet her safe arrival and with the stern sitting low in the water, she made a brave entrance. The faces of those on board told their own story: it was clear they had gone through an emotion-filled night.

Sir Robin took charge and a team of engineers was already standing by to sort out the problems caused by the flooding. The damaged sails were sent off for emergency repairs and on *London* we relaxed into a couple more days on the warm loo seats of chilly Yokohama.

With our rubber-stamped group entry visa for Shanghai no longer valid, a new race was hastily organised and it was agreed that we would head south-west towards the Japanese island of Okinawa instead. The forecasts were still looking unpleasant, but we had all now been in sixty-five knots – a Storm Force Eleven. We had stared straight into it, dealt with it, understood it, respected it, and if such a blow should occur again, we would be ready.

Which is exactly what happened.

After three days of repairs we were at the same start line, setting course for our new destination. Just as before, it was a congested few hours dodging between the mass of small freighters and as night fell, so the wind got up once more. We watched astonished as the sea built and the wind grew in strength until a regular fifty-five knots blew across the deck.

We knew what to expect, though, and braced ourselves for another night of intense wind chill, wetness, noise and confusion. It really was *déjà vu* as the same people succumbed to seasickness, the same bruises got hit as we were tossed around the boat, the same helms took the battle to the storm and showers of gravel again hit exposed skin with unerring accuracy.

The only difference was that we were in last place. A general malaise had descended, helped by a vicious flu bug that laid half of us low. Stuart and Aki were hit particularly badly and our skipper confessed that he was finding it very hard to motivate himself to even come on deck.

By the morning the storm had tracked over us and twenty-four hours later we were becalmed in complete millpond serenity. Looking at the gently undulating surface, it was hard to believe that the ocean had been so untamed. Once again nature was humbling us, making it clear that we were mere riders who had only partial control of our destiny.

The calms coincided with our tracking across a strong easterly flowing current and in the slow slop we got pushed further and further away from our destination while the rest of the fleet seemed to make better headway west.

At each radio sched we had lost more and more miles and the famous *London* spirit was once again being sorely tested as the ignominy of our position sunk in. Ali and I, as watch leaders, ran the boat as best we could, trimmed sails, ran the generator to charge batteries, made water, played to our crew's strengths and managed the watches, assessed the currents and the winds and took our views to the skipper for debate. Under the red cabin lights that burn at night, Stuart would stare at the ceiling from his sick bed and advise on the best plan of action before breaking off for another bout of phlegm-filled coughing.

It looked likely that this short race was already out of our control and, with series leader *Bristol* and *Plymouth* well placed, the single point we would get for eighth place looked like the worst scenario possible.

Stuart tried hard to overcome the malaise, came on deck as we flew the spinnaker and took over the helm just as a small squall appeared out of nowhere. Just when he – and all of us – needed a lift, a twenty-knot gust kicked in and blew our heavily repaired medium-weight sail into tatters again.

Top: Easter Monday in the Philippines and locals prepare their boats for night fishing.

Bottom left: Taxi cab Philippino style, and the opportunity to become Wallace and Gromit for a few bone-shaking minutes. *Photo credit: Alan Wells.*

Bottom right: A lofty view over Flying Fish Cove on Christmas Island. Despite the remote location, the FA Cup Final from the Millennium stadium was shown live on TV as the locals celebrated Liverpool's win over Arsenal.

Top: Flying Fish Cove, and the race fleet sits at anchor in the Indian Ocean waiting for a spare part to arrive for *Bristol Clipper*. The race to Mauritius is delayed and the five-month separation from my family is extended by a few extra agonizing days.

Bottom: This eight-inch long monster centipede that lives on Christmas Island delivers a fierce sting – as Ellie discovered when one took a liking to her big toe.

Top: Rounding one of the Capes is a major moment for any sailor – and we've just done it! (*Left to right*): The author, Jane Gibson, Nieves Heathcote, Anne Kellagher, Alan Wells, James Bedford-Russell, Perry Cleveland-Peck.

Bottom: Table Mountain and the Twelve Apostles slip astern as *London* heads for Brazil.

Top: The Clipper race fleet lined up in Salvador after race 13 was complete. *London* sits proudly at the head, having crossed the finish line in first place.

Bottom: A hundred and twenty floors up in the World Trade Center after the happiest of dinners, we celebrate as a family, blissfully unaware of the tragedy that would soon unfold.

The Clipper fleet parades along the Hudson as it leaves New York for the penultimate race in the series. Ten days later, the World Trade Center was reduced to rubble.

Top: *London* at speed. *The Times* newspaper used this image to support one of James Landale's despatches.

Bottom: The frustration of going nowhere very slowly.

Top: A school of dolphins plays around the bow of *London* 400 miles east of Ireland. It is one week on from September 11 and on dry land the world continues to hold its breath at man's madness.

Bottom: We had the privilege of being the only people on the planet to witness some of the greatest shows on earth. This sunset lights up the ocean 200 miles off the coast of West Cork.

Top: *London Clipper*. *Photo credit: Gary Bower*

Bottom: The waters around Jersey become more crowded as the island welcomes the fleet in.

But perhaps it was the sheer shock of its ripping that pulled the boat back into form. There is nothing like a good disaster to bring out the Blitz spirit, and Anna, a very sick Aki, Ellie and Jane spread out around the accommodation area and began two days of round-the-clock repairing. The sewing machine refused to work, so they hand-stitched the vast tears back together while up on deck a reduced watch of three made do with a spinnaker too heavy for the job. As a result, we lost yet more miles.

But even down in last place, there was still the faintest glimmer of hope. We were south of the fleet with the wind on the nose and further north the main players were having the same conditions. If the wind remained the same, every boat except *London* would be forced to tack.

The forecast did not seem favourable, but as each hour passed, the gusts continued from the same direction. Lady Luck was at last smiling on us and as *Plymouth*, *Portsmouth* and *Bristol* tacked, we started to eat into their advantage. At the same time the weather grew perceptibly warmer and as winter was shrugged off, the crew turned their faces upwards, gaining new energy and life from the sun.

We had endured a seriously tough few days and several of the crew really started to wonder what on earth they were doing on board. But it was such moments that made the journey so memorable. When we splashed back down into the mad, chaotic 'real' world again, it wouldn't be the sunsets, or the dolphins or the rainbows that we would remember. It would be these truly bloody, awful, miserable times, when each of us had to dig really deep to discover new strengths to get through it all. Those were the moments to recall with deep satisfaction.

It is rare to get the opportunity to discover how deep one can dig and what one is prepared to go through to come out the other side intact, and it is a rewarding, private, intense moment. And when others go through it with you, the bond built on that shared experience is a strong one that lasts a long time. Everyone has their limits, their boundaries and their foibles, but on this adventure each individual bit off far more than they had ever chewed before and still managed to come back for more. It may have been less than happy for a few days, but it was an important part of our year of discovery.

We moved up to seventh place and then on one night took sixth as well. In a flat-calm morning, the sails of fifth-placed *Bristol* came into view and we sat working the light winds as hard as we could, under a now revitalised Stuart. He was back to the form that we had enjoyed from the first few months of the race and people responded well to the heady energy that flowed around the cockpit. The novelty of what we were doing had faded over the previous couple of legs and our approach had become too intense, too introspective and too serious. But having been at the nadir of lows, the freedom we felt on coming out the other side brought the joy back again and we laughed and flew with a new optimism as we tried to gain another scalp.

As the light and patchy winds continued, *Glasgow* closed up behind us and for twenty-four hours the three yachts were never more than a couple of miles apart, doing barely one knot on the smooth surface.

As Okinawa grew slowly closer, so the wind teased and taunted and the night watches were a busy time of frantic sail changing as we tried to match the canvas to the wind. Finally it started to kick in and we all surged forward once more. *Bristol* moved away up ahead, while *Glasgow* closed in from behind as the three of us fought for each vital point.

With land in view and the wind coming tight on the bow, *Bristol* bore away towards the coast to generate better speed and, in doing so, handed us their position on a plate. We had to tack out to miss a headland, went too far and handed the advantage back to them again.

Under cover of the night, the three yachts closed up again and for five hours we sparred, duelled, luffed each other, leant on each other, covered each other as the line drew ever closer. Up ahead, we were closing in on *Portsmouth* and *Plymouth*, and suddenly a result that we hadn't dared dream of looked like a real possibility.

The helming was intense and my wrist, now braced by a splint, struggled with the pressure as my tendons creaked under the input from five intense months at the wheel. Ellie had given it an exploratory feel and advised that complete rest was the best cure for the repetitive-strain injury. We were still racing, though, so that would have to wait for a while.

Here was an opportunity that needed to be capitalised on and I did three hours without a break before Ali took over. He took the fight on into the night, doing a sterling job for a further three hours, before handing back to me again for the final hour's dash to the line.

In the cockpit, all the crew were in action and Stu called out the tactics as he watched the yachts on either side of us. The call of 'bear away' was followed by a shout from the helm as he eased the course by ten degrees. Further calls came from the winch trimmers as they shouted, 'Easing yankee', 'Easing staysail' and 'Easing main' to the foredeck crew, who watched the sail shape with a critical eye, before adding a shouted 'stop' to the steady stream of exchanges. Thirty seconds later we needed to cover the other yacht and the call to 'harden up' brought a repeat of the long line of communication, this time as the sails were ground swiftly in. Failure to talk to each other would compromise the boat's speed and the fact that we were inching ahead spoke volumes for the team effort going on around me.

The three yachts were never more than a couple of hundred yards apart and *Glasgow*, defending her place with a real aggression could at one point have stepped across on to *Bristol*'s deck, so close were they. The crew had leant across the small patch of water and snapped a couple of pictures of their rivals, sitting tight-lipped as they worked the boat hard.

Up ahead, we looked slightly more secure, but back they came, *Bristol* on one side and *Glasgow* on the other, making it difficult to know who to cover. One slip and they would both be through, and an acceptable fifth would become a depressing seventh.

This was sport at its best and it was a shame that the race was not attracting greater publicity. Here were three crews sailing their hearts out and putting on a grandstand finish that was being witnessed by no one. It is not often that ordinary people get the chance to put themselves right into the heart of such a demanding sporting arena and by so doing, come to understand the pressures, the elation and the gut-wrenching sickness of winning or losing.

As *London* crossed the line just eight seconds ahead of *Glasgow* we were scoring the winning goal against Man U in extra time of the FA Cup. We were kicking the vital conversion into a tricky crosswind at Twickenham while France held its breath. We were putting against Tiger Woods for the Open. We were passing Schumacher around the outside of Woodcote on the last lap of the British Grand Prix.

We were spraying the champagne, punching the cup into the air, kissing the medal and really understanding how Damon felt on the podium's top step, why Dennis Wise grinned from ear to ear on his last visit to Wembley and why tears freely fall as the national anthem celebrates such sporting achievements.

Fifty seconds behind us, after 850 miles of ocean racing, came series leader *Bristol*, the prize scalp of the fleet. Here was the other end of the sporting spectrum. Here were the slumped bodies of Oxford as they trail Cambridge home in the Boat Race. Here were the weary handshakes for the losers. Here were the recriminations of a tack not taken quickly enough or a piece of helming not sharp enough. Here the gut-gnawing cancer of just missing out on a medal ate into the favourites and their mood was not helped by the enthusiastic energy that flowed from both *London* and *Glasgow*.

Up ahead at the marina, the boats who had finished ahead of us (all this drama was for just fifth!) had followed the grand finale with rapt attention, gathered around the radio like a family settling down to listen to a play in years gone by. When they heard the news that *Bristol* had lost out, a huge party developed and *London* was the toast of the fleet as we came alongside at 01.00.

Bristol's attitude over the previous few races had become increasingly confident and bullish, with several rather too confident taunts thrown down to the other crews. There was mutual delight at the result – there always is when a giant is slain – but we were realistic enough to know that they would come bouncing back.

But the moment was a good one and the pooling of an exotic mixture of drinks from every boat (including *Bristol*'s) fuelled a riotous party that lasted until lunchtime the following day.

The remnants of winter still gripped Japan and, through a heavy mist of torrential rain, the fleet got their first view of an island I had never heard of. A visit to the capital, Naha, and a look at the tourist information there introduced me to a story that was shocking, moving and ultimately inspirational.

The story dates back to 1945, yet it was retold with all the raw pain of a much more recent tragedy. Even now the people are still rebuilding after a battle that was one of the bloodiest of the war. It was fifty-six years ago, yet still they grieve for the souls who were killed. It was fifty-six years ago and they continue to fight for peace with a passion, a desperation almost, so fresh are the memories of what war visited on this idyllic oasis.

The Americans landed on the island in the spring of 1945 and the casualties from the resultant battles were so great – on both sides – that it prompted the use of the atomic bomb on Hiroshima and Nagasaki in August of that year. The Americans believed the loss of life under a mushrooming explosion would be far less than if the battle crawled slowly north-east towards the Japanese mainland. The Imperial army had shown that, out of respect for the Emperor, they would continue fighting until no one was left. At the height of the first set of battles the commander of the underground naval headquarters in Naha sent a message to the Emperor in Tokyo saying that nothing was left standing on the island. No buildings, no trees, no shrubs. 'Even the weeds are burnt,' he said.

Having sent the message, he and several hundred fellow officers then committed suicide in their bunker, rather than be captured by the enemy. Across the island, the civilian population followed suit as their own soldiers spread word of what the Americans would do to them.

The tales were so horrific that mothers strangled their own babies, before slashing themselves open. Sisters stabbed brothers and brothers pulled the pins on grenades given to them by their own soldiers, in order to blow their own families apart.

Whole villages leapt into ravines as the battle closed in on them. A class of school girls flung themselves off a cliff and were followed by their teachers, rather than face the imagined horrors of capture and when it was all over, when the final breath of the final baby was squeezed out and the blood drained away from its anguished mother's heart, some two hundred and fifty thousand people lay dead.

Fifty years later the people of Okinawa created a monument in a cliff-top Peace Park. Line after line of black marble stone radiates out in a series of semicircular waves towards the ocean and on the stone faces, front and back, in columns of three, are the names of every single person who died.

They are listed irrespective of which side they fought on. The names of American soldiers are remembered alongside Japanese airmen, who are remembered alongside the school girls, the babies, the brothers and sisters. The British are listed too, with some two hundred surnames appearing on this roll call without racial boundaries.

The memorial is an elegant gesture that points to solutions achieved through brotherhood, rather than through creating divisions and war between peoples. The Okinawans desire peace passionately and have adopted the slogan 'Brothers at first greeting' as a demonstration of how they welcome strangers – no matter where they come from – to their island.

But they do so under the steady sound of clattering helicopter blades from American gun ships and the scream of jets from a mixture of US Air Force fighters and heavy bombers. Despite their desire for peace, the islanders have to endure the presence of a huge number of American bases crammed full of military personnel.

The Americans refuse to leave Okinawa because it is of 'strategic importance' to their country some eight thousand miles away. Their presence is at odds with the hopes and dreams of the local people, and when three thick-headed US Marines kidnapped and raped a twelve-year-old school girl a few years ago, it brought back all those fears that decades ago led to so many suicides, and around eight hundred and fifty thousand people marched to the city hall in protest.

At the start of my year away I didn't even know of Okinawa's existence. After a couple of days on the island, my mind had yet again been broadened, my eyes opened, my political views questioned, and the history books, which put the use of atomic weapons into context, made more sense.

Much more importantly, it was deeply gratifying to find that no matter what culture I was dipping into, the fathers and mothers who belonged there had the same hopes and dreams for their children as I had for mine. In Okinawa, they know that dialogue is key and that as long as people communicate, talk, share and have hope, then nightmares like the one that island endured might just be avoided in the future.

Our arrival on Okinawa coincided with St Patrick's Day and predictably, even in this far-away outpost, we managed to find an Irish bar. The Irish community seems to extend to just about every corner of the planet and everywhere their welcome remains rich and genuine. Several of the crew had not managed to get to a cash machine for more supplies of yen, so the gregarious and red-faced Irish bar owner gave them great piles of his own cash. He did so in order to help them to buy drinks, and then joined in with their enthusiastic toasts. When the yen ran out, he dipped into the till to lend them a bit more, taking another drink here, saying another 'Slainte' there. At the end of a very long and loud night he stumbled off to bed, having counted the takings with a growing gleam in his eye.

It was clear he had completely forgotten that the piles of cash he had just thumbed through were his in the first place, and to him the night's takings had clearly been worth celebrating. By the time morning arrived, such minor details of accounting would be lost as he greeted the dawn in a thick, hungover blur.

Also in the bar, standing out like sore thumbs, were several military personnel from the nearby airbase. Crew-cut US clones surveyed us with deep suspicion and couldn't decide if there was some gentle ribbing going on, as we chatted to them over pints of imported Guinness.

Andy Howe, the man responsible for getting weather information for our route planning on *London*, found himself chatting to a meteorologist from the US Air Force. In an amiable, Brits-always-talk-about-the-weather sort of way, he asked what the forecast would be like in three days' time. The serviceman, deadly serious, gave the straight-faced reply, 'I cannot give you that information. I don't know who you are.'

Andy tried again, suggesting that he was not looking for military secrets but just wondering if it might be wet and windy at the start of the race. Again he got the robotic reply: 'I don't know who you are. That information cannot be shared.'

So the weather on Okinawa was a secret, known only to US goons who had yet to discover that there was life beyond their perimeter fence. And of course we gently teased.

A few of us hired a car to go and see the battle sights and visit the Peace Park. At the cemetery I bought flowers from a stooped and wrinkled old lady who peered up at us from under a straw coolie hat. In the midst of a glade of trees, I set them down at the base of a bronze statue depicting three life-size young children. The work represented all those innocent lives lost and I placed the flowers on behalf of my own children, who I pray will never know such a time, one where hope is not given even the faintest glimmer of a chance.

Out in the countryside, we drove through little villages before stopping at a café for lunch. Away from the capital, there were no English-language or even illustrated menus to guide us, and the waitress giggled as we took it in turn to shut our eyes and place a digit on a random line of Japanese script.

Ten minutes later four great platefuls of food came steaming out from the kitchen and we sampled a mixture of unknown delights. The waitress looked on anxiously to make sure that we were happy and through a series of nods, smiles and exaggerated 'mmmms' we relayed our thanks.

Back at the yacht club they gave us a party that fully lived up to the 'Brothers at first greeting' motto and amid the smiling 'Kampai' saki toasts, Okinawa became another place the fleet would be happy to return to.

The weather is warm all year round (oops, a US military secret, that), the life expectancy is the highest in Japan, the island is a popular holiday spot with idyllic beaches of fine white sand and the food, whatever the impenetrable menu might say, is delicious.

We left in a rain storm (darn, another strategic slip by me) and motored out to the start with a new crew member on board. *The Times* was the media sponsor for our race and with Hong Kong a major PR stopover, all the stops were being pulled out by the organisers.

On board *Glasgow* was the paper's Marketing Director and joining us was the man responsible for liaison between *The Times* and Clipper. We assumed that he would be on board simply for a jolly, until we saw his CV.

Justin Packshaw was his name. An ex-army officer in the cavalry with a Para and Commando course under his belt, and a bit of SAS thrown in on the side. He was also a keen sports skydiver and, most importantly for us, an ex-crew member of a joint-services entry in the Whitbread Round the World Yacht Race. Justin also turned out to be a Chelsea supporter and I suddenly had a new best friend.

We chatted on the foredeck as the boat prepared for sea and realised that we had been moving in similar circles in London, knowing many of the same people at agencies and galleries. He skydived at Netheravon and when I spoke about Tiger Moths he said he knew Charlie Shea Simmonds's wonderful G-AGZZ.

He brought a fresh supply of energy to the boat and enthused a crew who had started to become just a little jaded. His experience provided a sound backbone of support for Stuart and as the race started we were a flurry of activity under the dual commands that came from the pair of them.

Stuart is of the school that says there is always something new to learn, and relished the opportunity to share his theories on how to make the boat go faster. We agreed that Justin would be on my watch for the first half of the race and then move over to Ali's so that we would all benefit from his knowledge.

Justin blended in quickly and we sailed the boat better, sharper and more accurately than we ever had before. Unfortunately, the winds were not kind to us at several critical moments and as the first night at sea fell, we had slipped down to eighth place. But, fired with the heady new drive energising the boat, everyone pushed themselves hard, and twelve hours later we had clawed our way back up to fourth. The sailing was idyllic, with warm sunshine bringing out shorts and T-shirts, and a steady wind meant that speeds were consistent for hour after hour – something that we had not enjoyed for several months.

A closely packed fleet headed to a waypoint off the coast of Taiwan, put into the race course to avoid a large patch of vicious overfalls marked on the chart. The sea close into the land would deliver a sharp and uncomfortable large chop, which the organisers were keen for us to avoid.

As we closed in on the mark, *London*, *Portsmouth*, *Glasgow* and *Leeds* tacked around each other with just a couple of miles separating us. As we got to the turning point, the wind, which had gone back to a frustrating mixture of variable strengths and directions, chose to pick on *London*. As the other yachts sailed away in selected patches of breeze, we struggled and found ourselves back down in seventh place. What's more, the wind direction was forcing us towards Taiwan and into the overfalls that the waypoint was supposed to counter.

The sharp chop caused us to stop dead in the water as each wave hit the bow, and despite the best assembled efforts of the helm, the trimmers and the tactician, we were clearly struggling.

Stuart, Justin and I sat at the chart table and weighed up the pros and cons of heading south. Doing so would take us away from the fleet and put us out on a limb. We were getting no useful weather information, so had no idea of what was in store. A brave and imaginative tactic was needed, but it would have to be a gamble inspired by a gut feeling. What we did know was that with a fleet of identical boats all on the same tack, it would be very difficult to make up places by simply following.

It would either work brilliantly, and we would get the best winds first and romp into Hong Kong hours ahead of the rest, or the opposite would happen, which would leave us at the very back.

As racers, the crew thought the risk was worth taking, so in a move that confounded the fleet (*Glasgow* even came on the radio to check that we were all right) we tacked and left the other seven boats struggling with the large chop. Pretty quickly the seas calmed, and as we made good progress south we hoped that Lady Luck might favour the sun-kissed *London*.

At the next radio sched the fleet had indeed struggled and *Jersey* had taken a similar flyer to the north. At that point it was clear that one of us would be in the driving seat as we closed on Hong Kong. By Sod's Law, Neptune decided to give *Jersey* the helping shove.

Down south, we slopped along in a light breeze, aware that a large swell was coming down from the north. A big blow was going on a hundred miles away and when we saw the next set of positions our worst fears were confirmed. *Jersey* were romping along, surfing down waves and making speeds of over twenty knots.

By comparison, we struggled to make seven and knew then that it was probably all over. Stranger things have happened, though, so we continued to race as hard as the conditions allowed and waited to hear if spinnakers were being blown out or halyards snapping on our rivals' boats.

Eventually, some twenty-four hours later, the winds arrived from the north and we too started to speed towards the finish. But it was way too late, and with *Jersey* already over the line and *Bristol* and *Liverpool* following close behind, we began to prepare ourselves for the ignominy of coming last.

But morale was good, despite the result and the disastrous effect it would have on our points standing. All of us knew that we had sailed better than ever, with Justin's keenness working us back up to our old level of enthusiasm. We accepted that taking a tactical risk was a do-or-die thing and enjoyed the fact that we had been brave and bold in our thinking.

It was hard for Stuart, though, and in a very public arena he had to face up to the fact that when all the excuses were spent, we were still last. It would be the first time in all of its circumnavigations that our boat would finish in such a position, so bitter pills were being swallowed and he needed lots of reassurances. Justin was quick to oblige and was full of praise for the way the boat ran, the competitiveness of the watches, the competence of our sailing ability and above all, the atmosphere that was *London*.

Such good spirits were brought to light on our final day at sea. Gary was doing a short piece to the boat's camcorder and speculated that our bad luck was down to the fact that Neptune was upset with us.

We were supposed to have performed our crossing-the-line ceremony when *London* first sailed across the equator in December. We had been busy racing *Bristol* at the time, so had put it on hold. The crew had every intention of observing the tradition, but for some reason we never quite got round to it.

London had sailed on to Hawaii and then Tokyo and from there to Okinawa, but still we had failed in our promise. It was decided that the run of bad luck was Neptune's way of reprimanding us and as Gary speculated to the camera, I decided it was time to put things straight.

The ceremony takes the form of a court, where dubious charges are levelled at the crew and then ridiculous penalties imposed, usually in the form of much dousing in flour, water and any other messy substance available on board.

As the videotape continued to roll, I crept up behind Gary and deposited a full bag of flour over his head. It was swiftly followed by a bucket of water as the camera caught it all and the entire crew cried with laughter as great globules of floury paste dripped from his nose.

We needed another victim and with Danny about to leave the boat in Hong Kong as well, he was sent for, quickly tried and then soaked with even more gunge, which left the cockpit ankle deep in muck.

The court was well and truly under way and one by one every member was brought before the saki-sipping judge (me) and then publicly humiliated by order of Neptune (Stuart). Everyone was 'done', even if they had 'crossed the line' before, and when it came to my turn I could taste an exotic blend of flour, sea water, scone mix, mustard, tomato ketchup and maple syrup dripping from my nose.

Here we were in last place and the boat echoed to the sound of deep laughter, as the ghost was finally laid to the King of the Sea's satisfaction.

Such good spirits had been in evidence the previous night as Danny and Gary spent their last night at sea. The pair of them had been brilliant crew mates, bringing only positive energy to the boat, and to have had them both in my watch made times on deck a real delight.

Back in Colón, James and I had found an illuminated magnetic taxi sign in a supermarket and had secretly added it to the ship's supplies. Now, on his final night on board, Gary rigged it up on deck while Danny slept, wiring the light into the boat's electrics.

Three hours later, at 23.00, the watch changed and I asked Danny to take the wheel. Normally the departing watch vanished below to their bunks in seconds and he vaguely wondered what they were still doing on deck. As he settled down to concentrate on the compass and steer a course, someone asked him what was the best way to attract a cab driver's attention in a busy London street. Like a lamb to the slaughter and in broadest cockney, Danny the cabby offered up the following advice:

'Just raise yer arm and shout, "TAXI!"'

At that moment Gary flicked his hastily made switch and, in the darkness of the South China Sea, the yellow light on the coach-house roof shone out, turning *London* into a floating minicab.

We all cracked up with laughter, while Danny grinned from ear to ear, enjoying the joke hugely. He and Gary would be sadly missed.

In a stiffening breeze, we romped over the last hundred miles, keeping a sharp lookout on the radar set as a grey gloom hid a mass of fishing boats and small coasters from view. Visibility was down to around half a mile and time after time a ship would appear out of the murk and cross our bow before quickly disappearing back into the swirling mist.

As night fell, our GPS homed in on the lighthouse on the tip of Waglan Island and we crossed the finish line with Gary, Danny and Phil (our three leavers) driving the boat. The darkness hid the hugs that marked our end-of-race ritual, which was probably a good thing. Our departing crew mates' eyes glistened wet in the moonlight and both Gary and Danny spent time alone on the foredeck, watching as the mountains of Hong Kong Island grew ever nearer and their adventure crept closer to ending.

It was a spectacular time to arrive and as the city started to reveal itself, it seemed that every light in every tower block, apartment and office had been turned on to greet us. A vast array of futuristic skyscrapers, each with its own neon sign, soared up towards the Peak and our trio on the helm dodged around sampans, junks, huge cruise liners, pilot vessels and the ubiquitous Star Ferry as we crept towards the typhoon shelter at Causeway Bay and the Royal Hong Kong Yacht Club.

All the crew sat at the bow, taking in the extraordinary vista and reminding ourselves with firm pinches that we had sailed to this point all the way from Portsmouth. We had crossed the two biggest oceans in the world and were now arriving in Hong Kong by sea. It was a great moment of achievement, a rare opportunity and a sight that we wanted to drink in and remember for ever.

As we approached the pontoon, we changed into our boat uniform of blue-checked trousers and red-and-blue *London* shirts. 'Jerusalem' went into the CD player, the volume was spun round to max and, with the stirring anthem ringing out across the water, there was a massive stampede from the bar.

The rest of the fleet came out to give us a welcome that would melt the heart of the most cynical. There were waves, shouts and cheers, ribald abuse, good-natured teasing, blown kisses and broadly smiling faces. Seven boat crews meant that the pontoon was dangerously overflowing and the ninety colleagues who welcomed us each wanted to be the first to catch our thrown lines. I came ashore and into the halfway-point celebrations with a real spring in my step and warm feelings of love for the people who were sharing the adventure with me.

The previous six months had offered me so much and the intense experiences and emotions merged into a kaleidoscopic blur. It had been a privilege to sail with so many good people and with three now leaving the boat and six new members joining, we would all have to work hard to ensure that the same spirit remained.

But all that was a few weeks ahead. For now, we could celebrate the end of the outward half and every mile sailed in the months to come would bring us a little closer to our loved ones again.

And although I was far away from home and had not seen my family for four long months, a warm and enveloping welcome awaited me. There on the quay was a familiar figure, and as the teeming mass of clipper crew members wound their way back to the bar, I got a hug to welcome me ashore from an old friend.

Alex had run a photographic gallery in London and for many years she and I had worked on a broad range of projects together. She had resigned a few weeks before me and headed to Hong Kong to fulfil two passions. The first was to set up her easel, brushes and stretched canvas in order to paint. Paint every day, as the mood took her, and learn if she had the talent and the energy to make it a full-time profession. And just as important was the second reason – the man who she thought might be the one to partner her through life.

She looked great and the giggles and hugs at this unreal reunion made me feel instantly at home. Making me feel equally at home a day later was a family whom I had never met and who knew next to nothing about me. But because a friend of mine was a friend of theirs, an open invitation had found its way to the boat via e-mail. So thanks to David Constantine, I found myself stepping out of a cab and gingerly opening the gates of the most amazing house on the edge of a small village called Shek O, for my first night in a proper bed.

Bird song filled the air as twilight slipped in across the distant ocean. The crags were bathed in the gentlest of golden glows from the setting sun, which picked out small patches of rock that rose out of the dense green vegetation in the hills behind me.

From the veranda, with its cane furniture, louvred white shutters and terracotta pots of white lilies in full bloom, I looked across a manicured lawn and over a low stone wall towards the sea.

I appeared to be in paradise, a guest of the Watkins, who lived a lifestyle surrounded by the old colonial qualities of Hong Kong in its British Empire heyday. The gentle garden beckoned and I sat on the veranda of this perfect house gently unwinding, taking on board the deep satisfaction of what we had achieved.

Sailing into Hong Kong harbour is a pretty special experience for anyone. But the fact that we had sailed there from Portsmouth was only just starting to really sink in.

We had truly sailed halfway around the world.

To circumnavigate half of the planet, to traverse the Bay of Biscay, the Atlantic, the Caribbean Sea, the Panama Canal, the Pacific – all of it – and now the South China Sea, made us privileged members of a unique club. Because we had been so engrossed in the intense competition of the journey, the realisation of what we had achieved had been hidden away.

And as I sat with an ice-cold beer in my magnificent old-world splendour, amid the peace and quiet of the end of the day, it started to sink in big time.

And it felt deeply, deeply good.

A huge guest suite awaited me and when my hosts announced that they had to attend a charity dinner, I wondered what I was supposed to do with myself for the evening. And while I wondered, I relished in the comforts of my room, taking a long, hot bath in a good old-fashioned English tub. My mobile phone could talk to a transmitter for the first time since leaving Portugal and as I soaked, it rang repeatedly as news of my arrival spread. Bowlsie and Goldie called, as did my sisters, brother and parents. I spoke to James Landale at *The Times*, who would shortly be flying out to collect his wife off *Jersey* and I spoke to my friend Jem back in his studio.

As I lay in the water I idly flicked through a copy of the Hong Kong edition of *Tatler* and as I looked at the beautiful people at the beautiful functions, I wondered if my friend Richard Young ever came out to photograph the parties. Then the phone rang again and a familiar voice came winging in from London.

'Hello, mate – thought we would surprise you!'

Bloody hell. It was Richard and his wife, Susan. How spooky was that? And as if to prove that magic was in the air, a knock on my door announced that dinner would be served in the dining room.

I was surprised to find a couple ready to eat, sitting at the table patiently awaiting my presence. They turned out to be Lisa Watkins's parents, out from the UK to visit daughter, son-in-law and their brood of delightful grandchildren.

We went through the formality of very English introductions and in response to my 'Ian Dickens', Lisa's father, whom I had known for all of fifteen seconds, asked, 'Any relation to Peter?'

Peter, my uncle. Peter, who had commanded Royal Navy vessels in the South China Sea, from where we had arrived. Peter, who had married in Singapore, which was where we were heading next. Peter, who, along with his father and brother, had been based in the dockyard at Hong Kong. Peter, the decorated MTB skipper, whose old boat still existed and, I had recently discovered, was lived in by a friend of both mine and Sir Robin. Peter, with whom I had spent several years cruising up the east coast of England on a thirty-two-foot ketch and learnt the art of sailing. Peter, who would have thrilled to the adventure I was undertaking.

So his ghost joined us at the table and I wondered what surprise would visit me next.

Being made temporary skipper was the answer, as Stuart had decided to head back to Wales to get a real break from the race after so many months of intense emotions. It was an unplanned trip but when he found a well-priced flight the temptation was too much. In a couple of hours his bag was packed and he was off, up and away back to the green green grass of home.

Less than twenty-four hours later I spoke to him and the sound of a contented baby gurgling happily in the background was the clearest indication that his trip had been worthwhile. Having worked alongside each other for so long, both of us found the telephone call to the old stone home overlooking the ocean in north Wales a strange experience.

Back in Hong Kong, *London* had been lifted out of the water for her halfway refit. Propped up on wooden blocks, our beautiful sleek craft looked distinctly ungainly beached in the yacht club car park, as the local team set to, power-washing the hull in preparation for a new coat of anti-fouling.

My colleagues sat way up in the cockpit, listening to the list of jobs that needed completion before Stu returned. It was extensive and I was eager to get the work completed as quickly as possible, so that we could all get a break. Much of it relied on the delivery of spare parts from the UK, the boatyard meeting deadlines and the weather being kind for the outside work on the rigging and superstructure.

Pretty soon the boat lay in pieces as parts were stripped down, serviced and reassembled. Predictably, it took way longer than anticipated and as spares remained sparse, half-assembled bits remained half-assembled. The kind hospitality of the Watkins had been replaced by boatyard living again and a bed smelling of fresh paint replaced the luxurious guest quarters. At least the Royal Hong Kong Yacht Club offered five-star facilities and the smart showers, swimming pool, terrace bar and restaurant provided a decent start to the morning and a good supper at the end of the day.

A trip to the Peak, where I joined Alex for an engagement-celebrating, sun-baked lunch surrounded by fragrant Hong Kong ladies who picked timidly at plates of lettuce, was a welcome relief as she showed me her diamond-encrusted ring finger. Otherwise my time was spent in the yard, cajoling Clipper and the Chinese workers to get on with the work. Joining me were Gary and Danny, who had plans for Stuart's cabin. They wanted to leave a permanent reminder on board and had found rolls of sticky-back wallpaper in powder blue, complete with teddy-bear, steam-train and sailing-boat motifs. The perfect adornment for a small boy's bedroom.

As we now expected from Gary, the workmanship was immaculate. After adding the final detail, a tiger-skin print throw over black satin sheets, they stood back, admired their handiwork and signed Stu's cabin wall with a flourish. A queue of envious skippers from the other boats came to see the finished article and we were all eager to see our leader's response when he returned.

What should have taken three days dragged on into four, then five and then six as I continued the chivvying. Torrential rain did not help and the work continued in a depressing grey downpour. Stu returned, laughed deeply at his cabin and as he settled back into 'home', the cottage on a hill in Wales returned to being a fantasy. The rest had done him good and as we went through the list of completed jobs, he was itching to get the boat back into the water and up to speed again.

The break that I really needed failed to materialise and we were into new crew members, work-up periods, training sails and getting the boat restocked for another fifty days at sea. After ten days I got bored with the same view of the fetid waters, a boat in pieces and the overcrowding, overbearing city. I got fed up with the trudge over the yard to the showers and the lack of privacy when I got up and went to bed. I got fed up eating in the same place with the same people and went off to find a hotel. A charmless offering with a tiny bedroom and no bath, looking out over bleak, dirty walls, did little for my mood and when that became too oppressive, I moved on to a guest house.

'Guest house' might sound charming but in reality it was a polite description for a cheap and nasty backstreet knocking shop. When I asked for a room, the man in a dirty vest smoking a fag end looked over my shoulder for the inevitable companion. He was more incredulous when I looked at the dirty sheet and asked for pillows and a blanket and he finished up completely flummoxed by my desire to spend an entire night there – on my own. And so the Hong Kong break I so desperately wanted took place surrounded by wafer-thin walls with the wallpaper peeling off them. Through the shaking plywood came a steady stream of moans, pants and groans as the energetically worked and long-suffering mattresses were put through their paces.

I was thoroughly depressed, lonely, fed up and totally out of love with the teeming, manic, rude and soulless place that filled my ears twenty-four hours a day. Forgetting the excitement of our arrival, I found myself falling off a bar stool from an overdose of red wine, and on the next headache-filled morning I viewed the city through a heavily jaundiced eye.

Pulling back the blackened net curtains on the desolate view, I finally cracked. My fist hammered hard at the glass as I shouted out of the seedy window to no one in particular, 'This place stinks.'

In the typhoon shelter at Causeway Bay, the water was awash with raw sewage. A thick brown scum floated on the surface and clung to discarded plastic cartons, carrier bags, floating shoes, the bedraggled fur of dead rats and the hulls of the smart yachts.

Closer to shore, it clung to the granite walls and traced the mooring lines from rusting thick metal rings out to the slum sampans. It clung to the sides of the floating homes, with their canvas roofs patched with plastic tarpaulin and bamboo poles strapped to the sides, which were bedecked with shit-encrusted old tyre fenders. Small window boxes with flowers lined the decks, but the bright-orange blooms couldn't provide a scent strong enough to beat the smell that ripened in the sun.

Each sampan had a series of smaller craft that also floated in the shit. They were stacked with a curious assortment of flotsam and jetsam picked up from the foul harbour. There were odd clothes, piles of wood, an incongruous Pimms umbrella, stained and faded but still intact and opened at a jaunty angle.

Marooned on one sampan was a small dog, constantly yapping at its leash. Its fur was thick with oil, grime, scraps of food and its own waste dripped off the side and mingled with the human excrement in the harbour.

On the wall beside the constantly busy main road sat the Noon Day gun, a relic of a more illustrious past and still fired at midday for the pleasure of tourists. Its history – inevitably – is linked to Jardine Matheson and its ceremonial unveiling in front of banks of video cameras played out a silly charade that all is well with the Empire.

I shouted my anger out louder.

'HONG KONG STINKS.'

The lights of the chrome edifice that was the Porsche showroom were reflected in the foul waters where the poor lived and the dirty dog yapped. Inside, several examples of the latest turbo were on display. Rich swathes of leather adorned the wall for the customers to pick their trim. The varnished brochures, aligned symmetrically in a black polished rack, related with clipped Germanic pride how fast their products could travel. In Hong Kong, getting out of second gear would be an achievement, but that is not what the owners of cars like these are seeking.

Up on the hill towards the Peak, such badges of ownership are just part of showing how successful you are. All the time newly built high-rise apartments climb above slightly older high-rise apartments in order to give the owner of a brand-new Porsche a smarter address from which he can shout his wealth from the rooftops.

Down below, the luxurious apartments in the seething streets are the ugly nouveau towers that make Hong Kong tick. They are the banks, the financial houses, the institutions with their odd codes of conduct, their taipans, their masonic-style secrets, where pinstriped workers play the games they play in London and flirt and gamble with the capital reserves of the world. Their work is identical to the weekly ritual that goes on at Happy Valley Racecourse every Wednesday night, where they take a punt, putting vast, really incomprehensible amounts of cash all on number seven.

Invariably they win, and the Porsche showroom, the exclusive clubs, the champagne houses, the yacht brokers and the golf courses are delighted. But once in a while it all goes wrong and a Nick Leeson flop flees into the hinterland, leaving his Filipino maids confused and unsure and a clutch of car keys swinging on a hook. In the clubs and air-conditioned restaurants, grave words are shared, incredulous heads shaken and the money movers made nervous until the Bollinger numbs the pain.

Like Dustin Hoffman rattling on the glass at the back of the church in *The Graduate*, I continued my moment of pane-banging frustration.

Another yell of 'Hong Kong stinks' stopped my frantically shagging neighbours mid-frenzy and the words echoed off the seedy brick wall opposite my window, unsettling the roosting pigeons, which flapped noisily away.

Hong Kong stank because it wanted money by fair means or foul and it would do all it could to help itself to it. Cash machines existed every few hundred yards and in between lay shop after shop to help relieve anxious consumers of their wealth. Rolex and Cartier, Porsche and Bentley, Tiffany and Louis Vuitton. Hand-made suits. Hand-made shirts. Monogrammed slippers. All essential items in the quest to portray just how well life is going.

The wives of the money movers do the shopping, while at home the maids and the house servants get children ready for school, shop for food and prepare every meal. They are the trophy wives, who dutifully play the game, name-drop, score points, wave from the higher balconies and take lunch in the Peak Café. Up in the rarefied atmosphere and away from the gawping tourists, they sit, Gucci glasses pushed to the forehead, toying with their sensible salads before heading for the gym to ensure that they keep immaculate for their husbands. A bit of tarnish in the trophy cabinet means that the side is let down and then the only solution is a new, younger, sleeker model.

And if the trophy wife does not thrill any more, it is off to the bars at Wan Chai, where the stink of Hong Kong grows ever more rotten.

Knickerless girls flash their abused crotches across the street, pull down lycra tops to reveal their boobs and make a lunge for the passing pinstriped fly to entice the randy punter in. In the thick red velvet confines of a hundred clubs, over-chewed gum is pushed to the back of the mouth as warm, overpriced champagne arrives and the fleecing commences. The florid-faced expats know it is all a game and roar headlong into it. Their wallets are bulging with credit and they play merrily along, even upping the stakes in a double-or-quit moment before walking into a backroom with a couple of girls, each wearing a fixed smile that seemingly ignores the stale tobacco, alcohol and saggy belly of their client. The bored bar girls have seen it all before and go through their tired pantomime of simulated lust as Mr Important shoots out his frustrations in a seedy room that looks past the air-conditioning ducts and into the grime of a darkened back alley.

His Porsche will eventually weave a drunken path back up the hill for home, where his wafer-thin, fragrant, dutiful wife (who knows better than to ask why he is late) ends up listening to the rasping, dribbling, rumbling snores reverberating through the luxurious apartment and reflects on how lucky they are to be enjoying such a good life.

With a final hammer at the window and without a backward glance at the sad room, I headed back for the comfort blanket of my precious boat. And while the guest-house residents continued their enthusiastic coupling, I reckoned that my chances of ever working for the Hong Kong tourist board might have taken a bit of a dive.

Day after day and night after night of stress-free, pure, simple living with the elements as the only company, away from politics and materialism and greed and backstabbing – frontstabbing too, when the greed got too big – meant that experiencing Hong Kong at its most squalid was a nasty shock to the system.

We had been to Tokyo, Hawaii and Panama, plunging into big-city life, and it had been fine. But Hong Kong seemed to be a pastiche, a cartoon version of money at its most powerful, and the cancer that fed off that wealth was ugly for an outsider to suddenly observe.

My mood was fuelled in part by a sharp pang of homesickness kicking in, helped along by a mild dose of panic. It had been nearly five months since I had last seen Anne, Holly and Mike, and suddenly I could only picture them in the abstract. I couldn't remember how they smiled or looked when they were asleep or how they smelt when I hugged them – all the little details that go into a look, a move, a moment. We talked daily on the phone but the sounds were of voices rather than people in tune with each other because of their shared experiences.

I learnt that my daughter had her first serious boyfriend. Was she radiating with pride? Did she blush? Did she look adoringly at him?

I didn't know.

I discovered that my son had got into performing magic tricks and apparently practised for hours. What were the tricks? Did he do them well? Was there an elegant twist that made audiences gasp?

Again I was clueless.

Six more weeks to Mauritius and then I would find out. For the first time in my year of discovery, I willed the time to pass as quickly as possible, and I hated that idea as well.

Danny decided that goodbyes were not for him, headed on impulse to a travel agent, booked a flight and swiftly departed. Unbeknown to him, friends would be waiting at Heathrow in a large stretch limo, ready to whisk him off to watch England play at Twickenham and help him through the pain of returning.

Gary also dreaded the thought of cashing in six months of travel experience with a twelve-hour whizz back to the normality of day-to-day life in London. To stave off the moment, he booked himself a ticket on the Star Ferry to Kowloon. From there he would catch a train to Beijing and sightsee for a couple of days. The Trans Siberian railway would then take him out of China, drop him off in Mongolia for a further break and carry him into Russia. From Moscow, another train would deliver him to Berlin and once he had his fill of those great cities, a train to Paris would allow him to catch the Eurostar back to Waterloo. It would be two weeks before he would emerge with the commuters from Surbiton, Clapham and Wandsworth and stride out into a London morning identified only by a bright-yellow Clipper jacket and a well-travelled kitbag slung proudly over his shoulder.

With two loyal friends leaving and six new eager arrivals, *London* had to go back to square one and all the lessons, short cuts and shorthand communication that we had developed as a crew suddenly stood for little.

After they had watched us from the comfort of an armchair for six months, we had to patiently listen to a litany of fresh-faced enthusiasm. A few of the newcomers were not shy in coming forward, and with an astonishing lack of sensitivity, one told us, 'Changes need to be made – you need to be more efficient.'

We were curious to know how someone could decide this without having yet set sail, but they remained adamant that changes were needed. When pressed, they were not exactly sure what these changes might be, but stuck to their views anyway.

Another newcomer was positive that he would be spending his time at the nav desk helping Stuart make better tactical decisions, rather than being on deck as a working crew member. In the excitement of finally getting their part of the adventure under way, it seemed that tact and humility had been temporarily forgotten.

Like patient parents, we bit our tongues, listened politely and knew that after a few weeks at sea it would all bed down and people would begin to appreciate what long-distance racing is all about. No matter how many hours someone has spent at the helm of a small dinghy or how many weekends he or she might day-sail, being part of the crew on a large ocean-racing yacht with more than a dozen people packed into a tight and very public little space would need an open mind and an honesty about learning new skills.

It was the start of a difficult period of adjustment on both sides and it served to illustrate just how far we had come as a crew. What to us was now second nature was a slow and clumsy moment of discovery to the joiners and it was far too easy to simply take the task out of their hands. The boat had tried numerous techniques over the months since the start and developed, through trial and error, operating systems that worked well. It took a lot of restraint on our part when someone who had been on the boat for five minutes attempted to advise us how to do a job better.

The new team took part in a small regatta with several of the Royal Hong Kong Yacht Club boats and sailed a large triangular course around the harbour, dodging out of the way of coasters, tugs, cruise ships, pilot vessels, Star Ferries and dirty sampans. All the bravado heard in the bar was soon swept away as Stuart worked us hard, and I think that the critics began to understand how much application was needed.

We were beaten by two fast and lightweight racers but were the first clipper home, which boded well for the next leg of the race.

13

SECONDS OUT, HEAD FOR HOME
HONG KONG TO SINGAPORE
VIA SAN FERNANDO
12.04.01–26.04.01

The next morning the fleet finally left Hong Kong behind and prepared to join a mass start for the race to San Fernando in the Philippines. The event is a bi-annual classic of the Royal Hong Kong Yacht Club and several notables, including Laurie Smith in *Rothmans*, had taken part in the past.

The clippers are heavy boats and while the local racers stripped and pared whatever weight they could, we loaded up with another fifty days' worth of tins, which would take us to Mauritius. I didn't hold out too much hope for our chances of overall success.

Motoring away from the typhoon shelter with 'Jerusalem' doing its fanfare, we passed the lone figure of Gary standing at the end of the breakwater. A video camera concealed his face and one arm was held aloft in a permanent wave. We shouted out farewells but got no response as he struggled with his emotions and from way down the bay we could still see him there, the vertical arm still raised in a lengthy silent salute of goodbye.

Taking his place, James Bedford-Russell began the long journey back towards his much-loved *Etchell*, moored at Cowes. The ever-smiling Nieves Heathcote took the place of Danny as the other second-half circumnavigator. David Sage and Graham Parker would be with us until Mauritius. Bella Abrahams, now engaged to the skipper of *Jersey*, would sail as far as Brazil, willing us to beat her intended at every opportunity, and Trevor Crowe planned to come as far as Singapore before heading home.

Down at the start line, in front of the Watkins's beautiful home, some forty yachts milled around each other, waiting for the off. Three helicopters chased around the sky filming the action and when the gun went off we got a reasonable start, running in the top ten of the pack.

The race is supposed to be primarily a downwind event, but yet again we found ourselves beating into a fresh breeze with the wind on the nose. It had been two months since we had last enjoyed protracted spinnaker runs and the rising and falling bows soon sent several of the new joiners in a pale-green rush to the rail.

I was eager to get the new people on my watch up to speed as quickly as possible, so they found themselves at the helm on their first night at sea. We observed with zipped lips as the wake fell back in a series of sweeping S shapes and looked on in astonishment when the cry of 'Watch out, huge wave' went up. The experienced round-the-worlders in the crew scanned the sea long and hard but could see nothing other than a small ripple heading towards us.

On the previous few legs, Stuart had been able to enjoy uninterrupted periods of sleep while the boat, complete with sail changes, spinnaker peals, reefs and trim had taken place without the need for twenty-four-hour supervision.

Now with new blood on board, people were subconsciously establishing a pecking order and were keen to ensure that their skills were made known. Decisions that I made were being questioned, with several members of the watch having an opinion or a 'better' solution to what experience was offering them. I was happy to let them have their head for a bit, aware that it would be wrong to stamp on their keenness. But as the days went by, it became an increasing source of frustration, not just to me but also to Stuart.

He would come on deck and offer a bit of advice to a new joiner on the helm, which would be promptly ignored. The new helm apparently knew better and stuck to a line that was clearly making us go slower. Things had to get heavy-handed and once Stuart had given the deserved bollocking, the mood of my watch descended into a quiet flatness.

The race was going well, despite the steep learning curve on board, and we ran a course direct to the Philippines while other boats explored the options to the north and south of the rhumb line. It meant that we could run in the middle of the pack and keep an eye on the progress of the groups both above and below us. If one pack moved faster than the other, we could simply take our choice and head over to where the better winds clearly were.

In the clipper pecking order, *London* was running third behind *Jersey* and *Leeds*. Stuart – without any help from the tactical expert who had just joined the boat – picked his moment perfectly and made the decisive move as the winds started to lighten after two nights at sea. As Luzon came closer we ducked underneath *Leeds*, picked up a good wind from the south and closed in on the race leader.

With the race lasting only a few days, there was no margin for error and as the last twenty-four hours unfolded it was clear that we had made the correct choice in our heading. Up ahead lay *Jersey*, in sight and struggling in the lightest of breezes. Much to the delight of Bella, there was a glimmer of a win, but we almost rolled to a stop ourselves and ended up slopping over the finish line around twenty minutes behind her fiancé.

London was back on the podium in second place, though, after three trying months and, more impressively, we had finished seventh overall, beating many of the lightweight specialist racing boats. It was a fast race too, with Laurie Smith's record broken by a couple of minutes and the result did Clipper's reputation a power of good. We were quietly impressed at our performance against professional crews and started to appreciate just how competent we had become.

Getting to a safe anchorage inside the reef required local knowledge, so a speeding *banka* came out to meet us, acting as a guide towards the shore. Looking like a huge water boatman insect, the hand-made canoe had spear-like outriggers on either side of its brightly painted hull and a puttering lawnmower engine that sent it screaming across the water at a rate of knots. Each clipper was assigned its own personal carrier and once at anchor, the lime-green hull of our own narrow water taxi hung off the stern as its owner, Marshall, chatted away happily to the crew while we put the boat to bed.

In the intense heat, the warm waters beckoned and our swim was quickly joined by kids from the beach, who paddled out inside giant inflated black inner tubes. Their dark-skinned faces bobbed around us as they shouted their 'Hello, sir!' greetings and showed off passing jellyfish by picking them up to a reveal an underside alive with stinging tentacles.

In groups of four, the crew crammed into Marshall's canoe and watched him wind a dirty piece of cord around the flywheel before giving it a pull start. Sounding like a Suffolk Punch or an Atco, it sped off across the water, and with eyes shut one might have been in an English garden on a sunny Saturday afternoon as the old-fashioned two-stroke kicked in.

At the beach, amid the long line of *bankas* pulled up on the sand, more kids gave their eager greeting, happy to do a high five or two as I passed by. The race organisers had based themselves at a beach-side hotel complex straight out of a Robinson Crusoe movie. It was built on gnarled and bleached wooden stilts, with a combination of thick thatch and painted corrugated-iron sheets for the roof. We were welcomed to the bar by the gregarious owner, Robbie. A character who had lived life to the full, he was born in Lincoln, grew up in South Africa and hated the Philippines when he first went there, but was now deeply in love with both the place and his stunning Filipino wife.

Robbie loved what we were doing, loved the fact that we had been brave enough to turn our back on convention for a bit, loved the fact that we were living life in the 'proper' way and as we chatted he bought Ali, Andy and I drink after drink, insisting that our paying was out of the question.

For two days life became really chilled in the simple, warm and genuine welcome that existed all along the beach. I took a stroll for several miles and everyone I met stopped to wave, smile and chat. Further down the strand, several *bankas* were kitted out for fishing and, to provide illumination during the night, beer bottles filled with kerosene were taped to the bow. The fuel in the bottle soaked the underside of a corncob husk and while such illumination might not amuse the powers who oversee marine safety, it seemed to work perfectly well.

I walked along miles of virgin white sand that scalded the soles of my feet, and after a while the small hotels, thatched beach huts and boats were left behind. Turning inland, I headed down a rough path, through fields of cattle and past small homesteads where cockerels crowed loudly and hens pecked at the dust. Again the local people waved happily and a small gang of kids followed me, chattering away in pidgin English.

Reaching a road just as a taxi was going by, I hailed it. 'Taxi' suggests a smart sedan with air-con and comfy seats, but in Luzon it is a rusty motorbike attached to a rickety sidecar. We were soon speeding down a main road, looking for all the world like Wallace and Gromit as we dodged into the main traffic flow in an alarming high-revving kamikaze manoeuvre.

The precarious machine dropped me off on the dusty hard shoulder and its rider flagged down a minibus to take me the rest of the way. Once again the term 'minibus' conjures up a certain picture, but here, in an explosion of chrome, bright emulsion paint and a heavily modified jeep body, I joined a group of happy travellers on the bench seats that lined both sides of the truck. Once more we kicked up the dust as we pulled out right into the path of a lorry, which swayed on to the wrong side of the road and sent a gaggle of oncoming sidecar taxis lurching into the hard shoulder.

The trees, bus shelters and buildings were festooned with posters urging the locals to vote and despite the iffy politics that make the world view the Philippines in a less than favourable light, the people who live there – the people who actually make a country and give it its personality – were nothing other than genuine, polite, welcoming and happy. Mrs Marcos and her shoe fetish or Mr Estrada and his coups seemed not to affect the people one jot and after the crassness of Hong Kong, it was a wonderful release.

We joined in the San Fernando race celebrations with gusto, doing a turn on stage with Stuart and his guitar, and our efforts went down so well an encore was demanded. At the bar, Robbie cut the heads off fresh coconuts, added a generous quantity of rum to the coconut juice and again insisted that the drinks were on him.

The crew of *Ffreefire* [sic], a super-fast eighty-foot racing 'sled', who had broken Laurie Smith's record in the race, took us under their wing and we struck up a very happy partnership. They had invited some of *London*'s crew for a sail earlier in the day and were clearly impressed with our efforts. As the sun set on a placid, velvet sea, they took us to one side and presented their huge battle flag to the boat. They wanted to be a part of our round-the-world adventure and whenever we arrived in port, they wanted their colours to fly alongside ours.

Marshall sped me out across the bay back to *London*, which was riding at anchor, and I hoisted our huge new flag up the forestay. As I did so, a distant cheer echoed out over the water from the two crews and a long series of toasts were proposed and drunk as they talked about the races to come. Back onshore, I took time out from the noisy shouts from the bar, strolled down to the edge of the beach, sat on the sand and stared out towards the ocean.

The setting sun bathed the palm trees, the *bankas*, the thatched beach huts and the small hotels in a warm golden glow. The beach was alive with locals promenading up and down the now cool sand. Children splashed happily between the boats in their inner tubes and as the sun slipped gently into the warmth of a tropical night, flocks of bats fluttered out of the trees. Behind the corrugated-iron walls of the small hotel, through the lush garden and its thick canopy of trees, the noise of the main road to San Fernando filtered in. There was the insistent buzzing from the motorbike taxis, eagerly touting for business. There was the rumble of trucks and coaches and an occasional air horn as someone made a suicidal attempt to join the traffic flow.

In the last of the light, the night-fishing *bankas* sped across the glassy surface, their lit corncob husks doing a valiant job to stay burning in the warm rush of breeze. The sun finally set on Easter Monday and I watched the parents quietly gather their children and stroll without haste towards home.

The next morning, while the rest of the racers slept off their hangovers, the clippers prepared to race on towards Singapore. Robbie, once again, bent over backwards to help us on our way. We needed to stock up on bread and fresh fruit, so he dropped everything, got in his car and shot off to markets, supermarkets and bakers, before returning with a bootload of produce. Transport his laid-back dress, wild hair and lived-in face to a tube train in London and I could uncomfortably imagine the down-the-nose sneers of dismissal and disapproval. For sure, he was one of life's drifters, but he was also one of the kindest and most genuine people I have ever met.

London was the last of the fleet to leave the moorings, following Marshall back out through the reef towards the race start. As we hoisted our sails and began to jockey for position, he gave us a huge wave, his bright-white teeth flashing his genuine warmth as he wished us luck for the next leg.

It was one of the closest starts yet, with all eight boats crossing the line within a few seconds and a few yards of each other. Straight away we ran into a field of fishing marker poles and sailed through them like skiers in the Super Giant Slalom. The six-foot-high bamboo poles had on the bottom end a huge rootball to attract small fish. These are a welcome nibble for larger fish, which in turn provide a catch for the local fishermen waiting to pounce.

Except we got caught as well. A pole lying flat in the water and unseen by the helm caught itself around the rudder and suddenly the boat was dragging a huge weight that refused to budge. Stuart ordered a series of zigzags to shake it off, but the pole stuck firm. There was nothing we could do except turn through the wind and heave to. As a result, *London* slipped down to last place.

Two hours earlier our team meeting on the beach had agreed that the boat should run at a deeper intensity of focus for the first few days in order to lead from the front. And now, here we were, with the race barely ten minutes old, having to play catch-up.

As night fell, the first waypoint of the race course slipped by with the entire fleet within half a mile of each other. It indicated a turning point and across all eight boats the spinnakers were being prepared for the new course. Upwind of us, running parallel, were *Bristol*, and with their kite hoisted and set early, they bore away, allowing the wind to fill it, and headed down toward us.

I was steering and watched their trajectory out of the corner of my eye. We were closing on each other at an alarming rate and although they were making good progress, it looked very tight for them to make it across the front of our bow. I checked with Stuart that we had right of way (*Bristol* was the windward boat) and he confirmed that we should hold our course. When it was clear that they could not pass ahead of us, he expected them to duck down under our stern. But still they drove on, course unchanged, until it was clear that a collision was inevitable.

We were not going to be muscled out of the way by an illegal bully-boy tactic and held our course until we were just a couple of feet apart. Exasperated, Stuart shouted for me to bear away, but as we did so *Bristol* leant even harder until her spinnaker enveloped itself on our stays. Such contact is deemed a collision and is one of the cardinal sins in racing. With the thirty-ton hulls moving at racing speed now just inches apart, Stuart again shouted out to their skipper that the tactic was completely out of order. All that produced was another lunge at our hull and another contact between the two yachts. I now had the wheel over as far as it could go in order to get out of the way and as we floundered in a mess of flapping sails, *Bristol* slid down our hull and off in front.

To add insult to injury, one of their crew gave us a derisive departing wave, shouting out that it had been 'nice playing with you'. Everyone on board was incensed and, while eager to keep the race running under the right sort of atmosphere, we insisted that Stuart protest about such actions.

Bristol was a good, fast boat and had notched up several wins. But they didn't need to sail like that and their actions suggested an unhealthy desire to make gains no matter what the cost. Boats could have been damaged, people could have been hurt, and when no word of apology came from *Bristol* on the radio, we fired a report back to race HQ and hoisted the red protest pennant.

The hearing would take place in Singapore, but as that was ten days away we knuckled down once more and started another attempt to climb up from the back of the fleet. Through the night the crew trimmed away, concentrating hard, and when the sun rose the next morning we had pushed up into second place.

The organisers had warned that this race would be the toughest of all. Winds would be either light or non-existent and the heat, as we closed in on the equator, would start to eat away at us and frazzle nerves on board. We altered our watch system and ran for three hours during the heat of the day and then worked for four during the relative cool of the night. It also meant that the off watch got a longer sleep when the air was slightly cooler.

The sun was intense and gallons of squash were consumed during the course of each watch. We tried to keep it cool in a bucket of sea water, but within twenty minutes the water had become almost too hot to drink. An egg was cracked on deck, where it fried merrily away, and a dousing with a bucket of seawater was less than refreshing thanks to a water temperature akin to that of a hot tub. Down below, sweat poured off bodies and attempts to sleep in the airless coffin-like bunks resulted in a clammy, sticky mess of discomfort.

A strong breeze would have helped, but as we closed in on the Doldrums only the most gentle of puffs kept our heavy hulls barely moving through the water.

Far off to starboard lay Vietnam, and at an equal distance away to port lay Brunei, Sarawak and Borneo. Our bow, however, ignored such attractions and pointed towards the next distant waypoint in the race.

Such light-wind sailing was the hardest challenge in racing but we worked away, changing sails to suit the breeze, trimming for every modicum of speed and then changing the sails again as the wind shifted once more. The hard work paid off and we found ourselves leading the race. With no consistent wind from any major weather feature, progress was simply down to the behaviour of the clouds above us. As one boat sat and stewed in a windless patch, another a few hundred yards away would be skimming along at a heady four knots as a breeze-delivering patch of vapour slipped by overhead.

Because of such vagaries, the organisers had set a series of 'gates' in the course and if the lack of wind prevented the fleet from making them, the race could be shortened in order to get everyone to Singapore on time.

We battled hard with *Bristol* for the best part of a day, pulling out some four miles on them over twelve hours. But just when our advantage looked like it was starting to stick, *London* ran straight into an unmarked fishing net. For the second time in this race, the rudder seemed to possess a magnetic appeal and despite our best efforts, the net remained firmly attached. Once again we had to stop the boat dead in its tracks, lower the spinnaker and go into wind in order to solve the problem.

Every second counted and Stuart stood at the stern, with harness attached to a safety line and knife clenched between his teeth, ready to dive in. Sharks were his worst nightmare and the idea of plunging down into the unknown to clear the net did not amuse him greatly. With the boat now motionless, he took a deep breath, dived in, cleared the net with one sharp shove and was back on board as if attached to an invisible and very tightly wound bungee cord. Even if there had been a shark, the immersion was so rapid the predator would have failed dismally to get even a leg.

The sails were shot up again, trimmed and set and our lead remained intact, with *Bristol* still wallowing in our wake. With *London* still smarting from their aggressive attack, the mood on board was, unsurprisingly, upbeat.

Jersey and *Liverpool* were now our sparring partners and we all slipped through the second gate on the race course with barely a quarter of a mile between us.

Squalls started to line the horizon and in one selected blow we sat in a wind hole of frustration, while our two adversaries, clearly visible, sped off and were suddenly nine miles ahead. Behind, the back markers were starting to struggle and after six days' racing the two tail-enders were told by the organisers that their race was over and began the long motor to catch up. A day later another three boats, including *Bristol*, had their race terminated and it was left to the three front-runners to continue the battle for another forty-eight hours.

The sea state changed during the night and we rode nose-on to a short, sharp chop. The waves acted like a buffer to our slow progress and any attempt to build boat speed was halted by the opposing slap of the ocean. It was deeply frustrating because we knew that with the sail choice and wind speeds that existed, the boat should be able to move a lot faster. We checked the trim and made small adjustments, but nothing would improve our progress. To make matters worse, even though we had established that we were sailing as best we could in the difficult conditions, the voices of dissent were back. My watch had a whole raft of different views and were not shy in coming forward with their opinions as to how the boat speed could be improved.

Stuart, trying to sleep in his bunk below, eventually lost patience and came up to prove a point. He was clearly frustrated at a group who seemed more keen on running itself as a debating society than as a team. Knowing full well what the problem was and ignoring the precious race, he insisted that everyone should put their ideas on the table. As the sun started to rise after a trying night at sea, he worked through all the suggestions and proved them wrong one by one. Nothing made any difference and he ended up repeating my view from an hour earlier, confirming that the sea chop was killing our progress. By going through the charade, we had lost more time on the leaders, but he was insistent that the carpers should learn a valuable lesson.

He urged the watch to respect the viewpoints and skills that had been learnt over seven months at sea, rather than dismiss them out of hand, but while the lesson proved a point, the atmosphere in the team I was supposed to be inspiring slipped to a new low.

It was a difficult moment. I had been a watch leader since Panama and for the first time the job I was doing was being questioned. Without tact or forethought, individuals repeatedly and forcefully made suggestions as to how I might improve my approach. The easy working relationship with Danny, Gary, James *et al* seemed a long way off.

It would be true to say that for a couple of days I was less than happy, and this feeling, combined with the pangs of missing Anne, Holly and Mike, led to my most miserable period on board since the start of the race.

I spoke to Stuart and offered my resignation, thinking that he might be happier with new blood running the watch. In the interest of making the boat go faster, a change may have been to *London*'s advantage. But he was adamant that I should continue and reassured me that my quiet, more intense style (compared with Ali's exuberant laughter-filled watch) was doing a more than acceptable job.

The race still had to be won and we knew that in such fluky winds and variable conditions there was still a chance. Sure enough, with twelve hours remaining, *Liverpool* and *London* reported identical distances to go in the radio sched and the last night saw a final burst of effort and energy from both clippers. When another perfect day in the tropics dawned, *Liverpool* was four miles off to our port and, most importantly, around a mile behind.

The winds were almost non-existent, though, and the boat speed, in a good spell, was a mere one knot. Jane was at the helm and her deft touch in the light conditions always seemed to find a little extra slice of speed. The outcome would be decided according to whoever might benefit from the lightest zephyr off a passing cloud. Meanwhile we willed *London* through the glassy water towards the final radio transmission that marked the end of the race. There was a collective holding of breath as the lat and long positions from the other boats were reported and then we sat in agonised silence, waiting for *Liverpool* to send her message. When it finally came, we were two and a half miles ahead and, for the second race in succession, had finished second, with another seven points to add to our tally.

A great cheer went up and Ali, Andy, Nieves and I rolled backwards off the stern as *London* slipped slowly on through the water. It had been an exceptionally tough leg in the incredible heat and emotions had run high as a result. The need to cool off and let it all drift away was a top priority, but before we could even start to think about a lazy wallow, there was a mad splashing panic in the ocean. Even crawling along at two knots, our yacht moved effortlessly away from the three of us and we were left treading water in the deep end, with a depth of six hundred feet beneath our feet. Much to the amusement of those on deck, our panicky breaststroke and wildly splashing crawl made a ridiculous sight as we attempted to catch up and in the unseemly scramble for the trailing rope ladder poor Nieves was muscled to the back of the queue. Between Ali, Andy and I, we liked to think it was so we could give her a strong helping hand up from the safety of the deck.

Liverpool motored over to give us the traditional three cheers of congratulations and after the compliment had been returned, we started to plan the rendezvous with the remainder of the fleet.

In the light of a setting sun the eight clippers converged and, with engines off and hulls drifting, the crews had a mass swim in the depths of the South China Sea. It was a stunning, tranquil moment, broken by an occasional scream as a sea snake wriggled between the swimmers. It was only back on board that we discovered that the snakes are among the most deadly in the world.

It was a lengthy motor through the busy shipping lanes, which gave us the chance to do all the maintenance work on board before we arrived. When the skyscrapers of Singapore eventually slipped silently past us in the darkness of Saturday night, we were ready for a break. Two short races had not allowed the new crew to slip into a routine and I hoped that the next leg, with its three-week sail across the Indian Ocean, would allow things to settle and the mood to calm a little.

More importantly, at the end of it all, would be a reunion with my family and if anyone could have suggested a bigger incentive than that, I'd have loved to hear it.

Singapore proved to be a good stopover. After the thrust of Hong Kong, I was curious to see how another large city where banking is a key influence would affect me. Remembering my shouted opinions from the squalid hotel, I wondered if I had changed deeply as a person. Becoming a vocal protester about the evils of consumerism would not be such a great move if I expected to go back to a job where the role of making products seductive was what paid the salary.

I need not have worried. The credit card was back with a vengeance and I loved the open spaces, the rich lush greenery, the parks and the quaintly named streets that made the city a delight to be a part of. Orchard Road, Raffles Boulevard, Somerset Road, Oxley Rise and Boat Quay all conjured up gentle images from the days when the radio was a wireless and the Home Service and the Light Programme brought listening pleasure to millions.

The city has had a chequered past, of course, and a visit to Changi Gaol, beyond the thrusting skyscrapers and bustling harbour, puts recent history firmly into focus. A newly opened museum there shared the horrors of the foul camp that housed so many Allied prisoners. Prisoners who, because they had not died for their country, were treated with complete contempt by their Japanese captors. The Geneva Convention was put in place to protect soldiers, sailors and airmen, but the prison commanders ignored such protocols because, in their eyes, true soldiers, sailors and airmen would have died rather than face the ignominy of capture.

At Changi, thousands of emaciated prisoners wizened down to almost nothing, and in the faithfully reconstructed prison chapel I read emotional messages in memory of the men whose bodies let them down before the war was over. Their memory burns bright in the eyes of proud sons, daughters, nephews and nieces, granddaughters and grandsons. Young hands had written numerous messages of love to souls long since departed, the visitors having come a long way to pay their respects to relatives from a past that still clearly hurt.

Up the road, the awful concrete block of the main prison could still be seen and indeed was still in use. The death penalty awaits anyone who tries to bring drugs into the country, and looking up at the foul and darkened walls, I wondered about the fate of nice backpacking girls from the UK who naively chance their luck, only to find that justice is swifter and far harsher than they ever imagined it could be.

The harsh city laws that go to such extremes as to prevent gum-chewing on the street have their benefits, though. These rules have left a scrupulously clean and courteous country where the locals quiz you on your opinion of their city, thank you for your custom as they take your cash, ask questions about your home and pat you fondly on the back in a final farewell.

Singapore is a rich, cosmopolitan city that is given vitality by its mix of cultures. Indians, Chinese, Japanese and Europeans, with large doses of Indonesians and Australians thrown in for good measure, bring a positive energy. But, by comparison with Hong Kong, the energy here is much more laid-back, less thrusting and apparently far more at ease with itself.

People were successful, it was clear, but they carried it off without the ostentatious need to show off through material possessions. The restaurants were full, but there was not a pinstripe suit in sight. Bars down on the waterfront were packed, but the conversation was gentle and mercifully free of the braying gloat that spills out of wine bars around Cheapside, Wall Street or Wan Chai. Mellow jazz oozed out on to the cobbled streets as sampans floated gently past, their decks lit by the warm orange glow of numerous paper lanterns.

Raffles Hotel lived up to its reputation of rakish charm, although the sight of long lines of ready-mixed Singapore Slings complete in souvenir Raffles glasses burst the bubble for us. But we ordered them anyway. It was Ellie's birthday and amid the toasts it was clear that a chap called Wil, sailing on *Portsmouth*, was proving to be an increasingly important person in her life.

Back at Raffles Marina on the western tip of the island – more a five-star hotel complex than a place to park a yacht – things were not going so well. *Bristol* had an engine problem that engineers were struggling to fix and a sudden intense thunderstorm had unleashed a massive bolt of lightning directly overhead which knocked out four of the yachts' electrics. *London* was one of them.

So while frantic repairs were attempted by Clipper, the crews enjoyed the smart surroundings, taking full advantage of the spectacular outdoor pool, the bubbling warm outdoor jacuzzi and the long line of sunbeds that cosseted a mass of exhausted bodies.

Stu was happy because Liz and Ben had become jet-setters again and the rest of the crew slotted comfortably into the warm embrace of camaraderie that existed between all the boats. Everyone knew everyone else and stepping into the Raffles Marina club was like entering a local pub and finding a group of your best friends waiting at the bar. The only difference was the group totalled around one hundred and twenty.

Every night there was laughter and after the official prize-giving the party evolved and developed. Once the VIPs had gone, the local band ended their set with a drum roll and the inevitable 'Thank you, Singapore, and GOODNIGHT', and with the lights brought up to full glare for the incoming cleaners, the noisy party moved downstairs to the pool. In the dark under our familiar ceiling of stars, more drinks were ordered as the crews bantered and joked, joshed and teased, argued and, in Ellie and Wil's case, hugged and kissed as the night wore on.

Swimming was inevitable and at some point in the small hours – a time that was by now comfortably familiar – the first bodies took to the dark, warm waters.

The smart clothes put on for the prize-giving were discarded without a thought and the pool filled with a mass of skinny-dipping sailors who dived into the waters with a loud giggle, encouraged by a huge cheer. All that Great British reserve had been left several thousand miles behind in our wake and the party showed no sign of dying down as more drinks arrived and the volume increased. In true tabloid reporter fashion, I decided to make my excuses and leave. I wanted an early night and thought that retiring at 05.20 would set a good example to my fellow revellers. At least I got to bed just before the sun made its first appearance over the celebrations.

A group of very quiet and rather fragile crew members gathered for a late breakfast, each toying with a croissant and sipping rather too much strong coffee in an effort to cut through the murk. By the pool, Ali – as always, the life and soul of the party – remained where he had fallen and the rasping snores from his sunbed drifted up into the sultry air.

Above, in one of the first-floor marina offices, a rather more serious and alert gathering was taking place. The skippers of *London* and *Bristol*, along with various crew members, assembled nervously outside the room where the race committee would listen to our protest about the previous race.

A panel of stern-faced officials sat behind a long table and one by one the witnesses shared their facts. As I had been on the helm, the event was replayed from my point of view – a recollection not helped by the energetic celebrations from the previous night.

With all the facts given, the committee went behind closed doors and debated what they had heard. It didn't take long – *Bristol* were found to be at fault and were penalised a number of points from their championship total. And while it was the correct decision, we took no pleasure from moving closer towards the leaders by such means. Bob Beggs, the skipper of our rival boat, and his two witnesses were generous in their defeat and we all retired to the bar for a no-hard-feelings drink. It was not what my liver really wanted.

Work continued on *Bristol*'s engine and our departure day loomed. With a steady stream of engineers still hard at it, Clipper decided that six boats should leave, with *Bristol* following as soon as the work was done. She would be accompanied by *Glasgow*, who would ride shotgun just in case of trouble. We would motor as a fleet at half speed until they both caught up and then travel together down towards the Indian Ocean, where the race would begin.

Motoring was tedious but necessary for two reasons. The first was the weather, as the very light winds would not ensure a fair and balanced race to Mauritius. We had already experienced just how localised the winds could be in the race from the Philippines and yachts stuck in wind holes would never get the chance to recover and catch up. The first boat into the Indian Ocean would most likely win the race to Mauritius and so it seemed fairer for all to start where the consistent winds benefited everyone equally.

The second reason for motoring as a fleet was the very real threat of piracy. The waters we were going through are the worst in the world for attacks on shipping and although the raiders are usually after much bigger prizes, the race organisers were not going to take any chances.

We were all briefed on the procedure should a suspicious boat close in on us and I was detailed to fire off a Mayday should things get really heavy. As if to confirm the fears, our on-board Satcom C set beeped off several emergency messages concerning attacks taking place in the seas all around us.

In one, a fast boat had come alongside a tanker and launched a grappling hook and line, which the modern-day pirates climbed up and then held the crew hostage with a sub-machine gun. Such drama usually netted just cash, watches and the crew's personal possessions, rather than the stock in the hold, but none the less it would be a deeply unpleasant experience to go through.

14

CHRISTMAS IN MAY
SINGAPORE TO MAURITIUS
VIA CHRISTMAS ISLANDS
04.05.01–27.05.01

Working in watches of three that rotated through the crew, we slowly motored away from Singapore and headed south-west towards the distant Indian Ocean.

The fleet of six yachts were forced to cruise even more slowly after a message came through on our first night at sea. The engineers had still not fixed the problem and *Bristol* and *Glasgow* would be delayed for at least another day. To conserve fuel on the long motor, boats paired up to tow each other and the crews settled into a period of languid stupor as the days and nights drifted slowly past.

The weather was hot and humid and in order to minimise the gap between the clippers, we stopped at regular intervals to change the tow and, more importantly, go for a swim. The dirty green waters were shallow and strewn with knitted mats of palm leaves, floating logs and numerous bobbing coconuts. Once in the water, bodies were immediately attacked by tiny sea lice that started to nibble away at exposed flesh. They were an irritant rather than a stinging menace but they added to the growing concern that was being felt throughout the fleet as we still waited for news on the race start.

Not only frustrated, we were also ashamed to admit that the days were mind-numbingly boring. Such moods were deeply out of character and once we had admitted it, guilt immediately set in at such negativity. We were now seasoned racers, though, and realised that we needed to get back to sailing hard and fast.

How could we be bored? We were travelling towards the straits between Sumatra and Java. Off to port were Kalimantan and Borneo, while off to starboard lay Indonesia. Small islands with beckoning deserted white beaches slipped by and while a driftwood-burning beach party was a tempting option, the race organisers forbade us to stop off as it would cause untold headaches in terms of immigration controls.

The equator was crossed again and the new crew members were invited to stand before Neptune for the ritual humiliation. A huge pot full of thick porridge oats mixed with water, mustard, ketchup and brown sauce was dutifully ladled over their grateful heads and the great man was appeased once again.

We motored under a full moon and watched giant birds flap slowly overhead from out of the rainforests of Indonesia. It was only when one of them flew in front of the moon and I saw the giant membrane that we realised they were bats with a three-foot wingspan. They came perilously close to the rigging, and Ellie, James and I mused at the mayhem it would cause if one were to drop in through the open hatch and on to the sleeping crew.

Ahead lay the Bangka Straits, a renowned pirates' attacking spot. According to the Admiralty charts, the area also contained an unswept minefield and there was the risk of underwater volcanic eruptions with the potential for producing large, ship-damaging waves. And still we were bored. It was so tedious, I even shaved my beard off, immediately regretting it as the blunt blade hacked at the skin and burned my face like fire.

What was gnawing away at me was the lack of progress and, with it, the growing threat of being delayed in reaching Mauritius. With the family on half-term holidays, my time was tight and any more delays would mean a reunion cut short.

The following year, when May bank holiday came around again, I imagined I might be waiting in a long checkout queue at B&Q. And if that were true, I knew I would stand there, head hung in shame for seeing, but not really seeing, the once-in-a-lifetime exotic vista that was now all around me.

Some of my fellow crew were a great deal happier. At the combined swimming sessions and tow-rope change-overs, guests from the other boats swam over and clambered aboard. Up in the forepeak, Andy slept contentedly with an arm around his girlfriend Sarah, who had joined us from *Jersey* for the day. Up on watch together under a romantic night sky, Ellie talked earnestly with Wil and from the overheard snatches it sounded like plans were being hatched for a life together.

As we entered our fourth day of motoring, *Bristol* and *Glasgow* finally hove into view and as night fell, the fleet crept through the channel running between Sumatra in the north and Java to the south. The port of Merak was well lit up to the left (another place rife with pirate attacks on boats at anchor) while the dramatic mountains overshadowed the lights of Tua to the right.

We slipped silently by, talking in whispers as lightning flashed behind a bubbling mass of moonlit cumulus, and it truly felt like we were escaping from a very foreign and far-away land of mystery. To add to the drama, a powerful searchlight suddenly swung across the water and picked us up in its beam. Our immediate fear was a pirate attack but the light came from a large merchant ship nudging gingerly east, which, it seemed, was equally jumpy about us as we made our noiseless way westwards.

The perfect symmetrical shape of Krakatoa passed by at three in the morning and we were awestruck by the energy of the phenomenon that could blow an island apart in an explosion that was heard two thousand miles away. For years after the last eruption, stunning sunsets marked the end of the day all over the globe, as the volcanic ash hung in the upper atmosphere.

Such a bang was what was needed to bring *London* out of its lethargy and as dawn broke, the radio announced that the race would commence just as soon as we ran into the first decent winds. The Indian Ocean greeted us with a huge swell that gently rolled up from the south, and it was so tall that yachts were hidden from each other in the rise and fall. It originated from Australia and the Southern Ocean. With Darwin just under a thousand miles away, it was frustrating not to be adding Oz to our collection of stops, but as a day of further setbacks developed, Australia suddenly became a realistic option.

Bristol's problems were still not over and despite the repair work by Singapore's finest, her engine and generator were once again out of action. As the eight yachts circled each other in the swell, several skippers were ferried on board to try to solve the problem. They discovered a sorry trail of unemptied water traps and blocked fuel filters and, as a result, an inoperative fuel injector pump. It seemed that, the world over, fitters could not be trusted to do a decent repair job.

There was no way *Bristol* could start the race without engine back-up. A man-overboard situation, or a serious injury that required a drive to the nearest landfall, dictated that. So the fleet drifted for more mind-numbing hours as the spanner men did their best and the e-mail connection to race HQ burnt red hot.

Clipper were adamant that the fleet should stick together whenever possible and it soon became clear that outside assistance was going to be needed. We could either turn around and head back towards pirate-infested Merak or motor on towards the tiny speck of Christmas Island, which was at least in the right sort of direction.

After a skippers' conference, a visit to Australia's smallest offering was agreed and an engineer would be standing by, hopefully to solve the problem quickly. And so we motored some more, and so my unease grew as the date of my return to the bosom of my family slipped out of my grasp yet again.

At least there was a bit of wind, so we were able to sail and the fleet in full flight made a great sight as we cruised south. We made good time too and were ready to hit the hot spots when the island came into view at 22.00 the following evening. But any thoughts of just downing sails and rowing ashore were banished by the harbourmaster, Don O'Donnell, who was determined to do things by the book. He had agreed that our ETA of 06.00 must stand and until then we were not to even drop anchor.

And so the yachts drifted up and down the coast for hour after hour as another long night of no progress ran its course. We did so just a few hundred yards from the shore, where no depth-sounder was needed. The seabed ran out from the beach for twenty or thirty gently shelving paces and then plunged in a vertical drop to a depth of over six hundred metres.

Don O'Donnell had clearly not enjoyed a stress-free day and it was he who had set the rules. Not only did he have a giant rusting phosphate carrier about to leave his precious harbour, but he also had to deal with the arrival of a boat load of illegal immigrants who had made the crossing from Java in a modified fishing boat and were now residing in the island's tiny detention centre. Eight yachts, with some one hundred and twenty crew, was a headache he could do without.

But Clipper HQ had been hard at work while we were at sea and had liaised with Canberra to smooth immigration procedures. They also had an engineer on standby and had scoured the world for a replacement pump, finding one in Darwin, which even now was on a flight to Christmas Island.

It all sounded too good to be true and I remained sceptical about whether we would enjoy a quick turnaround. I mused on the idea of taking a flight out of the island in order to get to Mauritius on time as I could see all too easily a delay of many days stretching ahead. I simply could not bear the thought of arriving just after my family had departed.

Describing the moment, my diary entry read, 'BUGGER BUGGER BUGGER BUGGER BUGGER BUGGER BUGGER.' Rather eloquent and restrained, I thought.

As we drifted through the night I spoke to home on the sat phone and was humbled by the support I continued to get. My idea of taking a plane was instantly banished and Anne gave me a thorough ticking-off for even suggesting it. She reminded me that the crew should support each other through thick and thin and there was no way I could walk away and let the boat down. She repeated her views in a stinging e-mail and I stood like a small boy before the headmistress, well and truly corrected. To receive such unselfish support from home meant a huge amount and did much to ease the pain.

The sun rose to reveal a lush green jungle-covered island that rose out of the sea in three distinct plateaux. From the towering crags, tropicbirds and frigate birds soared and swooped, minute specks emphasising the soaring rock faces that jutted out of the greenery.

A colonial residence complete with manicured lawns and white flagpole slipped by at the opening of Flying Fish Cove, the island's only harbour. It looked out towards the ugly scar of the conveyor belts and silos of the phosphate works that provided the only real employment. Underneath the rough quayside wall lay the immigrants' fragile transport, its roof lined with clusters of white plastic bags – the pathetic belongings of the hopeful refugees.

The boat was a typical Indonesian inshore fishing vessel that had been modified to afford some shelter for the one hundred and fifty men, women and children who had crammed on board. It had been painted battleship grey in an attempt to blend with the ocean and the fact it had got here meant that the protection and camouflage had done their job.

The occupants had come from Afghanistan and were clearly being helped by a well-organised chain that took a considerable amount of their money in return for a chance of freedom. The Australian government would decide on their fate and, even now, the hapless souls were on their way to a detention centre in Darwin while the authorities decided on the best course of action. More often than not, such people would simply be sent home, while the vessel that brought them on the last leg of the journey would be towed out to sea and sent to the bottom.

We learnt all this from a profusely sweating and grumpy immigration officer who regarded his posting to Christmas Island as the job from hell. His police colleagues were more friendly, though, and despite the tiny backwater feel of the place, they followed the law to the letter. There was something curious about sitting on deck in the sunshine, surrounded by jungle and tropicbirds as a uniformed policeman went about his job. The uniform was a slightly modified version of the one worn in Australia, with a baseball cap with a blue-checked band replacing the more formal headgear and a light-blue polo shirt instead of a stiff white collar and tie. The final essential detail was the wetsuit neoprene shoes, which were rather more practical than a pair of highly polished 'evening all' black brogues.

We sat at anchor and watched with glee as an Australian stamp went into the passport. Crews swam in the crystal-clear waters and we waited to hear the prognosis on *Bristol*'s problems.

An engineer had taken one look at the damaged pump and said, 'No way.' So that put paid to an immediate departure.

The part coming in from Darwin had failed to materialise – a mix-up over what had been asked for – so leaving the following day was out of the question as well.

A pump was now being flown out from the UK, which meant a minimum stay of three days and, being a cynic, I placed a silent bet as to which airport the pump would go walkabout at. Until then, there was nothing we could do but enjoy the hospitality ashore. The inflatable tenders were blown up for the first time, as crews ferried themselves to the beach, with its ready-built barbie areas, and started to explore.

The bank was warned of our arrival and extra cash had been flown in. The clipper crews crammed into the Nissen-hut-style building to get Australian dollars, the tellers counted out the notes, bearing the Queen's head, and then settled back to wait for Monday morning. Once the weekend was over, a steady stream of bar owners, hoteliers, café managers and taxi drivers formed an orderly queue and the Australian bank reserves were paid back almost down to the last cent as the cash passed over the counter once more.

The island gave us the warmest of welcomes and whenever one of us set foot on a road, every passing motorist, whether in a car, van or dustcart, stopped and offered a lift. Everywhere we turned there was a friendly wave, a warm hello and some lively banter about anything and everything.

Stuart, Andy, Ali and I repaired to a bar that sat amid the jungle, overlooking Flying Fish Cove. We were introduced to the delights of VB, or Victoria Bitter, and drank the health of the only other people in the room.

Roo and Bully became our latest best friends. Bully had the florid face of a heavy drinker and the piercing blue eyes of a prize fighter. Roo, by contrast, looked like Roy Wood from Wizard. He had the hair of a Hell's Angel that tumbled down over huge exposed tattooed biceps. He looked likely to bite the heads off new-born babies but had the smile of an angel, with a personality to match. Over several 'tinnies' (in less than a day half the fleet had become honorary Strine speakers) we learnt about the island from Mr Roo and Mr Bully.

As we talked, the sun sank lower in the sky and our lofty vantage point gave a grandstand view of the refugee boat as it was towed far out to sea. Roo and Bully knew the form and just before the prescribed moment, took their seats with us at the vast open window. The explosion was huge and a giant fireball, like an overenthusiastic special effect in a movie, burst skywards as the remains of a boat that had carried so many hopes and dreams settled back on to the surface of the sea in a million pieces and slipped beneath the waves.

Keeping Don O'Donnell busy was yet another arrival – this time of the monthly freighter full of stores. Roo told us that when the ocean swell gets up, the freighter has to stand off for several days, and if conditions fail to improve, it heads for the mainland once again without unloading.

'When that happens, it becomes a bit of a disaster area around here,' he confided.

I naively asked why and, in response, his swarthy bulging arm waved in the general direction of the bottles lined up behind the bar.

'Because we run out of drink, you Pommie idiot.'

Having been so described, I thought it wise to live up to the name and continued my penetrating inquisition.

'So then, what do you do?'

With a saddened shake of the head, he explained what clearly should have been patently obvious.

'We drink the VB and when that runs out, we move on to the yuppie beer. When all that's gone, we start on the white wine, followed by the red, and if the ship is still not in, we start on the spirits.'

Continuing my in-depth probing of the island's drinking habits, I asked what had happened the last time the ship had failed to land. This time the reply was positively gleeful and Roo grinned at the happy memory of it all.

'We got as far as the gin and vodka, moved on to the whisky, then the rum, and only had the brandy left before the weather allowed the ship to dock.'

In the supermarket, a large blackboard offered two prices for the same produce and shoppers could select a tired-looking cheap lettuce that came by sea or a slightly fresher, more expensive offering that came in on the twice-weekly flight. The supply chain is key to the island and with nothing other than a few bananas grown in the jungle, the inhabitants have learnt to stockpile in case of delays.

Crab is always an option. The island is seething with millions of red crabs, which are its claim to fame. In the mating season they pour in a non-stop carpet of red, out of the jungle and down to the sea. The roads are full of crushed shells and to peer into the jungle is to come face to face with crabs under every leaf, every twig, every branch and up every tree. The jungle floor is free of rotting vegetation as they eat everything and apart from a vicious giant centipede that delivers a burning bite, the island is otherwise free of nasty creepy-crawlies.

We toured the coastline in a bus especially laid on by the islanders, who were eager to show us their precious sights. The herded fleet marvelled at spectacular volcanic blowholes where vaporised sea water roared up through the rock from the sea a hundred feet below. When the vast energy was unleashed the noise sounded as if one of Tolkien's thoroughly unhappy monsters lay writhing in Middle Earth, somewhere beneath our feet. The camera-clicking tourists were taken to an old mining site that was the proposed launch pad for a telecommunications satellite and although nothing had yet been built, the lateral thinking of the islanders illustrated a deep desire to keep the economy flowing.

We were roped into a football match against an island team and a collection of lithe, fleet-footed locals arrived wearing a ragbag of football shirts – all from the English Premier League. It was a good, hard game in the afternoon sun, and when the final whistle was blown, a 2–0 defeat for the sailors was a respectable result. When the Millennium Round the World race came to the island, they lost 14–0 and by all accounts were lucky to get nil.

The two teams retired to the Christmas Island Club, our newly adopted watering-hole, and settled down to watch the FA Cup Final on satellite TV. It was strange to be a part of an annual sporting fixture from the other side of the world, but good to catch a glimpse of Britain and to see it bathed in lots of warm sunshine. A year before, Bowlsie and I had taken our sons to the last-ever final at Wembley and watched Dennis Wise lift the cup for Chelsea. Because of the tedious delay for the fleet, my thoughts were constantly turning to home and the reminder of a classic father-and-son day set off all the emotions once again.

And then, surprise, surprise, we learnt that the fuel pump, which had made it as far as Singapore, had missed the flight to Christmas Island and another delay of four days was on the cards. If that was truly the scenario, we would arrive in Mauritius the day after my family had left for home, and I wanted to sit on the paradise beach and cry.

But Clipper were starting to get cold feet about the delays as well. It was British week in Mauritius and our visit was a key part of the celebrations. After much debate it was agreed that the race should start with seven boats and *Bristol* would follow as soon as she could. Because there would be no race for the championship leader, the race committee would sit and decide how their non-participation would be treated in terms of the overall points tally.

The organisers were also concerned about splitting up the fleet – something that I could not understand. When we were at sea, we raced. It could mean that at the end of a three-week crossing, boats were several hundred miles away from each other and often finished two or three days apart. Having *Bristol* at sea, on her own, would be no different and we urged the argument on, so that we could get started.

I was not the only one who had family coming to Mauritius and there was a growing frustration among the crew as another wasted day crept by. But as things turned out, this actually worked to our advantage. When the race did start, we were so up for it, so ready, so focused, we zipped around the deck like fully fledged pro racers, leaving Stuart bathed in a glow of deep pleasure.

London hit the line in second place, quickly converting it to first, and knuckled down to protect its lead at all costs. The two watches settled immediately into the race routine and the personnel changes discussed with Stuart and my fellow watch leader, Ali, made for a much better-balanced pairing of teams.

We were off, the sun shone, a huge swell gave good spinnaker surfs for the first time in three months, our boat was in front and we were finally racing over a decent-size ocean again.

The only downside was the route. From Indonesia, the fleet would have had several tactical options to choose, but from Christmas Island it was a straight drag race for two thousand miles. It meant that we might be in sight of other yachts for the entire race and the pressure to keep sailing at the very maximum would be intense.

Experience had taught us that in such heavy conditions ropes and shackles were under huge strain and likely to snap. We doubled up as many lines as we could and when a brand-new shackle exploded under load and released the spinnaker into a flapping mass, we were ready to deal with it.

Stuart had been on the helm and as he went forward to supervise at the bow, I was left in charge at the wheel. Once again the crew were on fire and as they poured out into the cockpit from their bunks, I allocated positions as each individual appeared. Like a well-oiled machine, they slotted into the tasks with an easy understanding of the role, and the whole operation flowed smoothly. The foresail was hoisted to screen the flying spinnaker, the flapping sail was dropped, the spinnaker pole sent forward and lowered, a new line strung and attached, the heavyweight spinnaker attached and hoisted, the foresail dropped and packed and the spinnaker sent below also packed. The whole process took just ten minutes and, behind us, *Liverpool* had not even taken in the drama.

Other boats were having similar problems in the heavy conditions and after just a day at sea *Plymouth*'s steering cables snapped under the intense load on the rudder. *Jersey* were close by and had a spare, so they downed sails and motored towards them with the new part. For their troubles, they were given immediate redress by the race committee. *Plymouth* had contravened race rules by using a fleet spare once the race was under way, and while we appreciated the seamanship aspect of getting the correct parts to work as quickly as possible, we assumed that the organisers would take such actions into account when we arrived in Mauritius.

Twelve hours later it was *Portsmouth*'s turn to suffer a steering failure, which helped us considerably. We had been battling it out with them since the start, at one point sharing the lead with identical distances to go. *Portsmouth* too had a spare cable, so they were back in the hunt after just half an hour of repairs.

Glasgow was next on the list and when her cable snapped as well, there was no fleet spare and no boat to come to the rescue. As a result, things took a lot longer to fix and given the combination of heavy seas and temporary steering, there was no way they would risk flying a spinnaker. Their race was effectively run and the poor crew had to settle once again for an ignominious last place.

Such inconsistencies hardly seemed fair and it seemed unreasonable that two boats could get back into the race while a third was left to suffer. Again we assumed that Clipper would consider the matter when we reached Mauritius.

For a couple of days Stuart joined my watch and he and I shared the load at the wheel. It was the first time our Hong Kong joiners had seen such big conditions and they now began to understand how important precise helming was. It was all about equipment preservation and we could not afford to constantly collapse spinnakers, as this might in turn lead to bending spinnaker poles, breaking guys and snapping uphauls and downhauls, as we sought to protect our lead. It had been a long time since I'd had to deal with such seas and after a couple of hours my hands were stinging from a long line of raw blisters that had burst as I constantly played the wheel against the waves.

But it was great sailing, and speeds were constantly up above ten knots, giving us daily distance totals of over two hundred miles. The organisers had reckoned a sixteen-day passage and in our eagerness to get there we had set ourselves a target of fourteen. At such a pace, twelve days for the Indian Ocean started to look possible, which meant we would be back to the original schedule.

London buzzed like never before as we continued to try to build an advantage. Our slim lead of three miles over *Liverpool* was good, but try as we might, they refused to be shaken off. When the wind picked up further, the boat went into twenty-four hours of selected helming, but whatever we did, they matched and sat, magnet-like, off our stern.

For ten whole days and nights we hung on, each watch determined to be the one to pull out a little more on our pursuers and build a bigger buffer. The elusive win really started to look like ours and the yearned-for yellow pennant could just be glimpsed fluttering away in the distance on a very long piece of fabled string.

As each day passed, the string was pulled in a little closer and the crew could start to hear the rustle and crack as the pennant struggled in the brisk breeze. We could feel its fanning effect on our faces and soon would be able to almost reach out and touch it.

After our eleventh night at sea Stuart went off watch to get some well-earned rest and we followed him below for breakfast and four hours of total collapse in our fast-skimming bunks. Back on watch at midday, *Liverpool* could not be seen and *London* had committed a cardinal error.

With identical boats, all we had to do was cover the opposition. Do what they do, go where they go and there was no way, assuming both crews were sailing well, for them to take any advantage. The hard work from Christmas Island had proved that.

Leave them to their own devices, though, and the leader falls off his precarious driving seat. We were now blind to their moves and could not respond to any tactical changes going on over the horizon. Sure enough, at the next radio sched, *Liverpool* had made up the three miles and were now level with us. At the next report, twelve hours later, they had moved ahead and we wallowed in a mess of self-pity and disgust.

To make matters worse, my own watch took us off on an unnecessary journey to the south for several hours, which added insult to injury. I had been on the helm for most of the day and Stuart was adamant that I should get some rest. He too had been in desperate need of more sleep and when we both woke, a little more damage had been done to our race position. Being off deck, fast asleep and away from the decision-making going on in the cockpit was no excuse. Good, accurate communication was an essential part of briefing the teams and if they had not sailed to that brief, it was probably the fault of the communicator. I had clearly failed to get across the guidelines set out by Stuart and as a result we gave away a few more precious miles.

Second then became third when *Jersey* picked up better winds to the north and at the end of our first sub-two-hundred-miles day our splendid lead began to look very tarnished.

After we'd all been feeling sorry for ourselves for twenty-four tortured hours, Nieves took the boat in hand. She was adamant that the self-pity had gone on far too long and was not helping us over the last nine hundred miles. She announced herself to be 'Anti-Negativity Surveillance Officer' and stuck up signs that warned of serious punishments for negative behaviour and comment. She perfected the nasal tones of a Civil Service jobsworth and lifted the whole tone of the boat with her well-observed giggling banter.

Nieves is the sort of person who sleeps with a smile on her face and her sunny, positive personality was exactly what was needed to dispel the gloom of the moment. The 'if onlys' continued to quietly rumble, but only when we were certain that she was not looking. It was a perceptive bit of man management and illustrated the rich and varied qualities on board. And, as if to prove the wisdom of our long-standing boat motto, her input had helped make *London* go faster again.

The seas were still tough and we knew that a blown kite, a snapped halyard or broken steering up ahead would be all that was needed to deliver the lead back into our lap.

A twelve-day crossing now actually looked realistic and as squalls started to build, the boat kit was fully tested once more. We pushed as hard as we dared and drove our spinnakers on through the days and nights, through sharp showers of rain, blustery gusts and the more reliable winds.

Trimming the giant sail was best done from the stays halfway along the deck and each crew member took it in turn to watch and call for adjustments. It was a lonely, remote position and at night the trimmer was left alone in the dark, hanging on to the stays for support as the sea creamed by. Up above the sail, the vivid white cloud of the Milky Way revealed itself and we could clearly see a large black nebula of dense matter, known as the Coal Sack, next to the Southern Cross.

Trimming away in the dark with no one to talk to gave time to take stock. Whatever happened, we were still in a podium position and our overall third place would remain intact. All in all, not too much to be disappointed about.

Except, except, except. Without Nieves's support, I stood in the darkness and cursed once again over our lost lead that could so easily have been avoided. It was deeply, deeply frustrating.

As the weekend of our arrival loomed, the wind and sea state picked up again and we agreed to use the stronger helms through the night. I took the wheel for a very physical hour and for the first time I came away panting for breath as the sweat cooled in the chill night air.

It had been a rewarding ride, though, and seventeen-knot surfs had been regularly achieved. As I went below, Ali took over and immediately picked up a nineteen-knot wave. A couple of minutes later and a loud twang signalled that our steering cables had also given up the unequal struggle against the intense forces acting on the rudder.

All hands roared up on deck as *London* pulled herself into wind. The heavyweight spinnaker went into a death-throes frenzy, struggling to break loose from the wind pressure, and five of us fought like a rugby pack to tame it. We were all clipped on with safety harnesses for the wild ride, which was just as well. Just when we thought the sail was under control, it would refill and attempt to take us flying over the rail.

When it was eventually down, the forestay had sliced neatly through one of the clews and the sail that had stood us in such good stead since leaving Portsmouth was no more. We had worked so hard to protect it in the tough conditions of the Indian Ocean and while five of the seven boats had already blown their kites out, we had looked after ours almost to the finish.

The damage was caused by the steering failure rather than by pushing things too hard and it was a bitter pill to swallow. The emergency tiller had been readied for just this situation and the crew had got it in place and were already making way again. As in Japan, the direct link to the rudder made it impossible for one person to helm and Jane, Ellie and Nieves were working as a team, making adjustments to port and starboard, via the two winches.

With just the mainsail up, *London* was still doing eleven knots, but as we got down to repair the steering, *Plymouth* crept up from behind, reducing her deficit to zero, and slipped past in the night.

Once again we wondered how the organisers would treat the new third-placed boat, which had taken on board a fleet spare. There we were, a direct competitor for the place, who had suffered and lost out from an identical failure but with no spare on board to solve the problem.

With no replacement cable, Stuart, Andy and I braced ourselves into the rolling, rocking, crashing black hole of a generator room and made a new system out of Spectra cord. It was an impossibly fiddly job and in the torch-light conditions we did well to complete it in a couple of hours. But we put the system back together only to find that the wheel had more movement to port than it did to starboard, so we had to start all over again.

The three of us had all been on the helm for most of the day and were well and truly knackered when the cable snapped. Now we passed spanners and pliers to each other like zombies and after another hour agreed that it was impossible to continue without sleep.

An hour and a half later we were back at it and eventually got the wheel fully functioning again as the boat continued to surf down the huge swells. The helm needed to be as gentle as possible with the wheel, but the rolling sea quickly stretched the cord and as we tried to race again, it slipped off the guiding rollers and *London* was limping once more.

For the fourth time Andy and I joined Stuart in the Black Hole of Calcutta and started again. This time, though, we were really happy with the repair and felt bold enough to pole out the headsail to cover the final fifty miles into Mauritius.

We had lost even our podium position and fourth seemed a desperately unfair result after doing so well to tame the Indian Ocean. And as we predicted, *Liverpool* had blown out her kite as she battled with *Jersey* for the win up ahead.

If our steering had lasted for just another twenty hours, we would have taken second place and won another vital point in the world series standings. So it was thick-skin time, and by the time Port Louis revealed itself on the eastern shores of Mauritius, our rich stream of philosophical acceptance was flowing once more.

'Jerusalem' played loud, our growing collection of podium pennants flew alongside the *Ffreefire* battle flag in the stiff breeze and *London* entered port. The mood on board was alive with excitement. It was mid-afternoon and as we closed in on the harbour wall I could see a large gaggle of spectators waving enthusiastically across the water.

Long before the small figures grew into recognisable faces, the sounds of greeting poured out towards us – cheers and whoops and screams of delight, with the loudest coming from three distinct and identifiable sources. As *London* slowed and the mooring line team prepared to step ashore, there were Anne, Holly and Mike. As we waved, so too did Ellie at her mum, Ali at his parents, Jane at hers, Nieves at hers and, from behind the wheel, Stu spotted Liz and Ben. All along the quay, like anxious parents awaiting the return of the bus from a school trip, our fan club of followers waited impatiently for the first hug.

And then none of the recent hardships mattered, because I was on the quayside with my family, immersed in one huge embrace. And as we hugged again, the tears fell in the warmest of hellos.

We were together once more and had a whole week to luxuriate in the sounds of each other's voices and relax in the warm and silent contentment of togetherness. Stuart had been adamant that I should be excused from all the boat duties and after he had also embraced Anne with a warm bear hug of greeting, I was hustled off *London* with a packed bag and pushed into the back of a taxi.

Not only was the family in full flow, so too was the driver. He chatted amiably away like a true taxi-driving pro and in the first five minutes we had an update on the political situation on the island, the tourism issues, the state of the roads and the potential of the sugar-cane harvest. He also talked about football, taking his eyes off the road for a moment to ask me about my favourite team.

In answer to his 'Who you like? What team do you support?' I began with a childlike response, assuming he would not have a clue who I was talking about.

'Well,' I said, trying not to sound too patronising, 'my team play in the capital city of England, which is called London. They are based in the west of the city at a big stadium called Stamford Bridge. That ground is located in an area called Chelsea, and my team take their name from the London borough.'

Before I could continue and fill him in with essential details like 'they wear blue shirts and blue shorts', he cut me short.

'Not having the greatest of seasons and I'm still not sure about Ranieri. Zola still has what it takes, though, and isn't it a shame that Wise is leaving?'

Stunned by this encyclopedic knowledge of the Premiership, I asked who he supported, half expecting the answer to be Port Louis United FC.

'Bolton.'

'Bolton?' Michael and I echoed incredulously.

'Yes, Bolton. I got my Sky dish fitted and they were the first team I saw play, so now I support them.'

As we drove on through the dense sugar-cane plantations and caught glimpses of the ocean, he continued with his *Match of the Day*-style assessment of the UK leagues. Passing through small towns, we saw sport shops festooned with replica shirts and inevitably Man U's red strip appeared to be a major favourite. It was eye-opening to discover that the game of Association Football offered such a massive shop window for the UK.

Half an hour later just the four of us were in Grande Baie, looking out over the gently lapping ocean from a coconut-framed balcony at the Merville Beach Hotel. There were clean beds, a bath with running hot and cold water, a loo that flushed without the need for constant pumping, clean towels, colour television, a bag full of duty free from Gatwick and, most important of all, a decent lock on the door.

Despite all the tourist attractions that the island offered, I wanted nothing more than to laze on a beach, recharge my batteries and listen to the five months' worth of news that poured forth from Holly and Michael. Mornings blended into afternoons, broken only by a dip in the pool, a dip in the sea, a light lunch and a sumptuous supper. The odd game of table tennis, a bit of a kick-about, another swim and another read of my book. It was a complete contrast with a normal family holiday, where the need to go and 'do something' kicked in every forty minutes or so.

Stu, Liz and Ben came and joined us a few days later and they too slotted into the gentle pace, happy to chat and potter. We were all eager to hold on to every moment of the week and not fritter it away in a series of tourist excursions invaded by hordes of package tourists fighting for the ice creams or the best seats in the shade.

Out beyond the reef, a fleet of small sailing dinghies were cracking back and forth over the water. Eager to impress the family with my sailing skills, I headed out to join them. My first capsize took just three minutes and after seven further duckings and several abortive attempts to return through the tricky reef, where awkward winds did their best to unseat me again, I beached the boat on the sand five hundred yards away. The shamefaced walk back to my giggling family was worth their airline ticket price alone.

Despite our best efforts to slow six days down, the planet revolved and the week flew by. I hired a car and after checking out of the wonderful hotel where the staff had looked after us so well, we headed off towards the airport.

With the flight departing in the evening, it still gave us a full day, but the melancholy mood was back. We all knew the signs, having gone through the goodbyes twice before, and it clearly wasn't getting any easier.

Down at the south of the island, we discovered a picture-postcard beach that had a good-looking hotel with a view over the surf.

'Don't go back to the boat yet – enjoy another couple of nights,' was Anne's suggestion, so we approached the security gate with its Checkpoint Charlie-style barrier. All the good hotels were surrounded by such security and as we went to walk past, heading for reception, a uniformed guard stopped us.

'Can I help?' he asked, looking me up and down with disdain. I was dressed in the gear that was now completely comfortable. Fading Clipper shorts, a ragged T-shirt and my much-prized and very faded Mount Gay sailing cap that proved I had competed in the San Fernando race.

When I started to explain that I simply wanted a room, he cut me short.

'Full up,' he said, standing in the middle of the drive to prevent any further progress.

Taken aback by his rudeness, I tried again but got the same short response.

'Full up. Please leave.'

After months of delightful dealings with a motley collection of the world's inhabitants, it was deeply disappointing and not the ideal exchange to put me in the best of moods. Especially as the clock was ticking slowly towards the departure lounge.

As we walked away, a driver from a line of taxis awaiting the more fortunate guests beckoned me over. Taxi drivers had always been generous companions and earlier in the week one of his colleagues had invited us to his house for a drink and some supper.

'You look for somewhere to stay?' he asked and, with the facts established, he told us to head back to our car and follow him. He led the way down past the beach, around a couple of corners and into the driveway of a smart house set back from the ocean. At the far end of the garden path he opened the front door and, like a beaming estate agent eager for commission, showed us around the home.

It transpired that his brother owned the place, but was conveniently away from the island. The driver assured me that it could be rented for the knock-down price of £15 per night and I had no idea if his sibling was aware of this handy little enterprise. But it was a perfect base, so I took it anyway. The offer of a deposit was waved away and before I had parted with any sort of payment, the keys to the door were entrusted to me.

We took a walk to the beach and returned for tea, staving off the moment when it would be time for the fifteen-minute drive to the airport. But every half-hour or so the sky roared loud as a jet departed, reminding us of what lay ahead.

A few hours later and I was standing under a star-filled sky. An almost full moon bathed the undulating fields of rustling, swaying, sugar-cane plantations. The constantly shifting stalks were alive to the breeze coming off the Indian Ocean, and despite the late hour, the air was still warm.

I stood in the darkness alongside several other dark shadows, their presence defined by the glowing embers of burning cigarettes. My hire car creaked and clicked as the engine cooled on the roadside verge and my fellow watchers leant on their rusting mopeds, a pop-riveted old Austin Cambridge and a hand-painted Morris Minor as we stared through the chain-link security fence.

Above the runway lay my precious Southern Cross and off to the south my own star sign of Scorpio curled its stinging tail through the heavens.

We didn't have long to wait. At the Sir Seewoosagur Ramgoolam International Airport (almost as catchy as JFK or LAX), taxiing out from the terminal stand was an unlikely short hop. It took just a couple of minutes before the British Airways 747 series 400 turned its lumbering form into wind, held itself on the brakes and the four massive Rolls-Royce jet engines started winding up.

The roar echoed across the grass and shook the baked red earth under our feet. We watched the flashing red lights, the nav lights on the wing tips, the line of cabin lights extending from first class back into club and then down to the world traveller section as this magnificent giant of the air sat vibrating and shaking at the end of the runway. The lights snaked back over the vast wing and on down to the lit-up red, white and blue tail fin. Somewhere in among the sparkling trail was a cargo so precious and I wondered if their faces were peering out into the darkness, trying to catch a final glimpse.

The brakes went off, the lights shimmered through the heat haze of thrust and this special aircraft picked up speed, carrying my wife and children away from me at twenty, seventy, one hundred and forty, one hundred and eighty knots down the thin strip of tarmac and off, up and away into the scudding cumulus.

The take-off was routine and the spectators, who had watched it all before and dreamt of one day having enough money to visit their red-stained holy grail called 'Manchester United', quickly disappeared into the night. I was left alone, watching, until the specks of light dwindled down to a single star and then vanished altogether into a distant cloud.

All that remained was the darkness, the rustling sugar canes and me, hand still aloft in a final, tear-strewn wave of farewell. The skies soothed my mood and I looked again at the familiar comforting shapes in the heavens that we gazed up at every night from the oceans of the world. I wondered if they could also be seen from the seats in row 37 of the Gatwick-bound jet and hoped that they communicated my suddenly heavy heart.

I had waited five long, challenging, difficult months before we could be a family again and no sooner were we united in tearful hugs on the quayside of Port Louis than I was waving an unseen hand into the night as the miles between us once again began to grow.

I drove back to my darkened house, locked myself in for the night and left the tea things untouched. The marks of lipstick and fingerprints were comfortingly fresh, and provided a last tenuous link to the family.

Surprisingly, I slept like the dead and was only woken by the insistent ring of a telephone. It was Anne calling from Bedfordshire to tell me that they were home safely. It was raining, the dog was fine and they were having a roast leg of lamb for Sunday lunch.

The world had shrunk overnight and eight thousand miles of oceans, deserts, mountain ranges, cities, religions and cultures between us had been reduced to a simple chat across the garden fence. Anne had just bought the Sunday papers, so I asked her to look in the sports section and tell me how Bolton had got on. Somewhere on the island, a waterside-home owner with his taxi in the drive would already know the answer.

15

CAPE CRUSADERS
MAURITIUS TO CAPE TOWN
06.06.01–22.06.01

For the first time, I was frightened silly.

As the Cape of Good Hope crept ever closer on our last night at sea, the wind started to get up and the sea grew in size. There was no moon to light the way and a thick bank of cloud meant that we were screaming along at fifteen knots in complete darkness. With no horizon to position the boat against, helming in the wild seas became a real challenge and with thirty knots of wind filling the kite (ten more than its limit) not getting driven up into wind was proving a real challenge.

Time after time I had my entire body weight hanging off the wheel, forcing the bow back on to its trimmed course and after half an hour shoulders, arms, wrists and fingers all ached from the exertion.

There was way too much sail for the conditions and while the foredeck team prepared for a drop, I struggled on as the wind grew in strength. The bow was getting whipped around and there was nothing I could do to stop it. For several agonising seconds the boat was driving me, rather than the other way round, and as sails flapped, sheets flogged and the spinnaker pole rattled itself silly, I feared for the safety of my colleagues up at the bow. If the pole snapped – perfectly possible given the punishment I was unintentionally giving it – then it would scythe over the deck and take out the crew like skittles in a bowling alley.

Time and again I fought the wild ride and time and again it beat me.

And then into the equation came a large container ship, right on our starboard bow.

I could see from the steaming lights that it was coming our way and the twenty to thirty degrees of course variation that my out-of-control steering was giving put us first one side of it and then the other. Stuart was shouting back to me to ensure it passed us down the starboard side, but such finesse was easier said than done. As I frantically fought to keep *London* on a more even course, I looked up and saw both the red and green navigation lights of the giant ship, which meant that it was heading straight for us.

I could hear its engine above the scream of the wind and the thrashing sails. Its bow wave, lit by bright sodium deck lights, revealed the tormented sea spuming over its bow. It remained pointing straight at us and I fought the wheel with a new-found frenzied energy.

Stuart continued to shout from the foredeck, the sails continued to thrash and the bow bucked and reared like an untamed stallion. With a distance of less than half a mile now separating the two boats, I was finally able to get things on more of an even keel and we watched as the giant steel bow sliced past through the waves. It had never varied from its course and I wondered if we had been even noticed by the bored watch keeper, half asleep in his warm, dry bridge.

It had been horribly close and for the first time in eight months I had experienced one of those moments when the sea proves that it is way mightier and way stronger than man's feeble efforts to tame it.

Despite Stuart's reassurances that I had done a decent job in the conditions, I sat exhausted and dejected at the end of the watch. The crew at the bow had come under risk, we had narrowly avoided a collision and the boat had driven me for several out-of-control moments.

Sleep, when it came to me in my sopping-wet sleeping bag, was confused and unpleasant, and when we woke and prepared to do battle with the three oceans that swirl together off the Cape of Good Hope just three damp, tossing and turning hours later, I felt unprepared and lacking in confidence for the task ahead.

The Southern Ocean kicked up from Antarctica and smashed into the South Atlantic driving in from the west, which in turn entwined itself around the Indian Ocean driving smartly in from the east. With the dawn came a grey, dank light as a heavy sea spray of mist concealed both the sun and the fabled headland.

The ocean surface was alive with streaming, breaking, spume-filled wave crests that rode in on top of a giant swell and a wind in excess of forty knots howled its way through the rigging. The spinnaker had been replaced with a much more controllable poled-out headsail. Despite the breeze, we selected the biggest one in our wardrobe and hung on as it hurled us ever closer to the African coast.

Astern of *London*, the giant surfs picked up our hull and set us off on a crazy ride.

As the huge wave picked up the stern, the bow pointed down at an ever steeper angle. The hull teetered on the brink of the precipice, like a roller coaster at the top of its slow climb and then started a suicidal plunge downwards. Thirty tons of boat weight helped the acceleration, as did the hard-blowing wind in the sails.

The trick on the helm was to pick up the wave and surf it. As soon as the boat was being carried, the driver concentrated on keeping the balance straight and then hung on to enjoy the wild ride.

As the boat speed increased, the hull started to hum and vibrate madly as *London* began to tramp through the water. Astern, it looked like we were in a Formula 1 powerboat and as twenty knots came and went the ride seemed destined to end in disaster. Finally, though, the wave moved on, but before the helm could gather his thoughts another towering monster was tapping at our stern and the whole crazy process started all over again.

It was hairy, scary but huge fun and the confidence-denting insecurities of the night were soon replaced by an intense elation, fuelled by the energy all around us. Stuart and I took turns at the wheel and we were romping towards the finish, going around one of the most dangerous points on earth. This was our Everest and we were doing it on the sort of day that could never be described as 'easy' or 'lucky'.

I should have known better.

We gybed in the wild seas and as the mainsail slammed on to the other tack, a thick steel U-bolt that held the main sheet block in place snapped clean in two. It meant that the sail and the boom were now being kept in check by just one fragile line. Because of that, it was impossible to sheet the sail in to sort out the problem, but with the boom potentially out of control, the problem had to be fixed and fixed fast.

The only solution was to keep everything exactly as it was and take the risk of sending someone out along the thick aluminium spar in order to attach a jury rig to its end.

In the rolling sea, the boom was constantly dipping deep into the waves and having someone on the end of it was a huge risk. The predicament, when it came right down to it, was not really a predicament at all. Quite simply, the precarious high-wire act was our only solution.

Stuart was adamant that he should attempt the hazardous job, although, typically, Anna was quick to volunteer. Preparing himself by the mast, he asked me to take the wheel, adding that there could be no repeat of the previous night's loss of control. Allowing the boat to roll to the point where the boom dipped deep meant that he would be plucked off and swept away into the wild, foaming surface. Although he had a safety line, getting him back on board would be hazardous and very probably damaging. And that was assuming the safety line held in the fast-flowing waters roaring past.

Our skipper gave the thumbs up and began the cautious crawl away from the safety of the hull, as he edged out along the broad Clipper Ventures-branded spar, set ninety degrees to the mast. Once he had started the journey, I whispered urgent words to Ali and Alan and had them standing by the emergency dan buoy and the man-overboard button, just in case the worst happened. I decided not to tell Stuart of my plans as I reckoned he had quite enough on his plate already.

For the next ten minutes my mind, heart and soul focused on every nuance, every shift, every little kick and spin of the ocean as I concentrated like never before to give the smoothest possible ride. Out of the corner of my eye, I could see Stu attaching the Spectra cords that would give us control over the mainsail, and I could sense the uneasy shifting from Ali as his fingers closed around the dan-buoy fittings.

And all the while, the vast waves rolled in from behind and again and again the roller coaster hurled itself over the precipice and the boat speed rocketed up into the twenties, irrespective of the fragile repair taking place.

Eventually the job was done and Stuart eased himself back along the boom and down to the relative safety of the deck. He looked back down the boat and as our wide eyes met, he gave a simple thumbs up of thanks.

I have to confess that I was glad to be wearing dark glasses. My eyes stung with sharp pinpricks as the barely concealed emotion showed signs of bursting forth. I managed a single nod in return to the thumb and was humbled for the second time in a few hours.

The levels of trust and faith in such moments demonstrated an exceptional bond. All of the lives on board were well and truly in the hands of our crew mates, time after time. The bond between those involved in such moments had an incredible intensity and it is little wonder that the experience was way in excess of anything that a team of corporate managers on a team-building course will ever come close to discovering.

And so we roared on. The brooding mist lifted a little and there in the gloom was the fabled Cape. What a moment of intense achievement, and as Africa drew closer and the sun started to break through, we left the intensity of our experience just beyond the horizon and prepared to be part of a shore-based life once more.

An hour later, as Table Mountain soared above us, we could hear police sirens, were able to look into homes along Camp's Bay, could identify cars driving along the coast road and watched as the high-rises of Cape Town grew in size. The secret world back at the wave-strewn Cape was ours and while we waved at the crowds and got dressed in our Clipper uniform to play the corporate game, we were all still lost in an intense twenty-four hours of raw sailing adventure that will, quite simply, live with each of us for ever.

It frightened me silly. Yet at the same time I was inspired by and in love with every second of it.

We knew what we were in for right from the start, though, when Stuart gave us the bleakest of views at our pre-race briefing some fifteen days before.

If you were watching a movie, at this point the sound would waver and the picture would start to ripple as we swirl back in time. As the ripples settle and the picture clears, the sound man fades up the dialogue again.

The viewer now sees that the Cape has disappeared and been replaced by an open-air pizza restaurant on a boardwalk somewhere. The director of the movie, inspired by the use of such helpful titles as 'London, England' or 'Paris, France' over images of Big Ben and red buses or the Eiffel Tower and chaps in stripy jumpers, might well have added 'Port Louis, Mauritius' and a bit of Cajun or sitar music to help set the scene.

As the sound fades up, Stuart's voice can be heard telling his startled crew about the dangers they are about to face. And he pulls no punches.

We were setting off on the final part of the Indian Ocean and could expect the first few days to be heady trade-wind blasts. As we closed in on Madagascar all the experts from the Admiralty pilot books, previous racers, Clipper chairman Sir Robin Knox Johnston – they all said keep well clear. Electrical storms, wild, confused seas, currents and counter-currents said, 'Bad place to go.' The books suggested we should be at least 150 miles south of the island's southern tip and that was just what we intended to do.

No sooner had Madagascar been dealt with than we would be heading towards the fast-streaming Agulhas current, which runs south parallel to the African coast. This we could use as an express travelator to speed up the journey.

The only problem is that down in the Southern Ocean, vicious lows were streaming up from Antarctica, bringing with them winds of seventy to eighty knots. When the wind blowing north hits the fast current flowing south, the seas erupt into the most dangerous place to sail in the world.

The freak wave is a common occurrence and hundred-foot-high breaking surfs would pulverise our boat in seconds. Supertankers break their backs in such seas and the coast is littered with wrecks of those unfortunate enough to get caught out.

Because of the risks involved, the game plan was to cross the current at its narrowest and get inland of it. We would monitor the weather by the on-board fax system five times a day and when certain that no low was coming, we would dip out into the current and use it to our advantage. If the blow got too much, there were numerous bays along the coast and all the experts who had written about this stretch of water said, 'Seek shelter at the first opportunity.'

Normally one would do the exact opposite and stay far out to sea in order to have safety from lots of sea room. Doing that off Africa would mean having to cross over the Agulhas current in order to reach land and the further south a boat journeyed, the wider the band it would have to cross. There was no way we were going to risk crossing the fast-flowing current at its widest, only to get caught out by a rapidly moving low-pressure system. As Stuart said in his brief, seamanship would be his number-one priority and if staying safe meant we came last, then so be it. As it turned out, he was pretty close to the mark.

The fleet set off under the eyes of the President of Mauritius, who started the race from a coastguard cutter in the bay just off Port Louis. As soon as he was safely onshore and heading back to his palace, the show start was halted and three boats returned to port. Once again mechanical difficulties were causing problems and we had to have more work done on our generator before we could depart properly. Our return to shore was a great relief to the two local engineers, though. They had continued to work on board as we went through the charade of the presidential 'start' and didn't really fancy a trip to South Africa.

In the end the work was still not fully completed and we were sent off to sea with a temporary repair which the engineers assured us would be all right. It failed within the first twenty-four hours and with no generator, we had no water maker. On our first night at sea, water went on to an immediate ration and the team of oil-stained spanner wielders were roundly cursed.

Stuart was justifiably furious and decided then and there that such compromises would never happen again. In future he would refuse to leave port unless completely happy, and if that caused a problem for the organisers, then he would walk away. As a crew, we were in complete agreement.

The suggestion that the first few days would offer gentle spinnaker runs was banished on the first night. The wind grew in strength, peaking at around fifty knots. And to make matters worse, it was on the nose, forcing us to beat hard into it. Poor John Williams and Andy Harris – our two new joiners, known to one and all as 'Fester' and 'Doris' – were quickly heaving into buckets as the boat ran on into the night.

We went down through the wardrobe of sails, until the small No. 3 Yankee and bright-orange storm staysail flew at the bow and the main powered us along under three reefs. *London* still heeled way over, though, and vast quantities of sea water rattled over the downwind rail and threatened to spill into the cockpit.

As the island of Réunion appeared, with its spectacular nine-thousand-foot mountain, we found ourselves in second position and rolling along pretty well – despite the conditions.

My usual position at the helm during sail changes was adapted and I became a member of the foredeck crew for a few hours. We had two headsail changes to make with a deck heeled over at forty degrees, and with the bow rising and plunging into the waves, it would be a long and very physical job.

Stuart watched, grinning and dry, from my usual position at the wheel as we started on the task. Wave after wave slammed in, bursting over us and within seconds the three of us were completely soaked. Shouted conversations were interspersed with the spitting out of salt water, and the sails flogged and slapped as we manhandled them on the deck.

Anna was the first to get badly caught out by a wave. A breaking wall of water smashed in and as it broke down the hull, it whipped away her feet. She was left helpless and struggling on the downwind deck with only the safety rail and her harness preventing her from going overboard. As she struggled to get up, another wave burst on top of her and knocked her flat once more.

A new crew member and I managed to scramble to her and eventually pulled our dripping colleague back to the relative safety of the upwind side. Already Perry Cleveland Peck, a writer from *The Times*, was proving a valuable new member of the team.

And then it was my turn. As we packed the downed sail into its bag, another huge wave whipped me off my feet and in a trice, I, like Anna, became a floating passenger being swept away down the deck.

My face was covered by the confusion of breaking waves and all I could see was swirling water and snatches of sky. I was aware of the safety harness pulling me up short and being thankful that it held. Like Anna, I was pinned on my back and two more waves immersed me completely before I was able to get upright again.

The job was eventually done but it had taken us a knackering one and a half hours. We returned to the cockpit soaked through and completely spent, to sit slumped and panting, like the losing crew in the Boat Race.

As Madagascar came closer, we went off to the south as planned and watched with amazement as the rest of the fleet flew in the face of all the experts and closed right up on the coastline of the island. It appeared that some boats were prepared to win at all costs.

And win they did. We sat in an unforecast area of high pressure with absolutely no wind and the sea a millpond calm just twenty-four hours after its huge confusion, while the rest of the fleet made stunning progress in the supposed no-go area.

In twelve hours we had travelled just seven miles and with the rest of the fleet banging in distances of ninety miles-plus, we were instantly on the back foot. At each radio sched the African coast came slowly closer and the boats up ahead put themselves right into the heart of the Agulhas current, gaining even greater distances.

We were aware of the dangers ahead, which the sky confirmed with an ominous warning. Black, gloomy yellow and greenish swirling clouds stretched across the horizon and, behind them, lightning flashed. As the sun was snuffed out, the scene became an all-pervading grey and in the lowering light the blinding distant blue sheets of electricity backlit an oppressive cloak of gloom. As the rumble of thunder reached us, sharp gusts rattled into the sails and *London* trembled from the impact. It looked like we were sailing inexorably towards the gates of hell.

Stuart called me to the nav desk. Opened out in front of him was the chart for the African coast and he had marked it up with all the dangers, all the safe havens, all the offshore and onshore currents and all the relevant radio stations that we might need along the way. He wanted to talk it through with me just in case the boat was caught out in one of the infamous huge storms and he was washed over the side.

If we were unable to find him in the chaos, it would be disastrous to sail on into those highly dangerous waters without having a full and thorough understanding of how to navigate to the safety of dry land. And while that was a chilling thought, it spoke volumes for Stuart's attention to detail and thoroughness in planning for the safety of survivors on board.

To make the moment more bleak, Ellie, who had been looking over our shoulders, asked what would happen if we both went overboard. My safety line became a permanent attachment to the deck, even when the weather eased.

After ten days at sea we were still playing catch-up and languished many miles behind down in eighth place. The first sight of land appeared and a stampede on deck caught the first views of Africa. No matter how many miles we had sailed, the sight of the first landfall, particularly when it was that of a new continent, never failed to thrill. Now we were inside the Agulhas current and preparing to dip into it and go for an express-train ride, the barometer started to drop as a huge low approached.

We were back, once again, to the smallest sail wardrobe and as the storm hit with a vicious ferocity, *London* beat slowly up the coast, making around three miles per tack towards our destination. The boats up ahead were worse off and many had either hove to or were simply holding station in the storm.

Their disregard for the experts' advice was now starting to hurt them and both *Liverpool* and *Portsmouth* reported extensive damage as they rode out the huge blow. And as they struggled, so we crept slowly up towards the sixth- and seventh-placed boats until we were in striking distance of at last making up a place.

Conditions were foul. The wind and the waves were doing the gravel-hurling routine again and in the cold South African winter we were adding more and more layers to keep warm. Down below, trying to keep upright was almost impossible, and during a watch change the metal clasp of someone's safety harness slipped from their hands and struck Ellie a blow on the head. She went down as if hit by Mike Tyson.

For half an hour she drifted in and out of consciousness and we readied ourselves to make an emergency dash into Port Elizabeth. Ellie, the ex-nurse, was the one we turned to for advice on injuries and as she was still out for the count, Stuart turned instead to Tim, a retired GP, on board *Plymouth*.

We relayed our medical observations over the SSB radio and in another wildly bucking clipper Tim listened carefully to the words. His response was encouraging and it seemed that we were safe to continue on to Cape Town. The wild night eventually blew itself out and as dawn arrived we entered another period of light wind, drifting off Africa's southernmost point of Cape Agulhas. And to complete a beautiful start to the day, Ellie was up, smiling ruefully and making more sense than she had for several months.

The forecast suggested several more days of no wind and at the next radio sched a number of the boats who had been badly caught out by the storm urged that a message should be sent to Clipper to end the race immediately. Down in the Southern Ocean, another huge low was building and if motoring began immediately we would make it to Cape Town before getting caught out.

Now the boats who had suffered damage in the last storm wanted to cut and run. *London*, with all our kit intact, were less than happy with the idea. If our competitors were now unseaworthy, then they should retire from the race, make for a safe haven as quickly as possible and accept the loss of championship points as a result. It was a bit like Schumacher having a problem ten laps from the end of a grand prix and then asking the organisers to end the race early, so he still might win. Ridiculous.

Fortunately, back at Clipper HQ, Sir Robin agreed and so we raced on and into the storm described earlier.

As that mad, final, scary night ran its course, we slipped past *Leeds* half a mile off our starboard beam, and with the extra point gained from coming seventh, just held on to our overall third place.

The drama had a final twist, though. As Stuart was doing his high-wire act out on the boom, *Leeds*'s steering failed and our place looked secure. Imagine the frustration then, when we hit a massive wind hole a few hundred yards off Camp's Bay and sat drifting just a mile from the finish. As we sat going nowhere, our repaired rival appeared over the horizon and closed in, until she too hit the wind hole.

The two boats sat a few hundred yards apart and after all that we had been through it seemed that fate was going to deal us a final unfair and twisted hand. In the end we just hung on and *London* crossed the line, motored towards the marina and tied up under the shadow of Table Mountain.

Surrounded by the warm hospitality of the Royal Cape Yacht Club, the crew could not settle. Despite our being on dry land with a beer and a plate of good food, our thoughts were still out in the wildness of the previous night, replaying and reliving the experiences in our heads.

At some point after 01.00 I sat on the carpeted floor, my back resting on the flower-patterned wall next to Stuart as we shared our deepest thoughts and emotions on the last twenty-four hours. He told me that his trip out to the end of the boom had relied implicitly on the helm keeping things balanced and the fact that we were in Cape Town, safe and secure, confirmed his extraordinary level of trust.

The faith he had shown was humbling. Without being melodramatic, he had quite literally handed over his life to my care for ten precious minutes. In turn I had looked after it – not only for him, but also for Liz and Ben – and the emotional bond that it created was profound. I confessed about preparing the team for an imminent man-overboard moment, telling him that I had decided not to share the decision for fear of causing undue alarm. Stu smiled, responding that he had thought about briefing for that too but already knew that, as a crew, we would put things in hand.

And then we talked it all through again and then again, reliving every tiny detail in order to exhaust the subject and allow us to move on to the next challenge. It was getting on for 02.30 before the repeatedly hugging mutual admiration society finally retired to bed.

After the tough, eye-opening sail and the adrenalin rush that it produced, I suppose it was no surprise that my body went into shutdown once the excitement was over and we settled in for a few days on a South African shore.

The moment I hit dry land with an immune system that was as flat as a dead battery, I caught a cold, with a vicious sore throat and racking cough. While my mates headed off to Table Mountain and Stellenbosch, I locked myself away in the Cullinan, a brand-new hotel in the Las Vegas mould, which rose proudly out of a dreary suburb. I looked out over an uninspiring dual carriageway towards the docks and away across the water past the impressive Waterfront shopping mall, to Robben Island – Mandela's place of imprisonment for so many years.

A day of housekeeping, plus a haircut and trips to the post office and postcard shops, followed on from working on the boat and, with a major victualling session also planned, my days in South Africa were well and truly tagged. But help was at hand and the welcome sight of James and Cath Landale joining in was greatly appreciated. They had won a holiday to Cape Town and were adamant that the bulk of it would be spent on board their respective special boats, sleeves rolled up and hands deep in the bilges.

Several crew members were in the wars after the tough seas we had experienced around the Cape. While Ellie was fine, another member lay in a hospital bed as a doctor gingerly inspected her back. Bella Abrahams appeared to slip down the companionway steps in the storm and aggravated an old injury. Ashore, the pain in her spine grew worse and the experts were worried by what they saw. In the end she had to leave and needed several days of further treatment in South Africa before being allowed to fly home. She was as devastated as her future husband, on board *Jersey*.

A crew member from *Liverpool* underwent surgery to wire up a shattered eye socket, a round-the-world crew member from *Glasgow* headed for home to marry his fiancé and Perry Cleveland Peck, who had proved such a good team member for *London*, was drafted into *Glasgow* to replace him.

The clipper fleet were also in the wars as their mileage continued to bring an ever-growing list of mechanical problems. Major changes to the fuel system for both the generator and engine were planned after *Bristol* found that a piston on their main engine was about to give up the ghost. Contaminated fuel was deemed to be the cause.

After being sent off to the start of our previous races with repair work that was, at best, unreliable, Stuart was adamant that *London* would not leave until he was fully satisfied that the kit could survive the rigours of a long ocean passage.

He had our full support and the fleet eventually delayed leaving by twenty-four hours as engineers worked through the night to complete the long list of modifications. Even so, both our generator and engine refused to run cleanly, and while the rest of the fleet headed out for the start, we had two Cape Town engineers emulating their Mauritian colleagues by working frantically to get the jobs signed off.

In the end we hoisted the mainsail in the marina, motored out with the engineers on board and dropped them off on to a pursuing launch as the ten-minute gun went. There was no time to evaluate sail selection, so we stuck up what seemed right and, without the opportunity to time runs to the line, sat ourselves in the middle of the pack and waited for the start gun to fire.

16

SENNA-SATIONAL
FROM CAPE TOWN TO SALVADOR
01.07.01–22.07.01

As usual for Clipper starts, the wind was horribly light and the unleashed energy was more a slopping drift. We crossed the line in second place, though, and pointed the bow north for the long slog up towards where the trade winds blew. A big surf was rolling into the shore of Robben Island and behind us Table Mountain stood majestic against a crisp, clear, sharp blue winter sky.

My watch went straight back into their familiar routine and as we headed into the afternoon I still felt dreadful and was not the only one who was knackered. The five of us sat in energyless, slumped heaps, struggling to get the motivation to race again.

Very strong sweet coffee with Mars bars all round ensured the energy levels perked up a little and my team knuckled down to maintain our good start.

As night fell and a bright full moon lit the distant mountain crags of the Twelve Apostles, we slipped along in the lightest of breezes and watched the water for any sign of more consistent winds. The watching paid off and we were ready to catch a big wind shift with the right sail already in place, making five easy miles on a less alert *Bristol*, a few miles off our port quarter.

The wind grew in strength and while the gentle trade winds beckoned, we were still firmly in the clutches of the Cape and the big winter storms that rush up from Antarctica. The blow continued to revolve until we were beating into wind and, with thirty-five knots pushing us headlong into bow-smashing waves, two reefs in the mainsail and the small No. 3 headsail drove us on through the South Atlantic.

The conditions were just what the boat didn't need and the crew members who regularly suffered from seasickness were soon barfing away into buckets and dragging their spinning, turmoiled bodies into the sanctuary of a bunk. My cough showed no sign of letting up and suspicious diesel fumes seeping up into the cockpit from the generator room had me erupting in phlegm-rattling, spitting, wheezing, smoker-style explosions through the night.

If the fumes were bad in the cockpit, they were all-pervading down below and the off watch eventually succumbed, with crew members queuing to throw up in the heads. Stuart was particularly badly hit and if my cough sounded awful, his sounded distinctly terminal.

I had a quick look in the generator room, as some worrying knocks were coming from the steering, and nearly passed out from the strength of the fumes. The bilge was awash with a mixture of diesel and sea water and I staggered out, eyes smarting, to turn on the pump and get the bilge to shift the content into the ocean.

It was clear that the modifications carried out in Cape Town had caused the problem but it was impossible to identify where the leak was coming from. The new system had all worked wonderfully in the flat calm of the marina, but with the boat now on its side and rising and falling to boot, flaws in the design were immediately found.

I reported our problem at the 03.00 radio sched and three other boats confirmed that they were also experiencing difficulties. It seemed that there were several things wrong with the installation and we would have to set to and rectify the work as soon as the weather calmed.

Everyone was unhappy with the news. Stuart's role should have been navigator and strategist, but for the previous few legs he been forced to spend more time wielding spanners. As a result, the boat was not being as competitive as it should be while the fixing continued. But even that was going to be impossible for a few days, as he lay in his bunk sweating through the cold that I had struggled through onshore.

I looked after things as best I could above deck while the amazing Ali Baxter started to try to isolate the leak. For hour after hour he sat wedged against the generator in the dark, airless, cramped, rocking, fume-filled room and tinkered away, clearing up the mess. We had to make repeated checks to ensure that he had not passed out from the unhealthy air, and at dawn he emerged exhausted from a filthy, unpleasant, dangerous and sick-making time in a space akin to the foulest of prison cells. Once again the level of selfless commitment was astonishing, but Ali brushed off the universal praise with a wave of the hand.

With the dawn came a squadron of albatross – ten in all – that wheeled and spun in ever-closer circles around the boat. They passed by low and fast, often coming to within a couple of feet of where we sat, allowing us to look deep into their huge, black, beady eyes. They are the most beautiful, inspirational birds and I could watch them soaring the waves with millimetric precision for hours and hours.

The smell of frying bacon meant that Nieves and Ellie had risen to the mother-watch challenge and were doing their bit to lift spirits. When the galley plunged into the wave troughs with a sharp smack that sent everyone flying, the easy option of a bowl of cereal was tempting. But there they were, breathing in the fuel fumes, frying pan wedged into place, eggs spitting in the fat, and producing rolls to remember. The breakfast moment built on Ali's exceptional gift to the boat and the mood on board improved by a couple of notches.

Stuart missed out on the feast, though, confined to his bunk apart from hurried trips to the heads in order to be sick yet again. A boat full of fumes, faulty kit, half the crew laid low by seasickness, more crew suffering from colds and a skipper who was unable to move from his cabin was not the dream start we had been looking for.

Ali and I ran our individual watches, managed the boat between us and made calls on sail choice, wind angles and route, with Stuart giving an occasional croak of approval from his sick bed. The cold winter wind continued to pound in on the nose and meant that the warm-layer wardrobe was plundered once more. Thermals, fleecy mid-layers, foul-weather kit, hats, scarves and gloves were all pressed into service on this run up to the tropics and sea boots stayed permanently wet for day after day.

We were running with the pack, though, and a steady fourth place in the middle of the fleet was as good as it was likely to get, given the state of the crew and the boat. After a couple of days it was my turn to fade, and when Stuart made his first visit to the cockpit, he caught me in mid-cough.

I was sent to bed straight away, apparently looking 'effing dreadful', and despite an attempt at protest, it was where I wanted to be. I slumped on to my bunk and, still dressed in thermals, slipped into a fleece sleeping-bag liner, added the sleeping bag, piled a damp duvet on top and tied my lee cloth up tight.

In a sweaty haze, I was vaguely aware of the sea getting rougher as the wind increased and half heard torrential rain hammering on the coach-house roof. And then it all slipped away and I fell into a deep, deep sleep that gripped me for hour after hour. Sail changes were made and I was oblivious to them. Meals came and went and I knew nothing of them. Watches changed and changed again as Anna took over the reins and I missed it all.

For twenty hours my knackered body demanded shutdown in order to repair its exhaustion. Unbeknown to me, Ellie had gone back to her old career and in between working the boat she played the part of nursie again, quietly checking in on me at regular intervals. When I did eventually wake, it was to a gentle shaking from not her but James Bedford-Russell.

'Can you manage to do mother watch today?' he asked. 'Ellie was due to do it but has caught whatever you've got.'

In an 'out of body' dizzy haze, I stumbled into the galley and set to on lunch as the cold weather and high winds continued to stretch us. With lots of fresh vegetables on board, I added a whole stream of ingredients to boiling water and pretty soon had an impressive pan of vegetable broth simmering away. In went onions, peppercorns, garlic, a dash of Lee & Perrins, a bit of tabasco, a spoonful or two of mustard powder, some broken-up spaghetti, potatoes, leeks, celery, carrots – a bit of anything and everything from the array in front of me and as it all blended together the smell was terrific.

It tasted pretty good too, and a large second helping fuelled us up as we pounded through the day. Mashed potato with mustard, parmesan, garlic, olive oil and melting pools of butter featured in my dinner menu as comfort eating was clearly a popular route for the damp souls up on deck.

I looked in on Ellie, now flat out in her bunk, but I didn't have the medical training to do anything other than wipe a fevered brow. And what's more, the uniform looked far better on her.

At the end of the impromptu cooking session, I too went back to bed and slept for another fourteen hours. Even as a student, I never slept so much, and it was a strange experience to go through. Despite the rest, I still felt totally spaced out, with legs like lumps of lead and Stuart confirmed that he had felt exactly the same.

Dolphins know when they are needed and the wild sea became alive with maybe two hundred of them. They burst from the waves and the breaking rollers were crammed full of bodies as they became the crests and the wave faces, muscling out the sea and tumbling over each other so they could have more space.

They rode and leapt and swooped and dived all around us for several minutes before disappearing as quickly as they had arrived. They were clearly on a major journey to somewhere and this was no time to stop and play. It had been an extraordinary sight, though, and the boat buzzed from the moment of restorative magic that they brought.

Vicious squalls still dominated the horizon, although the distinctive 'cloud streets' of long bands of cumulus associated with trade winds suggested that the more consistent breezes were near. But there was no sign of the tropics and although a feeble sun shone, there was little heat to be had from it.

With the breezes came more consistent daily runs and our first two-hundred-mile day started to look realistic. The mood on board was still flat, though, and we sat and stewed as yet another race and another month at sea took shape. It began to feel a little too much like a chore and all the wide-eyed freshness experienced when we first sailed the Atlantic was replaced by a leaden weariness. Everyone felt it and at that particular low moment the end of the race could not have come soon enough for one or two individuals.

The pessimist would observe that we were back to where we had started. Routine constrained us all, and the only difference from acting like robots on the commuter special was that our current duties went on all day and all night. We got up, went to work, had a break, went to work again, struggled with bad news, had a sleep, dealt with major problems, minor problems, irritations and politics in exactly the same way as in the onshore life we had rejected.

It was a sound reminder that there's no such thing as escaping to Utopia. Wherever one heads, the bad times will always share an equal status with the good. And all of the good that had fuelled us for so long could only be ultimately valued as long as we had bad times to compare it against. The two forces balanced out – ying and yang, black and white, high and low. But with that understood and accepted, we knew that if the bad times were currently clinging like a limpet, good times were surely just round the corner. And as if to prove the point, when the wind kicked in again from the beam, we were into a big, vivid, speedy, adrenalin-surging, breaking-free-from-the-chains period of high-speed surfing. Fuelled by the simple reward of progress, the smiles returned.

It was tough, though, and very physical, but to keep the mind focused we started turning the screw a little on our rivals. Conditions were such that Ali, Andy, Stuart and I went into a helming roster with one hour at the wheel followed by three of rest and we ran through a wild moonlit night taking advantage of the huge following seas rearing up in our wake.

Sleep was still coming very easily to me, despite falling into my bunk fully kitted up in foul-weather gear and life jacket. Once the aching muscles found a position that was half comfortable, I was out like a light for two hours, fifty-five minutes before someone was shaking me awake. Five minutes later I was at the helm, screaming along on a knife edge of surf, spinning the wheel this way and that, reading the waves through my feet and singing out the speeds from the instrument panel as the hull started to race wildly through the water. And as I was doing it a nugget of sleep was wiped from eyes still getting accustomed to the dark.

As the nine-hundred-mile mark came and went, the hard work proved worthwhile and we closed right in on *Jersey*, up ahead in third place. As the day dawned, the wind increased some more and with thirty-five knots blowing into the kite, we stood a good chance of doing it some serious damage. Down it came and up went the No. 1, poled out as the wind came almost directly astern. This gave us similar speeds to the spinnaker, but it was a much more easily managed package that allowed everyone to helm and develop their surfing skills. It also protected our power source, which, with two more weeks to go, was prudent sail management.

Such moments of de-tuning are a recognised part of a good skipper's strategy. Have a bit of a breather, get everyone involved, run at ninety per cent for a day and let the much-jaded batteries recharge and take time to re-evaluate our plan.

Like the North Atlantic, the South is dominated by a huge weather system, named, with great originality, the South Atlantic High. In the southern hemisphere, winds from an anti-cyclone spin out anticlockwise and the best breezes would be several hundred miles north of the high's centre.

That was where we were heading and as other boats pointed straight towards South America and took advantage of the early breeze, we continued north, losing miles to *Portsmouth*, *Plymouth* and *Bristol*, who had all chosen the direct route.

Portsmouth were positively romping away and built up a

worrying lead of over a hundred miles to our fourth place. Joining us on the northern-route strategy were *Jersey*, *Liverpool* and *Glasgow* and for several days we were all in sight of each other as the latitudes reduced in number and the longitude counted down towards the Greenwich Meridian.

If we wanted a good result, the weather would have to be kind to us. And with our track record for finding wind holes or picking the exact moment when the weather turned against all the forecasts, trends and history books, we were starting to worry if our chosen route was the right one.

With the championship placings so tight between third and sixth, we could easily tumble down the rankings to our lowest position since the start of the race. As *Plymouth* sped along in *Portsmouth*'s wake, it looked as if there was an uncomfortably good chance of that happening.

Friday night came around and as the sun set, first Mars, then the Southern Cross and then Scorpio appeared against the dark-blue sky. It was 19.30 and with another fifteen degrees traversed, time to change the clocks on board by another hour. Doing so put us back on the same time as the UK. It was warming to think of family and friends going through their routine at exactly the same time as us as we breakfasted 'together', worked through the day 'together' and shared our dreams.

And while we sat in the chilly cockpit looking up at the starry winter sky, I thought of England at the end of a summer day. The sun would still be up and several hours' more daylight would bathe the countryside in a warm twilight glow. Birds would still be singing and the fields of wheat and corn would colour the vista from the back of the house as far as the eye could see.

In my imagination, it was the sort of evening to take the dog for a walk across the fields towards the village of Northill and sit in the dragonfly-filled garden of the Crown, looking at the brightly coloured hanging baskets and enjoying a pint of Abbott.

Oh! To be in England and is there honey still for tea?

In such a poetic, nostalgic haze, I turned on the SSB radio set the following day and managed to pick up a weak signal from the BBC World Service. It was the weekend of the Wimbledon Finals and I wanted to try to catch a small spark of the idyllic summer I imagined I was missing. At five o'clock in the afternoon, the crackling voice of a reporter was describing the covers coming off for the first time that day after rain had heavily interrupted the playing schedule. My idyll was shattered but it was equally deeply reassuring to find that nothing at home had changed at all.

We continued north and at each sched lost more and more miles to not only the leader but every other boat as well. Now *London* and *Glasgow* resided in joint-last place and the mood on board slumped again. I was still very tired and missed a watch to try to shake the malaise once and for all. I slept for another eight hours and, with the naps taken between earlier watches, spent another fourteen hours in total unconscious. It was all very odd and very unsatisfying.

A couple of days after we logged into the GMT time zone, the moment came when the GPS position slipped over from reading eastings to westings and on 8 July, at fifty-four minutes and thirty-two seconds after midday, we passed the mark at Greenwich, four thousand four hundred and thirty-four miles to the south. The Namibia Abyssal Plain lay immediately south, the Angola basin to the north, to the east lay the Mid Atlantic Ridge and the nearest coast was Namibia, eight hundred and three miles away to the east.

The next time I crossed the line in this direction would be on the M25 heading for home. I reckoned that Hoddesdon was about the correct spot and delightful though the Hertfordshire town is, it could never be quite as uplifting as making the transit on latitude 023° 34.715', one thousand seven hundred miles south of Ghana.

A day later the longitude relayed that we were now due south of Portsmouth and I sent a message to the Clipper office, reporting that we had now officially circumnavigated the planet. It was an amazing realisation as I looked at the inflatable globe on board and spun it slowly all the way around. We had sailed away to the furthest point possible, crossed the International Dateline and come all the way back again, driven only by the winds and the tides.

I had wanted to send the signal so that I could emulate my Uncle Claud. Some fifty years before, commanding a destroyer returning to the UK, he managed to position his ship where the Greenwich Meridian bisected the equator. To make it more elegant still, he ensured that they steamed through the point on the stroke of midnight. The resultant signal, as it was Morse-coded back to the Admiralty building in Whitehall, read: 'My position at 00 hrs 00 mins 00 secs was 000° 00.000', 000° 00.000'.' My delight on hearing the story was way in excess of the reception it got from the Navy, who were less than amused at such frivolity.

To mark such a special moment, we held a completely childish competition when the crew came together at the teatime watch change. At last the buzz so obviously lacking was back with a vengeance as we celebrated our circumnavigating achievement, and a passing remark about Alan Wells's thin white legs in a pair of baggy shorts was quickly turned into a major event by John Williams. We had a knobbly knees contest.

There was a parade, a full running commentary, a blind feeling test which Ellie volunteered for and even talk of a swimwear section. It was all very silly but exactly what was needed. People were crying with laughter, although to an outsider it would have appeared, at best, mildly amusing. Tears streamed down faces, people shouted and screamed and it was clear that the missing release valve had at last been located and firmly pressed.

John had joined the boat in Mauritius, and raced over leg five to Brazil. He brought with him the perfect balance of energy and enthusiasm, tempered by an understanding of the sensitivities that he knew would exist on board. Acutely aware that we had been a team for many months, he had stepped on board with a clear understanding of the potential pitfalls and trod a balanced path with great intelligence and elegance. He was great to have around and quickly became a hugely popular member of the team.

And to add to the good feeling, the trades from the top of the high-pressure system were kicking in and as our speed increased, so the southern boats started to slow. Their positions were plotted and as the picture emerged, *London* started to look very handily placed.

Up into second place, and if the trend continued it was clear that we would be in the lead before the day was out. With renewed energy, the boat really flew. In my off watch, now free from the constant tiredness, I gave my bunk a good clean, washed clothes, had a bucket wash, trimmed my beard, cut my nails, slapped on some deodorant for another week. I felt refreshed and ready for anything.

Which was just as well, as this was the moment the main heads chose to block up. There were two separate heads, but most people tended to use the main one located in the middle of the boat. The cubicle also doubled up as shower and had a small sink where teeth-brushing took place. 'Compact' and 'bijou' would be an estate agent's description.

It had a door of sorts, a vinyl flap that zipped down to give a modicum of privacy to the user. Trying to stay on the seat when the boat was bouncing through the water was an art to be mastered and unless mother watch remembered to pump away their dirty washing-up water, it would bubble back through the shower drain and seep into the shorts gathered around the ankles of the seated crew member.

Removal of the loo's contents relied on pumping the waste out by hand. Thirty strokes of the pump were needed to flush it through the system with the help of sea water and a further fifteen to expel the remaining water and prevent any slop coming out of the bowl when we next hit a wave. Because of the small bore of the pipes, strict rules specified the number of sheets of tissue that could be used per flush and the rule was generally strictly observed. No one really wanted to have to deal with a blockage. But now we had one.

In the middle of the South Atlantic, one can't pick up the Yellow Pages and ask someone to deal with the unmentionable problem. A yacht at sea has to be a self-sufficient unit and when a problem occurs, someone on board has to fix it. Faced with a blocked loo, the crew suddenly all seemed incredibly busy on a whole series of deeply engrossing projects around the boat and Stuart handed me the rubber gloves, a screwdriver and a can of air freshener before fleeing to the deck.

I am not a plumber, but as with any other task on board, a logical approach would eventually determine where the blockage lay.

I gingerly unscrewed the pumping mechanism that controlled the flush and what remained in the system poured out over my Marigolds. But no sign of the actual blockage yet. Putting it all back together, I traced the direction of the waste pipe and undid the jubilee clips holding the first section of tubing. I nearly choked on the overpowering smell, but this tube did not seem to have a blockage either, as daylight made it from one end to the other. With that section back in place, I tried the pump again, but still nothing budged the way it should and all I achieved was to add yet more water into the system.

With the floorboards up, I continued to trace the waste pipe's path and removed the second section. Again the smell was fierce, but again there was no sign of a blockage. In the saloon, more boards came up and the rusting tins of food that covered the third and final section were carefully removed. The blockage *had* to be here, and as I undid the first jubilee clip with an accomplished aplomb, the pressure that had built up from my repeated pumping found itself an escape route. The blowback was spectacular and my face took the full force from a high-pressure explosion of the pipe's content.

If you want to truly learn about humility, scraping the digested contents of crew mates' intestines from your hair and violated nasal passages is a pretty honest place to start. But at least it meant that people were able to use the loo again. Someone offered a vote of thanks for my efforts and someone else seconded it – the motion, they decided, had been carried.

The weather fax showed a cold front that was expected to pass close by and, true to form, the blue skies were replaced by an ominous band of threatening cloud. It built and swirled around us, reducing visibility to just a couple of miles and we sat squall watching in a constant drizzle, keeping the spinnaker up for as long as possible to try to press home any advantage.

The wind shift that the weather change brought put us right on track to Salvador and when we spoke to *Jersey* on the radio, they, along with *Liverpool*, were sailing along in brilliant sunshine just a few miles away. It seemed that the change brought with it a massive advantage unique to *London* and when the next reporting moment arrived, we were off, up and away into the lead. Poor *Portsmouth* had seen a lead of over a hundred miles dwindle away to nothing and now languished in seventh place.

From bitter experience, we could imagine the mood on the boat and knew how low they would be feeling. And in response we turned the screws even harder and started to increase our advantage, seemingly without even trying.

All the crews sailed hard and we were doing nothing different from how we had sailed for the past nine months. Yet there we were, making ten miles on some boats, twenty on others, and it all appeared to be ridiculously easy. And all because the vagaries of the weather had decided to settle on the small patch of sea occupied exclusively by *London*.

Liverpool were tracking us closely, though, so there was no time to let up as we headed west, some two hundred miles south of the tiny British island of St Helena. Eighteen hundred miles still separated us from the finish line and we knew all too well the pitfalls that could lie in wait and burst the longed-for bubble of victory.

We ignored what the future might hold and just got on with sailing the boat, following the normal routine and doing what we always did. Winning was not even spoken about as the crew simply concentrated on the here and now with a firm dose of realism.

As *Liverpool* drifted ever backwards along with the rest of the fleet, our lead went up to sixty miles and it became harder not to start dreaming about the yellow pennant. The eight days to the finish started to stretch away amid all the painful longing that overexcited children go through when they are waiting for Christmas Day.

The trades continued to blow breezes, now warm, into our lightweight kite and the sea sparkled like a million tiny diamonds in the sun. Our wake hardly broke the surface and the white bubbles that spread from our bow looked like the remains of tired detergent in a washing-up bowl. It carried a trace of our passing for a few seconds before giving up the ghost and a look at the surface of the water fifty yards behind the boat revealed no trace of our ever having been there.

As I looked down into the clear water, some five kilometres deep, the sunlight refracted through it, creating constantly swirling translucent light patterns like the markings in a jellyfish. It was engagingly hypnotic until a brightly coloured piece of paper floated by, followed by another. Ali was pumping out the heads and the only consolation for the shattering of the tranquil moment was that my unblocking efforts were clearly still proving effective.

But no matter what we looked at or where our thoughts went, the days still crept by with excruciating slowness.

The weather continued to favour *London* and after a half-day when the entire fleet, spread out over two hundred miles of ocean, sat in horribly light breezes, the southern boats were rewarded by a fresh blow coming up from the south. Usually that would give them an advantage of several hours before the wind got up to our position in the north, but on this occasion *London* got the wind at exactly the same time.

Up ahead, we could see a problem, though. The high pressure that we had hoped would drive us all the way to Brazil had split. It would mean making a leap between the isobars we were on and a second band that was rapidly developing away to the west. In between the two zones sat a large wind hole that widened as it went north and this meant that the gap between decent breezes would become much worse for us. The skippers of *Plymouth* and *Bristol* had spotted the trap and were already turning south. *Liverpool* also headed down as well and as *London* led the fleet west, so we were the first to grind to a halt.

Our healthy lead ensured that we stayed at the front for several more days, but the inevitable happened and we finally dropped back to third place as *Plymouth* inherited the lead.

We all knew it would happen and had several days to prepare for it, but none the less Stuart's explosion of anger was still a force to be reckoned with, as our advantage was lost. His mood was not helped when the South African-modified fuel system gave up the ghost (again) because a brand-new pump failed. He and Ali worked through the night bastardising our water pump in true *Apollo 13* fashion and managed to create a system that worked after a fashion. But once again it meant that our skipper's mind was taken away from the tactical decisions of the race.

The crew sat and stewed for several more days until another cold front came through and, with it, the wind again. We went up through the spinnaker wardrobe, going from lightweight to the all-purpose and, as the wind still increased, we changed again to the heavyweight. All three sails had been flown within a half-hour period and the living area was strewn with wet cloth as the sail packers dealt with them all.

With the wind a big following sea returned and quickly we were back into surfing territory, making twelve to fourteen knots towards the Brazilian coast. Having been teased and tempted by the conditions, I wanted the win really badly and started to appreciate just how gutted I would be if we lost out once more.

We had led for several weeks on the way to Hawaii and ended up third. We had led towards Panama and lost out to *Bristol* and *Liverpool*. We had led most of the way across the Indian Ocean only to end up fourth. And now, if we were not careful, we would lose again. I became cross at the banter and the games that were going on around me, irritated at people's apparent lack of focus and concentration on the job they were supposed to be doing. I was cross with Stuart and Ali for working on the foredeck in a heavily rolling sea without safety harnesses. Their excuse that it restricted their movement too much did not impress and I had no desire to be the one to communicate the bad news to their next of kin.

The mental stress of the race was getting to me and as each day went by, we all had to work hard to control the mood swings fuelled by the growing desire to win. Stuart got everyone together and reminded the watches that first place would only come if we worked at it. Deserving the accolade was not a good enough reason and had never helped in the past. A single-minded focus was what was needed now for every second of the next few days, and his words were timely.

The increased wind took us back into the lead, but as the fleet narrowed in towards Salvador, the advantage of being the northernmost boat started to dwindle. We built a small gap over the first couple of reporting schedules and then held steady with a fragile twenty-nine-mile advantage, with three days left to run.

And still we were tested. The spinnaker pole came crashing down the track in mid-gybe, missing Stuart's head by millimetres. The weight of it would have caused a serious injury and, in addition, the force of the crash could easily have broken the pole and the sail. But we got away with it while *Bristol* lost their kite in a spectacular blow-out and *Portsmouth* lost their kite, pole and track in an incident similar to ours.

On the helm, Nieves contrived to wrap the spinnaker around the forestay but we were able to use the wind to untangle it without a hitch. It seemed that at long last fate was smiling kindly on us and we could breathe again.

If we could have removed the worry about the result, we would have been enjoying ourselves like never before. The helming was easy – a real delight – and *London* ran down satisfying waves in the warm tropical breeze. Several sei whales surfaced right next to the boat, each easily as long as our hull, its giant dorsal fin cutting lazily through the water.

One of them dived beneath us, giving the hull a firm nudge on its way past and with just sixty thousand of these beautiful creatures left in the world, it should have been a perfect moment to reflect about what we were doing and the environment we were doing it in. But with a couple of days to go, there was still everything to play for and the whales were quickly forgotten.

The winds would get lighter as the race fleet closed in on the coast and the lead boat would hit them first. And as *London* wallowed, everyone behind would play catch-up all over again. Sure enough, the reports showed our lead dwindling and it looked like the finish might become a real lottery, with any one of five boats, separated by just twenty-five miles, in with a chance of taking line honours.

As the distant glow of orange light pollution revealed Salvador's location seventy miles away over the horizon, the lights of *Liverpool* appeared to our north and gradually closed in until the gap stabilised at a mere four miles.

We struggled along at five or six knots and then wallowed at two or three as the breeze failed again. With the speed cut in half, the finish line, which had been twelve hours away, suddenly extended to twenty-four hours and every single person had to find another twelve hours of focus and concentration from somewhere.

Our silent yacht crept up on the coast like alien invaders taking a distant look at life from the outside. All the lives along the shore had no idea of our presence as we had our first sight of civilisation for three weeks. Up ahead, oblivious to us, Saturday night was starting to kick off.

As we watched, someone was dying in a downtown hospice, while somewhere else in the city a baby was born and families rejoiced. In the bars, eyes met and bodies moved to the African-influenced rhythms of the drum. In one street, people fought and noses were bloodied. In another, a flash of a plunging knife was lit in the moonlight. In cars, on beaches, in cheap hotels and in dimly lit bedrooms couples loved and made love. In smart restaurants, the rich ate at candle-lit tables, while in the shanty towns children cried with hunger and mangy dogs scavenged in the gutters.

Jets arrived at the airport and jets departed. On the roads, someone got a speeding ticket, someone else inspected a broken tail light and someone else shook a frustrated fist. People walked the sidewalks, talked their talk, as the trees overhead whispered and the traffic hummed to the music of life.

Creeping closer from our secret world, we could smell the city as well and then hear it too. An ambulance screamed on its way to the stabbing and the lover, on his motorbike, roared smugly home, sending exhaust fumes out to us across the glassy water.

And as the city revealed itself in the dawn and the energies of the night passed away, yet another wind hole stopped us in our tracks. But it hurt *Liverpool* too, and when we made five miles on them, the long-anticipated moment looked like a reality. I had been at the helm for four hours and kept urging my fidgeting colleagues not to celebrate until every inch of *London* had crossed the line.

But when we got to within nine-tenths of a mile I too started to really believe and unscrewed the tightly sealed jar to let a little of the excitement out.

Fatal.

The six knots of breeze died away and a strong counter-current, just half a mile off the coast, picked us up and started carrying us back towards *Liverpool*. Half an hour later our distance to go had increased to a mile and a half, with the instruments showing that we were still making negative headway.

I couldn't bear to watch and went below, sat on a sail bag, looked at the words in my book and failed to read any of them, despite moving on ten pages. Ali's watch tacked the boat for another run at the finish and this time the breeze held on, the current missed us and we crossed the line in a screaming, cheering, hugging, kissing mass of boiled-up emotion.

Everyone had donned dark glasses, even though the sun was still low in the sky, because we all knew the feelings that lurked just under the surface. And true to form, as the three weeks of tough, tough mental and physical digging came to the surface, the emotional outpouring was, well, damp.

We won.

A simple, stark, matter-of-fact word that confirmed *London* as the first boat across the finish line when the thirteenth race of the 2000 Round the World series was run.

Simple words that hid twenty-two days of intense battling over three thousand eight hundred miles of ocean and concealed a race that was physically taxing at the start and mentally exhausting at the end. It was a race that had given a deep, long, intense awareness of the pressures professional sportsmen go through and we could appreciate at first hand the gut-wrenching pain of living right on the competitive edge day after day after day.

Ocean racing is unique in the pressures that it brings. Grand prix drivers step up to the high wire for two hours before they can sprint up to the top step of the podium. Footballers have ninety minutes to perform, while golfers have to keep it all together for perhaps four hours.

Cricketers in a five-day test have a bigger challenge, but even they are allowed to head for a hotel the moment bad light stops play, and take a rest. On a yacht, in the lead, with weeks still to run, there is nowhere to hide. The pressure, with us every second, every minute, hour, day and week, through the long hot days and the cold, star-filled nights, was relentless.

But we won, so all the pain, the anxiety, the tiredness, the frustration and the slog of what suddenly was becoming a very long year went under the carpet and we celebrated with an energy that impressed the locals and delighted the bar staff.

With the rest of the fleet in, we sat in pole position on the pontoon with our yellow pennant flying proudly at the shrouds. In preparation for the prize-giving we had decided that yellow should be the theme to match our first-place flag and a steady stream of crew returned clutching a variety of peroxide mixes from the local chemist. As the instructions were in Portuguese, we were left to guess at what to do, and the galley was filled with a long line of hardened sailors looking in the mirror and anxiously checking the results. Concerned cries of 'Is it all rubbed in?' and 'Does it look even?' rang around the boat as the blokes crowded out the girls in front of the lone mirror. And while we all went increasingly yellow, Aki's Japanese DNA refused to let him into the game. His thick Far Eastern follicles refused to yield to the bleach and despite repeated coatings, his hair stayed resolutely black.

The mass of blond heads seemed to amuse and at the prize-giving we were fêted, applauded, cheered and fêted some more. We shook hands with the great and good, including the Governor of Bahia, gave TV interviews and paraded *en masse* for the cameras.

We sat and partied, danced and partied, hugged and partied and nursed hangovers from hell. We did everything that was expected from winners emerging from a titanic battle of physical as well as mental will power.

And in between it all I sat at the nav desk and savoured writing the diary I had dreamt of writing for far too many months.

London Diary, Tuesday, 24 July 2001

> *So all in all, not a bad day at the office!*
>
> *I apologise for hardly referring to race 13 in my last three diaries and you had to instead endure tales of knobbly knees, breakfast preparations and the toilet arrangements of those on board. For every day of those last three weeks, we have been on a knife edge, a roller coaster of emotion, where we believed that at last London would get the win that was deserved.*
>
> *We have been so close so often and know through bitter experience just how fickle the gods can be. No one dared mention the 'W' word on board and the last week at sea was probably the most nerve-racking, constant, ever-present period of intense pressure that any of us is likely to experience. Thumbs were chewed, sleep was impossible, tempers became frayed and nerves stretched tighter than a Brazilian beach thong.*
>
> *Even when we had nine-tenths of a mile to go and a cautious rumbling of celebration was starting to seep out, the wind died, a counter-current picked us up and swept us*

back towards the hard-chasing Liverpool. Half an hour later our distance to the finish was back to one and a half miles and we had to do it all over again. Those of you who know Stuart can imagine the intensity as his favourite expression, 'PANTS!', echoed out towards the shoreline of an unsuspecting Salvador.

But then, after nine long months of trying, we did it and the cheers, the whoops, the hugs and kisses and a plentiful supply of tears as well, burst forth as the finish line slipped by and the coveted yellow pennant was ours at last.

The prize-giving was last night and this morning, as a rather fragile crew continue with the programme of boat maintenance, the fabled pennant flutters above our blues and reds. Down in the galley, a spectacular silver mermaid trophy, who we have christened 'Wanda', has been kissed, caressed and kissed again. Locals stare down at us from the spectacular waterfront setting and wonder why we all have bleached blond hair. With the yellow finally ours, we decided to prepare for the prize-giving by having hair to match and the nearby pharmacy did a roaring trade in Wella's finest peroxide, before we paraded for the cameras at the local yacht club.

There were twelve, now blond, crew on board for this leg and each of them can be justifiably proud of their achievements. But the win belongs to far more than those of us who went through the gut-wrenching agony of the last three weeks.

This win belongs to every member of crew who has raced London around the world. And more than that, it belongs to our legion of supporters who keep things running back home and support our dreams with an unbridled energy and ongoing good humour.

Many have come out to add their encouragement at stopovers and having met the Baxters, the Kellaghers, the Gibsons, the Howes, the Heathcotes, the Wells and the Satos, I know just how much this will mean to them and how ear to ear their grins will be. On hearing of our victory, Jim Baxter was quick to pledge two rounds of drinks for the crew. Such generosity from a Scotsman indicates the depth of feeling that buzzes through the *support network back home and we shall drink his health with alacrity.*

And while I am in full Oscar-winning acceptance speech mode, I abuse my journalistic privilege and use this space to thank my wife, children, family and friends who have rallied round and provided the stability at home that has allowed me to participate in such an extraordinary year of experiences.

And finally. Behind every great man, there is a greater woman. Liz Gibson has been an absolute pillar of support for our much-loved skipper. She is the one who scoops up the fragmented, soggy, broken pieces after each emotionally challenging race and gently rebuilds them in order for us to stress him out a whole lot more. Her constantly smiling face has been a tonic for all of us and it is Sod's Law that Brazil is one of the few countries where she has not been on the pontoon to cheer us in.

To all of the above, as you pop open the champagne and celebrate the win, the crew here hold up a giant mirror and reflect your support, energies and good wishes directly back. As they say at the end of such emotional outpourings, 'We couldn't have done it without you.'

Ian Dickens, Centro Nautico, Salvador de Bahia, Brazil.

In the midst of all the partying, I wanted to pay an important pilgrimage and booked an airline ticket from Salvador to the teeming city of São Paulo.

It fulfilled a promise made to myself at the start of the race to Brazil and I was adamant I was going to honour it. If we won, I wanted to go and pay my respects to one of the most focused, dedicated, brilliant winners that Brazil has ever had.

He was a man I was privileged to meet on several occasions and the charisma he exuded, his passion and compassion for life were a real inspiration. I watched and listened to his approach to winning and was moved by it. Now, as a much less worthy winner who had struggled through every emotion possible to play a part in winning our own minor sporting event, I wanted to acknowledge the inspiration that he brought me.

A couple of days after the rowdy prize-giving, a lone yachtsman could be found in a lush green cemetery in the Morumbi district of São

Paulo, kneeling at a simple brass plaque set in the grass. He laid a pair of vivid red roses over the wording 'Ayrton Senna Da Silva. Nada Pode Me Separar Do Amor De Deus' ('Nothing can separate me from God's love').

It was a privilege to be able to complete my promise, and I did so with pride, humility and silent tears.

17

New York New York
Salvador to New York
29.07.01–20.08.01

Now, with one win to our credit, we wanted nothing more than to repeat the feat and were really buzzing for the challenge. Salvador had given us a fantastic welcome and looked after us with the warmth one expects from a Latin-American country bursting with smiling energy.

But, predictably, there were last-minute problems. An hour before the start we gave the generator a final check and it chose that moment to fry the alternator. An engineer who had been working on the unit for a couple of days took a quick look and confirmed the problem, but nothing could be done in the few minutes available. We would have to rely on the main generator to charge the batteries and while such a back-up system would work, it would be far less efficient and much more fuel-hungry. With the rest of the fleet heading for the start, we headed for the fuel barge and added another eight heavy jerrycans to our payload.

Our plans started well enough and with the wind blowing through the crew's yellow hair, Stuart timed the run over the line to absolute perfection, crossing it some five seconds and several boat lengths ahead of the rest of the fleet.

For a change, there was a decent breeze and the spectator boats were soon wheezing along in our wake as they struggled to keep up. We headed down the now familiar shore of Salvador, took a turn past a marker buoy for the crowds at the yacht club, headed over to the lighthouse that had indicated the previous race's finish line and set course for the eastern tip of Brazil.

The need to generate power for the first time arrived and it was quickly apparent that there was a problem with the main engine alternators as well. We were not getting anywhere near the charge needed and what should have taken two hours turned into a marathon four hours of engine running. In the intense heat from the motor, Stu did the fuel calculations and realised that there would not be enough to complete the trip.

Battery power would have to be conserved, so the electric fans were turned off, leaving the off-watch crew sweating in their bunks. We switched off lights and prepared to use torches. The radar was turned off, then the telephone, then the computer, in order to conserve power. However, doing this started to compromise the boat's safety.

This leg would have the threat of hurricanes spinning in from the Cape Verde Islands across the Atlantic towards the Caribbean and tracking them was an essential part of our route. Getting caught in hundred-knot winds would require a guaranteed radar signal and radio connection, in case we needed to call for help.

Going to the radio to shout 'Mayday' only to find no battery juice would be less than satisfactory. When one of the alternators on the main engine also gave up the ghost completely, the decision was made for us. We were going to have to stop.

Race director Colin de Mowbray was still in Brazil and he offered to have the replacement part and an engineer standing by in Recife, some 150 miles up the coast. It would be our decision alone, though, and ducking out of the race would obviously put us at the back of the fleet.

It was assumed that *London* would get some form of redress as the parts had failed after a period of maintenance and before the race start, but we had no idea what form it might take. It was up to us to decide what to do, and Stuart agonised long and hard. Ali and I had a talk together at the chart table about the pros and cons and it was clear that stopping was the only real option. Seamanship had to come first and with Clipper offering a solution, our boss would be crucified if we opted to sail past the pit stop, only to run into problems later.

Recife lay twelve hours ahead, so the two watches pushed on hard as our first night at sea fell. Off to starboard, *Jersey* and *Bristol* matched each other's every move under white sails, both desperate not to lose any advantage as the title race hotted up. *Plymouth*, *Portsmouth* and *London* ran under spinnakers, which we were just about able to hold in the acute wind angle, in order to make the best course. *Leeds* and *Glasgow* brought up the rear and the whole fleet was covered by just three miles after twelve hours' racing.

With a constantly collapsing kite, *Portsmouth* bore away a little and crossed our bows a couple of hundred yards away. It was good to see another clipper under full sail and understand how we looked to an outside observer. She was a great sight, her beamy hull riding the waves with effortless purpose, streaming a frothing wake of bubbles as she cut through the ocean at a steady ten knots.

On the stern, a frantically waving figure turned out to be Wil, desperate to communicate with his brand-new fiancée on *London*. As hearts flew across the expanse of water, the fleet 'Aaaah'd' to another relationship that had just tied the knot in this year of discovery.

Also watching us were fleets of tiny fishing boats, riding the swell precariously into the night. Some ten miles offshore and overloaded with crew – some just young boys – the tiny, dinghy-like craft braved the sea in order to scratch a living. The poverty ashore had been extreme and it was humbling to see the risks that needed to be taken, purely so a few bronze coins could drop into a grateful, hard-worked hand.

As more twinkling white lights appeared on the sea, they looked temporarily like a bulk carrier on the distant horizon. And then suddenly the fragile small boats, not revealed on the radar, were just a couple of hundred yards away. Sometimes, through the darkness, the boys called out a greeting towards us, the sea appearing not to thwart their energy for life, despite threatening their low-lying gunwales.

Through the night, our engine ran yet again, as the on-board kit drained away the hard-earned battery power and the off-watch crew struggled to sleep through the heat and noise. We are all unified by the decision to stop and knew that every second made might have a bearing on the result of the race.

We bore off ten degrees, left the front of the fleet and headed to the shore once more. As the sun rose, *London* surged past the fairway buoy of Recife harbour and the crew dropped sails as if our lives depended on it. With the engine gunning us swiftly over the surface, we motored at full speed up through the entrance and pointed the bow towards a line of buoys away in the distance. As the gap narrowed we could see a ramshackle building made from a mixed assortment of timbers and, perched on top, what appeared to be the bridge of an old trawler. It turned out to be the city's innovative and somewhat underused yacht club.

In front of it was Colin and Igor the engineer, waving the new alternator at us. They clambered into a zooming inflatable, which we assumed had been commandeered from a friendly local, and headed out to guide us in. As they drew near, the man on the helm throttled back and, in the best Birmingham accent, advised us where to moor. The tones of this ocean gypsy from Dudley combined with Colin's refined English and Igor's Portuguese to create an incongruous welcome.

Anna had logged the time of stopping down to the last second and, like anxious parents, the crew monitored progress on the engine as the smells of breakfast wafted up from the galley. Igor, who felt responsible for the failure as he had been the engineer in charge in Salvador, set to with a vengeance. The first thing he confirmed was that the problems with the main engine alternator were serious and we were right to stop.

That was good news, particularly for Stuart, who had cursed his lack of mechanical knowledge through the night, not knowing if he could have improvised a repair. The skippers of *Bristol* and *Plymouth* had been full of advice on the radio, urging us to press on with a bodged solution rather than stop, although some of their suggestions sounded a little alarming.

One idea was to wire up a number of light bulbs in series to bypass the generator regulator and act as a kind of fuse. We had already had a small fire when the alternator became overloaded back in the marina, and encouraging wires to overheat miles out to sea did not seem such a great idea. The skipper of *Jersey* had been more supportive and endorsed the decision to stop. He recognised that if we ran into trouble and people got hurt, Stuart and Clipper would be crucified for not taking up the option of a professional repair.

While Igor worked below decks, our two new team mates sat in the sun and looked at the distant traffic grinding across the bridges spanning the numerous canals that led off from the main harbour. David Sage – back on board for the final leg, along with Alastair Standring, read aloud from a guide that the description of 'The Venice of Brazil' was, perhaps, a tad hopeful. The dusty factories, derelict buildings, bleak wharves and rusting ships rather confirmed the view.

We had fully expected the stop to take the best part of a day and when the generator burst into life after just four hours of repair work, the sweating but profusely smiling Igor emerged triumphant into the cockpit. We let things run for a while just to make sure and when all seemed as it should, Stuart sent off our pit-stop crew with a hurried and grateful farewell.

The crew on *London* were really pumped up and ready to race. We motored back towards the sea and watched as huge breakers cleared the sea wall on our starboard side – the wind and sea state had clearly got up. It made sense to hoist sails in the lee of the wall before motoring out into such a huge swell.

The boat rolled alarmingly as Ali steered across the wave pattern and headed for a point south of the marker buoy that had sped by a few hours before. We turned back on to course, raised the white sails, trimmed for speed and roared past the marker, noting the GPS time as our race got under way again. Four hours and thirty-two minutes had been the total down time, which would put us something like forty-five miles behind the lead boat. The chase was well and truly on.

Back on our track and with the 2.2 heavyweight spinnaker flying, we made great speed but knew that the boats ahead would be enjoying similar conditions and making equally good progress from the same winds.

We pushed on hard, though, with a new focus and commitment coming from everyone on board. Through the day, kit was taken to the limit in order to try to close up on the pack ahead. As night fell, a vicious, evil-looking, black and writhing bank of cloud appeared, and with it a torrential deluge. A nasty, twisting following sea came with the wind and my watch were on red alert to drop the kite if the conditions took a turn for the worse.

On the helm for two hours, I watched the wind instruments like a hawk, bearing away a little when the gust became too strong and then coming back on to the wind to get maximum speed. It was a real game of Russian roulette and our hearts were in our mouths on several occasions when the sail-ripping limit came close. *London* was running at ten-tenths for hour after hour, which put a real strain on the crew.

And just when the worst seemed over and I relaxed a little, an awkward wave sent the hull one way and the sail another. The result was a spinnaker wrapped round the forestay, which initially refused to budge. I could clearly see what had happened and didn't really need the slightly hysterical 'You've wrapped the kite' shriek from one of my team. I didn't need it, first because I could see the cock-up with my own eyes, and secondly because it didn't offer any help to actually solve the problem.

After a couple of minutes' gentle persuasion with a turn of the wheel and the help of the wind, we managed to get the spinnaker free again and at the end of a trying and mentally challenging watch I went below, angry with myself for making such a slip. If the boat wanted to catch up, we would need to sail better than the rest of the fleet and not make any errors ourselves.

Stuart was sat at the nav desk and as I removed my life jacket and damp oilskins, he mentioned that a message had come through from *Jersey*. They had received an e-mail from Anne (*London*'s system was out of action again) and although Stu assured me it was not urgent, he nevertheless suggested that I call home straight away. His nonchalant words were like an electric shock going through me and I suddenly feared the worst. Why would I get a message from home via another boat with an instruction to call right away? Something dreadful must have happened and all the darkest fears of accidents involving the children roared into my head in full, X-rated, horror-story Technicolor.

While the rest of the watch carried on undressing around me and headed for their 02.00–05.00 sleep, I took Stuart's place and reached with a trembling hand for the sat phone. As I entered the pin numbers and codes, the nightmare thoughts grew ever bigger. House fire, car crash, Mum or Dad – something really bad had surely taken place.

I got through first time and from the confused seas off the easternmost tip of Brazil, I spoke a tremulous greeting.

Everything was fine. On the Clipper website in the UK there had been a problem accessing *London* and Anne had set to and sorted it out. The message she had sent to *Jersey* was simply to reassure us that e-mail contact was about to be re-established. That was it, nothing more. There were no problems, disasters, illnesses or accidents. The message, relayed through several people, had lost the vital element along the way and my relief at the discovery was immense.

After hanging up, I stumbled past Stuart and stepped into the darkened sanctuary of the main heads, zipping up the PVC door behind me. The pressures of the race, the intense focus of the last watch, the drive of the last day, the desire to earn another win, the pressures of being at sea, in competition for ten months, and then having to potentially face my worst fear of all, suddenly took their toll and chose that moment to seek out the chink in my fragile armour.

Now I understood the tears shed by Mikka Hakkinen when he crashed out of the Italian Grand Prix a few years before. I remembered Michael Schumacher breaking down in sobs at a post-race press conference a year later, and in the private cubicle I too had my moment of emotional outpouring.

As *London* roared on through the night, I sat on the tiny loo and shook as the previously hidden pent-up emotion gushed out in great, gasping, draining sobs. It was a release that came completely out of the blue, triggered by the most innocent of things and as it subsided I questioned whether I should allow myself to become so totally focused on the race. Perhaps I should chill just a little and not take it all quite so seriously.

But that has never been my way. When I get involved in a project I do so with a complete dedication and a desire to get things done to the very best of my – and everyone else's – ability. I give a hundred per cent and I expect the same from whoever I am working with. Such an attitude might mean a roller coaster of a ride but that goes with the territory when you set high goals and come close to achieving them.

I headed through the darkness to my bunk and tumbled into bed, looking forward to the fact that the next day was my mother watch. A full day away from sailing, a day of no-brainer moments spent slicing onions, cleaning walls and drying dishes. It was exactly what was needed.

Except the conditions had other ideas. As breakfast was cleared away, the wind picked up and the seas started to rise. They were coming in from the stern quarter, though – ideal conditions for spinnaker surfing. But as the conditions changed, so the helms found it tougher to stay on course. As the morning went by, I listened to the kite collapse time and time again as the hull went too far through the wind, and I winced as the spinnaker pole shook itself at the mast in its death throes.

We had learnt during the night that *Glasgow* had already damaged her kite and that *Portsmouth* and *Leeds* had damaged spinnaker poles. Now was the time to press home the advantage and damaging kit ourselves would be less than ideal. Stuart decided that we needed to go to selected helms and in between preparing lunch and dinner, I joined the roster of Stuart, Ali and Andy to do battle with the tricky, steep facing waves. This approach had become a recurring feature of my mother-watch days and once again I had to forgo the eight hours of uninterrupted sleep to help drive the boat ever onwards. Yet I wouldn't have missed those helming conditions for the world.

The sea state was tough but as long as the helm kept *London* in the very narrow groove, she simply picked up her skirt and flew. Through the next day and night we creamed along at fourteen to sixteen knots, each driver taking an hour at the wheel before going below for three hours of bicep-resting kip.

At the next radio reporting moment, the lat and long numbers showed we had overtaken *Glasgow* and *Leeds*, had *Liverpool* in our sights and were closing in on *Plymouth*, *Jersey*, *Portsmouth* and *Bristol*. Now, around the tip of Brazil, a strong current headed up the coast at three knots and *London* was placed firmly in the middle of it. The rest of the fleet had chosen to follow a slightly shorter route pointing directly at the finish, some three thousand five hundred miles away, and as they rolled towards the Doldrums, our current-assisted speed never let up.

Through the following day we set new standards for boat speed. Stuart led the way, with a new spinnaker record for *London* of twenty knots. I took over and banged along in a surf, achieving 19.8, then 20.7 and finally a roaring 21.7. Andy joined in the fun and took off with a maximum speed of 22.4. This was huge fun and the testosterone surged around the cockpit as we played with the ocean.

As the waves picked up the stern, the bow pointed vertically downwards into a *Star Wars*-inspired black hole. As the boat started to plunge, a gentle turn on the wheel put us on to the surf and the racing surge began. As the speed increased, so too did the noise of rushing water, and the bow wave started to rise. As the speed increased, so the wave moved aft until it resembled a pair of giant swan's wings that enveloped both sides of the cockpit. The rooster tails of spray shot some ten feet into the air as we rode through a tube of water and the speed dial relayed the increase in velocity.

The whole hull vibrated and shuddered at the speed, and on the helm we had to be quick to deal with the moment when the surf ended. Allowing the hull to round out and then get laid flat by a broadside broach would spoil all our efforts and by the time that fear had been avoided, the next wave and the next and the next arrived. Each brought its own trademark kick and spin, and as the intense racing continued, the four of us worked away at taming these subtle differences.

We ran like this for two days, storming along at an average of thirteen knots over an eighteen-hour period. It meant that we completed over three hundred miles in twenty-four hours, which set a new record for the Clipper Ventures fleet. It also meant that we were closing in on the front of the pack and the impossible suddenly looked possible.

Plotting the position of the other boats, we could see that *Plymouth* had the benefit of watching our charge from behind and was now moving across to take advantage of the obvious current. She was in joint-first place with *Bristol* and *Portsmouth* and when the sun rose on the third high-speed day of charging catch-up, her sail was off our starboard side.

More importantly, it was behind us.

After four days at sea and a pit stop of four and a half hours, we had come from behind and taken the lead. Up at the halyards, the Brazilian courtesy flag still flew and I asked for it to stay there. Moved by the visit to Ayrton Senna's grave, I saw this as an opportunity to emulate his legendary drive. True to form, we had achieved what looked impossible and taken the lead from the back of the grid. Senna's national flag at the mast might bring good luck, I thought, and if nothing else, it paid homage to his inspiration.

One would have hoped that our amazing progress would unite the crew, but in certain quarters heads were down. Stuart's plan had been to sail as hard as possible while ensuring that no kit was damaged and, to do so, he picked the helms who he knew could cope with the conditions.

And while the speeds increased and our juvenile whoops shot around the cockpit, there was an ill-concealed resentment from others at not being given the chance to helm themselves. As we sped onwards, the new records were met with a stony wall of silence and studied indifference from the sulkers.

When news came through that a girl on board *Glasgow* had achieved a new fleet speed record of 22.6, the dam broke and out poured the resentment. It was two of our female crew who did not like the fact they were not allowed to helm and now that news came through of a woman hitting new records, they made their feelings felt. They seemed unwilling to acknowledge Stuart's strategy – which had the support of everyone else, both girls and boys – and our old maxim of putting the boat first, our crew members second and ourselves last seemed to have been forgotten.

It had nothing to do with a battle of the sexes and everything to do with selecting those crew members who were most capable of managing the conditions. On board *Glasgow*, their female star driver had been chosen for those reasons and was at the wheel for her skills alone. On every boat, each individual had special talents that helped make the boat go faster and they were utilised irrespective of their gender. Apart from having the clear benefit of speed, we were also the only boat in the fleet not to suffer from equipment damage caused by out-of-control moments. So it seemed that the strategy was correct.

When the complaint came, it did so in the form of an ill-considered, whining harangue rather than a reasoned debate, which did little for Stuart's temper and the overall mood on board. As a result, the parties involved festered and whispered chats took place in secret huddles around the cockpit.

A day later the conditions eased, Stuart immediately changed his strategy and straight away I offered the wheel to the loudest complainant, who, of course, now refused to take it.

Ah me, it was better than *Coronation Street*.

We had a crew meeting as our first week at sea came to an end. It gave everyone a turn to share their views and, in the light of the pressures, I spoke about the journey we were undertaking and how I planned to take time out to remember just how special it was. In a few short weeks our circumnavigation would all be over and I was not thrilled to sail along with miserable, complaining individuals unhappy about a piece of race strategy.

Sports psychology is a fascinating subject and I remember watching Martina Navratilova overcoming the pressures of her game. She sat down, thought about it and decided to stop scowling and shouting at the frustration and started instead to smile and laugh. When a pressured shot went wrong she would grin to herself and go for the next point with a look of detached amusement.

I felt that we should be doing the same and if the tension could be resolved, the whole mood on board would become more relaxed. Stuart agreed and asked us all to put aside the festering differences and simply enjoy our last month at sea.

Matt, the skipper of *Plymouth*, came on the radio and straight away launched into a debate about redress for the pit stop. His view was that we were unlikely to be awarded anything and he felt it would be wrong if we were. Already ahead of the game, we had planned to run the race ignoring such benefits, knowing that they would incite controversy. It seemed much better to take the battle to the race track and do things on merit, which was what we had just done.

Surely *London*'s own unhappy brigade should be content with that.

Arriving at the equator for the third time in our round-the-world odyssey brought the laughter back. Stuart, Ali, Andy and I went into the well-rehearsed routine of Neptune and his 'crossing the line' ceremony. Like a bunch of am-dram luvvies, we took to our usual parts with Stuart as the King of the Sea, Andy and Ali as the policemen and myself as the judge.

We mixed up the usual foul concoction of porridge, curry powder, flour, water and ketchup and initiated Alastair and Doris into the grand, if slightly messy, world of the great king. When the curtain went down and the foul slop was being picked from their matted hair, the players congregated on the stern, congratulating each other on the performance.

'I thought you were wonderful as the policeman – you really became the part.'

'I simply loved your judge. Witty juxtaposition of wild and stern, twinkle and severity.'

'You are marvellous as Neptune. You took it to new heights and I adored the wig.'

Kenny Branagh, eat your heart out, baby.

Up ahead, the boats further to our east wallowed badly in the Intertropical Convergence Zone of no wind. As they did, so our lead extended and we hoped beyond hope that a slice of selective luck would hold and the Doldrums would be kinder to us.

Looking at the updated weather reports, it seemed there was only a little further to go before we cleared through it. We had yet to hit any real wind holes and up ahead the familiar 'streets' of cumulus were starting to form again.

It looked like *London* might be through with only a slight reduction in speed and if that was the case we could be off and away, leading the pack onwards past the Caribbean islands and into the next danger area with its threat of hurricanes.

And just as we looked forward, the ITCZ shifted north and the gift of any type of wind went with it. The sails started their familiar slap-slap-slap taunt and *London* and *Plymouth* wallowed around, sniffing for any sort of breeze. To make it worse, the current that we were relying on to continue our progress fizzled out as well. The routing chart showed it to be there, we had expected it to be there and our tactic had relied on it being there, but our speed over the ground told a different story.

As the wind died, so the heat rose and the temperature, particularly below decks, climbed to a humid and uncomfortable repetition of the slow journey towards Singapore.

The lack of wind stuck with us for first a day, then a second and then a third. At times it was so aimless and fluky that *London* got pushed into completing slow, 360-degree pirouettes, which, more often than not, were aped by *Plymouth*. By the time the first gusts spun in off the Azores high-pressure system and filled our sails, *Bristol*, *Portsmouth*, *Jersey*, *Liverpool* and *Plymouth* – the last had grabbed the initiative while we were facing the wrong way – had all slipped ahead. We were about a hundred miles behind the leader, in sixth place, and had it all to do again.

As we finally emerged from the ITCZ, the confused weather put on one last amazing display for us. In just one vista, there were squalls, towering cumulus, layers of nimbostratus, a layer of elliptical cloud that looked like a giant flying saucer, a quarter band of a rainbow, dark blues, deep oranges, bright whites and jet blacks, with shafts of setting sunlight piercing the gaps. A breathtaking, threatening, seductive, hypnotic piece of nature for our exclusive benefit.

We left the brackish green waters that oozed out of the Amazon some one hundred and fifty miles away to port, and now the wind freshened and finally took *London* off on some decent spinnaker runs up past the Windward and Leeward Islands. To know that Barbados, St Kitts, St Lucia and Antigua were all slipping by was a tremendous magnetic pull. It seemed wrong to be so close to so many magical places yet allow them to slip through our fingers and disappear in the bubbling wake.

As we headed north, the night sky started to change. My beloved Southern Cross had been visible only in the early evening, low on the horizon behind us, and for several days cloud had blocked the view. It never reappeared and as the southern hemisphere slipped away, it was replaced by the old familiar shapes of the north. As we headed onwards, so the shapes started to gently track their way across the night until the star patterns, familiar since childhood, settled back to the points where they belonged.

It was a sure sign that the final chapter of the race was upon us and the realisation was a bitter-sweet moment as we counted down in days rather than months or continents.

But even without the Southern Cross, the skies still performed. On one clear night a high bank of 'mackerel' cloud appeared out of nowhere. The ice crystals that formed the cloud built a translucent barrier in front of the moon, until its diffused light resembled a giant eyeball staring down at us from on high. At the very centre, the moon itself became the glint in the eye, while the cloud created a larger, opaque ball around it. Bringing colour to the 'eyeball' was a dense ring forming a perfect circle, as the light refracted through the ice in reds, oranges and yellows that merged into greens, indigos and violets.

Who needs mind-expanding drugs when nature could do this for you? Half an hour later it had vanished and the moment had become an exclusive show for the six of us lucky enough to be on watch – perhaps the only people on the planet to witness it.

My second mother watch of the race came up and for a change the weather behaved impeccably. I enjoyed the time out, despite baking a pair of disastrous loaves that resembled miniature breeze blocks. In fact, I was so ashamed, I baked another two and chopped up the still-warm bricks to go with lunch. And just to prove that I was half capable in the galley, the fish pie I produced for the evening was a bit of a *tour de force*.

Being paired with Ellie for the chores was always a delight. I knew that the day would be full of laughter and together we giggled our way through supper preparations like a couple of kids at the back of a Home Economics class.

Take a baking tray and add a couple of tins of salmon and a couple of tuna. Melt some butter in a pan, add some flour, stir in some milk and once the white sauce is made, add dried parsley. Pour the sauce over the fish. Then mix up instant mashed potato with boiling water. Add some mustard, garlic and pepper and layer the potato over the fish. Sprinkle with parmesan and put knobs of melting butter on the layer of potato. Bake in the oven for half an hour and stand by for applause.

There was not a fresh ingredient involved, but I defy anyone who chooses to copy the masterpiece to be anything other than overwhelmed. Rick Stein must surely be nervous at such talent.

Cooking, cleaning, eating and sleeping on board was second nature and no one thought our living conditions the slightest bit odd. It was a chance glimpse of Andy Howe clipping his toenails over breakfast that reminded me how far we had come and I decided to share the moment with the readers of *The Times*. If we were going to be put off our breakfast, then so too should they.

London Diary, Monday, 13 August 2001

> *So when was the last time you cracked twenty-eight eggs into a bowl and whisked them up for breakfast?*
> *When did you last slice up two loaves (baked the*

previous day) and attempt to create twenty-six perfectly browned pieces of toast in a tiny, 'it's either furnace or cold' recalcitrant grill?

Can you remember when you last provided cereals, teas, coffees, jams, Marmites, peanut butters and lemon curds for thirteen demanding clientele who were desperate for breakfast NOW, so they could either get out on watch or go to bed?

Yes?

Well, did you prepare the toast while sitting on the floor of a cramped galley with your entire home skimming along at a rocking, rolling fifteen knots? If you did, you will know the frustration of seeing the carefully placed slices come shooting back out of the grill like departing Exocets and land all over the floor as the boat rolls alarmingly on a huge wave. Butter side down, of course.

And all the while a bubbling kettle and a spitting frying pan full of bubble and squeak hang, Damocles-like, above your head.

If it is still a 'Yes', you will know that familiar smell of burning bread that pervades the air the minute you turn to make someone a mug of tea. But then perhaps you are thankful as the smell helps to disguise a number of less pleasant aromas that the morning brings.

Crammed into the living quarters on board London *are eight healthy adults (with five more sniffing the air impatiently in the cockpit) who sit wherever there is space in the six-b- fifteen-foot area. Actually, half that space is available, as the galley space is out of bounds in order that the two mother watches can work around each other, as the well-oiled routine gets the day under way.*

One place someone will always find a seat is in the heads, as this too occupies part of the living area. Only a thin (non-soundproof) and flimsy (non-aroma-proof) PVC zip-up door divides the breakfast preparations from someone's noisy constitutional, which is often accompanied by singing in order to create a distraction from the, er, motions coming from within.

Freshly removed sea boots with week-old damp socks add to the swirling flavours blending with the scrambled eggs, and as smelling feet are exposed to the toast-burning, sweat-filled, bowel-cleansed air, perhaps a bit of toenail clipping might be started by one crew member, as his colleague, squeezed in next to him, munches from a plastic dog bowl of cereal, oblivious to the fact that by the time he has finished, one or two minuscule additions may well have joined his diet.

If a group of thirteen political refugees were found housed in such conditions in a suburb of Birmingham, there would be a moral outcry, with angry editorials thundered out in the national press. Questions would be asked in the House and Social Service chiefs would cringe to the stinging criticism that would deservedly come their way from a Paxman-esque TV grilling for all to see.

On board London, someone might raise their toast-munching head out of a well-thumbed copy of Yachting World and wonder vaguely what all the fuss was about. The person in the heads might let off a ripe ripping of wind in response to the disgust and follow it up with a great roar of laughter. The toenail clipper might well pick up a few bits of his choicest harvest and marvel at them with whoever sits next to him or her.

For the crew, such moments are the absolute norm. No one bats an eyelid as breakfast unfolds this morning, just as it did yesterday, last week, last month, last year, and such conditions seem completely natural and acceptable to all of us on board.

And now that the heads has been vacated, I need to go and scrub it clean.

Good morning.

Ian Dickens

A day later there was very nearly fresh fish for supper. Occasionally we trailed a line astern, but had only once caught anything. As the sun set, the reel gave its telltale whizz and Stuart rushed on deck with a great leap of excitement. For fifteen minutes he played the catch and by the time the fish came close to the boat, the light had all but gone.

Torches were eagerly played on the water and just as he completed the final flourish and pulled the potential supper from the sea, the image of a rich and juicy tuna was replaced with a writhing, snarling monster of the deep. I have no idea what it was, but the eel-like body, with two vivid blue stripes and a madly gnashing jaw containing a nasty set of very sharp and large teeth, sent everyone into a *Dad's Army* 'Don't panic' moment.

No one was brave enough to go near the thing until the thrashing had all but subsided and by the time the obscene creation could be freed from the hook, it was more dead than alive. If it had been a stunningly beautiful fish, we would have whacked it on the head and eaten it without a second thought, but back it went into the ocean.

Being dead ugly can sometimes have its advantages, I suppose.

As the miles to the American coast counted slowly down, Andy continued to watch the developing weather coming from the Cape Verde Islands and Africa. Several tropical waves had formed and tracked across us, but none had developed into the spinning deep lows of hurricanes.

In the Caribbean to our west, tropical storm Barry failed to cause concern and when finally the first hurricane of the season, Chantal, started to track over the Atlantic, we were well clear of the danger zone. While Barry and Chantal are fine enough names, they don't really suit the whirling-dervish nature of a hurricane. The weather forecasters need to pick something a little more macho or a tad more fierce if their TV broadcasts are going to work. I'm sorry, but if someone tells me that Hurricane Eric is bearing down on me, I would not be able to take the threat seriously. But if girls' names are absolutely essential, I reckon 'Gail' might suit.

Stuart gave us a weather lecture and I was amazed to discover that, despite the high winds at the centre of such storms, the low-pressure system tracks very slowly, moving over the sea at just fifteen knots. And even if it were to come close, we could expect relatively light winds just a couple of hundred miles away from its vicious 100mph centre. The theory, fortunately, could not be properly tested.

Miami came abeam and the jungles surrounding the Amazon and the Orinoco were replaced by the concrete ones of the USA. It seemed to me that the similarities between the two, apparently disparate, locations were actually pretty marked.

Down south, piranhas stalk the swamps ready to tear you from limb to limb. Wherever you go, a deadly snake, a stalking wild cat or a nervous, blowpipe-wielding native is intent on looking after their patch and removing you from it.

And if the creativity of the tropical jungle is smart, up north the camouflage is way cleverer. The evils in the concrete jungle are hidden behind doors marked 'Boardroom', where the flashing, joshing, false smiles betray the most venomous of poisoned tips. Even in the vacation season, the phenomenon of Brad getting one over on the holidaying Chuck does not let up, and in the country clubs, behind the studiedly casual disguise of freshly pressed Ralph Lauren chino shorts and shirts, the ever-present threat of danger lurks. As the Timberland deck shoes kick a ball along a beach, corporate knives are out, ably assisted by calculating, perfectly formed, orthodontically immaculate, wafer-thin wives.

There were no snakes hanging off the street lamps or alligators in the pool along the east coast beaches, but the terrain for the unwary was far more treacherous than that on the floor of the steaming rainforest, a thousand miles away to the south.

As New York neared, we expected a period of variable weather which might slow the leaders up a little. And while the weather did change, bringing with it unpredictable squalls and intense thunderstorms, the basic wind patterns refused to help our cause.

Stuart has perfected the art of reading the marginal conditions and on several occasions called for the kite to be dropped just seconds before a sail-cloth-ripping blast hit the boat. Sometimes I had to bear away dramatically to prevent the loss of our power source, but it meant that we were maximising our time under the fastest sail plan and all the while closing in on more vital race points.

Time and time again our skipper's calls were perfect, and as news filtered through from other boats who had been less fortunate, we started to make up places once more. While they were kite-less and living in an environment cluttered with chattering sewing machines and sail-repair glue, *London* sailed ever onwards until we were back in fourth place and closing in on *Jersey*.

The thunderstorms were spectacular and for several hours during the night the sea around the boat took hit after hit as forked lightning struck into the water. We could smell the energy and the entire cockpit was lit up in tableau after tableau as the light cracked off like the cameras of a thousand press photographers, freezing the moment for a split second.

It seemed prudent to turn off and disconnect all the boat's electronics, so convinced were we that a direct strike was imminent from the deafening bolts of lightning. With the storm directly overhead, strands of blond hair raised themselves to meet the swirling cloud as an intense static filled the air. But, rather than worrying about the kit on board, the watch was more concerned that the conditions were revealing a worrying set of darkened roots at the base of our growing locks.

Putting that concern to one side, the crew worked the conditions well and when the finish line lay just one hundred and fifty miles away, *Jersey* was just three miles ahead. The race committee had contacted the fleet to report that *London* had been awarded a time redress of four hours thirty-two minutes – our pit-stop down time. It would be more than enough to put us comfortably into third place.

We were still eager to do the business out on the race track, though, and pushed on hard through the final tough twenty-four hours. Up ahead, both *Bristol* and *Portsmouth* had slowed dramatically as the wind died close to the coast and all of us knew from bitter experience that anything was possible.

The last night was as trying as the previous week and another line of nasty squalls and crashing thunderstorms kept Stuart on his mettle. Once again he read things brilliantly, but as the sun came up the wind died again, leaving us doing a mere two-knot crawl towards the finish line.

There was no sign of *Jersey*. Indeed there was no sign of New Jersey. Or New York, or Long Island, as a heavy mist sat overhead. Huge container ships appeared out of the gloom in the shipping lanes around us and we fretted over the possibility of losing the last podium position at the eleventh hour.

The final radio sched of the race crackled into life and *Jersey* had indeed crossed the line ahead of us. But only an hour before. It meant that we had three and a half hours in hand, but with the wind dying again, our chances of even finishing third now looked horribly slight. Behind us, *Plymouth* had found a pocket of breeze and were closing in, along with *Liverpool*.

Eventually the odd, tripod-like structure of Ambrose Light (which the GPS had been aiming at for the past eighteen days) slipped by close off our port side and the third place was ours. It was not quite the way we wanted to get the points, but our speed throughout the entire twenty-one-day race had shown that *London* had lived up to her desire to be on an all-guns-blazing charge from beginning to end.

The two watches downed sails and as we started the long motor in, the gloom finally lifted to reveal first Coney Island and its derelict parachute jump ride along the boardwalk, then the Verrazano Narrows bridge, then the yellow Staten Island ferries, the Statue of Liberty and, finally, the thrusting towers of lower Manhattan.

As we docked, the skipper and crew of *Jersey* were leading the cheers, stood by to take our lines and give enthusiastic hugs of congratulations. It must have hurt badly to lose a much-needed extra championship point and their generous display of sportsmanship was very special.

In the heart of the city – especially one as big and important as New York – life continued unabated, totally ignoring our arrival. We may have been sailing round the world, but there were more pressing issues to think about.

Despite the city's being totally unimpressed, we were happy with our result and happy to have arrived a couple of days early. It allowed *London* to be put to bed for a well-deserved rest, talk to the family before they headed for Heathrow and the flight to JFK and go and check out the apartment we had rented. It also allowed me to check out a local barber, even though I had promised Holly not to get my hair cut until she had inspected the blond look. I loved the idea of a middle-aged, one-time suit-wearing, briefcase-carrying, ex-board director of a multinational discussing his peroxide highlight root problems with his teenage daughter.

Throwing caution to the wind and blowing a budget I did not have, I got a local firm to meet me at JFK with the biggest stretch limo on their books. The family had not been to New York before and I wanted to greet them in style. Saving cash on a one-way ride, I headed out to the airport in a much less glamorous bus and waited expectantly at the gate, ignoring the curious looks at my oddly coloured hair.

No tears this time (apart from those that followed Holly's laughter) and we hugged in the middle of the concourse as disgruntled New Yorkers picked their way around us. Outside on the pavement, I gave the nod and my driver arrived – and kept on arriving. Darkened window after window slipped by until eventually the door at the back of the white limo stopped beside us. Mike's eyes lit up and the happy ride back into the city was accompanied by electric windows gliding up and down, fuzzy in-car TV pictures, drinks from the fridge and chats to the chauffeur via the intercom system on the back seat.

The magic that is New York hit them instantly and its urgent buzz remained as we became a summer-holidaying family for a whole week and the city introduced itself.

Steam rose from the subway vents and mingled with the sultry heat of summer. Up three blocks and into Central Park, the air was full of flying frisbees that skimmed perfectly past ranks of elegant bodies baking gently in the sun. In Sheep's Meadow and Strawberry Fields, New York chilled in the August sunlight, before heading back to work.

Yellow taxis hooted their horns at pedestrians, who shouted back, pointing angrily at the 'WALK' sign. And as the cabs slowed, they brought another cacophony of horns from the cars backed up behind.

The subway clattered beneath the baking streets, taking an oddball collection of $1.50-paying punters towards Brooklyn Bridge, Queens and the Bronx. Uptown girls headed for Downtown worlds and people in suits and carrying briefcases turned towards Wall Street and their Bears and Bulls.

On 33rd the exit of the subway was filled with the Empire State, its Art Deco tower piercing the deep blue of the sky. Helicopters, Piper Cherokees and Cessna float planes skimmed the air at low level while above them 737s, MD9s and 747s headed into JFK, LaGuardia and Newark.

On Mercer and Spring the traffic clattered over the cobbled streets of SoHo, and down beyond Tribeca the unsuspecting twin towers of the World Trade Center blocked out the light.

From the yacht harbour under their shadow, a small yellow ferry cut across the Hudson River every half-hour, taking the occasional commuter, tourist and wide-eyed clipper crew member away from the film-set excitement of Manhattan and depositing them at Liberty Landing Marina on the New Jersey shore.

For a week we were tourists, swallowed up by a city much too busy to worry about round-the-world races and our tales of derring-do. Thanks to Bowlsie back in London, I went to the New York offices of his ad agency and collected tickets to a Yankees ball game. Despite my not being a client any more, Lowes continued to look after me, and as well as supplying the tickets they provided an office and a telephone so I could talk to my parents and collect e-mails. Their ongoing support was deeply touching and made a memorable evening for the family, even though we had no idea what was taking place on the pitch.

In between trips to the park, Tiffanys, FAO Swarz, Grand Central Station and a hairdresser, the family crowded on to a Circle Line ferry that ploughed through the waters of the Hudson. It dropped us at the Statue of Liberty and then moved on to the deeply moving Ellis Island museum. As the ferry returned to Manhattan, and the sights were pointed out to us, the familiar mainsail of *London* hove into view. Some of the crew had volunteered to stay on board for a day's corporate work and they were busy entertaining potential sponsors, handing out elegant, toenail-free nibbles and topping up glasses of wine.

To the tourists from Denver and Milwaukee, Houston and Atlanta, Paris, Birmingham and Hamburg, hiding their faces behind banks of video cameras along the ferry rail, the blue-and-red-striped sail belonged to just another boat out on a Saturday cruise. It made a nice picture in front of the amazing Manhattan skyline, but that was all.

I watched with puffed-up pride as *my* boat slipped by. I wanted to call order on the hundreds of people lining the rail and tell them, via the ferry's intercom, what a special yacht they were looking at. That sixty-foot hull concealed so many stories, so many miles, so many cultures, sights and sounds and smells, among which the self-important NYC was playing only a walk-on part.

Most likely, though, I would have been dismissed as one of the crazies who harangue you on the Big Apple's sidewalks, amid the constantly shifting crowds. But that was OK. With the race end less than one month away, it didn't hurt to have our achievements pricked a little and to appreciate that in some parts of the world life remained much too busy to stop and take in our adventure.

Another reminder of why the year of living at extremes was so important also hit home in New York. My aunt Audrey, who had waved from the deck of HMS *Glasgow* at the race start and loved the adventure I was undertaking, had gone. Audrey, who had been tickled pink when I relayed back to *The Times* her late husband's story about all the zeros when he crossed the Greenwich Meridian. Audrey, who had planned to come out to New Jersey and surprise me. Audrey, who was planning a picnic on the beach with her friends from the Royal Lymington Yacht Club for when we sailed back into the Solent. Bright, sprightly, flirty, always laughing Audrey, who had gone to bed making a list of things to buy in New York and never woke up. She had suffered a massive haemorrhage in the middle of the night and time crept up and stole her away.

Having thrown caution to the wind with the limo, I decided that the holiday should finish as it had started. It was only money, after all, and although we could ill afford to spend it, Audrey's passing was a salutary reminder to live for the moment.

A charming receptionist high up in the World Trade Center took our booking for dinner and reminded me that they had a policy of jackets and tie for the men. Mike had arrived with a typical teenager's wardrobe stuffed into a bag and, with the best will in the world, his football shirts and tracksuit trousers would not be acceptable. Macy's did the trick, and as we rode the express elevator up to the one-hundred-and-twentieth floor I was the proudest man in New York.

Mike looked great in his new blazer, tie and chinos, and Holly sensational in her first little black number. As we were shown to our table, heads turned and I wallowed in a warm fug of pride as my family settled down around me. The maître d' was a delight, the wine waiter gentle, and the choice of food and drink was acknowledged with a warm nod of approval. The children weren't patronised and they too were praised for their clever selections. With a growing confidence, they made bold choices, trying tastes not tried before and communicating it to our waiter with a blushing charm. The conversation was good and as we talked about our four individual adventures and observations, they made intelligent comment on all that the year had delivered. They showed a warmth and a compassion for each other and for the people they had met along the way. They also showed a rich streak of gentle, teasing humour, and unselfconscious laughter rang out from our table as the evening elegantly unfolded.

The lights were set low and from our high vantage point we could look out over Manhattan, across the lights of the city to the dark rectangle of Central Park and the Upper East Side, where our apartment awaited. The bill eventually came and despite it being the most expensive meal I had ever paid for, I handed over the Amex card without hesitation. A healthy tip acknowledged a wonderful night delivered by the most caring attendants, our chairs were gently pulled back and a steady stream of staff bade warm goodnights as we headed back for the elevator. I had my camera with me and took a picture in order to capture the moment and remember for ever a very special night.

The following day was 31 August. They boarded a plane for London, I stepped back on board for our last ocean crossing and New York breezed unsuspecting into September.

18

RACING IN PERSPECTIVE
NEW YORK TO PORTSMOUTH VIA JERSEY
31.08.01–26.09.01

Clipper wanted us to start the race alongside the towers of Manhattan but with no wind (and much to the relief of the race crews) the plan was shelved. The idea of starting off the Statue of Liberty and racing out through the Verrazano Narrows, dodging Staten Island ferries, pleasure craft, container ships and tugs, would have been a nightmare and with a small window on the tide, one boat could gain a serious advantage before the race had even reached the ocean proper.

So instead of racing, we formed up in a large V, motored across the Hudson and began our parade down the Manhattan shore. Crowds maybe ten deep lined the route for mile after mile and cheered our brave departure.

Not.

New York had remained blissfully unaware of our presence throughout the stay and as the grand parade of ocean-going yachts readied themselves for the might of the North Atlantic, not a soul stood on the banks to see us go.

But as the fleet came abeam the yacht harbour under the shadow of the World Trade Center, the small yellow ferry that had shuttled crews back and forth from New Jersey to Manhattan gave us a blast from its foghorn. The other luxury cruise yachts moored there quickly joined in and the combined hooting ricocheted off the tall aluminium walls and came spinning back over the water towards us. It was a moving gesture from sailor to sailor and meant a lot to us.

We turned downstream and motored past the Statue of Liberty, the crews snapping away at the extraordinary skyline for one last time, unaware that when their films were developed three weeks later, the photographs would take on such a powerful significance.

When Ambrose Light came abeam, the fleet formed up in a Le Mans-style start and set off for our third crossing of the Atlantic, out of sight of any spectators or support boats. The GPS showed the next waypoint as the Lizard Light, on the coast of Cornwall, and Clipper were eager for us to set a brisk record for the classic route between the two points.

The race was departing at the start of the autumn equinox, and low-pressure system after low-pressure system should help to sweep us across.

The Great Circle route would take us towards Newfoundland and the shallow Grand Banks. *The Perfect Storm* was set here and the fishing boat sent to the bottom of the ocean made its final, fateful journey at the same time of year as our crossing. It would mean some feisty sailing in feisty conditions and I was looking forward to a final sharp workout as the sea threw us its worst.

We had a familiar face back on board, rejoining the team for the first time since Hawaii. I was delighted to have James Landale back in the team and on my watch. He was a good helm too and would strengthen our position when the weather turned.

As we slipped away from Long Island, the winds remained light and we tracked away from the coast, along with *Bristol* and *Jersey*, in order to get into deeper water first. We had reckoned on there being helpful current at the thousand-metre depth mark and hoped it would sweep us on past the inshore fleet.

It was a track that would also take us over the very tip of the Grand Banks, so if the weather did turn, we would be in the steep waves for the smallest amount of time.

Ice, which could be a threat, had, during this mild autumn, receded further than my hairline and gave us one less thing to worry about. Small 'growlers' did not show up on radar and at night would be impossible to see – the first glimpse would be made by the crew in the forepeak, as the ice burst through the thin hull skin and joined them on their pillows.

Frustratingly, our instruments showed we were losing two knots of boat speed to a counter-current that should not have been there, and although we were sailing along well, the daily mileage total suffered.

The chart clearly showed that the current should be with us and every other boat in the race seemed to be making healthy distances yet again. It was horribly frustrating and as each radio sched came in, we found we had slipped further behind.

As the Grand Banks loomed, the position of the leaders was plotted as they headed close to the Newfoundland shore. According to our charts, there appeared to be plenty of counter-current that would stop them in their tracks, but it refused to find them.

Nor was there any sign of the series of lows we were bracing ourselves for, and despite a couple of decent spinnaker runs, the wind remained horribly light. Down at the wrong end of the fleet, we looked anxiously at the performance of *Liverpool*, *Plymouth* and *Portsmouth*. If we stayed where we were, they could all overtake us in the championship points tally and from our solid third place overall we would slump to a lowly sixth.

As if to make amends, a profusion of sea birds and whales joined us, providing the best wildlife display of the entire trip. A huge whale surfaced right alongside us, its massive, spouting form the same length as our hull. We had comical-looking pilot whales sticking their stubby noses out of the surf as a great pod rode the Atlantic with us. We had dolphin after dolphin clearing their blowholes with a distinctive puff right next to the cockpit, and, with a trust that was frightening, they all seemed to want to share their home.

The sun shone on a glassy sea and for day after day we continued the struggle to complete decent distances. On the way up from Brazil our run of three hundred miles in twenty-four hours had set a new record, but now *London* was not even managing to get into three figures.

The storms failed to materialise and the Grand Banks turned themselves into 'the Perfect Yawn' as everyone became affected by the conditions and we slopped oh so slowly eastwards. The radio scheds, run by *Leeds*, turned into a 'last day of term' round of nonsense chat as we all struggled with the tedious progress.

As we gathered around the radio at lunchtime on 11 September for the latest positions, the race suddenly ceased to be of importance. Simon, skipper of *Leeds*, relayed the news that an aircraft had crashed into one of the Twin Towers and suggested we tune into the BBC's World Service.

The vision of a Cessna being flicked off the World Trade Center like a tiresome tic grew in nightmarish proportions as the news erupted like a mushroom cloud outwards and upwards until it towered over us in a deathly grey pall.

We had all been there. We had shopped in its mall, drunk in its bars, used its subways and licked its ice cream. The dinner I had enjoyed on the top floor, looked after by the nicest people, so sensitive to my family, was recalled in a disbelieving haze. I could picture the kind face of the old waiter who had made such a fuss of us. I could recall with real clarity the elevator attendant, the barman, the cloakroom lady. What had happened to them and everyone else who earned their living within the walls of those towers?

News from the radio was reported with an assumption that the listener also had access to a TV set. When they said an aircraft, surely it would be something that the tower could withstand. When they said it was a passenger jet, surely it was empty but for some nut at the control. When they said it was full and not one but two aircraft, surely it was a mistake. When they said the buildings had collapsed, surely it was journalistic licence for a floor or two of crumbling rubble.

As the reports carried on through the day and into the night, growing in detail and adding more facts, the picture became horribly clear.

My mind raced ahead and I started to think what the reaction might be to such a calculated act of terrorism. Having been away from world news for a year, I had only the sketchiest idea about America's new president, but I had learnt enough to know that George W. Bush would be spoiling for a fight. The BBC reporters were still trying to establish who the perpetrators were, but even as that was being discussed, there was talk of hitting back.

I became a news junky, acutely aware of where such an attitude could take the world. The very real scenario of the planet tearing itself apart was cruelly at odds with the peace, tranquillity, freedom and pureness of the endless vista all around us.

The wilds of the world's oceans suddenly seemed the safest place on earth to be.

But despite that, I desperately wanted to be at home. I wanted to wrap myself around my children and tell them it would be all right. I wanted to look into their eyes and promise that no harm would come to them. I wanted to offer parental reassurance that they had a safe future and, even though that was what I wanted, I had heard enough to realise that such words of comfort could not be trusted.

I knew that they would be shaken to the core by the uncomfortably familiar sights on the TV and spent a long time on the sat phone, trying to put a part of me three thousand miles ahead of our slowly moving bow, in order to ease their pain. Michael's voice was broken by shock and he asked me if the newspaper headline proclaiming 'Armageddon' was true. Holly's tears fell into the phone and splashed back out in mid-Atlantic as she cried for the wretched souls captured on film as they plummeted to the ground.

Overnight my children's innocence had been brutally blown away and I heard second-hand about the tears and the fears that filled my home, in a moving follow-up e-mail from Anne. I fired up my laptop and looked at the picture I had taken of us at the end of our special dinner.

I wanted desperately to reassure them and offer a small crumb of support to help ease the pain they were feeling. While the watch around me slept, I lay propped up in my bunk and started to tap away at the keys, writing a piece specifically for my children. Forty minutes later it was done, and from the nav desk I dispatched the file to *The Times*.

London Diary, Saturday, 15 September 2001

> *In my forty-five years on the planet, that was a defining week in a year of defining moments.*
>
> *I lie in my bunk and look at a picture stored on my laptop taken the day before we left New York. There, smiling back at me, is my family. Confident, happy, assured, at the end of a wonderful dinner in a gently lit dining room 120 floors above Manhattan.*
>
> *It was taken in the World Trade Center and the confidence of youth shines like a bright beacon from my children's eyes.*
>
> *A few days later, that innocence, faith and trust had been raped and overnight the child became tarnished with the foul and sordid problems of the world. Having been there, the abstract, for them, was replaced by raw reality and the people we touched, responded to and created a bond with, probably now lie, a tragic statistic, crushed under a million tons of rubble.*
>
> *Too far away, I have to try and offer support and reassurance to young minds coming to terms with a loss*

they take personally and who are rightly worried when the word 'Retribution' is bandied about with cavalier abandon.

I hope that my circumnavigating circle, concluding this week, might offer them a beacon of hope in a world that seems destined to self-destruct on greed, jealousy and lack of respect.

And if it helps, then this year-long odyssey becomes way more than a mere sailing adventure, or a highly charged sporting event.

We have sat for thousands of hours and witnessed the days and nights as planet earth gently breathes. We have witnessed its light and its dark. We have endured serenity, solitude, tumult and, occasionally, chaos. Its presence is total and recognises no borders, no cultures, no class or divides.

It belongs to all of us, in equal proportions, and we, wherever we live, are responsible for it. Without care and without respect, it will simply cease to be.

No matter whether you are a Cuban or a citizen of Brazil or a fisherman in Portugal with your Catholic faith. No matter if your home is in Yokohama, Tokyo or Nagasaki, with your Shinto temple. Irrespective of the Hinduism of Mauritius, the Anglican faith in South Africa or the Buddhist shrines in China, the world remains a shared possession. In the Galápagos, they pray in a corrugated-tin church and on Christmas Island an almost identical building brings the community together.

For me, the simple sight of the Southern Cross is all I need to feel secure, humbled and inspired in equal measure.

And into those cultures, those beliefs, those ways of lives, we have stepped ashore and found new friends in the most unlikely of places.

In Hong Kong, we left a bond and a link with the sampan drivers who ferried us ashore throughout the days and nights. In the Galápagos, Ecuadorian Panama-hat-wearing George looked after us with all the care of an attentive father. In Yokohama, Frank took us under his wing like long-lost relatives and in Mauritius the pedlars of tatty beach souvenirs took time out for a kick-about on the sand with my son.

In New York, we bantered comfortably with the doorman of our rented apartment and in Cape Town the taxi drivers included us in their lives for the few days of our passing. In the Philippines, as I walked between a poor farmhouse and a small field of mangy-looking vegetables, the owner gave me a beaming smile and shouted out, 'Hello, sir' as I slipped by his plot.

In Okinawa, where the memory of mass destruction sits fresh in the mind, strangers are greeted warmly and the desire to have dialogue, above all else, remains their eager mantra.

And in the shadow of such dastardly, foul-minded, greedy deeds that have tarnished the world this week, I have seen enough hope from the last forty-eight weeks to know that there are enough people on this planet, irrespective of their cultures or beliefs, who are big enough and brave enough to stand up and be counted for the sake of the home we all share.

I make no apologies for not giving you a report of our painfully slow journey towards Jersey. Coming first, fourth or eighth into St Helier this week becomes deeply insignificant when the last year has suddenly justified itself with such clarity.

To my precious Holly and Michael, to baby Ben Gibson – indeed to all those young lives who will inherit the earth – I hope that my observations help, just a little.

Dad (Ian Dickens)

It seemed that my personal words helped others besides Holly and Mike when they were published a couple of days later. The observations and the reminder that hope still existed amid the madness seemed to touch a wider audience. Most importantly for me, it helped put things into perspective for my children. As more people saw the piece, so the sentiments travelled and it eventually became syndicated and was broadly read across the USA, bringing a steady stream of gratifying thanks.

The skies became silent for the next week and the blueness above us remained free of vapour trails, as the airways to America closed down.

We willed the wind to arrive and help speed the journey for a crew whose hearts were no longer truly in the race. Overnight the sporting element had become a trivial bit of nonsense but the more we willed the winds to arrive, the lighter they became.

Even the days of a hundred miles in twenty-four hours seemed a lifetime away. Forty-five-mile totals looked decidedly racy and the whole fleet bunched right back together again. With the weather faxes bringing pictures of high pressure after high pressure, it was clear that we were going to be late into Jersey.

On one particularly entertaining day, *London* shot from seventh to joint-first place in one period of windless slop and then slumped back down to eighth again just twelve hours later. It was clearly going to be a complete lottery and any boat that got moving would do so thanks to the flukiest of gusts rather than through skill and tactics.

As the coast of Ireland drew slowly closer, the weather dictated that we sit at the southern flank of the fleet, now strung out in a vertical line to the north, all with almost identical distances to go. South looked good and when *Bristol* headed towards us it seemed to endorse this view. But then the first decent breeze in weeks cut in from the north and we were at the back once more.

It was so painful it was laughable and the whole stopover in Jersey, complete with its big crew reunion party, looked to be in jeopardy. There was some thought that the race might be called off, but with the top three positions so close, it would cause huge controversy if the organisers chose such an option. We, like *Jersey* and *Bristol*, could still win the event outright and no one wanted it to end with a whimper.

It was a nightmare dilemma for Clipper. They had a huge amount of sponsorship from the island of Jersey, and its people were expecting a big event to come sailing in during the next couple of days. They had three hundred guests coming to a party in order to meet round-the-world yachtsmen and women, and they had a race that needed to maintain its credibility in the world of sailing.

After a long silence it was announced that the race would continue for as long as it took and everything else would be rescheduled around it. That was good news as far as we were concerned, and the crew settled down to going nowhere with renewed vigour.

Getting a thirty-ton boat moving in the lightest of breezes and maximising every little bit of puff is the most technical sailing possible. It required incredible patience, total concentration for hour after hour and constant trimming to reap the maximum benefit. With such short distances being covered by the fleet, an extra mile could mean the difference between first and last place, so we worked the boat as hard as we could.

When an Irish coastguard turboprop (identified as an Italian passenger plane by one of the crew) swooped low over us, we were up to second place and starting to feel a little more hopeful of a decent result. They had also flown over *Bristol*, now to the south, and as the wind holes continued we crossed the continental shelf and headed towards the Celtic Sea.

Wildlife still abounded and for night after night, *London* was tracked by dolphins bursting through the richest phosphorescence we had seen. They zoomed in and out of our wake like torpedoes running amok and the night watches were dazzled by the raw and simple beauty of their presence. Out on a windless sea, they kept us company, languidly breaking the surface through the following day and at one point we had around forty riding with us as constant companions for several hours at a time.

Shipping started to increase and after several false starts, a decent wind kicked in and pushed us towards the winking light of Bishop Rock. The wind, after such a benign, tedious fortnight, whipped into the sails but not, unfortunately, into certain members of my watch. As we changed jibs, reefed and tacked, every manoeuvre seemed to turn into a Fred Karno cock-up of amateurism. Everyone reported they were ready to put in a reef, yet this simple and familiar task descended into farce. As we tried to correct the problems, losing valuable seconds along the way, my fellow watch leader offered a shoulder of support. Ali could see where the trouble lay and, like me, he knew that one or two of my team were clearly struggling to get through the final week at sea.

In the debriefs, the pressures of eleven months of intense racing started to break to the surface. There was backchat and muttered asides and no matter what was said to try to resolve things, the next manoeuvre became an even bigger disaster area.

Stuart got involved and he too seemed to be battering at a brick wall, as more of the same was aimed at him. Just when we were about to complete our thirty-six-thousandth mile, it appeared that nothing had been learnt and that the summit of sailing knowledge I thought I was approaching was proving to be no more than the bump of a foothill. If nothing else, it was a valuable lesson in humility to discover that one never, ever stops learning.

We had a crew meeting at which everyone was urged to hold it together for just a little longer. Stuart asked for patience from those on the receiving end of the frustrations, calling on them to rise above it, count to ten and refocus, but the mood did not improve much.

And to worsen the frustration, the wind that had got us to the Scilly Isles started to tail off again. As we tacked through ridiculously big angles created by the fast-flowing tide, real progress was once again proving a challenge and *Liverpool*, *Leeds* and *Jersey* started to close in. As we crept towards the Lizard, their sails appeared astern and a real scrap was developing over the last couple of hundred miles.

The *QE2* steamed past close by and despite the fact that the high-flying jet vapour trails had restarted, I wondered if we were looking at the possible future of transatlantic travel. Stu called them up on the radio and learnt that the two thousand people on board would be delivered into Southampton just four hours later. Twelve hours after that, the liner would be off to New York again, fully revictualled, cleaned and laundered, with a new complement of passengers. In order to get to America, it seemed much more appealing to spend five days moving at a heady twenty-five knots, with some decent food, an evening movie, spectacular sunsets and a surface alive with wildlife, rather than face the nightmare of Heathrow and then hours of inertia as trolley-pushing flight attendants, with their sing-song 'Ice and lemon?', brushed by at thirty thousand feet.

Whatever. She looked stunning with her rich blue hull, smart red lines and the understated Cunard logo below the bridge. The *QE2* was our first sign of England and when the dark-blue haze of land grew in size, a perfect autumnal day revealed home proper. Above the cliffs, a patchwork quilt of stubble fields showed that harvesting had only recently been completed.

The green and pleasant land so often remembered by our playing of 'Jerusalem' surrounded the ultra-white buildings of the Lizard lighthouse, perched precariously above the sea. Beyond them lay more fields, some brown, some green, with the tiny white dots of sheep and, further away, a coppice and a house or two. Down below the cliffs, inshore trawlers motored home with determination, chased by flocks of seagulls, and as we struggled to get around the GPS mark that we had aimed at all the way from New York, a bloody-minded freighter decided to head straight at us, forcing a last-minute tack. He had all the sea room in the world and his belligerence was a fine reminder of some of the less attractive qualities of home.

We just scraped around the mark by the skin of our teeth. A big tide was on the turn and starting to sluice back out towards the Atlantic, almost taking us with it. With not much wind, it was a close-run thing and the boats behind us were well and truly caught. Both *Jersey* and *Leeds* were in sight but, trapped by the fast flow, they were unable to make the turning point until either the wind increased or the tide turned again.

London had been closing in on *Liverpool* all day and we thought we would get them at the mark. When they turned to *Jersey* some half a mile before us, Stuart wondered if there had been some sort of error in our data. He checked the waypoint co-ordinates from the race file, then double-checked them with the skipper of *Jersey*. He checked with *Liverpool* to ensure that they were following the same race directions and, having done that, he rechecked our own waypoints. It seemed clear that we had turned around the correct mark and *Liverpool* had not.

But Stuart being Stuart, he was not even going to begin to suggest that *Liverpool* were cutting corners in order to stay in front. He firmly believed it to be a genuine mistake and didn't really want to follow the crew's desire to take matters further. We believed that a missed mark, mistake or not, had to be reported – especially when our hard work at closing the gap to just half a mile had been lost and we were now back to three. He fired off a message to race HQ and waited to see what would happen at the finish.

It transpired that *Liverpool*'s computer showed the same GPS position as our own, yet their turning point was a good half-mile further away from the coast. After the attacks on America, information relayed from the American-controlled GPS satellites was being classified as more sensitive and, as a result, it was less reliable than what had been available previously.

As we headed for Jersey, the wind got up again and with the rest of the fleet struggling to make the Lizard, we beat into the stiffening breeze with three reefs and the No. 2 Yankee up at the bow. It was Sod's Law that the on-the-nose breeze we had battled with to the Lizard, now swung round and did its best to bar our path to the Channel Islands.

At some point we were going to have to tack, and with ourselves and *Liverpool* being forced well west, timing would decide the second and third places. With a firm eye on the overall standings, Stuart decided to go early and stem a long period of foul tide, in order to have a direct beam reach towards the finish when it turned.

The tack was another complete cock-up by my watch and I went to my bunk desperately depressed at our inability to perform even the simplest of manoeuvres. Earlier a sail change had taken much longer than it should have, with no sign of any contribution from one grumpy team member. A further reef, which we should have been able to do with our eyes shut, collapsed in mayhem when lines were not ready and I soul-searched once more over how to combat such problems.

If I went through a verbal checklist with the team, I was scorned by the struggling individuals for being patronising. If I kept quiet, all the things that should happen suddenly failed to happen, and if I stepped in and corrected the problem, I was criticised for doing someone else's job.

Ali had been at my side again and put a comforting arm out in the darkness, understanding my deep frustration.

As the short, sharp, uncomfortable English Channel chop continued, the sun rose and we saw the Channel Islands for the first time. As the tide turned, Stuart's decision seemed to pay off, as two knots of current pushed us towards our target and into a direct run to the finish. We scanned the horizon for signs of *Liverpool* but had no idea where they were. Guernsey came and went and there, finally, was Jersey, with the Corbière lighthouse standing proud as the last waypoint of the race.

A large gin palace motored out and kept station off our starboard stern quarter, its crew waving and pointing cameras. As we closed on the island, so more craft joined in, until a flotilla of around sixty boats surrounded us. It was a generous welcome and when a powerful rib zoomed close in, complete with TV crews, we could see that a couple of friends of *Liverpool*'s crew had hitched a lift.

Surely they would not be out at sea if their boat had finished, and when Muir pointed to us and mouthed the word 'Second', we were ecstatic. Alan, celebrating his birthday, took the wheel and we crossed the finish line to a cacophony of horns.

It mattered not that we were a week late. On Sunday morning, Jersey had come to celebrate and in addition to the boats all around us, we could make out thousands of spectators lining the cliff tops. Poor old *Bristol* had won the race and arrived at 04.00 without so much as a single spectator to applaud their success. We milked it for all it was worth, and the closely following fleet saw every hug and embrace, every popped champagne cork and every silly dance recorded by banks of TV and press cameras. Stuart even did the

Ellen McArthur bit and let off a couple of hand-held flares for the hooting fleet.

Second place meant that we had earned a fourth red pennant and as the rest of the fleet arrived, we worked out the latest points tally. *Portsmouth*, our nearest rival, finished last and, with *Plymouth* fifth, our third-place position in the overall standings was untouchable.

With *Bristol* winning and *Jersey* finishing fourth, we could go no higher either, so for us it was the end of the race. It could not have been a better place to celebrate a podium finish in the championship and the island really responded with the warmest of welcomes. In shops, supermarkets, restaurants and bars, everyone knew about the adventure and wanted to talk about it with us.

I had a clean dry bed too, thanks to an enthusiastic welcome from Kathryn Fowler, my old PA. She whisked me home and with her husband, Andrew, provided five-star hospitality in return for my tales from the high seas.

Andrew's parents supplied supper and in exchange I gave them a potted history of our year away. I knew that this would become a recurring feature of my homecoming and relished the chance to see what effect it had on an audience. In this I was helped by the digital pictures stored on my laptop, and Joy, Chris, Kathryn and Andrew proved an exceptionally good audience, listening with rapt attention as they hurtled around the Cape of Good Hope in the comfort of their dining room.

I did my last victualling run in good old M&S and rather than having to buy hundreds of tins, we could opt for a few packs of fresh pasta, salads and ready-made sandwiches for our last twenty-four-hour race back to Portsmouth. Instead of relying on a truck to ferry it all back, I could simply stroll to the marina with all we needed packed into a few carrier bags and have it all stowed in a couple of minutes.

In New York, I had intentionally run down the food stocks to keep the boat as light as possible. The extra days at sea meant that supplies had dwindled somewhat and we saw an increasing inventiveness by the galley crew in using up what remained. Unlike many of the other boats, we never came even close to being hungry, but we were down to our last half loo roll when the sun rose on our final day.

The send-off from the island for the twenty-four-hour blast back to Portsmouth was equally spectacular. A large fire-fighting tug led the yachts out of the harbour, her hoses making a huge arc across the water. Four Yaks (one of them flown by my old friend Peter Scandrett) zoomed low in a really tight air display, and once again we were pursued by an armada of some seventy boats.

As usual, the winds were light and a new start line was set in order for us to make it to the finish on time for the assembled press. For several hours we motored in glorious sunshine and flat-calm sea until the island of Alderney was off to port and the French coast around ten miles to starboard.

Sailing to Jersey on a training race the year before had seemed like a major adventure, but after so many miles the distance really compressed into what was suddenly a ridiculously short hop. We lined up in the still-light winds and made a reasonable start, running in the front third of the pack. But the winds proved fickle, all the time shifting, and constant trimming was required in order to seize any advantage.

With one puff the breeze seemed to favour us and with the next we would drop back a little. The last night at sea fell, and up ahead a lighthouse shone its clear warning. It was coming from the Needles and already England had crept closer far quicker than we wanted it to. And even though our position in the series was secure, we wanted to end on a high note.

My watch finished and I got my head down for the last time in the narrow bunk. This small, personal space was home and for one more night I looked at the pictures of my family taped to the walls. The damp pillows, deeply encrusted with black mould, supported my head and the damp and equally blackened duvet was pulled up over the musty-smelling sleeping bag liner. To the gentle sound of water on the hull and with a slight heel from the increasing breeze, I fell into a confused sleep.

Waking early, I went to take a look at our progress on the chart table as the sounds of sail changes took place above me. I was spotted by Stuart, who immediately enlisted me to help, and I arrived on deck in T-shirt, boxer shorts and life jacket.

The other boats were a long way off and I learnt that Ali's watch had inherited the Fred Karno routine that I had begun to think was exclusive to me. Stuart was struggling to understand why he had not gybed with the rest of the fleet and Ali and Andy were furious with themselves at an apparently clumsy and slow piece of foredeck work in transferring the spinnaker across.

London was now dead last and the mood on deck was not good. Never mind that we were guaranteed third overall, we had wanted a last pennant for our swansong race and with hours, rather than weeks ahead, there was little chance of improving our result.

We arrived in the Solent around the eastern edge of the Isle of Wight before daybreak, which was good news for the race organisers and bad news for us. The finish had been carefully timed for 11.00, so to keep us hard at it until the allotted moment, the race course was extended. For the next few hours we dipped in and out of the Solent as a misty, damp, grey dawn fumbled its way out of the night.

With a good strong wind, the racers were making the new marks ahead of schedule and the radio was alive with course change after course change from the organisers. It meant a lot of swift manoeuvres, good tacking, spinnaker sets and drops, sail hoists and trimming, and to my delight, when my team came back on watch, all the cock-ups of the last week vanished into thin air.

The team were sharper than razor blades and as we dropped the kite yet again and tacked towards yet another mark, we were clearly closing on *Leeds*. The crew were really fired up and when we passed them and started to close on *Portsmouth*, the boat was back to her normal self.

Clearing the Nab Tower by inches, just holding on to the kite in a wind that had become brisk, the trimmers had to ease it right out before the rudder could get any purchase and make the vital turn. Behind us, *Leeds* followed the same frantic course and like us, they were nearly laid flat on several occasions as the spinnaker powered the boat right up.

And then there was the Solent proper. There was Cowes. There was Fawley power station and there, in the distance, Portsmouth. Because of our delays crossing the Atlantic, the lively weekend we had planned for the finish was replaced by a bleak and cold Wednesday morning. As it was midweek there were no great fleets of spectator boats or massed crowds along the shore and when one of Clipper's racy 'thirty-eights' motored alongside with training skipper Liz Green on board, we chatted across the water as if we had left England only that morning.

It all seemed dreadfully normal and the last forty-eight weeks, the previous 35,999 miles, the wilds of the Pacific, the South China Sea, the Atlantic and the Cape all vanished into a parallel universe that became a distant dream.

The musicians in Havana, the man who had spirited his lover and son away to America from the Hemingway Marina in Cuba, George in the Galápagos, the beautiful Polynesian girls who welcomed us with flower leis in Honolulu, Frank and his saki-induced rendition of 'Two Rittle Boys' in Japan, the US goons in Okinawa, the posing of the Royal Hong Kong Yacht Club members, the wonderful Marshall and his lime-green *banka* in the Philippines, Don O'Donnell and his boatload of refugees on Christmas Island, the Bolton-loving cabby in Mauritius, the adrenalin-filled adventures off the Cape, the warmth of the São Paulo taxi driver who led me to Ayrton Senna's grave and the restaurant staff who treated us with such professionalism at the top of the World Trade Center, just three weeks before – all retreated and suddenly became memories hard to hold on to.

The official Clipper spectator boat, crammed full of family and friends, motored by and I could hear Anne and the children long before I could see them. A huge banner held aloft by Peter and Isobel Sticklee proclaimed 'Welcome Home Ian' to their uncle and just a few minutes later our race was run.

We motored in with all the podium pennants flying, gulping champagne from the bottle and trying to take in that this really was the end. When the commentator announced '*London Clipper*' to the massed ranks, we slipped alongside for the last time as the Royal Marines played us in. In the sea of faces, I could see my Tiger Moth-flying friend Charlie and skydiving pal Simon Ward. There were family faces everywhere and I could see Henry and Sue, Jonathan, John and Signe. There was Kate, adamant that she should fulfil her mother's wishes and allow the spirit of Aunt Audrey to become part of the celebration she had so wanted to witness. There were Mark and Debbie, Bernadette and Tony, Liz and her banner-making brood, my best friend Jem and his partner Nicky, Gerry and Lucy, Dave Gunns and his son, Christopher – so many familiar faces, all smiling the biggest of smiles – and I hugged them all with the greatest of affection.

And then there was Anne, who planted a huge, big, wet kiss to assembled laughter and cheers. There was Michael, who impressed with the strength of his warm and all-enveloping bear hug. And then there was Holly, who, as she embraced me, sobbed with the intensity that is reserved for dad-and-daughter reunions. Together we fished out the now battered packet of tiny metallic stars that she had given me eleven months before and which I had carried faithfully around the world, and sent the last four into the water to complete a huge circle. I held on to her tight and wallowed in the sweetest of homecomings, that only a loving family can bring.

19

SPLASHDOWN AND RE-ENTRY
LONDON DIARY, WEDNESDAY, 26 SEPTEMBER 2001

L ondon *bobs gently at her moorings. The wake of passing ships sends her hull rocking and she strains at the lines holding her to the pontoon, as if eager to break free.*

Her decks are empty, her holds clean, her bunks devoid of life and her radio silent. Her sails that have driven us across the Atlantic Ocean, through the Caribbean, over the mighty Pacific, through the South China Sea, across the Indian Ocean and around the Cape of Good Hope to the South Atlantic, rest stained and weary in their bags.

The galley is silent, the nav desk is blind, the instruments unreading and the skipper's cabin zipped up and moved out. The logos are peeling, rust streaks line the once-white hull and halyards and sheets lie frayed in a salt-encrusted coil.

Ships have souls. Their personality is made by the crew, whose energy and drive, focus and dedication, determination and resolve make the hull sing.

And how she has sung. From the lightest of breezes in the North Atlantic to the fiercest of sixty-five-knot blows off Japan. From under vast thunder clouds alive with crackling lightning off the coast of Cuba to the huge rolling swells coming up from the Southern Ocean off South Africa. Under the watchful eyes of soaring albatross and gently inquisitive whales, London has taken us around thirty-six thousand miles of the world's oceans and delivered us safely back home again.

To an outside observer, as she sits at her lonely mooring, it looks as if that soul has departed. To her crew, though, it can never die. If we were to step on board again and take a nostalgic stroll around the decks – be it next week or next year – a thousand different memories would spring instantly to life.

In the galley, we alone would hear the sound of laughter as Danny rustles up beans on toast in impossible conditions. We alone can imagine the sound of a gently strummed guitar coming from Stu's cabin as it helps to soothe his fevered brow. We alone will look at the nav station and hear Anna's insistent call for log details and we alone will recall the mixed look of astonishment as the off watch are woken to do the graveyard 02.00 sail.

We alone will look at the spinnaker pole and see Aki riding it in the fiercest of storms. We alone will look at the cockpit entrance and hear Ali's ever-present greeting as he arrives on deck.

We alone will remember the elation of a good radio sched echoing around the cabin, and recall the tough times as people struggled with seasickness, a rolling bunk and their own demons, in their battle to complete the course.

At the wheel, the worn leather betrays a million turns and we alone will recall London's hull responding to every input as her thirty tons answered the call to dance.

Our adventure is over, but our love affair with the boat that carried us safely around the world will continue indefinitely. If you happen to see her awaiting refit in a boatyard in Plymouth or sitting at a desolate mooring in Southampton, go and say hello, pat her hull and let some of her magic rub off on you.

She has been on the podium for every one of her three circumnavigations and the twenty-seven of us who were privileged to take her around the world this time join Ras Turner and his crew from 1996 and Alex Thompson and his 1998 crew as fully paid-up, devoted members of her fan club.

Wherever she sails in the future and wherever the seas take her, a part of us will for ever remain on board. And as we splashdown back to normality next week, that thought alone is comfort indeed.

Ian Dickens

With a final push of the send button, my last piece of copy flew off to *The Times* and I gathered my belongings together. Around me, the people who had shared so much did the same and, like me, they completed it all as slowly as possible. Any excuse to stay on board a little longer was grasped at and my family, waiting expectantly on the quayside, started to get a little irritated.

Getting off was hard, though. Everything we knew, everything we needed, everything that had moulded the last intense year, was on board and, like a child with its comfort blanket, we were loath to let go.

Outside was a big bad world where an uncertain future would have to be faced. On board, the routine was so comfortably familiar and the desire to slip the lines and return to our proper home out of sight of land, with a kettle singing in the galley, the smell of fresh bread, the easy routine of making the boat work, the secret night skies and the warm respect for the members of the team who made it all happen, whispered a seductive call.

A final hug to Anna and Ellie, to Andy and the Baba. To James Landale, James Bedford-Russell, Nieves, Alan, Doris and David. To Aki and finally, especially, to Stuart. There was no sign of Jane, and her bunk was already clean and vacated as she headed for the sanctuary of home.

I stepped over the rail, handed my kitbag down to Anne and jumped ashore. A last look and a gentle pat on the side of *London*'s hull and we turned, damp-eyed, towards the car park and a drive into the future.

The welcome back to Britain was entirely predictable. The hotel Anne had booked in Portsmouth decided to let the room go to someone else and when we arrived in the afternoon to check in, there was nothing for us.

'It's not my fault,' said the girl on reception, blaming the computer for not showing the booking, now clearly visible on the screen in front of her. With no rooms anywhere in Portsmouth, we ended up at a cheap Novotel in Southampton, and had the added expense of a taxi to take us there after a final crew party.

The next morning we needed to get back to Portsmouth, and the staff in reception directed me to a free phone in the corner of the lobby. It provided a hotline to the local minicab firm, who answered with an uninterested, 'Yeah.'

'How much to Portsmouth?' I asked.

'Fifteen pounds,' said the bored voice.

'OK, fine,' I said. 'Hello? Hello?' She had hung up.

Ten minutes went by and with no sign of a car, I called again.

'I was after a car to Portsmouth and we're still waiting.'

'Yer didn't book it,' she replied.

'You didn't give me time,' I said, fighting the growing desire to have a full-blown argument.

'That's not my problem,' was the helpful response. 'D'yer want it or not?'

I wanted to become Captain Pompous and bark back, 'Do you want my business or not', but I was stuck in Southampton and she was the only cab firm answering the phone.

'Yes, please, and thank you so much for your help. Hello? Hello?'

Mmm. Welcome home.

We drove through the English countryside and on to the dreaded M25, each mile taking me further away from the sea. Having spent a year where speeds in excess of 15mph were treated with whoops of glee, 60mph seemed suddenly fast. All around me on this weekday morning, executive cars with suit jackets hanging in the back flashed by. The outside lane was full of senior execs and sales reps rushing from one appointment to the next in their Mercs and BMWs. They flashed headlights to shift a lane hog out of the way and the juggernauts played their own game of rushing aggression as they crawled nose to tail around Essex.

I sat in the slow lane, happy to cruise gently along. Now so in tune with accepting the vagaries of the wind and the current, I saw that rushing would achieve nothing other than an ulcer. The family were thrilled at this new me. For years I had led the outside-lane charge and gunned my turbocharged engine to prove who was king of the road, as their white knuckles gripped the seat.

And now we plodded along in a hire car, oblivious of the truckers creaming past inches from the window, listening to the radio and taking in the countryside. Eventually my slow, laid-back pace got to Anne, who uttered a line I never thought I would hear: 'Can you drive faster, please – we want to get home.'

Before leaving Portsmouth I had looked at the AA road map in the car, traced the Greenwich Meridian north and impressed myself by finding that it intersected the orbital road pretty much where I had imagined. This was the moment I had thought about several months before, from many thousands of miles away, and now we were closing in on the point.

Back then, we were sailing north-west, away from the coast of Africa, and heading towards the centre of the South Atlantic and Brazil.

We watched the GPS count slowly down through eastings until, for a moment, we, the crew, were neither east nor west. The display read 000° 00.000'' for a split second, and then westings, for the first time in several months, brought us back from the fleeting visit to nowhere.

The concept of being nowhere wasn't new because I had been there several times before. On childhood visits to my grandparents' home in Blackheath, we were taken to the Royal Greenwich Observatory and it was always a memorable day out, no matter how many times we did it.

Part of the routine was to stand astride the copper strip set into the pavement, which marked the imaginary line soaring off to the exotic and unimaginable places I was later to visit. Way back then, though, for the first time in my life, this small and impressionable boy stood confused by the notion that, for a moment, he was nowhere.

I had thought of those days as we slopped across the zero-degree longitude four thousand miles south and now we were crossing the point exactly as predicted. Our Vauxhall went from east to west at a heady, spray-filled 60mph, but this time there were no great swells, no albatross, no dolphins, no wind-flecked waves and no *Cutty Sark*-driving trade winds as the numbers whizzed, somewhat quicker, down to zero and, for a moment, nowheresville.

A strip of asphalt replaced the ocean, cutting a swathe through the countryside. There were plastic-clad warehouses that marked the edge of a trading estate. There were huge signposts warning of the upcoming turn-off and there were trucks, cars, buses and vans.

There were also blue flashing lights and a closed road.

All across the tarmac were bits of motorbike and a dented car that had slewed around to an ungainly halt, straddling two of the now silent lanes.

A yellow crash helmet sat on the soaking road amid torn-off chrome exhaust pipes, a ripped saddle and a buckled wheel. Underneath a blue tarpaulin that was being pounded by the incessant rain, lay the lifeless body of the rider. Round him, beside him, over him, the police silently worked, doing what was needed, with the minimum of fuss.

At some point a community officer would have the thankless task of knocking on a door and telling a white-faced loved one the dreadful news.

All of this happened within a hundred yards of the Greenwich Meridian. It happened a couple of seconds into the westings and the poor soul, as he went truly west, straddled the exotic longitude on his final and violent journey.

His start point, astride the glistening machine, had been exciting – exotic even. The end, unimaginable. And now, like everyone who straddles the line, he too was nowhere.

It seemed appropriate to slow right down again and continue the sedate journey away from the sea, home to our house surrounded by fields filled with wave upon wave of Brussels sprouts.

It was all very surreal. Everything was the same, apart from a kitchen wall crammed full of postcards and the map, now marked with a thick black line of progress. The dog seemed friendly enough, the lawnmower started at first pull, the garden looked good, Tesco's was its usual Friday-afternoon trolley-crashing scrum and the *Biggleswade Chronicle* reported that a bicycle had been stolen from a garden shed.

Back in my own bed, I woke on cue every three hours, attuned to the need to go on watch. I looked out through the gap in the curtain at the moon and struggled to see the stars that were normally so vivid overhead. With the dawn came a mug of tea as Anne restarted the routine halted the previous October. The dog spotted the signs and despite my having been away for a year, she knew that a spare biscuit would be on the cards.

A neighbour dropped in a welcome-home card and a couple called by to shake my hand. The telephone rang at regular intervals and I perfected the technique of answering the inevitable, 'So, how was it?'

The first few goes lasted around twelve minutes and were clearly too long. My romantic wallow through the South China Sea was interrupted by a 'must go – really busy – tell me more when we next meet – dying to hear it all. Byeee!'

I tried a more frugal approach but the listener demanded greater detail and in the end I settled on a tight spiel lasting around seven and a half minutes that included answers to the popular 'were you scared?' and 'favourite place' questions. It seemed to satisfy the madding crowd.

In addition to writing for *The Times*, I had also filed copy for the *Biggleswade Chronicle*, whose readers had shared my adventure. As the phone continued to ring, I began to appreciate how many individuals had lived vicariously through my travels and how much pleasure they had clearly got from it. Going into town for a paper, we knew that I had become a local celebrity when I caught site of the window display in Dave Gunns's bakery.

A cake with an iced map of the world complete with *London*'s route sat in the window. Posters, Clipper caps and newspaper cuttings accompanied a sign proclaiming, 'Welcome home Ian.' It was incredibly thoughtful and I bought a round of jam doughnuts to show my appreciation.

With the children back to school on Monday and Anne back at work, I had the house to myself. The crashing sameness of it all was deeply reassuring but also deeply depressing. The year had simply vanished and had it not been for the map, the postcards and the display in the baker's window, there would have been no sign that such an immense wealth of experiences had ever taken place.

The newspapers told tales of Tony Blair and John Prescott, the state of the railways, the roads, the economy and the euro. The tedium continued on the inside pages and it all seemed earnestly self-important and puffed up when placed in context of the global picture spinning in my head.

I had a much broader perspective now and the small snippets of world news from Manila and Singapore, East Timor and Quito seemed much more relevant. Even on the far-away speck of Christmas Island, our old friend Don O'Donnell was in the news, talking to Radio 4 about his latest immigration problem that had sailed into Flying Fish Cove. By comparison, the voyeuristic focus on Michael Barrymore and the secrets of Diana shrivelled into insignificance.

A look at the appointments pages in the *Sunday Times* suggested that finding a job would not be too difficult, although a long chat with Bowlsie made me realise that there had been a dramatic downturn in business following the terrorist attack in New York. But I was in no rush – we had managed the redundancy package well and there could be several months of gentle splashdown before the need for a second income.

I travelled to London to meet up with friends and stayed the night with Jem and Nicky. They had been generous hosts in Portsmouth, insisting on buying my first lunch ashore, and it was good to have enjoyed that meal with them. The following morning Nikki dropped me off at the tube and I joined the flow of commuters pouring through the barriers. Surrounded by suits, I emerged on the platform for the Piccadilly line just in time to hear an announcer report delays. A frustrated groan rippled through the assembled ranks and pink *FTs* were rustled in angry protest.

The first train came in but was far too packed to make it worth even attempting to squeeze on. A second arrived and it too was crammed full, although people managed to find space. When a third followed, it was still too busy for my liking, so I sat on my bench and simply waited for one that had a spare seat or two. I had no deadlines to meet and couldn't see the point of rushing. The platform guard eyed me nervously and, still dressed in my familiar faded kit, I guessed I didn't really fit in with the usual commuting crowd. I had no meetings to attend, no expense claims to file, no contact reports to write.

With all the time in the world, I walked between the next couple of reunions and ambled through London taking it all in. I kept catching sight of my former self – frantically hailing a cab, running for the tube, standing on a street corner shouting into a mobile phone as I gesticulated wildly at the person on the other end – and I found it all very uncomfortable.

After a gentle stroll from Kensington down to Chelsea, I had coffee with a friend who was eager to see my pictures and the stories that went with them. She had kept in touch throughout the year and was a gratifying listener to all my tales, demanding way more than the seven-and-a-half-minute version. I walked on to Mirella Ricciardi's house and revelled in the wonderful lunch she had arranged in my honour. Her passion for life and zest for following her own path were deeply infectious. She had really enjoyed my adventures and, being an adventurer herself, understood the early observations of the homecomer. She nodded wisely, appreciating the turmoil in my head.

'Better to be broke and free rather than tied and rich,' was her enigmatic advice, and it certainly didn't seem to be doing her any harm.

The thought of returning to the world of business and meetings, boardrooms and politics sent shivers down my spine. My mortgage dictated otherwise, though, and the lifestyle my children had grown up with required a significant salary to keep it going. And while I would be deliriously happy to sell the house, invest the proceeds in a decent boat and go and live the ocean-gypsy life, it was hardly fair to seriously suggest such a dramatic change to the family.

The simple way of life and the honesty that it brings, the stimulation that nature provides and the easy acceptance, by other like-minded souls, of a person for what he or she is, were an addictive drug. Anne was happy with my dream and was certain that our future should be based around such a life.

For now, though, our children were at a key stage of their education, and with GCSEs and A levels looming for Holly and Mike the one place we needed to be was in a settled home. I wanted to provide a stable base while they rode the pressures of exams. Like any parents, we were anxious for them to do well and gain the right bits of paper as passports to the adult world. Having got these, they could then choose the path that promised most fulfilment. If Mike found stimulation from being a surf god rather than a board director, then that was cool with me. If Holly wanted to become a hairdresser in the local salon instead of an actress, that was equally OK.

But before they could decide, the exams took priority and my boat, a gîte in Provence, a converted fisherman's cottage in Greece or a B&B business in Devon would have to wait for a while.

And if Elm Farm was to keep the name Dickens over the door for the next few years, I would have to return to the fray, become a grown-up again and find myself a proper job.

A firm of professionals who put together attention-seeking CVs was the first port of call. I sent off all my details and the end result made me appear eminently employable. Looking at the latest batch of recruitment ads, I reckoned that there were at least three or four positions to which my skills were perfectly suited.

The cocktail of award-winning advertising and marketing skills, the years of experience in a multinational company, the lessons gained from managing a competitive and focused team in the race, the bigger-picture view of the planet and the energy that was buzzing through me would all surely make me a fine catch for someone.

Off went the first batch of CVs with accompanying letters and back came an equal number of standard rejection letters. The following weekend another selection of plum appointments appeared and another round of CVs went into the postbox. Back came another bunch of 'sorry, no, very high standards, amazed by the response, not quite what we were looking for, good luck with your future career' letters.

As the weeks went by, so the pattern became horribly familiar and I started to learn that just getting a letter back was an achievement. Some employers, it seemed, could not be bothered to do even that – presumably because an accountant somewhere had worked out that saving on stamps and envelopes was more important than courtesy.

It was early days and I was not unduly worried. In honesty, a part of me was actually secretly delighted, because while the marketing post at Acme Drainpipes might pay a salary to meet the mortgage, I struggled with the idea of such a role. The thought of having to get passionate about trade shows where new concepts in guttering were presented to the trade media, or briefing an agency about a revolutionary diameter of waste pipe, did little to light my fire.

With September turning to October and the postman bringing a regular supply of letters whose content I could already guess, I changed tack, went on the offensive and approached the recruitment consultants direct. Armed with copies of *Marketing*, *Marketing Week* and *Campaign*, I wrote off to the advertisers in the back and felt sure that my details would fit someone's book.

Back came a stream of letters similar to the previous ones, replying that they had nothing on offer for my skills. Most seemed not to run any form of database and I was asked to reapply should a post catch my eye in the future. The CV, which I hoped would be winging its way on to an MD's desk or at least held in a pending file, was now sitting in a bin along with the four hundred or so other hopefuls looking for gainful employment.

One of the agencies seemed to carry more pages of positions than most, so I sent them my CV, along with a short, pithy note written with deliberate dry humour in order to stand out from the crowd. Marketing is about creating a personality and I wanted to prove that I had one in full working order. The company I approached specialised in placement of senior marketing people with experience in Fast Moving Consumer Goods.

In my last role, I remembered hundreds of thousands of my products whizzing off the shelves of Dixon's, Boots and Argos each year and those fast-moving products appeared, to my educated eye, to be goods that were purchased by, well, consumers. That educated eye belonged to a board director responsible for marketing, which I assumed to be a reasonably senior position.

Not according to the executive placement company who sent me a particularly soulless response.

'As you are aware,' they wrote, 'our company specialise in senior marketing staff with experience in the FMCG market place. As such, we have nothing that relates to you.'

When I sent off my CVs, I regarded such companies as the Santa's Grotto of instant solutions that would get me back into the world of earning. Now I realised that they had all the charm, skills and creative flair of a bad estate agent.

A telephone call put me firmly in my place and the person who had signed the letter appeared deeply affronted that I should dare to question their letter.

'Mr Dickens,' she sighed wearily. 'We *have* looked at your CV and regret that your qualifications do not match those sought by our clients. You have worked in the Consumer Durable sector of the market, not FMCG, and there is nothing for you. Goodbye.'

So it seemed that employers were looking for exceptionally precise and pigeonholed skill sets and, unless I matched them exactly, it was still 'sorry, no' time. I applied for an advertising job with a car company. 'Sorry, no. No experience in the automotive market.' I applied for a marketing job at a charity. 'Sorry, no. No experience in the charity sector.' A travel firm, an airline, a mobile-phone company. The response each time was depressingly familiar.

Unless I found a role that was a mirror image of what I had done before, I would remain unemployed. Twenty-one years of loyalty to one company, simply because I enjoyed that challenge, was now working against me. No breadth of experience, no breadth of jobs, that was what counted against me, even though the thought process involved in creating a marketing plan to flog 'consumer durables' was remarkably similar to that required to flog a car or two.

I wrote to my mates in advertising agencies only to learn they were going through a torrid time. Clients were slashing budgets and pulling work as they worried about the economy and the threat of war in the wake of September 11. 'A year ago,' they said, 'we would have snapped you up, but we're laying people off and it's only going to get worse.'

It would mean even more on the job market and even more applications to anything and everything on offer. I began to realise how sheltered my two-decade cocoon of comfort had been.

The welcome-back meetings with mates continued and I much preferred relating tales of the ocean to an appreciative audience to waiting for the postman. While all around me worked, I had the days to myself, enjoying freedom as Christmas approached.

Bowlsie and Goldie gave a predictably open-armed greeting and sympathised with my dilemma. Their agency was also feeling the pinch, but they vowed to spread the word and keep their ears open on my behalf. We talked about maybe doing some freelance consultancy work and I was put in touch with a couple of contacts who might be able to help.

Amid the latest batch of 'sorry, no' letters, a bank statement showed that we were not quite as flush as we first thought. Although funds could probably last until February, Christmas would have to be horribly frugal, and yet again both Holly and Mike were completely on side, with not an ounce of selfishness. They had been to the Galápagos twelve months before and if it meant no turkey and only the smallest of presents this time round, then so be it.

The offer of consultancy work moved along a notch and I went off to take a brief for a forthcoming brand-development project. Dusting down a jacket and tie, I joined the rush into the City and arrived at a lofty, glass-clad meeting room on the top floor of Lloyds of London. Over the next hour a series of facts and figures streamed forth from a laptop and around me the team from the agency made copious notes. Try as I might, nothing anyone was saying seemed to make sense and I could not grasp the new financial-services concept our excited client was sharing. We retired to a coffee bar to discuss what had been said and when the agency asked me to develop a plan and present it the following week, I ran scared.

Maybe the recruitment agencies were right. It all seemed so serious, so worthy, so lacking in personality, so vital to the future of the organisation and so unimportant to the planet at large, I got cold feet and chickened out. I didn't think I could do it and the realisation was a severe dent to my confidence.

Bowlsie was sympathetic, and although I felt I had let him down, he continued to call, encourage and cajole on a weekly basis. He appreciated how lonely it must be in an empty house where the phone didn't ring, the e-mail link sat idle and the postman delivered duds.

The up side was that I could take Holly and Mike to school and collect them again at the end of the day, while in the meantime perfecting my bread making and preparing creative suppers. It was great to have long periods of time together where we talked about anything and everything and Holly thought it cool to have the only dad in the class officially described as a 'bum'.

Conscious of the promises I had made to be a better parent and spend more time with my family, I booked Mike and myself into drumming lessons. We had agreed on the idea in Mauritius and now sat, side by side, beating out a four-beat bar under the beady eye of our spiky-haired young teacher. Within weeks I was left way behind and watched with real pleasure as my son raced through complex routines as if he had been doing it all his life.

As any sign of income refused to make itself known, Anne urged me to go on the dole and my initial pride gave way to practicality. I had paid into the system for long enough, so why not?

Visiting the local Job Centre was another new adventure-filled moment to add to my list. It was like stepping into a DIY store with a counter full of tradesmen with pencils behind their ears and being the only person unable to mutter 'two be four' or 'grommet washers' with any sort of credibility.

There was a desk with a woman behind it, so I went up, said, 'Hello' and sat down.

'Do you have a ticket?'

'Sorry – I thought this was reception,' I replied.

'You need a ticket,' she said, pointing over at a dispenser like the ones at a supermarket deli counter.

'Oh, right,' I said, and walked over to pull down the tab marked '52'.

No one else seemed to be waiting but, learning quickly, I sat down on the communal bench. Just as buttock met wipe-clean PVC, the woman's voice called out, 'Fifty-two?' and I went back to the desk.

I explained my situation and was delighted to discover that no form existed for someone who had stopped work a year before and then spent eleven months sailing around the world.

'Do you have your National Insurance number, Mr Dickens?'

'No – I haven't a clue what it is.'

'No matter,' she said, 'I can look it up. What's the address?'

With that information given, she embarked on some furious keyboard tapping and waited for the right page to appear. Lots of boxes and lots more tapping ensued until the holy grail came close. At that point the screen was turned away from me and she scribbled the vital details on to her form.

'So you've got the number?' I observed. 'Can I make a note of it for future reference?'

'Very sorry,' she replied, 'that information is classified. If you want it, you'll have to make your own enquiries.'

'But it's there, right in front of you. It's my number. It probably exists on a bit of paper at home if I knew where to look. Can't you just write it out for me?'

'It's against policy. Sorry.'

So we moved on.

'Mr Dickens, when you get home, can you find a clean sheet of paper and write on it all the previous jobs you have done. This is called a CV.'

I was on the verge of becoming Basil Fawlty and sending the whole thing up, but thought better of it.

'Oh, a CV. Cee Vee. Good old curriculum vitae. On a bit of paper, you say? How big? Will Basildon Bond do, or should it be A4? Ruled or plain? All my jobs? Including paper rounds? Or is it just the board director bit you require. You know, Sybil, the bit where I ran a multimillion-pound budget and employed a large department of staff. A CV, eh? Right you are.'

Delivering all this with a Fawlty-esque reddening face and a thick slice of pathos was clearly not the done thing. This was the system and the system would win. 'Don't get smart with me, sir, because *we* have the jobs and the cash and, at the moment, you have nothing.' Play the game, tick the boxes, do as you are asked. Wait in line, take the ticket, come when called and things will roll along just fine.

A week later a bundle of information arrived, along with my jobseeker's allowance book, which would put fifty quid into the bank each week. It was slightly less than the £100,000 salary I was seeking, but it was a start.

At home, suppers became more frugal, heating was turned low, lights switched off and Anne read through the latest batch of reject letters over supper. I was tempted not to bother applying for anything new and only kept responding because my £50 relied on proving that I was actively looking.

At each two-weekly meeting with the Job Centre, I collected my ticket, looked at the board full of positions and then sat with my assigned operative, who entered the top-secret NI number on the computer and surveyed the screen.

They were all exceptionally nice people who went through the motions according to the rule book, but with a distinct lack of need for either directors or world-circumnavigating sailors in the local area, I was sent on my way, box ticked and book stamped.

After one such meeting I headed to Sainsbury's in order to blow the cash on providing a suitable welcome for Liz and Stu, who were coming to stay for the weekend. The clipper 'old boy' network was working overtime as we shared experiences and were reassured to find that everyone was going through the same difficult emotions of settling down. In the wilds of Norfolk, Ellie was going through the identical £50-a-week charade and had just been offered seasonal work catching turkeys for Bernard Matthews – a fine role for an ex-nurse who was trying desperately to save funds for her wedding.

I wanted it to be a memorable party for my skipper and as I unloaded the contents of my chinking trolley, keeping the whites separate from the reds and the rum separate from the port, I looked up to find my Job Centre adviser staring sniffily down her nose as she waited to pay for her lunchtime sandwich. This was clearly not what the cash was for.

Three months after our arrival in Portsmouth, there was still not a glimmer of a job. My applications were going further and further afield, but the postmarks from Glasgow, Edinburgh, Leeds and Dublin came back with the familiar refrain. A Hebridean ferry company, a municipal art gallery, an aquarium offering an 'undersea' experience – they all felt able to proceed without my input, and the letters were crumpled up and used to light fires.

The Christmas tree was up and its familiar lights twinkled out through the leaded-glass windows of our farmhouse. A fire burnt in the grate but we used the logs sparingly to eke out the supply for as many weeks as possible. I really wanted to be able to repay my family for their support and love and felt ashamed that I had so little to offer in return.

But they too had learnt strong lessons from the year, and while a selection of shiny material possessions would certainly have made the kids happy, they were equally content with what would be on offer this year. We were together, we were happy, we loved each other and the scratched-together, home-made offerings would mean much more than a lavish gesture in Comet or the Vodaphone shop could ever do.

For years the Christmas sideboard had groaned under the weight of a huge spread of luxuries that poured forth from a series of hampers. At work, suppliers, eager to offer their thanks for a year's worth of business and doubly eager to ensure it was retained the following year, sent generous gifts of Stilton and port, claret and champagne, Belgian chocolates and wafer-thin mints. I always distributed the booty among my team in the office but even so, the sideboard still struggled under the weight from my share.

This year there would be none of that. It would be Christmas on a budget and a bottle of Bulgarian red and a box of dates would be about as far as we were able to go on the luxuries. But none of that got me down. On the boat, we had concocted the most amazing feasts from a selection of rusting tins, and with a bit of flair and some lateral thinking, Anne and I would still be able to create a special day every bit as memorable as those of the indulgent previous years.

As I was wrapping up the final small gifts on Christmas Eve – a set of drumsticks for Mike, a framed picture of us in the World Trade Center for Holly and a home-made tape of the music I had listened to around the world for Anne (her request) – there was a hammering at the front door.

It was eight in the evening and we weren't expecting anyone. I released the latch and standing in the darkened porch, dripping wet, was a leather-clad, helmeted dispatch rider.

Through the visor, a muffled voice asked if I was Ian Dickens, because he had a package from the advertising agency Lowes. The delight at finding the right place was clear, as he had obviously been on the road for some time and with the all-important chit signed, he handed over a huge box and vanished into the night.

In front of the fire, we opened the package and found a massive hamper inside. Down in London, Bowlsie had been allocating them to his important customers and had added an extra one on the bottom of the list for us.

Out came bottles of champagne, good red wine, some elegant whites, a bottle of excellent port and a pot of Stilton. Christmas could be celebrated loud and long and I was overcome with the thought and care shown by my mate. Advertising people are often accused of being shallow, lightweight and false, but here was a gesture that meant so much.

I called Bowlsie at home, my voice breaking with emotion, and thanked him for the gift. Typically embarrassed, he told me that he had almost dropped the idea just in case I felt his charity patronising. Anne was already searching for the corkscrew, but couldn't find it, so instead the foil was coming off the champagne, chilled by its journey north. No worries on that front – we were happy keeping it all.

I knew that January would be bleak and was determined to stave off the inevitable depression. Twelve months before, we had seen the new year in as we cruised through the Galápagos and the year before that it had been in the company of a million people on the streets of London. We drove up to Stuart and Liz's cottage in Wales and, in front of a huge fire, welcomed in the new year. It was a deeply cold night, with a clear sky bringing on a heavy frost. Outside in the remote darkness, I could see the stars properly for the first time in months and away in the distance, bathed in moonlight, was the white peak of Snowdon. We fired fireworks into the night sky and wondered what the year would bring.

For Stuart and Liz it would be a baby, conceived, much to the delight of the crew, at the New York stopover. For Holly and Mike, it was mock exams, followed by the real thing. For Anne, it was a new job in London with more money in an attempt to keep the mortgage payments going a little longer. For me, it was an unknown and I could see more months of 'not what we are looking for' letters, stretching out into the future.

I was adamant that I wouldn't feel sorry for myself and had a real need to go to work, to feel valued and have a purpose to my day. I wrote to Clipper and volunteered myself as a worker on their stand at the Boat Show. They would be busy recruiting for the next race and who better to talk about it than a satisfied customer. I didn't want any money other than expenses and as well as having a schedule to adhere to, it would provide free entry to the show.

They were enthusiastic and it was rewarding to share my experiences with people looking to do something bold and different. When I was asked to talk at a meeting of crew already signed up, the fresh and eager faces that stared back were a powerful reminder of just how much I had learnt and how far I had come. I may have been stony broke, but I was beginning to appreciate that I was richer than I had ever been.

As a result of my few days dressed in corporate clothing, Clipper came back and asked if I would be interested in interviewing applicants for the next race. Clearly I would have a good idea of the qualities required and their answers to my questions would provide valuable clues as to their potential. The money was not great, but it was money, and as I was required for only a couple of sessions a week I could continue to claim my £50 from the government. Operating like this meant that the house was safe for another month.

The local Rotary Club asked me to speak at their annual dinner and I gave a forty-minute illustrated lecture on the delights to be found all around the world. With the memories burning so vividly, I was able to do it without notes and the reaction at the end suggested it had been enjoyed. An agent for after-dinner speakers approached me, I signed up and almost immediately got my first professional booking.

The speaking circuit provides a lucrative income and after my first fully paid talk Elm Farm was safe for yet another month. All I needed was a booking every fortnight and we would be laughing.

I had hoped that working at the Boat Show or mingling at business dinners might generate a lead or two, but everywhere was the same. The economy was flat and no one was employing – certainly at the sort of salary that I needed to keep my home. With that in mind, I started to apply for any job I saw, accepting that fifty per cent less than what I wanted would still make me substantially better off than I currently was. We could always supplement the income with some form of weekend work stacking shelves or pulling pints, in order to keep up with the bank's demands. The appointments section of *The Times* shrank from a supplement to a couple of pages hidden within the business news and still nothing emerged for someone who could apparently only offer the world experience in 'consumer durables'.

The adventure of sailing around the world dwindled by the day and my early eager enthusiasm about what we had achieved lay like discarded gift-wrapping paper in a soggy dustbin.

The first rush of welcome homes had long gone and as life carried on, my crew mates returned to the cocoons provided by office, boardroom and company car. And while I knew I had to move on too, it was difficult to do so, as the sheer scale of our adventure continued to play on in my head. I read an interview with one of the astronauts who had walked on the moon and was asked about the difficulties of 'splashdown'. 'No matter what tomorrow brings,' he said, 'nothing can ever compare or live up to the experiences from my journey.' And while I had got nowhere near his Sea of Tranquillity, I understood exactly what he meant.

I stood out from the crowd in Tesco's and Sainsbury's. The only middle-aged man doing the shopping, surrounded by pensioners, harassed mothers and wailing toddlers. At the DIY store, tumbleweed followed me from aisle to aisle, free as I was of the pressures felt by craftsmen or even weekend handymen.

In offices everywhere, frantically ringing phones demanded instant answers while the e-mails piled up into a mountain of problems to solve. At home, the phone rang a couple of times and on occasion it was a wrong number.

On one exciting day my own e-mail frenzy brought three contacts. One told me that a meeting I had planned needed to be rescheduled and rescheduled again. Another did the same for a planned lunch and a third was from a company who had received my CV and responded with a polite 'please feel free to keep in touch'.

I went to the local railway station to buy a ticket for my daughter. Ever thoughtful, I stood aside to let the suited businessman behind me get a ticket in time to catch his train and make a deadline. He eyed me cautiously and took his place at the front of the queue without managing to say, 'Thank you.'

As I left the ticket office, another suited clone was on the way in and as my day was slower than his, I opened the door to let him through. There seemed to be a brotherhood of clones catching the 08.49, because he too looked straight through me and offered no thanks for the gesture.

Back at home, I learnt from a friend of the seething e-mail she had received from someone in her office. It was not about loss of profits, or a missed order or an expenses scam. It was about the way she parked her car in the company car park.

All of these sights and sounds were not making the transition from yachtsman to businessman any easier. It also highlighted why the transition from businessman to yachtsman proved so unbelievably comfortable.

One of the key benefits of my slow trip around our planet was an endorsement of a belief I have always had. Decent, honourable, humble, honest and all-seeing individuals do not judge by accent, clothes, car size or status. Within the fleet, I sailed and partied with a broad cross section of characters and all were accepted without prejudice or judgement, irrespective of their job, their accent or where they sent their children to school.

In the countries we visited I met, again and again, genuinely good people who took time and trouble for a fellow brother of the planet.

In São Paulo and the Philippines, in Panama City and South Africa, in Mauritius, Christmas Island, Singapore, Yokohama and Hawaii, I met people who had seen further than the end of a desk and knew what life had to offer. I met them in dingy hotels, in seedy bars, in beaten-up taxis and in rusting buses. I met them in steam-filled laundries, in supermarket checkout queues and in remote cafés where sometimes sign language was the only form of communication possible.

In environments where the mind was open and barriers raised, life could be conducted with courtesy, humour and warmth. Genuine feelings, far, far removed from the world of the ignorant, blind and soulless individuals I seemed to be continually coming up against. And the more I looked, the more I thought my voice would struggle against this all-pervading boorish attitude that could see no further than the end of an ego.

Which was a shame, because I knew that I still had an awful lot to offer.

Bowlsie continued his weekly call without fail and filled me in with stories from the advertising world. He talked about my old firm and described the strategies they were considering. There had been no contact from the team who used to work alongside me and after a couple of attempts at e-mailing, I gave up. Their days were clearly crammed full of meetings, deadlines and reports, and my simple desire just to talk was placed firmly at the bottom of their list of priorities.

Their boss was in touch, though, and one Saturday night he treated Anne and I to the very welcome luxury of being taken out to dinner. Other old contacts also continued to show a depth of friendship that I found deeply touching and in between interviewing potential Clipper crew, I met up with Anna Tully, Michael Hoppen and Mark Cramner, who, like Bowlsie, all offered gentle encouragement and genuine support.

As the interviews continued and a trickle of funds kept the wolf from the door, Clipper invited me to a reception where a new sponsor for *London* would be announced. London had agreed to back the boat again in the 2002 race and a City-based organisation would help to promote the entry around the world.

They planned to sell on sponsorship packages to London companies and needed someone to do all the legwork. Here, at last, was a chink of an opening and if I could sell the promotion, then a generous cut would come my way for the effort. In addition to that, they were planning a reception to welcome the race fleet to the capital in the summer and needed someone to organise the party. We talked through how I might contribute, and their 'big wig' liked what I had to say about it and sent me a letter confirming the deal. Fifteen per cent of all sponsorship raised and a separate fee for organising the party. At last I might be on my way.

I spoke to the Job Centre, telling them that I would now be working five days a week, but the work would be speculative, only earning if I succeeded. Despite this, the rule book deemed my enterprise to be full-time employment and the £50 payments were stopped. Now I was having to buy rail tickets, travel into London every day, sit at a desk in an open-plan office and try desperately to get some early sponsors into the bank. With no sign of any hard cash coming in for several weeks at best, I was worse off than ever before.

My trump card had been the big wig's contacts and I relied on him to make a phone call or two directly to the top and talk to his colleagues among the chairmen of multinational companies. If I could get in a convincing sales pitch at the highest level, I knew that a sponsorship department lower down the chain would be forced to listen and hopefully go along with the positive views that filtered down from on high.

I wrote presentations that made a persuasive case for the investment required and started to prepare a list of who I would like to share them with first. Unfortunately, it stayed a list, as the gulf between me and the all-important chairmen remained unbridged. The chap who had taken me on had much more important things on his mind and the trifling matter of sponsorship for a yacht race was ignored. I battled on as best I could without his support but knew full well what happened to most sponsorship proposals that arrived through the more conventional route. Unless I could talk face to face with the right people, the proposal would end up in the bin and the familiar sight of 'sorry, no' letters would enter my life once more.

With the economy still flat and my uphill struggle made worse by the need to plunder budgets already spoken for, after a couple of months' work I had nothing to show for my efforts other than an even larger black hole at the bank.

My arsenal was bare and the moment came when I had to call an estate agent and ask them to value the house. After showing the slick-suited local rep around the beamed dining room and pointing out the huge inglenook fireplace in the sitting room, I led the way through the gently undulating and creaking landing and bedrooms of our thatched home. As I explained our situation, he was surprisingly sympathetic. 'Something will turn up,' he said. 'Don't worry.'

But I *was* worrying. Standing in the house that all my years of hard work had achieved and having to face the very real threat of losing it just because I couldn't find a job was a gut-wrenching experience. But Anne and I had to be practical. Elm Farm had appreciated well, so at least we had a decent asset on our hands. Looking through estate agents' windows, we started to see what our cash might buy and began to mentally readjust to a new style of living.

Once again my family were amazing in their acceptance of the situation. Again the lessons from the year of learning shone through and reminded us what was really important. Togetherness, health, love, friendship, warmth and respect. All those qualities could exist without a GTi in the drive, a Hugo Boss suit on the hanger, an acre of garden with a ride-on mower, exotic holidays or a smart address. In fact the honesty it could bring might be refreshing, as we could remove ourselves from the circuit of dinner parties where fellow guests grill you about your job title, car type, holiday plans and where you went to school, before deciding if they are comfortable befriending you.

'Let's just hang on a little longer,' I pleaded to Anne as we drew up a list of other things we could start to sell off. A couple of insurance policies were cashed in and the small sailing boat I shared was flogged off, taking with it my last tangible link to the sea. The MG Midget that I had raced up to the Arctic Circle with Jem would be next in line and that might buy us another month or two.

Back in town, I began work on the summer party to greet the Clipper Ventures fleet and set about trying to find a sponsor for that event. I was pleased with the sharply benefit-driven proposal that now sat on my laptop and the big wig's PA reckoned that it was wonderfully persuasive. Surely this would do the trick.

In between this brinkmanship, a sniff of a job had come about through my old friend Simon Ward, who worked in the radio industry. A body of broadcasters had set up a bureau to promote digital radio and were looking for a marketing person to run it. The contract was for an initial one year but if I worked well, it might be extended. The salary was good and I knew it was an opportunity I could excel at.

Not only would the house be safe, I would be in a familiar marketing environment and leading the way with my own style of management. It sounded perfect and the job Anne and I had dreamed about for the previous nine months.

At the interview I must have said a few half-decent things, because they asked me back for the second round. Sitting in front of a panel of some of the biggest cheeses in radio, I took a deep breath and gave it my best. When one of the panel asked how I would manage the bureau's board, made up as it was of successful, opinionated, high-flying rivals, I told them about our motto from a year at sea.

'Does it make the boat go faster?' I asked and explained how the simple thought had worked on board.

Drawing an analogy with the business challenges ahead was a simple task. If what I proposed sold more digital radio sets, then there was a clear, board-uniting answer. If it didn't, then the answer was equally clear. If following that tack initially favoured a broadcast rival, repeat the mantra again. If it sold more digital radios, it delivered more listeners into the pool. More listeners would mean more marketing opportunities and this was good news all round. My mantra was based on a bigger, all-seeing vision. I sounded like a New Age guru spouting some ancient secret wisdom, but it was all down to pure common sense, from a brain washed clean by the purity of the ocean.

The panel nodded wisely and one or two wrote a note on the pad in front of them.

'How do you propose to lead?' they asked.

Again the lessons from the boat cut through. 'As a team,' I replied, aware that I was starting to sound like the old man of the sea.

Our yacht could only move forward if its crew worked as a team. The helm could steer but if the sails were not set, we would go nowhere. With the sails set, we relied on a good trimmer to harness the wind effectively and ensure that we went faster, more efficiently than our competitors. All that was useless if we headed in the wrong direction and a good navigator and strategist had to keep us on the most efficient course, while down in the galley someone was needed to ensure we were sustained and fully fuelled for the journey ahead.

It was like a gearbox full of cogs – each would only turn together if fully engaged with the next set of teeth. And it could only turn in the right direction, if the crew, as a whole, worked together towards a common goal.

My seafaring analogies were easily transferable to business but free from the destructive office politics where one cog did his hardest to prove he was way more important and bigger than the cogs in the next office. There would be none of that under my stewardship and we would treat the underlying serious goal as a huge adventure and challenge that should be enjoyed.

Three hours later I got a call from the chairman of the board which started with the word 'Congratulations'. I was a chief executive and could start as soon as possible. And with that simple message and job title, I suddenly became an acceptable companion at dinner parties again.

I fired off an e-mail to all the old contacts in my address book, informing them of my new role and grand title, along with my new contact details. A reply came back almost immediately from an old work colleague, who had been deafeningly silent through all my months of tribulation.

'Well done, mate,' it said. 'Once you have settled in, give us a call and we can do lunch. Cheers!'

I told the London organisation who had provided a desk, telephone and not many sales leads for the previous two months that I would be leaving. With a couple more days to go, I embarked on one last flurry of activity in order to help their summer party along. My very last task, at the end of a particularly happy week, was to fire off one last proposal to another potential sponsor, who I thought might possibly bite.

Six weeks later an invitation arrived to attend the event and I leapt at the chance to see *London* again. Anne joined me on the DLR out to Docklands and we were greeted with the usual warm welcome from Sir Robin, Colin de Mowbray and the rest of the Clipper team. All around me was the logo of the company that my last-ditch attempt at winning sponsorship had gone to and I was delighted that finally my attempts had proved successful.

We listened to speeches, clapped politely and then headed outside to watch a re-dedication ceremony for 'my' boat. Away in the distance, I could see the oh so familiar sight of eight seventy-foot masts with a profusion of flags flying from the stays, just as they had looked at the sixteen stopovers around the world. It was all wonderfully reassuring and my crew mate Andy Howe, Anne and I quickened our pace towards the water.

There she was at the edge of the dock, spruced up and looking smart, but exactly the same much-loved boat that I had last patted an affectionate farewell to, nine roller-coaster months before. As I stared at my precious former home, the tears started to well in my eyes and from nowhere an unbelievable sense of deep emotion washed through me. As I looked upwards in an effort to stop the tears from falling, I glanced left and saw that Andy was clearly having the same problem.

To my right, unashamed, Anne let hers flow freely down her cheeks as she paid silent thanks again to the precious craft that had looked after her husband and his new surrogate family of friends so ably.

I had a job. My house was safe. I had a lifelong collection of new and precious friends. I had been reminded again why I married the woman I did.

I had finally come home.

EPILOGUE

Slowly but surely, the crew found their way back to their own homes too. My struggle had been replicated right across the fleet and for those not married, lives took dramatic turns. They turned their backs on offices and commuting routines and some began to earn all the necessary tickets for a career behind the wheel of a boat. Some travelled and others planned their own businesses, free from corporate pressure.

Stuart led a party of teenagers on a kayaking trip through the wilds of Alaska and rediscovered his need for adventure by camping on ice floes and warning off approaching bears. Liz produced a baby boy in the spring and young Oliver is now my proud godson, ensuring a permanent link with the Gibson family.

Bella, fully recovered from her damaged spine, married Paul. 'Doris' realised how much he loved his girlfriend Catherine during their forced separation in the South Atlantic and returned home, proposed and was married within a year.

Holly got better GCSE grades than she had dared dream of, and up in Yorkshire, Ellie walked up the aisle led by young Ben Gibson (aged two) and married Wil. The first hymn was 'Jerusalem' and as its opening crescendo built, an entire pew of grown men and women were whisked back to sixteen proud arrivals and departures across the world, in a wave of keenly felt emotion. Outside the church, the men among the *London* crew took out blue-checked waistcoats made from our boat uniform trousers and slipped them on under our morning suits. When the doors of the church opened, Ellie and Wil walked under an archway of raised old sea boots held aloft by Stuart and James Landale, Danny and the Baba, Andy, John Williams and myself. The subsequent party was filled with laughter fuelled by an intense comradeship, and the crews sat in a warm and comfortable contentment that only living on the raw and honest edge together can bring.

I acknowledged the mass of lessons learnt. The political experiences of the workplace that led me to the race. The simplicity of living learnt during the race. The discovery of true friendship learnt in the unemployable months after the race. These had all left me a more enlightened soul. The previous three years had been spent on a giant seesaw. The old job had placed me right at one end. My year away had placed me at the opposite end. And now, with both sets of experiences on board, I sat firmly at the centre, ying and yang evenly balanced, at ease with what went on around me.

Which was just as well, because the capital seemed pretty much as I had left it.

Having seen the sponsor's logo at the boat re-dedication reception, I was reminded of the work I had done to win them over. Delighted at my success, I sent off an invoice, as per the original agreement with the organisation who had employed me to sell the concept. After eight weeks and several reminders, I got a letter refusing payment. But rather than take them to task, I replied with a reminder of our original agreement and simply asked that my £800 fee be paid to a London hospice charity for children.

At the time of writing, they are still waiting for the modest sum to arrive.

And on my first day at work as a chief executive, I rolled back into King's Cross, which is where this book started, a richer, calmer, more contented man.

Joining the suited throng spilling out of the train, I walked at my own pace, ignoring the jostling progress towards the tube. Walking against the flow was a familiar-looking figure and I did a double take as he headed towards me.

It was Barry Taylor, whom I had last seen in Honolulu. He had not spotted me, so I stood in front of him, blocking the way.

He looked up, did a double take of his own and exploded into a huge guffaw of a welcome, complete with hug. As the steady flow of commuters bubbled around us, we laughed loudly, bantered, exchanged news and hugged again. It was a wonderful start to the week and a genuine moment of warmth. Or it was until a passing worker, intent on getting to his desk in double-quick time, took exception to our temerity in stopping to talk.

'Can you please,' he loftily asked in a nasal twang, 'get out of the way and stand somewhere else? People are trying to get to work, you know.'

Barry and I looked at each other, searched for a witty rejoinder, couldn't think of one, so burst out laughing at the ridiculous, pompous, self-important vision now stalking off down the platform.

This was reality, though. All through my journey to work there was little sign of awareness or courtesy to others. People pushed past others without an apology. Bags clattered into shins with no sign of awareness. Shop assistants took customers' cash without thanks and out in the street drivers refused to let other road users into the traffic flow. And if they did, it only brought on angry displays of annoyance from behind.

As Barry himself had been fond of repeating when things got a little too heated in the workplace, 'If we are not talking about finding the cure for cancer here, then there's no need to get so wound up.'

I could not believe that the perpetrators of these deeds were mean people. At home, I assumed, they led a happy, perfectly normal, civilised existence with their husbands, wives, children and parents. But the moment the door was opened at the start of the day, it seemed that the rules of the city came into play.

Like the ocean, which behaves in exactly the way it wants to behave – and sailors must ride its back with a clear understanding of this – the city offered its own raw environment. If that was where you chose to be, then those were the rules to accept. What I had learnt would never change that world, or the blinkered people who seemed to frequent it rather too often. But my own lessons had changed the way I viewed it all and the laughter that Barry and I shared seemed to be a pretty effective antidote. Like an accomplished sailor, I set my course with a keen eye on the conditions and knew that I would find a comfortable path through it all.

The journey had amplified my sense of the fragility of life. The grim reaper had sat in wait beside a railway line in Hatfield, hovered above the slippery decks of a Vietnamese fishing boat in the South China Sea, stalked the streets of New York, lingered near the meridian bisecting the M25, just as he lurks at a million kerbsides as people simply cross the road. I wanted to be able to look him in the eye when the time came and know that I had squeezed all that could be squeezed out of the opportunity offered by life.

I was sure that within the seething throng heading for the tube on my first Monday back at work, there were individuals who felt like they were drowning. The sensation of water invading lungs would be fuelled by an insistent belief that there should be more to life than the nine-to-five routine, the treadmill, the stress, the pressure and the politics. For them, I hope my journey has shown an answer and lobbed a handy life jacket under their nose.

The crew of *London*, drawn from a rich diversity of backgrounds, had all wanted more. So much so, they made huge sacrifices simply to pursue that desire. Hand in hand we walked up to the edge of the kerb, looked left, looked right, then left again and took the first step.